SIGNS OF LIFE

SIGNS OF LIFE

The Origin of Astrological Symbolism
and Its Relation to the Human Psyche

Charles Astor & Polly Dukes

symbolistica

Published by Symbolistica Publications

ISBN: 978-1-0687567-0-2

Contents

Preface

Astrology, whether seen as a method of revealing someone's personality, or merely as an interesting repository of symbolism, is currently a most unfashionable topic for intellectual discourse. One might almost go so far as to say that the subject is taboo. Of course strictly, nothing *should* be taboo for rational analysis, but such seems to be the case for the discussion of astrology, certainly in mainstream scientific arenas. Even amongst the so-called 'alternative' community astrology has become somewhat 'old hat'. Astrology nevertheless stubbornly continues to find a place in various popular media. Dating websites and apps frequently list a person's 'star sign', and numerous publications, whether in print or online, will still give astrology some space for those who seem unable or unwilling to relinquish an interest.

In scientific circles however, it's taken for granted that astrology is the quintessential 'pseudo-science'. One mention of a genuine interest in astrology in an academic setting may be enough to convince your peers that you shouldn't be taken seriously. It's true that the influential Swiss psychologist Carl Jung saw great value in astrology as 'a symbolic language of archetypes', referring to the subject as *"the sum of all the psychological knowledge of antiquity"*. Jung's work, however, though frequently fascinating and often compelling, has in many ways suffered the same downbeat appraisal in mainstream academia as has the subject of astrology itself.

The decline of interest in astrology and moreover the implicit interdiction against its mere discussion are however, in our opinion, quite lamentable—and not because we think that astrology 'works' as a method of discovering an individual's personality, but because a survey into the nature of its rich symbolism sheds considerable light onto some of the most fundamental origins and aspects of human custom, folklore, myth, religion, psychology, and what we might term spirituality.

To rest content in the socially accepted view that astrology 'doesn't work' and so to shun the entire subject out of hand not only disregards the questions of why astrology is with us in the first place and why it has so obdurately persisted into an era of science, but also leaves us uninformed of these other valuable psychological and cultural insights. We have therefore taken the (some might say rash) decision to explore and discuss this almost forbidden subject, in the hope that the reader will be rewarded with some clarity concerning its origins, as well as with some fresh perspectives into the human psyche.

— *C. A. & P. D.*

1

The Origin of the Zodiac and Its Symbolism

If we could travel far back in time to ancient prehistory, one thing that would soon strike us about our environment would be the almost complete absence of artificial light after sunset. The world's first public outdoor street lamps were installed in London at the turn of the 19th century. For all the long history of humankind before that, only flaming oil-soaked rushes, or primitive lamps made from burning oil in hollow containers, and later candles, were used to illuminate small, personal spaces after the Sun had set. Even these basic lighting technologies were mostly confined to indoor use; anywhere out of doors at night with no moon would have been absolutely pitch-black—an experience largely unknown to us today. One consequence of this would have been that whenever the night skies were clear of cloud or a very bright moon, the vast panoply of the starry heavens would have been observable in all its glory.

Today we can be informed about the precise movements of the stars and planets by means of a multiplicity of electronic systems and devices. For the majority of us however, it's seldom that we go outside and actually look at these heavenly bodies with the naked eye. Indeed, we're rarely able to do so even when we try, since artificial light pollution makes it extremely difficult for us to appreciate what a truly clear view of the night sky looks like. By contrast, early humans could not have helped being intimately acquainted with the appearances and gradual movements of the Moon, the planets and the intricate mass of star-patterns in the dark and mysterious 'other world' of the heavens which starkly presented itself on every clear night. While not actually asleep, our early ancestors would have experienced this night-time presentation of the heavens in a psychological disposition that was ripe for thoughtful study, as the hours of darkness were a time for quiet inactivity and rest. A near-sleeping state would have augmented such perusal of the heavens with a more imaginative introspection.

Early humans therefore found themselves closely familiar with the appearance of the vast 'heavens' above. In the daytime the sky was of course dominated by the Sun, that all-important bringer of light and warmth. On a clear night however the heavenly realm was the more mysterious abode of the Moon, the discernible planets, and the countless stars. All these bodies dominated man's embryonic idea of the cosmos and of his place in it. They were things above him, both literally and metaphorically. Forever superior and beyond mundane matters, these enormous presences oversaw everything and everyone. They were clearly greater and more powerful than himself or any earthly creature, so they must have possessed incomprehensible, magnified, 'heavenly' powers.

These heavenly bodies were not however all the same, and each would inevitably have been apprehended and named according to its own particular characteristics and behaviour, being thus given by way of mental projection a rudimentary 'personality'. It would have been inevitable that, in so naming and animating them with personalities, he would have drawn upon those aspects of his own psyche which appeared appropriate to these separate characteristics. Thus man began 'observing' and categorising his own nature in the projective mirror of the heavens. So it was not that God made man in his own image; it was rather that man created his 'gods' by projecting images of the major aspects or functions of his own nature (both physiological and psychological) onto the heavenly bodies. The personalities of these planet-gods were thus prototypes, apotheoses or pure ideals of his own basic urges or functions. Contemplating the planet-gods as such reified, divine ideals, early humans would naturally have wished to identify with them, emulate their singular power, and perhaps propitiate them to avoid any harmful influence he thought they might have over him. If his attitude toward them was sufficiently venerating, perhaps they might even bestow upon him some of their idealised power, protection or practical advancement in return.

The Sun, being the most dominantly authoritative presence in the sky, was so evidently the One God, the all-powerful, supreme deity. The Sun's presence meant day, which brought light, warmth, activity and life; its absence meant the cold night, and the attendant dangers of the dark. It's not hard to see how, from the very earliest times, a very general association must have existed of day with life and night with death. Sleep during the night-time seemed to be a form of death. Even in modern times we speak of 'the dead of night'. This association would easily have been extended into the notion that when someone dies (when they assume the lifelessness that is so redolent of sleep in the cold and dark night) they go to 'heaven' (they are transported to the other-world of the heavens, or the night sky).[1]

But the Sun ruled the day, which was the heart of life. Meaningful activity could only be undertaken with the benefit of the light and warmth of the Sun. Crops would only grow in the fertile mother earth when they received the Sun's benevolent light and heat. In analogously human terms, the Sun would therefore have been comparable to the father, the impregnator and giver of life; thus the Sun became the heavenly or divine father. So overarching and obvious was the fact of the Sun's power that early humans would not have questioned its place as the prime deity, or even have thought about its status that much—except perhaps fearfully in the winter when its awesome power seemed to dwindle dangerously away. In terms of an analogous physical human function, the Sun would surely have represented the vital beating of the heart, the prime indicator of life: normally one hardly notices it, but the absence of its operation connotes death.

---

[1] Humans universally seem to think of the 'good' place, 'heaven' (or 'the heavens'), as well as God, the ruler of heaven, as being 'above', and the 'evil' place, hell or *Hades*, perhaps with its 'ruler' the devil, as being 'below'.

The Moon was somewhat more subtle and mesmerising as a deity, as it slowly changed its appearance in a regular, undulating ebb and flow of rhythms. Its habitual period, from full to new and to full again, was altogether more intimate and familiar, in a shorter time-frame than that of the Sun's long yearly cycle, and coincided more or less with the female period of ovulation, conferring upon this divinity a decidedly feminine and maternal aspect, to contrast with that of the paternal Sun. The five other visible 'classical' planets would have been of considerable interest to those who watched the heavens at night.[2] These bodies seemed special in that they 'wandered' apart from the stars, in their own particular courses.[3] Although appearing of lesser significance than the Sun and the Moon, the apparent purposefulness of their intricate yet regular peregrinations would have engendered much speculative interest. They appeared human-like in their variety and in the independence of their caprice and apparent intentionality. In the attempt to comprehend them, it was natural for man to project human qualities onto their separable characteristics, such as their appearances and movements, accordingly giving each its own 'personality'.

Thus the personalities of these planet-gods would so easily have been projectively fancied as corresponding facets of his own nature. Mercury—when it could be glimpsed—was seen to be the swiftest of the planets and would have reminded him of speed and haste in life, and the rapidity of his quick communications and mentality. Venus, appearing softly beautiful in the mornings and evenings, would have echoed his more sympathetic, artistic and loving nature. Mars, with its redness, redolent of blood and heat, would have reminded him of the martial and active passion that his own nature was forced to assume in the more combative moments of his life. The distinguished and lofty appearance of the often bright but slower-moving Jupiter was suggestive of a lordly and beneficent planet-god, while the faint and seemingly distant Saturn seemed to embody a colder and more austere nature.

Despite the interest that early humans must have had for the wandering planets, the Sun undoubtedly remained the most dominating god or spirit of the sky. For them, the Sun was, as it still is for us today, the sole giver of life, and it was upon this most majestic heavenly body that they utterly depended for their survival and welfare. Significantly, the Sun was the arbiter and measure of the year and therefore of the changing but ever-recurring seasons. Early humans would have had a natural intellectual curiosity to understand this cycle of the year and its seasonal periods; in addition, a close knowledge of the seasons was also of immense practical value, as it enabled accurate anticipation of the correct times to plant and harvest crops and to manage livestock.

---

[2] The 'classical' astrological planets—the Sun, the Moon, Mercury, Venus, Mars, Jupiter and Saturn—were those visible to the naked eye and thus known in ancient times before the invention of the telescope. In traditional astrology the Sun and the Moon are referred to, for convenience, as 'planets'.

[3] The word 'planet' comes from the Greek πλανήτης (planētēs) meaning 'wanderer'.

As we shall see, the cycle of the seasons has not only been one of the most principal drivers of the adaptation of life generally in Earth's complex ecosystem, but has also been one of the most fundamental ways in which humans have related to their environment and indeed to the entire cosmos around them. The dynamic effect of the seasons goes deep within our genetic nature and has shaped not only our physiological being but also our psychological and cultural habits and outlooks, and even what we think of as our spiritual nature. We'll explore these issues in more detail, but first it may be useful to remind ourselves just what the seasons are and how they come about. Figure 1 shows the cause of the seasons, depicting the Earth at the four 'cardinal' points in its yearly orbit around the Sun (not to scale).

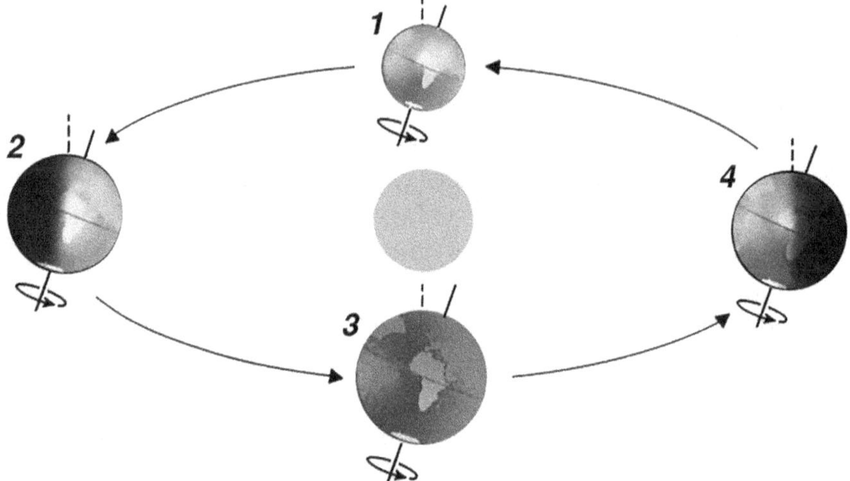

Figure 1. The Seasonal Points in the Earth's Path Around the Sun

Figure 1 shows the four cardinal points of the year. At point 1 we see the spring equinox in the northern hemisphere and the autumn equinox in the southern hemisphere. Point 2 shows shows the summer solstice in the northern hemisphere and the winter solstice in the southern hemisphere. Point 3 corresponds to the autumn equinox in the northern hemisphere, and the spring equinox in the southern hemisphere. Point 4 shows the the winter solstice in the northern hemisphere and the summer solstice in the southern hemisphere.

At each of these four points, one can see that the Earth's rotational axis is tilted (by 23.4°) away from the ecliptic (the plane of the Earth's orbit around the Sun, shown by the wide arrowed ellipse; lines perpendicular to the ecliptic are also shown by vertical dashed lines at each point). The Earth's equatorial plane (the line across the equator) is therefore also tilted from the ecliptic by the same angle. The orbital geometry resulting from this tilt means that different amounts of light and heat strike the Earth's north and south hemispheres at different points in the year.

The Earth's northern hemisphere is tilted *towards* the Sun at point 2 (the northern summer solstice) and thus it receives more light and warmth than the southern hemisphere, bringing the northern summer (and the southern winter). The Earth's northern hemisphere is by contrast tilted *away* from the Sun at point 4 (the northern winter solstice) and thus it receives less light and warmth than the southern hemisphere, bringing the northern winter (and thus the southern summer). At the equinoxes (points 1 and 3), the north and south poles lie directly upon the Earth's day-night terminator; then, the northern and southern hemispheres receive the same amount of light and warmth, and thus the days and nights are of equal length all over the globe.

The reckoning of the times of the seasons became an especially important and more extant practice after the Neolithic revolution, which began around 12,000 years ago, when humans began the transition from a hunter-gatherer lifestyle to one of settled agriculture. This immense social change allowed a food surplus, thus increasing the population and enabling people to live together in settled, socially complex communities. A surplus meant that at least some people did not have to spend all their time producing food; specialisations or trades appeared, as well as a comparatively leisured 'priestly' social group who were able to devote some of their time to the study of the heavens and the vital calculation and prediction of the seasons.[4]

The early astronomer-priests learned to predict or mark the times of the seasons in advance by becoming intimately familiar with the length of the day between sunrise and sunset, which changes as the year-cycle progresses. After the shortest day (the winter solstice, around December 22nd), the Sun begins to rise earlier and set later every day, the days becoming longer, until they become of equal length at the spring equinox (around 20th March). The days then continue to get longer until the Sun rises at its earliest and sets at its latest—the longest day—on the summer solstice (around 21st June). Thereafter the days gradually become shorter as the Sun begins to rise later and set earlier every day, until the days and nights are of equal length once again at the autumn equinox (around 22nd September). The year-cycle completes when once again the Sun rises at its latest and sets at its earliest on the next winter solstice.

An ability to determine the longest and shortest days (the solstices) and the days of equal sunlight in between (the equinoxes) gave ancient peoples an ability to mark the course of the year and its seasons. The use of sundials and water-clocks enabled the measurement of the length of the day from sunrise to sunset. Such measurements could thus reveal the shortest and longest days. The position of the stars at sunrise or sunset on those days, at fixed points either on the horizon or behind stable and unshifting structures such as solid stone menhirs, could be noted. It would have been perceived that, every year when (for instance) the shortest day was observed, the stars in the vicinity of the Sun but still just

---

[4] Barker, 2009

visible before sunrise (or after sunset), lying directly behind the unshifting point, would always be the same.

By such means humans in ancient times would have noticed that the background pattern of stars in the Sun's vicinity slowly changed as the year progressed, and that the same sequence of star-patterns repeated in the same way every year. Looking eastwards just before sunrise or westwards just after sunset, he would have noticed that in spring, certain patterns of stars were close to the Sun, but that by the arrival of summer, these had slowly given way to other star-patterns, and that yet others appeared at the time of later seasons. These patterns of stars close to the Sun changed throughout the year, until they repeated in the same cycle once more the next year.

In practice he would have noticed this seasonally changing backdrop of stars firstly with those star-patterns *close to* the Sun, in the east just before sunrise, or in the west just after sunset (known as the 'heliacal' risings and settings of such stars),[5] though it wouldn't have been long before he would have inferred which star-patterns were actually directly *behind* the Sun at any time in the year. Thus he would have become gradually aware that, in different successive periods of the year, the Sun was 'in' a certain pattern or group of stars. It was as if the Sun 'journeyed through' these different star-patterns in the course of each year, repeating the journey every year.

These star-patterns behind the Sun at different seasons would thus have been given special status, as they appeared to be the ones that the life-giving solar deity chose to 'inhabit' at those identifiable times of the year. Importantly, each star-pattern would have been naturally bestowed with imaginatively projected characteristics that corresponded to the salient features of the current time of the year in which they were observed. Thus the patterns of the stars behind the Sun at each seasonal period became imbued, by fanciful projection, with characterisations *of* those periods. These projected seasonal star-patterns, in what seemed to be the 'path of the Sun', were the essential precursors of the signs of the zodiac.

As these important star-patterns thus became familiar markers for the successive seasonal times of the year, man's focus became especially trained on that path, band or circuit in the background of star-patterns through which the Sun slowly moved in its annual cycle (now termed the 'ecliptic' or 'zodiac') and in which these seasonal star-patterns could be seen. This great band in the stars appeared not only to be the province of the life-giving Sun in its year-cycle, with its changing seasonal star-patterns, but was also that part of the sky where the mysterious god-planets were always to be found, somewhere along it, as if they were attendants to the Sun's royal presence.

It therefore became important for man to consolidate an overall knowledge of which star-patterns were behind the Sun in this ecliptic path at any given time of the year, as these patterns marked out and characterised for him the corresponding parts of the year-cycle. Thus people in ancient times noticed that the

---

[5] Hartner, 1965

Sun rose and set against different background-patterns of stars as the year progressed; each discernible 'seasonal slice' of the year having its own star pattern 'behind the Sun' (Figures 2 and 3). The deified planets could also be seen wandering in this 'path of the Sun', sometimes appearing in one star-pattern, sometimes in another.

In the orbital path shown in Figure 2 (Earth and Sun sizes and distances not to scale), the apparent position of the Sun against the background of stars moves along a delimited 'band' or great circle of star-patterns (constellations) known as the 'ecliptic'. Thus, different star-patterns appear behind the Sun at different times of the year. Figure 3 shows how, looking to the horizon at sunset, the Sun appears to be placed in front of one particular star-pattern at one time of year (top), whilst later on in the year, the apparent course of the Sun has moved along the ecliptic and so the pattern of stars 'behind the Sun' has changed (bottom).

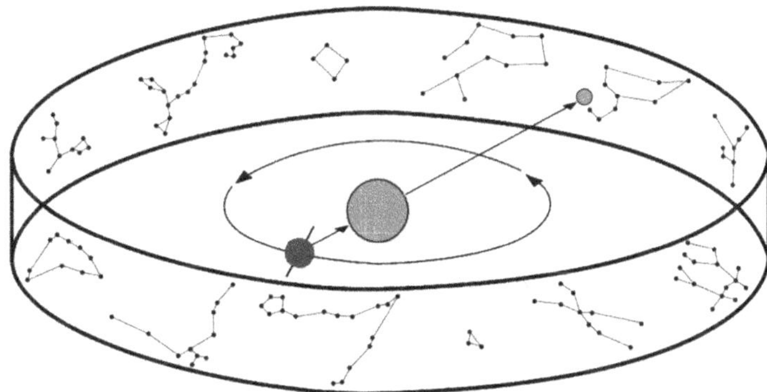

Figure 2. The Apparent Position of the Sun Against the Star-Patterns Along the Ecliptic as the Earth Rotates Around the Sun in Its Year-Journey

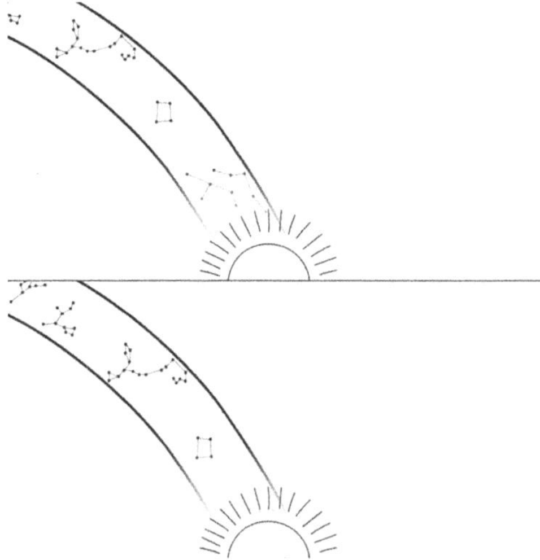

Figure 3. The Star-Patterns or Constellations in the Ecliptic as They Appear Behind the Sun at Different Times of the Year

Early humans therefore had such serviceable methods of determining the times of the seasons of the year fairly precisely: by observing where, on the terrestrial horizon, the Sun rose and set at significant times of day-length, and by discerning which particular star-patterns were behind the Sun at such times. Thus the times of the four important 'quarter points' of the year (the solstices and the equinoxes) could be ascertained. One particular star-pattern would, by careful reckoning, have been inferred to be behind the Sun at the winter solstice, while other star-patterns would have been similarly observed to mark the summer solstice and the spring and autumn equinoxes. Knowing which stars were always to be seen behind the Sun in the path of the ecliptic at these times would have been a reliable way of establishing these four cardinal points of the year, and thus of reckoning—and anticipating—the seasons.

Single bright stars, as well as star-patterns, became useful indicators for marking the times of the four cardinal points and thus the four main seasons of the year. Between 4,400-2,200 BCE the projected star-patterns or constellations seen as the Bull, the Lion, the Scorpion and the water-pouring 'angelic Man' Aquarius contained the spring equinox, the summer solstice, the autumn equinox and the winter solstice, respectively.[6] These star-patterns therefore took on considerable importance as marking the significant 'quarter points' of the year. Each contained very bright ('first magnitude') stars, namely Aldebaran, Regulus, Antares and Fomalhaut respectively, which by virtue of their proximity, at their heliacal rising, to the four cardinal points of the year, gave them special status, becoming known as the 'royal stars' in later Persia.[7]

The pre-eminence of the four constellations of the Bull, the Lion, the Scorpion and the angelic Man as the most significant markers of the year continued in myth and tradition to the time of the writing of the Old Testament Bible—with Scorpio assuming its 'higher' aspect as the Eagle.[8] We read their descriptions for instance in the Book of Ezekiel and the Book of Revelation.[9] So enduring was the influence of this group of four ancient figures that they have been incorporated into numerous features of Christian iconography up until modern times, as the 'tetramorphs', being regularly identified with the four 'evangelists' of the New Testament.[10,11] They are often depicted in the four corners of panels and paintings, typically with a representation of Jesus or other holy image in the centre (see Chapter 6).

---

[6] Hartner, 1965; Rogers, 1998

[7] Rogers, 1998, p. 24

[8] See the section on Scorpio in Chapter 3. Rogers (1998) has suggested the co-option of the constellation of Aquila (the Eagle) as an alternative reason.

[9] Ezekiel 1:10; Revelation 4:7

[10] Most Christian sources attest Matthew as the angelic man, Mark as the lion, Luke as the calf, ox or bull, and John as the eagle, though other early Christian commentators have postulated different combinations.

[11] Wikipedia, 2024

Babylonia-Mesopotamia

The four main points of the year—the solstices and equinoxes—certainly seem to have been the starting-point for the creation of the star-map of the heavens in ancient Babylonia, the cradle of astronomy and astrology. A study of the evolution of the earliest named constellations in ancient Mesopotamia has described how *"the solar stations of the solstices and equinoxes seem to be the all-important defining points of the whole system* [of the constellations]", how major groupings of associated constellations were imagined in the path of the Sun at the time of these solstices and equinoxes, and how their names and pictorial natures were reflections of the corresponding seasonal conditions. The study describes the Babylonian star-map as *"a pictorial calendar, where the succeeding seasons are represented by sets of characteristic symbols"* which *"impart to the constellations much of their symbolic character."*[12]

Thus by the time of the civilisation of ancient Mesopotamia, the periods around the four cardinal 'quarters' of the year were marked by the rising of groups of constellations which were named after pertinent, seasonally-associated themes. That these constellations' themes were specifically *seasonally* associated is attested by an example that is counter-intuitive but which nevertheless shows this to be the case. The constellation rising at the summer solstice was known as the Serpent, as a symbol of death and the entrance to the underworld, despite the fact that in more northerly and temperate climates this time of year is more positively viewed as the welcome and beneficent summertime. The more malevolent Babylonian attribution was due to the fact that the time of the summer solstice in ancient Mesopotamia was characterised by a scorching Sun so fierce that it resulted in drought, famine, plague, and in turn an inevitable association with death.[13] Thus the thematic characterisation of the seasonal star-grouping is a projective reflection or embodiment of the character of the corresponding prevalent conditions—whatever they might be.

Over time, the year was naturally further divided into shorter periods of twelve moons (months or 'moonths'). In Mesopotamia a 'luni-solar' calendrical system was established, where twelve months were calculated for the year, each beginning with the sighting of a new moon, the whole year beginning from the new moon closest to the spring equinox. Since the year doesn't comprise exactly twelve moon periods, an extra or 'intercalary' month was inserted roughly every three years to maintain an 'ideal year' of twelve months. The rule was that *"when a constellation rises a month later than its ideal rising date, it is time to add in the extra month".*[14] These monthly periods, like the year's quarter-points, could be approximately marked by the heliacal rising of appropriately themed constellations.

---

[12] White, 2014

[13] *Ibid.*

[14] *Ibid.*

The Role of Projection

From the foregoing we see that the people of ancient times imagined pictures in the random star-patterns that lay 'behind the Sun' at twelve seasonal moon-periods in the year. It is our strong contention that they would have imagined pictures with meanings (and therefore names) which would have been appropriate to the part of the year or season that they marked, rather than applying random designations. The characteristics of each of these twelve time-periods in the world around (the main spheres of life and the current seasonal matters that were being observed and engaged in) were psychologically projected onto the corresponding twelve star-groupings that were seen in the ecliptic 'behind the Sun' in these periods, as stylised characterisations. That is, the random patterns of the twelve star-groupings took on imagined depictions that reflected the themes of their associated *seasonal* characteristics. It was as if the Sun was 'expressing' himself in the different seasons in these star-patterns, with different patterns apparently mirroring the current seasonal characteristics (though really these pictorial and symbolical depictions were in fact psychological projections *of* those seasonal characteristics).

Thus, twelve major themes, approximately corresponding to the mundane conditions of the twelve seasonal 'slices' of the year, gradually became represented in the special star-patterns which appeared behind the Sun at those times. This is how the signs of the zodiac originated—in the seasons, *not* in the random star-patterns which happened to be behind the Sun at the corresponding times of the year (and which were fancifully given pictorial characteristics *of* those seasons). Each of the twelve seasonal characteristics was imaginatively *projected* onto the current star-pattern that the Sun was 'in' (i.e., onto the star-pattern that was inferred by observation to be currently behind the Sun).

Just how natural would it have been for the ancient sky-watchers to project the characteristics of each season onto the corresponding pattern of stars seen to be currently in the Sun's path? Psychological evidence points to the fact that it was almost certain to happen. Seeing meaning-laden patterns in ambiguous or random visual stimuli is inborn in us, and is even central to the way we cognise the world. Humans are pre-eminent pattern-seekers, and perceive largely by testing intuitive hypotheses about the things they experience, based on stored or innate knowledge and expectations. In other words we very often see what we want or expect to see.[15]

The innate readiness to perceive imagined orderly patterns in random visual stimuli has come to be known as *pareidolia*.[16] Most of us will have been acquainted with this phenomenon when 'seeing' faces or creatures in the embers of a fire or in clouds in the sky, or in any randomly-patterned surface. Humans moreover have an especial innate readiness to see, particularly, faces and animals in such

---

[15] Neisser, 1976

[16] From the Greek pará (παρά, 'beyond, beside, instead [of]') and eídōlon (εἴδωλον, 'image').

random visual stimuli.[17] This form of perceptual preparedness has provided significant evolutionary survival value: to be able to discern the lurking predator is an advantage, and instances of false positives ('seeing' a predator when it's not really there) is more than worth it for the times when it is there and we are able to detect it and escape with our lives. It's notable that this preparedness to see salient images in random stimuli occurs rapidly, at an early, unconscious level.[18] Research has shown that in modern times, pareidolia is more likely to occur in those who believe in religion or the paranormal;[19] one can therefore easily see how the more fearful and credulous minds of early humans would have been especially ready to engage in the process.

The images that we project onto random stimuli are those which tend to have particularly salient meaning for us. This is evidenced by the fact that the images or pictures which are 'seen' are likely to be appropriate to important facets in the prevailing culture of the observer. There are innumerable instances of projections of pictorial representations of Jesus Christ onto random patterns in various everyday objects in Christian cultures, in contrast to projected orthographic representations of Allah or of fragments of the Koran in Arab countries.[20] The fanciful projections we fabricate onto random stimuli therefore tend to reflect facets of the collective unconscious mind of the perceiver-projectors which are particularly *appropriate* or salient.

The fact that the images that we project onto random visual stimuli are those which tend to have some sort of important meaning to us has even been used in applied clinical psychology, in the form of 'projective' techniques, such as the Rorschach inkblot test. This test is designed to allow a person to respond to ambiguous stimuli (in this case, the random patterns made by inkblots) by describing what images they might 'see' in them. Advocates of the test (usually those of the psychoanalytic schools) suggest that it is 'projective' since, being unstructured, it enables the person being studied to project images freely from his or her unconscious mind. The images perceived, along with any recurring themes or otherwise telling responses, are analysed. The test makes practical use of the fact that, when we fancifully project images onto random visual stimuli, we tend to incorporate themes that are particularly *meaningful* to us in very deep, unconscious and fundamental ways.

Random stimuli have been used in other ways in order to project unconscious content, in various forms of so-called divination. Such practices have usually attributed any insights gained to supernatural factors, since the psychological processes involved have not been understood. Different cultures and traditions have chosen various sources of random patterns for this purpose. In all cases however the practitioner observes an essentially random stimulus and projects his or her unconscious insight onto what is seen. Examples of random stimuli

---

[17] Caramazza & Shelton, 1998; Delorme *et al.*, 2010; Nelson, 2001; New *et al.*, 2007
[18] Hadjikhani *et al.*, 2009
[19] Riekki *et al.*, 2013
[20] Wikipedia, 2018

used include the flights of birds ('augury') in Etruscan and Roman civilisations, and the spilled entrails of animals ('extispicy') in early Middle eastern times. The practice has continued up to modern times with practices such as the observation of the patterns of tea leaves in the dregs of a teacup. What all these practices have in common is that they are essentially a means of gaining access to the subtle insight of the unconscious mind, by gazing at random visual stimuli and projecting meaningful images onto them. The unconscious mind has a greater scope and fewer taboo systems or other perceptual filtering mechanisms in place than the conscious mind, and so may reveal truths that may be unavailable or repressed by 'normal' conscious perception.

Auditory stimuli have also exhibited this basic process that underlies pareidolia. Konstantīns Raudive studied random noise such as radio static and found that he was apparently able to discern human voices.[21] The voices that Raudive seemed to hear, like their counterparts in forms of visual 'divination' and in the Rorschach test, had great subliminal *salience*, as they appeared, even to Raudive, to be those of deceased family and friends. More common examples of auditory pareidolia taking place in everyday life can occur, as for example when, in the shower, we may easily seem to hear apparently important sounds such as the doorbell or a phone ringing. In this case, the nervous readiness or expectation to perceive certain stimuli (no doubt enhanced by the modicum of anxiety produced by the confined circumstances) constructs what sounds like a meaningful noise from the wide array of sounds produced by the shower.

It is immaterial to our present discussion whether the modern exploitation of pareidolia in projective techniques like the Rorschach inkblot test might be said to have any use as psychological testing tools. It's enough for us to note the powerful mechanism behind them; namely, that when presented with visual stimuli that are essentially unstructured, ambiguous or simply random, our innate cognitive preparedness provokes us to impose or 'see' ('project') orderly, recognisable and moreover *meaningful* images in them. Since these projected images are obviously not really 'there', they are perforce constructed by the prevailing unconscious partiality or saliency of our minds. For early human observers, the star-studded night sky was a major random-stimulus percept, and the Rorschach test-like process of projecting currently important (often seasonally based) facets of their own mind as fancied images onto the random star patterns must have been easy, extensive and protracted.

Our especial innate readiness to see animals in particular in random stimuli is interesting in the light of the fact that the twelve star-patterns which make up the zodiac are for the most part comprised of images of animals. Indeed, the word 'zodiac' is likely to stem from the Greek ζῳδιακὸς κύκλος (zōdiakos kuklos), meaning 'circle of animals', derived from ζῴδιον (zōdion), the diminutive of ζῷον (zōon) 'animal'. Even today astronomers can't seem to help projecting meaningful images—often of animals—onto the randomly-patterned objects they

---

[21] Raudive, 1971

study, such as the 'horse-head' or 'crab' nebulas. If today we were beginning the business of naming star-patterns that had seasonal significance, we would no doubt unwittingly invoke the process of pareidolia to supply seasonally apposite names. The tendency would have been more emphatically employed for peoples long ago whose livelihood and expectations depended in very direct ways upon the different and varying characteristics within the yearly seasonal cycle.

The unconscious projection of meaningful or appropriate images therefore influenced the way early humans saw pictures in the twelve star-patterns in the path of the Sun throughout the corresponding seasons. They would have projected appropriate current seasonal themes onto the fancied star-patterns which were behind the Sun at each relevant time of year. These projected themes would have been important and salient facets of their lives, especially those involving the concerns that were germane to the corresponding time of year, such as those involving the exigencies of their livelihood, the current needs of agriculture, and generally how that time of year made them view and reflect upon what they felt about the world and life. When, for instance, the Sun rose on the spring equinox, the mind of early humans would have been very much taken up with the new, fresh and seemingly forceful rebirth of life in nature, and an appropriate theme and name would have presented itself for the star-pattern seen behind the Sun at that particular time of year. They would have supplied similarly appropriate names for the other star-patterns in the Sun's path at other times of the year.

When there were no particularly bright stars or very obvious patterns for the twelve-fold seasonal divisions, even faint stars were co-opted and cajoled by the projective process of pareidolia into patterns for the purpose of marking the Sun's seasonal course through the year against the stellar backdrop. The stars that comprise the constellation of Cancer the crab, for instance, are not very bright, but they marked the seasonally significant summer solstice from around 2,000 BCE to 1,000 BCE, so these were endowed with a meaningful pattern or 'constellation picture' beyond any that would have appeared had there been no strong reason to imagine one. This was essentially the cognitive process behind the Rorschach test in action—the tendency man has to project unconsciously meaningful material onto random stimuli. The groups of stars that lay in the Sun's path at any given 'moonth' of the year therefore became a sort of 'Rorschach backdrop' onto which generations projected and refined a summary symbol or representation of the conditions of that seasonal segment. No doubt it would have taken many such generations for the characterisation of the current season to become a commonly-held conventional association of an imagined picture made from the random scattering of star-patterns—a traditional 'symbol of the season' in the starry sky.

The Rorschach test in formal psychology was concerned with the ways that an *individual* will project pictures onto random visual stimuli and so elicit unconscious aspects of his or her psyche. However, the Rorschach test-like projection of the mind of early humans onto the star-patterns behind the Sun for the different seasons of the year wasn't the work of an individual, or even of a few individuals; it was a *collective* process, eliciting not just salient facets of an individual's unconscious, but general human themes from innumerable people. The huge 'data set' of generations of interpreters meant that the twelve seasonal signs were shaped by the archetypes of the collective unconscious—core concepts of the primal concerns of all basic human experience. It was not a process that occurred at a particular time; it was rather one that took thousands of years to refine. Such a long-term reworking of these projections of the collective unconscious caused the themes which humans projected onto the zodiacal star-patterns to be elegantly emblematic and extremely salient to the general consciousness of mankind. Since the fancied names and themes were refined over millennia, they reflected major psychological issues or archetypes that apply to mankind as a whole.

What was climatically and culturally salient to mankind in each seasonal segment of the year was therefore projected onto the twelve 'star pattern segments' of the year, and conventions of the most appropriate, recurrent and popular pictures and meanings attributed to these segments would have become refined and consolidated by successive generations to become highly appropriate, archetypal representations of what 'this time of year' meant to the mind of man—more than any other conceivable stimulus. In this way the stars became a mirror for the unconscious mind of mankind, in which he could discern the major archetypal elements of his existence and of his concerns throughout the life-cycle of the year (which, as we shall see, also mirrored to a large extent his own life-cycle). Gavin White adumbrates some sense of our 'projective' hypothesis of the origins of the zodiac signs when he points out that elaborate pictures were imaginatively forced upon even sparse constellation-patterns in the 'canvas' of the heavens in ancient Babylonia:

> The [Babylonian] star-map can rightly be regarded as the fulfilment of man's desire to create a meaningful environment that encapsulates his understanding of the world and his place within it ... the season in which a particular star has its annual rising [i.e., is inferred by its heliacal rising to be 'behind the Sun'] lends to that star its characteristic symbolic nature. For instance, the familiar figure of Aquarius with his overflowing water jars is a pictorial allegory of late winter and early spring, when the rains of heaven fall in their greatest abundance and swell the rivers towards their annual flooding. In a similar fashion, the overpowering radiance of the summertime sun is symbolised by the radiant mane of the zodiacal Lion, and the springtime, which is characterised as the time when lambs and calves are born in the cattle-folds, is symbolised by the celestial figures of Aries and Taurus.[22]

---

[22] White, 2014

White goes on to note that the Babylonians, unaware of the psychological projective origins of the star-patterns, went on to endow these constellations with deific causative powers over the seasons (this confusion and misunderstanding of causation will be discussed further below). Thus the twelvefold zodiac was born, originating from the patterns of twelve months of seasonal characteristics and the human activities which attended them. That this is the case is evidenced by the close correspondence between the theme of each sign of the zodiac and the characteristics of its time of year, which we shall explore in more detail later. The naming of the star-patterns according to the characteristics of the prevailing seasons of the year and the culture of astronomy generally emerged mostly in the northern hemisphere; the process therefore produced projections of the themes of the seasons of that hemisphere. The twelve star-patterns thus came to embody, by way of this projective process, humanity's personal experience of life in each corresponding season.

To summarise: early humans, observing a night sky unfettered by light pollution, imagined pictures in the random star-patterns that were behind the Sun at different times of the year. Due to the naturally evolved process of pareidolia, these imagined pictures in the star-patterns were unconsciously afforded meanings which were appropriate to the mundane circumstances and conditions of the part of the year or season in which they were observing. Over time, these projected pictorial seasonal characterisations were grouped for convenience into twelve distinct clusters, roughly one for each moon-period of the year.

This projective symbolising of the seasonal characteristics of the twelve parts of the year in the star-patterns behind the Sun took place over a long time. During this time, people were of course not aware of the psychological projective process of pareidolia that was taking place. On the contrary, the fancied pictures were laid down in tradition and in time became so entrenched, over generations, that eventually they were simply taken to be naturally occurring tokens or correspondences *of* that time of year, as if the heavens supernaturally reflected—or even caused—the characteristics of the time of year.

In other words, ignorant of the projective process of pareidolia that was in operation, people began to assume that the deified pictorial representations in the twelve heavenly star-patterns (constellations) were in some way divinely responsible for, or in some way naturally related to, the characteristics of the parts of the year with which they were associated. It even came to be proposed that these constellations *caused* the corresponding personality-characteristics of people *born* in those parts of the year. To this day, many people believe that the stars of certain constellations have some sort of causal influence on what happens on Earth.

Some theorists, notably Carl Jung, have skirted the obviously misguided notion of such a causal connection by proposing a 'synchronicity' or an 'acausal connecting principle' between seasonally observed stars and the putative associations they have with terrestrial events.[23] As we have seen, the far simpler truth is

---

[23] Jung, 2015

that, in its origins, *astrology has nothing to do with the stars*, except in so far as certain star-patterns behind the Sun at different times of the year were employed by humans' collective unconscious as random stimuli upon which to project a characterisation of the mundane associations *of* that time of the year. The notion of a mysterious causative influence of the star-patterns upon the corresponding times of the seasonal characteristics (or, for that matter, of an 'acausal' correspondence) only came about because of ignorance of this cognitive process.

Confusion About Precession: Seasons, Not Stars

From the foregoing we see that, when humans first started noting the different star-patterns which lay in the Sun's path at different times of the year, it happened that, by way of the natural cognitive process of pareidolia, they came to project imaginative pictures (and thus names) *onto* those star-patterns— pictures and names which reflected the important seasonal activities and concerns of the time of year in which they were observing. In this way the sequence of seasonal conditions through the year became mirrored in the sequence of these pictured star-patterns behind the Sun. With no understanding of the true cause of the seasons, or of the psychologically projective origin of the star-pictures, and not anticipating any change in the season-to-star-picture correspondences, people in ancient times came to believe that those star-pictures were in some sense real and eternal; that they forever marked these twelve seasonal segments, by virtue of some divine or supernatural order. (It was, after all, an implicit assumption of the apparent fixity of the star-patterns that had been the reason that they had come to be used as markers for the different seasonal times of the year.)

The themes of the star-pictures in the course of the Sun's yearly journey therefore became virtually deific in character, until it became natural to suppose that the godlike powers in these celestial images in some way *accounted for* the corresponding seasonal conditions; that, in some sense, these heavenly signifiers or agents *caused* those seasonal events to be brought about or instantiated in their nature. The personification of the projected pictures having thus become bestowed with something of a numinous nature, appropriate myths and rituals came about to magnify, celebrate or honour them and their associated seasonal activities. In an age when writing had not yet been widely developed, such divine celestial associations were not only usefully memorable in the calendar, but also extremely powerful in a mythic or religious sense.

As the signs—the projected symbolic representations of twelve seasonal segments of the year—were divinely reified in this manner, they began to incorporate a divinatory or predictive aspect. It began to be assumed that those who were born when the Sun was 'in' a certain seasonal sign would naturally exhibit the characteristics *of* that seasonal sign in their make-up or personality. So, for instance, a person born at or shortly after the spring equinox was seen to be inevitably bold, forward and thrusting in character—just like the spring itself (and just like the image of the ram which seemed celestially to signify it). Just as there had become established in folkloric belief the assumption of a form of correlative inevitability or even of a causal connection between these divine star-constellations and their corresponding times of the year, so the notion grew that there was a similarly fated connection between these seasonal celestial daemons and 'native' births at those times. This is of course nonsensical, but one can see how such causal fallacies and beliefs came about.

The actual star-patterns that comprised the twelve 'signs' of the zodiac had become, by established tradition, firmly associated with the parts of the year whose seasonal characteristics had originally given those constellations their imagined pictures and names (by virtue of being behind the Sun at those times of year). However, to complicate matters, a phenomenon known as the 'precession of the equinoxes' (commonly referred to more simply as 'precession') causes these constellations, very gradually, to cease to appear behind the Sun at the times of the year that they had once traditionally marked and personified, and thus no longer to be such precise indicators of those year-segments. In order to explain precession we first need to refer to some basic astronomy.

Precession

As a preliminary we need to explain what is meant when we refer to the astronomical terms 'the celestial equator' and 'the ecliptic'. The celestial equator is the imaginary plane of the Earth's equator extended into space, while the ecliptic is the imaginary plane of the Earth's orbit around the Sun, similarly extended into space. We must also note that the Earth's rotational axis—and thus also the plane of the celestial equator—is tilted from the plane of the ecliptic by about 23.4° (Figure 4).

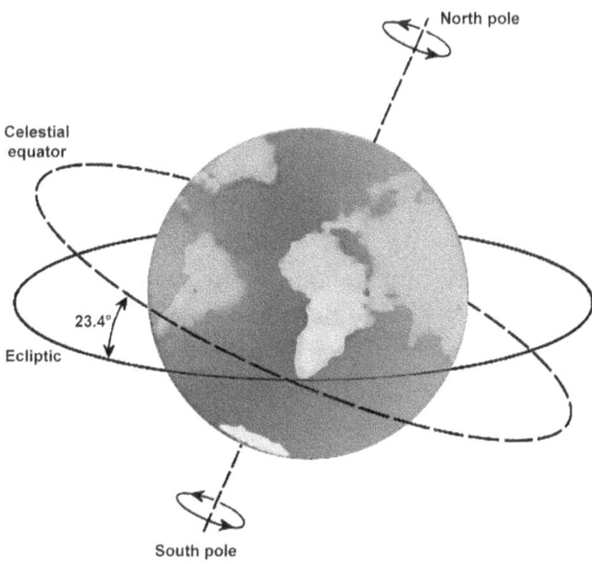

Figure 4. The Earth's Polar Axis and the Planes of the Celestial Equator and the Ecliptic

As the Earth orbits it, the apparent position of the Sun to an Earth-bound observer moves around the great circle of the ecliptic (Figure 5). There are two points in the Earth's yearly orbit around the Sun where, from a terrestrial viewpoint, the celestial equator exactly intersects the centre of the Sun's disc on the ecliptic, one at the spring equinox, or 0° Aries, which marks the beginning of the zodiac, and the other at the autumn equinox, which marks 0° Libra.

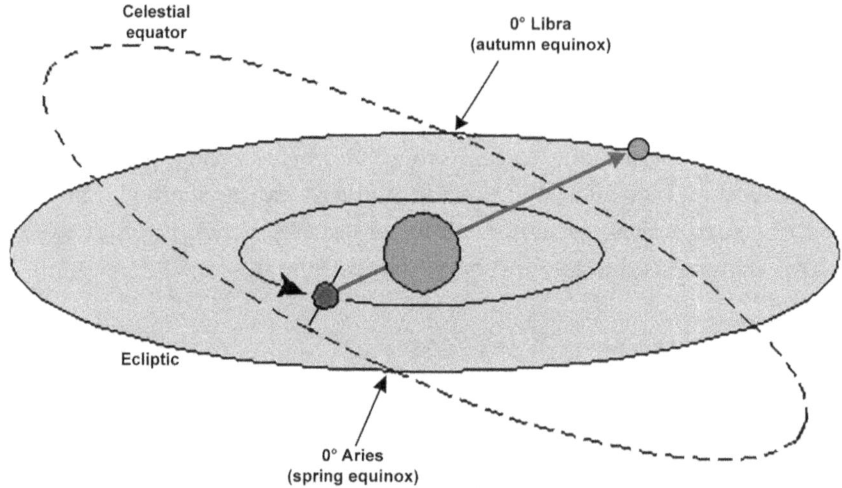

Figure 5. The Earth's Rotation Around the Sun, Relative to the Planes of the Celestial Equator and the Ecliptic

From the viewpoint of the Earth, the Sun appears each year to journey through a familiar, annually repeating series of star-patterns or constellations which appear along the 'band' of the ecliptic. These star-patterns along the path of the ecliptic contain the familiar constellations of the zodiac. The band of the ecliptic as pictured in Figure 5 has been redrawn in Figure 6 to show these constellations, which, from the Earth's viewpoint, appear 'behind the Sun' at different times of the year. As we indicated above, although the positions of the star-patterns seen 'behind the Sun' seem to be always fixed at particular times of the year, these apparently static positions in fact very slowly drift around the band of the ecliptic. For instance, at one of the two points of the year where the celestial equator intersects the Sun's disc on the ecliptic—the spring equinox (Figures 5 and 6)—the Sun appears for many years to be 'in' a certain point against the backdrop of stars. However, very gradually, that point in the star-field behind the Sun at that moment of the spring equinox will shift slightly along the ecliptic. This phenomenon is known as the 'precession of the equinoxes' (or more simply 'precession').

The reason for this gradual shift is because gravitational forces from other bodies in the solar system cause the alignment of the Earth's pole-to-pole rotational axis (Figure 4) to 'wobble' in a circle, like a spinning top, over very long periods of time. Thus if in our imagination we could see the Earth's polar axis extended far up into space, we would see that, over many thousands of years, that point would describe a circle against the backdrop of stars. The celestial equator necessarily also moves along with this polar axis 'wobble'—and thus *also* does its intersection with the ecliptic (Figure 5), causing a gradual backwards shift (or 'precession') of the apparent position of the spring equinox against the distant stars.

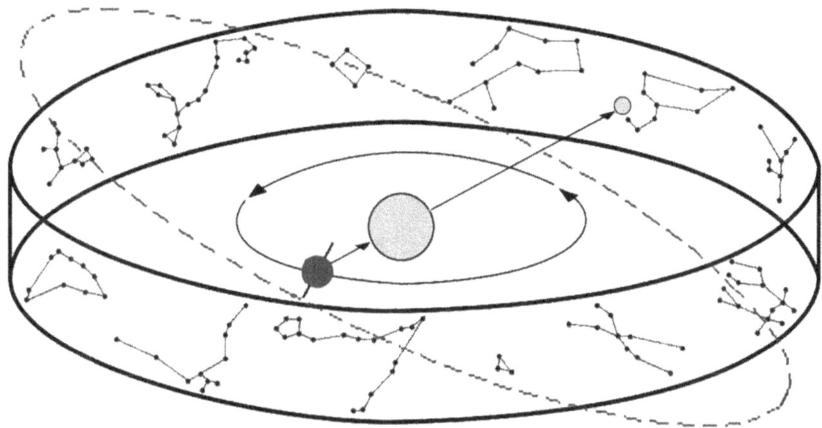

Figure 6. The Earth's Rotation Around the Sun, Relative to the Planes of the Celestial Equator and the Ecliptic, With the Ecliptic Expanded to Show the Constellations It Contains

Four stages of this very slow precessional 'wobble' are shown in Figure 7. Looking clockwise from top left, we see that, over time, the polar axis gradually describes a circle, causing the plane of the celestial equator (the planar extension into space of the Earth's equatorial line shown) also to move, in tandem. The rate of this precessional change is extremely slow—completing one full revolution approximately every 26,000 years, thus shifting just one degree of arc roughly every 72 years—but this nevertheless means that the apparent position of the Sun against the backdrop of stars at a given time of year does, even if extremely gradually, shift over time.

Precession means that a fancied constellation or 'picture made of stars' in the path of the Sun at a particular time of year, although giving

Figure 7. Four Stages in the Earth's Precessional Wobble, Showing the Movement of the Polar Axis and of the Equator

the impression of being fixed for observers within their own lifetimes, will nevertheless appear to be in a slightly different position in the sky for observers of successive generations. Thus, for instance, a star-pattern (or a particular star within that pattern) that is seen to be exactly behind the Sun at the spring equinox will shift that position very slowly over time, so that eventually it will no longer mark that time of year so precisely.

One observer in history might have discerned that one particular part of an appropriately fancied star-picture marked (by way of its heliacal rising) the exact point of the spring equinox; a few generations later, however, a later observer would have seen that the exact point of the spring equinox now lay in a slightly different part of that (now well-known) star-picture—or even, after a very long time, in a different star-picture altogether—perhaps an adjacent star-picture that had long been imaginatively pictured as denoting a completely different seasonal representation. Figure 8 shows the changing position, through the ages, of the point of the spring equinox (represented by the central dots along the dashed timeline) against the background of star-patterns.

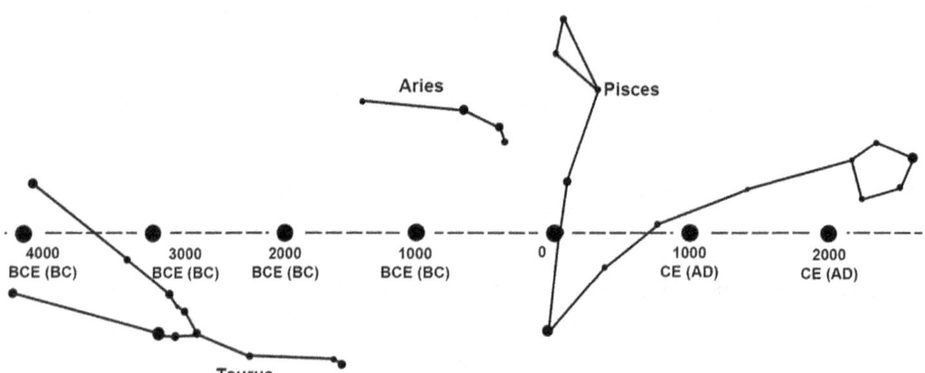

Figure 8. The Changing Point of 0° Aries as Seen Against the Backdrop of Star-Patterns, Through the Ages

The fact of precession was reputed to have been first discovered by the Greek astronomer Hipparchus in the second century BCE. However most people in ancient times were unaware of it, and the star-constellations that had once been fancied as corresponding to the twelve seasonal year-segments continued to be associated with those seasons, even when they no longer did quite correspond. To the ancients, this gradual mismatch of course had confusing implications for the utility of the star-pictures as supposedly precise markers for specific seasonal times of the year.[24]

---

[24] The initiates of the secretive cult of Mithraism, which originated in Rome around the middle of the first century BCE, might have known about precession. The cult constructed hundreds of instances of a 'bull-slaying' scene involving intricate iconography which may well have been a mythological account of the appearance of the phenomenon. See *Appendix 1: Mithraism.*

20

Stars in ancient Babylonia were probably arranged into constellations around the 5th or 6th millennium BCE, but by the 3rd millennium BCE, many these were removed and replaced by alternative figures. White (2020) has speculated that this may have been due to an attempt to correct for precession. Traces of the thematic characteristics of the 'old' constellations remained which may account for the apparent repetition or fusion of constellation figures in adjacent areas of the sky. Examples of this may be found in the ancient 'goat-fish' constellation, which may have been a later version of both Pisces and Capricorn, and possibly in the ram of Aries being a later form of Taurus the bull.[25]

Notwithstanding such interesting speculations about the possibility of early adjustments for precession in Babylonia, after a period of time that was long enough for the effects of precession to become plainly evident, the discrepancies between the seasonal times of the year and their erstwhile associated constellations certainly began to cause confusion, as they were only generally noticed long after the original 'season-to-star-pattern' associations had been firmly laid down in tradition. In other words, despite the effects of precession, the old, original associations between the seasonal parts of the year and the names and images of their linked star-pictures had stuck. Even if the Sun at the spring equinox no longer appeared *precisely* against the star-pattern that had once been fancifully imagined as portraying 'Aries the ram' in characterisation of the thrusting, forward nature of the beginning of the newborn lamb in spring, but instead appeared somewhat in the star-group of the 'Pisces the fishes' (which once characterised the last part of winter), the actual *star-grouping* known as the 'constellation of Aries' nevertheless still held on to its traditional name—and its old thematic association deriving from its originally associated season.

The effects of precession, though known to a few philosopher-astronomers like Hipparchus, were not known well enough in everyday popular culture for there to be deliberate, ongoing and regular revisions of the fancied star-picturing process over successive generations. The process of projective fancy in random star-patterns had long ago done its work to characterise the seasons, and the resultant pictorial representations and descriptive names of those star-patterns remained, despite the fact that they had become somewhat out of synchronisation with the seasons which had originally given rise to their themes. To rectify matters, Hipparchus decided that, regardless of the positions of the stars at any given time, twelve equal sections or 'signs' of a 'tropical' zodiac should begin at the point of the spring equinox. These signs' accurate thematic associations with the seasons—even if now slightly out of synchronisation with the originally associated star-patterns—was preserved and could continue indefinitely. The tropical zodiac of Hipparchus, by virtue of this continued seasonal associative utility, became the accepted zodiac that the greater part of the Western world adopted.

---

[25] White, 2014

The old erroneous conflation between the seasonal thematic signs and star-patterns nevertheless continues to this day by those who do not understand the origin of the zodiac signs, when they point to the fact that the Sun at the spring equinox no longer lies exactly in the backdrop-constellation of stars still called 'Aries' but rather to that star-pattern known as 'Pisces'—not realising that *the zodiac signs never had their origin in the star-constellations*, but in characterisations of the seasons, which happened, once upon a time, to be marked *by* those star-constellations. A truly serious criticism of *divinatory* (predictive) astrology would be one which pointed to the lack of evidence showing any correspondence between the characteristics of the zodiacal sign behind the Sun at birth and thematically related personality factors later in life. Such a reasonable criticism would however be completely irrelevant to the gradually increasing mismatch between the Sun's occupation of the zodiacal signs as fixed seasonal segments of the year and the Sun's apparent position against the star-constellations that were once associated with those seasons' signs, but which no longer are.

The truth is that it makes no difference what particular stars actually lie behind the Sun at (for instance) the spring equinox: the important point is that it was the theme of the time of year that was originally characterised by an appropriate picture, projected *onto* those stars; that is, the star-grouping behind the Sun at that time of year was merely once used collectively as a random stimulus upon which to imaginatively project a representation of that current time of year, in the form of an imagined and suitably associated picture, and those star-groupings just happened to retain the original name.

When the discrepancies due to precession became larger, some people even developed a divinatory 'sidereal' (star-oriented) zodiac (notably in Indian astrology), rigorously calculating twelve signs according to the positions of the once precisely-associated star constellations—not realising that these star-patterns were once twelve projected pictorial characterisations of twelve seasonal segments of the year, and that those characterisations of the actual star-groupings had simply stuck in long tradition—though, due to precession, they had wandered away a little from being behind the Sun at the appropriate time of year. The discrepancies brought about between the precise positions of the stars that still bear the emblematic names of the seasonal segments to which they once corresponded, and those seasonal segments themselves, began not to matter to most other astrologers, since they had begun to use the tropical zodiac wherein twelve signs of equal length always began at the spring equinox. Some of these astrologers may well have realised that it was the seasonal 'sign' that mattered, not the stars that happened to be behind the Sun at the time.

However, because the named identification of the star-groupings with the seasonal 'signs' had taken a firm hold in tradition before the slow effects of precession were widely appreciated, astrologers using the sidereal zodiac made the mistake of identifying the year's signs with the traditionally-named constellations, regardless of their 'time of year' association. The sign-to-constellation correspondence in the two systems (tropical and sidereal) actually still overlap considerably, so discrepancies have been to an extent minimised. But this is still an issue of misunderstanding, due to a lack of awareness of the pareidolia-like projective origin of the signs, and thus of the fact that the origin of the signs was not in the stars, but solely in the seasonal times of the year, for which the star-patterns originally acted as pictorial markers, by virtue of their being 'behind the Sun' at those times.

The true origins of the zodiac signs as markers of seasonal segments of the year became supremely obfuscated in the bizarre notion of the 'Great Year', which was a further result of the erroneous identification of the signs with the constellations and the unawareness of their seasonal or 'tropical' origin. Long ago, the random pattern of the constellation of stars behind the Sun at the spring equinox was, as we have described, used projectively to construct a symbol of the current time of the spring—a lively and thrusting newborn ram (Aries), as the spring itself is characterised by thrusting new life and rebirth. However, as we have also described, after long periods of time, the background of stars in relation to the Earth shifted due to precession, so that the stars behind the Sun at the spring equinox became those once associated with the preceding zodiac sign of Pisces the fishes, a sign originally bound up with a characterisation of the preceding season. After even further periods of time, the stars behind the Sun at the spring equinox will become those once associated with the next preceding sign, the sign Aquarius, the water-bearer. The point of the spring equinox will in fact go on to move through *all* the old named constellations which originally marked the seasons, in a circular fashion, until those behind the Sun at the spring equinox become once again those now called Aries. The entire cycle takes approximately 26,000 years, which means that the equinoctial point appears in one of the originally identified constellations for roughly 2,000 years at a time.

Ignorance of the origin of the zodiac signs as markers of twelve seasonal segments of the year, and a confused identification of them with the star constellations that once merely served to mark these seasons, caused a strange 'explanation' for this cyclic motion of the equinoctial point: its 2,000-year presence in one star-constellation was held to represent a 'great age', supposedly corresponding thematically in a global sense to the characteristics of the season that was originally associated with the constellation, the entire cycle being labelled a 'Great Year'. Thus, fanciful notions appeared about 'great ages' such as the 'age of Pisces', said to have begun around the start of the Common Era (or AD, the time roughly reckoned as the birth of Christ), ending around the beginning of the 21st century and supposedly endowed with characteristics usually associated with the zodiac sign Pisces. The 'age of Aquarius', purportedly having characteristics of that sign, is supposed to be starting roughly at our time of writing. How far removed indeed this is from the true origin of the signs of the zodiac as seasonal divisions of the year conveniently marked by (apparently fixed) star-patterns behind the Sun!

2

The Characterisation of the Planets

We've seen how in ancient times humans projected fundamental aspects of their subjective world onto the heavens. We've looked in particular at the way they projected salient characteristics of the current seasonal conditions onto twelve star-patterns that lay behind the Sun at the corresponding times of the year. There was however another process of psychological projection at work when early humankind observed the heavens. This concerned those celestial bodies which appeared distinct from the stars, namely, the Sun, the Moon and the other planets. In astrological terminology, the Sun and the Moon are referred to as 'planets'. We now know of course that the Sun is the star at the centre of our solar system, and that the Moon is the Earth's satellite. The very earliest explications of the heavens however simply regarded and characterised the bodies that could be observed, without a more advanced astronomical understanding. It has only been comparatively recently that scientific astronomy has revealed the precise mechanics and distances of these bodies in relation to each other, thus disclosing their true framework. Before that time, man was able to discern with the unaided eye that there were seven important bodies in the heavens which followed their own paths separately from the motion of the myriad stars. These were the Sun, the Moon, Mercury, Mars, Venus, Jupiter and Saturn.

Those fainter planets 'beyond' the Sun and the Moon in the night sky must have been objects of extreme interest, 'wandering' as they did from the general path of the mass of stars. They appeared to be attendants, or even perhaps children of the Sun, since the one thing they had in common was the fact that they all followed the path of the Sun (the ecliptic) as it made its year-long journey against the background of the familiar star-patterns. Yet they were all different to one another, both in appearance and behaviour, giving them apparent individuality and intention. In attempting to make sense of these lofty heavenly bodies, it would have been natural for early man to be unconsciously reminded of (or to 'project') facets of his own nature which seemed appropriate to the appearance and the behaviour of each.

Important seasonal characteristics or themes, which can be thought of as 'ways or modes of being in life', or 'types of expression', were projected onto the star-patterns that became the twelve signs of the zodiac. In the case of the visible planets, fewer in number, what was fancifully projected was rather the most basic human life urges, functions or principles, having physical, psychological and social aspects. These fundamental functions, assigned as it were to their embodiments in the heavens, are what humans have from the beginning understood as their major classical 'gods'. Each planet thus became a god in myth; an idealised personification or apotheosis of a fundamental human function. This is how some of the most important mythological gods had their birth in humankind's consciousness, the celestial planets being their visible representations or proxies in the 'heavens'. We may now turn to examine in more detail the characteristics of each of these these 'planet-gods' and the basic human functions that they represent.

The Sun

Astronomically the Sun is the star at the centre of our solar system. From our earth-bound or 'geocentric' point of view the Sun takes about a month to journey through each sign of the zodiac and a year to make one full cycle through them all. In astrology the Sun is seen to be the most significant and important of the 'planets'.[26] This may not be surprising: it hardly needs stating that, for every human in every era, the Sun

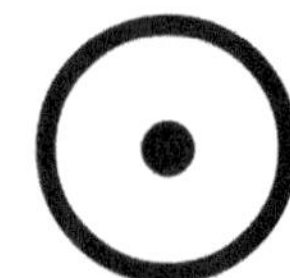

Figure 9. The Astrological Symbol for the Sun

means light, warmth and active life; without it there is a fearful cold and a death-like darkness. We might ask: why does sunshine make us happy? As obvious or idle as the question might appear, there seems no obvious answer, though worldwide, people agree that sunshine makes them happier. It cannot be due simply to the warmth or light it provides us, for other sources of the same amount of light or heat don't give us quite the same happiness. There's a special sense of happiness that comes from sunshine. Even an indirect view of sunshine, such as in a photograph or a video, can give us some sense of this special happiness. A person with a 'sunny' disposition is happy. An image or icon of the Sun is universally seen as one of happiness. But why? And why is it so difficult to articulate an answer? Perhaps it is because the salience of our collective internal representation of the Sun as *the* primal life-giver is so deep-rooted, so heartfelt, and embedded so profoundly in the core of our psycho-physiological and evolutionary nature—as far back as to the time when our ancestors crawled out of the oceans—that in the most fundamental part of our beings we recognise it as the one known bringer of life and the better part of the year.

The Sun has therefore been revered as a powerful deity—perhaps *the* primary deity—since the earliest times. Much of the deification of the Sun must have been bound up, often perhaps almost indistinguishably, with practical considerations. As we've seen, the Sun defines the year and consequently the seasons. Post-Neolithic cultures, who adopted settled communities and who thus developed a distinct sense of place, locality and orientation, needed reliable methods to know precisely the times of these seasons for the purposes of agriculture and the rearing of livestock, upon which their very survival depended. This initially practical knowledge of the solar year eventually became expressed in the most foundational expressions of their culture.

---

[26] In astrological tradition both the Sun and the Moon are referred to for convenience as 'planets'.

A dependable way of identifying the winter solstice in particular would have been especially useful and significant to these people, marking as it does the first subtle but real indication of the year's return to light and therefore to renewed life. The Neolithic people were not content with simple or makeshift technologies to ascertain the Sun's course through the year and its indication of the seasons. Massive stone circles were erected during this era which were specifically constructed to align with the Sun and its movement around the local landscape across the course of a year.[27] Stonehenge, perhaps the most famous of all standing stone circles, is aligned to the sunrise of the summer solstice and the sunset of the winter solstice. The passage tomb at Newgrange in Ireland, constructed between around 3,300 to 2,900 BCE, incorporates a carefully crafted aperture designed to capture the light of the winter solstice Sun and illuminate part of its interior at that specific time.[28] The Neolithic chambered tomb of Maeshowe in Orkney also forms an intricate astronomical solar calendar, intimately connected with its geographical location.[29] Many other ancient structures that served the purpose of ascertaining and magnifying consciousness of the Sun's yearly course can be found around the world.[30] As one author expressed his admiration for such ancient constructions:

> At Stonehenge in England and at Carnac in France, in Egypt and Yucatán, across the whole face of the earth, are found mysterious ruins of ancient monuments, monuments with astronomical significance ... They mark the same kind of commitment that transported us to the moon and our spacecraft to the surface of Mars.[31]

Such literally monumental technology established the precise times of the solstices and thus the year, and so facilitated the reckoning of the months (including 'intercalary' months, inserted into a calendar to harmonise months with the solar year) and enabled the fixing of appropriate dates for planting, harvesting and related agricultural activities.[32] It can hardly be doubted however that these impressive constructions inspired a geomantic and cosmological significance far beyond their initial practical advantage. The methods whereby such incredibly huge structures were transported and erected is still not understood even today, and suggests a consciousness of and a devotion to the solar year that transcended mere utility or even celebration, into a positive deification of the Sun and a numinous significance of its annual journey.

---

[27] Higginbottom & Clay, 2016
[28] O'Kelly, 1982
[29] MacKie, 1997
[30] Ruggles & Cotte, 2010
[31] Krupp, 1980
[32] oldeuropeanculture, 2014

Since the earliest times the Sun has been the pre-eminent object of worship and adoration in the heavens. Its powerful, resplendent nature has permeated every notion of God, greatness and glory. The *Isa Upanishad*, one of the oldest sacred texts of Hindu philosophy and spirituality, has symbolised the universal self (or *Brahman*) as the Sun.[33] The classical Latin word for God *Deus* (from which we derive 'deity') stems etymologically from the Proto-Indo-European root 'Dyēus' from *di or dei- , 'to shine' or 'to be bright', ultimately denoting the radiance of the Sun in the day (as opposed to the darkness of the night) and has many cognate forms in other Indo-European languages (such as the Sanskrit 'Deva', meaning a class of divine being).[34] The Sun has long represented the notion of God as the archetypally authoritative and masculine father principle (more latterly depicted as Michelangelo's venerable, grey-haired, mature man on the ceiling of the Sistine chapel). The Sun as the Father God is the creative spirit of power and vitality in nature, the sole bringer of light and warmth, by whose influence alone all earthly life, drawn up as if in adoration to its joyous face, is made possible. The Sun is in some sense a contrasting masculine counterpoint to the feminine Moon. In this central mythical dichotomy the Sun can be seen as a constant, beaming, smiling face, full of joy, whereas the Moon has often been seen as a changing, afflicted face, reflecting various moods, frequently those of sorrow.

Around the world the Sun has been revered as a powerful (and often, as we have noted, *the* all-powerful) heavenly deity. In ancient Egypt, whose hot, desert lands are dominated by its appearance and extreme influence, the Sun was the most important of gods, and was given many names. In the aspect of the solar disc he was *Aten*; when he rose, *Khepri*; at his most powerful at the zenith, he was *Ra*; when he set, *Atum*. The Sun gods *Horus* and *Ra* were later conjoined to make *Ra-Harakhte*, to reign over all Egypt. Many other ancient Egyptian deities were also identified with the Sun, reflecting the pre-eminence of this most illustrious heavenly presence in the spiritual tradition of this ancient culture.[35] As may befit the Sun's appearance to early humans as a phenomenon which appeared as overwhelmingly sole, unique and undeniably One, the earliest monotheism in the world was that instituted by the Egyptian pharaoh *Akhenaten*, who replaced all other deities with Aten, the god of the solar disc.[36] The ancient Egyptians and many other cultures often portrayed the Sun god as riding in a solar boat across the sky in his daily course.[37]

The ancient Greeks personified and revered the god of the Sun as *Helios*.[38] This deity was depicted as a beautiful young man who, in a similar fashion to

---

[33] Prabhavananda & Manchester, 1947

[34] West, 2007

[35] Ames & Viau, 1965

[36] David, 1998

[37] Siliotti, 1997

[38] The Sun has sometimes been associated with Apollo, though strictly Apollo represented the *light* of the Sun, whereas Helios personified the Sun itself.

portrayals in the Egyptian myths, drove a chariot across the sky each day.[39] The Hindu sun-deity *Surya* was also represented riding a chariot, drawn by seven horses which may have been representations of the remaining *Navagraha* or astronomical body-deities in Hindu astrology, excluding the Moon.[40] The Inca civilisation of South America worshipped the Sun as *Inti*, the supreme god. They considered their king, the *Sapa Inca*, to be the 'son of the Sun', and the people were seen to be the 'children of the Sun'.[41] The South American Aztecs also venerated the Sun as *Tonatiuh*, the leader of heaven. The Aztecs as well as the South American Maya built structures aligned with the Sun and developed sophisticated solar calendars.[42] Interestingly, historic civilisations which developed specifically solar religions tended to be those which had also established urban societies with a strong ideology of sacred kingship, where the Sun's power was symbolically vested in a single, 'royal' individual.[43]

Since at least Neolithic times, myths and cultural traditions have ascribed important significance to the beginning of the solar year at the winter solstice, for reasons that may have begun as largely practical but which soon gained a more all-embracing or spiritual significance. It is shortly after the winter solstice that careful observation can determine that the Sun's light is 'returning' (i.e., that the hours of sunlight in the day are once again increasing) and it is at this point in the year that the Sun can be said to have been 'reborn'. Similarly important 'stations' in the Sun's journey through the year (such as the beginning of spring at the vernal equinox, the apparent culmination of the Sun's power at the summer solstice, and the incipient demise of the solar year at the autumn equinox) have long been surrounded by similarly important rites, rituals and myths (see Chapter 3). The 'birth' of the solar year just after the winter solstice may obviously therefore be particularly significant and inclined to be associated with notions of a glorious nativity.

The Romans celebrated the festival of *Dies Natalis Solis Invicti* ('the day of the birth of the unconquered Sun') on 25th December. In the Christian tradition, Jesus is reputed to have been born on that date,[44] despite the difficulties which that proposal raises with the New Testament's purportedly historical account of the story of his birth (for instance, that shepherds were supposed to have been *"abiding in the field, keeping watch over their flock by night"* at the time,[45] when farmed animals would have been penned indoors). Later Christian commentators have strenuously attempted to disassociate the birth of Jesus from 'pagan' connotations of the birth of the Sun at the winter solstice, even going so far as to suggest, as did St Augustine, that for the day of his nativity, Jesus *"chose the*

---

[39] Guirands, 1967
[40] Dalal, 2014; Jansen, 2001
[41] Conrad & Demarest, 1984
[42] Bingham, 2004; NASA, 2005
[43] Britannica, 2017a
[44] Irenaeus, 1885
[45] Luke 2:8-20

shortest day ... the one whence light begins to increase" in advance of his actual birth.[46] The co-occurrence of the date of the birth of the Christian Jesus and that of the winter solstice, along with their obvious thematic similarities,[47] has however seemed to many unlikely to be mere coincidence.

Indeed there has been and still is a recurrent and pertinacious speculation that the story of the life of Jesus Christ and of many other dying and resurrecting 'god men' may have been fragmented re-tellings in the collective unconscious of a core ancient solar myth, in which the hero undergoes adventures in a journey which is essentially an allegory for the Sun's passage through the year.[48] This theory has been somewhat reinforced by modern scholarship which has argued cogently for the non-historicity of Jesus Christ.[49] We are wary of passing judgement upon this 'solar myth hypothesis', or upon the historicity of Jesus, though it is certainly interesting to note the great proliferation of solar symbolism and motifs in Christian texts and iconography, both before the putative life of Jesus Christ and after, up to present-day representations.[50]

In orthodox or evangelistic religious iconography, representations of Jesus or of some text from the Christian Bible are very often illustrated against a background which shows the Sun. This pictorial solar context has become so ubiquitous and obvious a theme that we hardly notice it any more—we just somehow accept it as a given that the Sun is a fitting motif to accompany a Christian religious representation of God. Christian saints and those associated with divinity in Christianity are also frequently depicted with a Sun-like corona, nimbus or halo around their heads. Christians do not seem to notice the obvious solar reference in uttering prayers to the 'heavenly father', despite the fact that the Sun is indeed in the 'heavens' and has for millennia been the symbol of divine fatherhood. The Jesus figure in the Christian story can be seen to have been referring to the symbolic principle of the father Sun when he likened the 'kingdom of heaven' to a mustard seed,[51] tiny yet powerfully potential, as the dot inside the Sun-glyph, the seed of potentiality in the reproducing living thing, the 'image' of the father that lives on through reproduced creation—an exact restatement of the meaning of the Sun principle in astrological symbolism. We note that the Christian 'Lord's Prayer' is easily interpretable as a collectively unconscious devotional hymnal reference to the principle of the father Sun:

> *"Our Father, which art in heaven, haloed be thy name,*
> (Our Father the Sun, which is in the heavens, the halo of the corona
> shines around you,)

---

[46] Augustine, Sermon 192
[47] Jesus said, *"I am the light of the world"* (John 8:12).
[48] Deley, 2019; Dupuis, 2001; Murdock, 2011; Murdock, 2011a; Stowe, 2010; Taylor, 2006
[49] Carrier, 2014
[50] Murdock, 2011a
[51] Matthew 13:31

"Thy kingdom come,
(Your year-cycle will continue,)

"Thy will be done
(Your power is inevitable and absolute)

"In Earth as it is in Heaven.
(You rule what happens on Earth and in the heavens.)

"Give us this day our daily bread,
(Continue to give us your warmth and light which make our crops grow and which therefore feed us,)

"And forgive us our trespasses, as we forgive those who trespass against us."
(As the Sun shines his light on all, whether good or bad, let us, like him, be good to all.[52,53])

The astrological symbol for the Sun is a circle with a dot in the centre (Figure 9). This glyphic representation of the Sun dates back at least to ancient Egypt.[54] It is also now the universally recognised symbol for the Sun both in astrological and in scientific notation. This glyph is known as the *Monad* (from the Greek μονάς, 'monas', 'singularity', in turn from μόνος, 'monos', 'alone') and represents the supreme being or essence, the indivisible and primal One, or God, the circle as the Sun, being the physical proxy of the universal spirit. It's interesting to note that the symbol resembles a stylised representation of the astronomical solar system, if the dot in the centre is taken to be the Sun and the surrounding circle to be the orbit of bodies.[55] Since antiquity the circle has been seen to symbolise the universal divine spirit, without beginning or end, eternal, unchanging and life-giving, whose principal attribute is oneness, unity, wholeness or completeness. The dot in the centre has been seen to represent the unique spark or seed of that divine and immortal spirit as manifested in the individual.[56] The symbol has been described as the *"seed of potential individual manifestation of human spirit or consciousness within the Collective Unconscious sphere."*[57]

In developed astrology the Sun is a symbol of the generative or creative life-force of the archetypal masculine father.[58] Psychologically it is seen to represent a

---

[52] Matthew 6:9-13; Luke 11:2-4

[53] In Chapter 4 we explore how the Christian New Testament story is interpreted by some as an allegory of the Sun in its journey through the year, with Jesus as the central, heroic solar figure.

[54] Gardiner, 1927

[55] It's notable in this context that in ancient times a precise topology of the solar system was obviously unknown.

[56] Mayo, 1972

[57] Mayo, 1964

[58] *Ibid.*

person's overriding or general nature, their underlying core self or spirit; the person's power, vitality, sense of aliveness; their creativity and consciously willed, purposeful self-expression (as opposed to their unconsciously-driven, involuntary or habitual behaviour); their image of self; their ability and urge to integrate each feature of themselves into wholeness of being, into an impressive and unique individual represented by the whole pattern of their psyche. It is thus a person's true (and unique) self, the vital core which nevertheless apprehends the whole.[59] The Sun therefore corresponds to the creative, conscious vitality of the core *and* whole of the life-spirit, whose urge is to express, imprint, reproduce or recreate its unique self-image.

In astrological symbolism the Sun is physiologically associated with the heart and circulatory system, and the immune system.[60] The central and purposive action of the heart and circulation integrates the entire organism via its network of cardiovascular vessels, while the pulse is a register of the *overall* vitality or the integrated equilibrium of the physical system as a *whole*. The state of the heart's action and the circulatory system is therefore not the cause of 'health' (cognate with 'whole') but an *index* of the health of the system taken holistically. Like the psychological function of the Sun, the heart is the core of the *organism* as an *organised* system, yet it represents the whole. It's notable that 'organisation' is the setting up together, correctly and inter-dependently, of organs, which, taken all together as one, make up a whole. The physiological correlate of the Sun's psychological sense of 'self' is reflected in the body's immune system,[61] which attempts to establish a sense of whole identity; that is, of 'self and other', so that it can repel or destroy the 'other' (in terms of malefic infection, etc.) and preserve the self. The Sun's symbol or glyph may be said to depict, physiologically, the 'seed', nucleus or potentiality of the unique self (the dot) in every cell (the circle); a coded representation, blueprint or 'repeating pattern' of this whole being (in biological terms, the DNA).

We noted above that historically, the Sun in religion and myth is particularly symbolised in urban cultures that have a strongly developed sense of divine kingship, as if in primordial acknowledgement that the king is the heart or index of the realm, while the people or subjects are the individual cells of the 'body politic'. Certainly traditional astrology closely associates the Sun and its ruled sign Leo with the theme of monarchy, royalty or kingship. The king is seen not only to rule but also to represent the entire people, as the Sun-Leo heart function acts as a representative index of the health of the whole organism (the word 'health' itself, cognate with 'whole', is a key Sun-Leo concept). As the functioning of the human heart in the heartbeat or pulse reflects the integrative equilibrium, health and vitality of the whole body as a system, so the monarch symbolises a country's whole or summary 'state'. The king is seen to belong to the whole of society in so far as he is their holistic representative or image.

---

[59] Mayo, 1964; Mayo, 1972; Mayo, 1995
[60] Mayo, 1972
[61] Mayo, 1964

The monarch in this symbolic sense is thus the 'image' or embodiment of the country or people who comprise the realm as a whole, and who thus integrates all of the people, without exception, in the role of an organising principle, as the Sun does the solar system and as the heart does every organ and cell of the body.[62] In traditional folklore the 'touch of kings' was said to heal or make one 'whole'. Both the king and its individual counterpart, the heart, are therefore 'holistic representations' of the system. The monarch is the heart of the people, as image, coherence and integration, as the physiological organ the heart is the core and general index of the physical person.

The word 'king' comes from the Anglo-Saxon *cyning*, cognate with Old English *cynn* meaning 'family', 'people' and the modern 'kin'. Originally, the king was 'the representation of the people',[63] or their embodiment.[64] Of the king it has been said that *"in geometrical terms we may picture* [the king] *at the centre of a circle rather than, as in the later medieval idea of monarchy, at the pinnacle of a pyramid"*.[65]

The heart and the king are therefore both astrologically associated with the Sun, and both embody the holistic aspect of the systems which they govern or rather represent. In this sense they are both akin to the conductor of an orchestra, maintaining or rather expressing the overall equilibrium or homoeostasis of subordinate, specialised functions within a system as a whole. As the heart brings or exemplifies wholeness to the body, so the monarch brings or exemplifies wholeness to the country. The physical symbol of kingship, the crown, is fashioned to be, like the Sun, a circle of gold, and is provided with a nimbus-like outer decoration reminiscent of the Sun's actual corona ('corona' being the Latin word for 'crown'). The crown reinforces and draws attention to the magnificence, uniqueness and 'soleness of the king, as the actual solar corona does to the Sun. It is like the function of a (usually golden) frame around a picture. In traditional astrology the Sun is particularly associated with (or 'rules') the sign Leo (the lion), which shares many of its descriptive attributes. The lion is the 'king of the beasts', and even appears to possess a 'corona' in the form of its majestic mane. The metal traditionally associated with the Sun is gold.

The Moon

Figure 10. The Astrological Symbol for the Moon

Astronomically the Moon is the only permanent natural satellite of the Earth. It was most likely formed about 4.5 billion years ago when a Mars-sized planet named *Theia* collided with the Earth. In the resulting gigantic cataclysm, part of the Earth and part of the remnants of Theia coalesced to give birth to the Moon, the now-familiar heavenly body whose

---

[62] Mayo, 1964
[63] Bosworth & Toller, 1954
[64] Ushigaki, 1982
[65] Carruthers, 1994

apparent shape changes through its familiar phases during each month. It is regarded as an important 'planet' in traditional astrology, second only to the Sun in symbolic significance.[66] Since the Moon takes the same time to rotate upon its axis as it does to orbit the Earth, it always keeps the same side or face turned towards us. As the Moon orbits the Earth, and as both orbit the Sun, the apparent shape of its sunlit portion, as viewed from the Earth, changes from complete shadow (at new moon), to no shadow at all (at full moon), with the familiar crescent shapes appearing in between. Each whole cycle takes one month ('moonth'), or approximately 29.53 days.

This repeating cycle or periodicity, with its incessant ebbing and flowing 'phases' of light and dark, has always been the most noticeable and important aspect of the Moon from our Earth-bound point of view. It has also been a convenient way of apportioning divisions of time in the year. From an initial 'quartering' of the year into the four periods between the points of the solstices and equinoxes, further divisions of three equal periods per quarter were eventually made to mark twelve in total, each corresponding roughly with the duration of one moon period, or month. Although there aren't exactly twelve moon-periods in any one year, the division of the year into twelve 'moonths' influenced the now-familiar number of signs of the zodiac, as well as the twelve civil months set by various calendrical systems.

The slowly undulating appearance of the Moon with its rhythmic oscillation of recurrent rounded shapes resonated with appropriately related aspects of people's experience. The Moon seemed naturally to symbolise the more fluid and changeable aspects of the psyche, in contrast to the fixed and unchanging vitality seen in the Sun. Characteristics of human life which are typically manifest in flux or in states of rhythm were thus collectively projected onto this ebbing and flowing vision in the sky, and the Moon's character as a 'deity' became an externalised symbol of such typically fluctuating factors. The Moon's association with the ebb and flow of fluids and with generally changeable phenomena in human experience also naturally connected it thematically with the tides of the sea and shoreline, which are in fact caused by the Moon's gravitational pull on the Earth's oceans. The Moon is at its most noticeable and mysteriously beautiful at night, and thus in the collective unconscious it has had, symbolically projected upon it, associations of darkness, a certain element of fear, wild imaginings, sleep, dreams and mystery. In dreams, irrational and amazing things happen, and the boundless range of our unconscious imagination comes to the fore.

Deities that distinctly represent the Moon and its fluctuating periodicity are relatively rare in mythology, though they do exist.[67] In the Mayan civilisation of South America, the Moon goddess *Po*, daughter of the Earth god, was seduced by the god of the Sun. Fearing punishment, the two lovers fled, but the Earth father killed his daughter in anger. The Moon's blood was stored in thirteen containers;

---

[66] In traditional astrological terminology both the Sun and the Moon are referred to for convenience as 'planets'.

[67] Britannica, 2017b; Dunn, 2019

when these were opened, out of twelve came insects and plants, which populated the earth, but out of the thirteenth came the spirit of the Moon goddess, who was thus reborn. The Mayan Moon goddess was associated with all aspects of female fertility, and with water.[68] It is interesting to note the appearance of twelve or thirteen units in this Moon mythology, which may well have been associated with the (roughly) similar number of lunar periods in a year.

The ancient Greeks personified the Moon as the goddess *Selene*, daughter of the Titans *Hyperion* and Theia, sister to the solar deity Helios, and adored and courted by the mortal *Endymion*. Selene is personified driving her chariot across the heavens, much as the Greek Helios and the Indian Surya were depicted in the case of the Sun god. Her equivalent in Rome was the goddess *Luna*. The ancient Greek deity *Artemis* was, in addition to being a goddess of hunting, also associated with the Moon and childbirth, her Roman equivalent being *Diana*. It may not be surprising that most lunar deities are characterised as female, since it must have been from the earliest times that the approximate correspondence was noticed between the length of the Moon's cycle and that of the human female period of ovulation. Indeed the word 'menstruation' is derived from the Latin *menstrualis* meaning 'monthly' (of the Moon's period). Some research appears to confirm a relationship between the moon and menstruation,[69] between a bright light during sleep (such as that afforded by the Moon) and the length of the menstrual cycle,[70] and between the type of lunar phase at conception and the sex of the offspring.[71] The association of the Moon specifically with the feminine can only have been reinforced by the rounded curves of its apparent shape, swelling and contracting rhythmically in a manner so suggestive of a pregnant woman's bodily outline.

The astrological symbol for the Moon is the double-curve crescent shape, representative of a common view of the Moon in a waxing phase (Figure 10).[72] The symbol has come to represent 'night-time' or 'sleep' in the icons of modern electronic devices. It is reminiscent of a shut eyelid (and often appears so, in the form a 'wet' or 'Cheshire' moon nearer the tropics), in contrast to the 'open eye' of the Sun's glyph. The symbol has been said to depict *'the incomplete circle: the mind, evolving human spirit. Or the dual nature of human spirit, part conscious, part unconscious'*.[73] While the circular symbol for the Sun represents the complete and unchanging spirit, the Moon's crescent is rather evocative of constantly altering phenomena and so represents the incomplete spirit, or the mind, evolving by changes and attachments to the world of things which are apprehended in time. The Moon is therefore a changing face, reflecting various moods, often of anguish and sorrow (whereas the Sun is popularly a constant, beaming, smiling face, full

---

[68] Thompson, 1998; Thompson, 1939

[69] Cutler, 1980; Law, 1986

[70] Lin *et al.*, 1990

[71] Sarkar & Biswas, 2005

[72] Waxing in the northern hemisphere; in the southern hemisphere the symbol would be representative of a waning phase.

[73] Mayo, 1964

of joy). The dark-light nature of the Moon's face can also be seen to represent the dually-layered aspect of human consciousness which has both conscious (bright) and unconscious (dark) elements.

In developed astrology the Moon is a projected symbol of the feminine and maternal principle, in contrast to the masculine and paternal Sun. Psychologically it's seen to represent or to be associated with a person's moods, emotions and emotional security; one's instinctive, unguarded, 'automatic' or involuntary emotional responses and behaviour, often due to unconsciously assimilated early conditioning in infancy; one's habit-patterns or mannerisms, developed over time (often of a crudely protective nature); rhythms, memory, reflective imagination, the subconscious and sleep. The Moon is also traditionally associated with one's emotional relationship to one's mother, family, ancestry and the patriotic identification with one's land or country.

That the Moon is closely associated with emotional factors seems appropriate, since, as noted above, it is the heavenly body which influences earthly ocean tides, the 'element' water having long symbolised the emotions. Our language reflects the portrayal of emotions in terms evoking water when we speak of 'still waters running deep' or 'wellsprings of emotion'. The changing aspect of the Moon has been seen to reflect symbolically the fluctuating characteristic of human emotions—now happy, now sad. Like the ocean, our emotions are typically changeable, fluid, often turbulent and hard to control. The salt tears of our emotional expression are also reminiscent of the salty water of the oceans.

The Moon is associated with time-based phenomena (as opposed to the Sun's 'eternal' appearance) and symbolically it is strongly tied to the past and to memory generally. The need for sleep, like the Moon's monthly phases, occurs with rhythmic periodicity, not only in terms of the nightly cycle of the period of sleep, but also with regard to the different periods or stages of different types of brain activity during sleep. It is interesting to note that the Moon's astrological association with both sleep and memory is reflected in the fact that physiological processes during sleep appear to be essential for the consolidation and the healthy functioning of learning and memory.[74]

In a similar connection to 'influences of the past', the symbolism of the Moon is associated with upbringing and early infancy (connecting again to the lunar maternal aspect) and with the learned habit patterns implanted in that developmental period; thus it is associated with the habitual, instinctive and responsive nature, prototypically instilled by the mother-infant relationship. It is therefore seen as apparent in one's unconsciously conditioned and unguarded outward manners; one's fluid and altering emotional moods, mannerisms, fluctuations, rhythms and habits. The Moon is also seen to be the changeable flux, reflection and emotional response of the mind, rather than the static, deliberate and willed creativity of the spirit seen in the Sun.[75]

---

[74] Rasch & Born, 2013; Yang *et al.*, 2014
[75] Mayo, 1964

The association of the Moon with changeable emotions and moods, such as those which often present during the female period of menstruation, has gone so far as to link its symbolic nature with 'lunacy'; indeed the word 'lunatic' is derived from the Latin word for Moon, *Luna*. Even in recent times, the periodic phases of the Moon have been proposed to be correlated with, if not causally responsible for, such various factors as fertility, reproductive behaviour, birth rates, blood loss, mental disorders, social disorder and sleep. Modern scientific commentators have been sceptical of these notions and have tended to doubt the validity of studies that link the phases of the Moon with such factors, though some research results have been so well supported that they have not been so easily dismissed.[76]

In terms of human physiology the Moon's astrological associations are traditionally said to be with functions that govern the regulation and flow of rhythmic and fluctuating processes, particularly those involving fluids, such as in the stomach and the digestive system generally, the lymphatic system and synovial fluids; in females, menstruation, the breasts, lactation, the uterine reproductive system and the instinctive urge towards the nurturing of young.[77] As we noted above, the Moon is also strongly associated with mechanisms that govern habitual and conditioned or 'automatic' responses, and with memory, dreaming and sleep.[78] Traditionally the Moon is associated with (or 'rules') the zodiac sign Cancer, which shares many of its descriptive attributes. The metal traditionally associated with the Moon is silver.

Mercury

Astronomically Mercury is the innermost planet in our solar system (the closest to the Sun) and the smallest—if one discounts Pluto, whose official planetary status was 'demoted' by the International Astronomical Union to that of a 'dwarf planet' in 2006 (see the section on Pluto). It is also the fastest in terms of its orbital rotation around the Sun, from which it is never more than 28° when viewed from the Earth. Because of this proximity to its parent star, Mercury is never far away enough from the Sun to be seen from Earth in the dark of the night sky and is therefore

Figure 11. The Astrological Symbol for Mercury

only visible at the times of dawn and dusk, and even then with some difficulty. Mercury's speedy journeyings and short-lived appearance makes the planet difficult to glimpse. Amongst the planets, it presents as the very heavenly embodiment of swiftness. Not surprisingly it therefore became associated with those aspects of the human psyche that are concerned with rapidity—such as with thought, the mind, and all forms of quick communication.

---

[76] Cajochen *et al.*, 2013
[77] Mayo, 1964
[78] Yang *et al.*, 2014; Cajochen *et al.*, 2013

It seems appropriate therefore that Mercury appears in mythology as a 'messenger' god, known as *Hermes* in the Greek tradition and *Mercurius* in the Roman. The deity personified communication, often of the messenger or herald, but also that of commerce and merchants, of trade-routes and roads. As the pre-eminent communicator, Mercury represented eloquence and quick-thinking—sometimes the artful and sharp thinking of the trickster or thief, being quick-witted enough to outwit others. Hermes-Mercury also frequently symbolised the 'guide who knew the way', notably as *Hermes Psychopompus*, the deity who conducted or communicated souls to the afterlife.[79] He was typically represented holding a staff or 'magic wand' known as the *Caduceus*,[80] around which are depicted two coiled snakes—tokens of his quick, strong mental powers. He was often portrayed as having wings on his feet or footwear, and on his cap or head, to convey his particular ability for speed and swiftness. At times he was associated with the exemplary swiftness of athletes.

The astrological and astronomical symbol for Mercury is a half circle (inverted dome) positioned over a circle, with both of these being placed over a cross (Figure 11). The pattern of the symbol's components has been said to represent the mind (the half circle) taking precedence over the spirit (the circle) and over matter (the cross).[81] Certainly the predominance of thought and communication that is emphasised in the symbolism of Mercury would agree with this iconography. Interestingly, the symbol is itself visually suggestive of the shape of Mercury's Caduceus, and the half circle above the circle at the top may be said to be reminiscent of the god's winged cap.

In developed astrology Mercury signifies a person's nervous co-ordination of sensory information, the logical processing of thought, and the subsequent communication of its message or meaning. It is a person's ability to adapt to the ever-changing immediate environment through their thinking mentality, their intellect; their urge and ability to know or cognise; to gather and encode information, and to interpret it by mentally representing and manipulating it as abstract, logical concepts, as well as their faculty to communicate or transmit such information, either in speech or in writing, or by motion and transport (for instance in the communication necessarily involved in trade).[82,83] Mercury is often taken to be unemotional, being principally concerned with the purely logical relations between concepts, and the interpretation and nervous transmission of information.

---

[79] From the Greek ψυχοπομπός, psychopompós, meaning the 'guide of souls'.

[80] From the Latin Caduceus, from the Greek κηρύκειον kērúkeion, 'herald's wand, or staff', derived from the earlier Greek κῆρυξ kêrux, 'messenger', 'herald' or 'envoy'.

[81] Mayo, 1972

[82] Mayo, 1964; Mayo, 1972

[83] The sense of Mercury's communication by way of physical carriage in trade may be reflected in the likelihood that the words 'market' and possibly 'mercantile' might be derived from the Latin word for Mercury, *Mercurius*, as the god of exchange, the term being borrowed from the Etruscan; see Online Etymology Dictionary (2024).

Mercury is physiologically associated with the sensory and nervous systems, especially the brain and its close relationship with the respiratory system, the arms and the hands—the primary psycho-physiological faculties whereby a person selects, receives, stores, processes and communicates salient information about the environment and its logical implications.[84] In traditional astrology Mercury is particularly associated with (or 'rules') the zodiac signs Gemini (the twins, emphasising the planet's characteristic mode of duality) and Virgo. The metal traditionally associated with Mercury is the element mercury (or quicksilver).

Venus

Figure 12. The Astrological Symbol for Venus

Astronomically Venus is the second planet from the Sun. Apart from the Moon, it is the closest heavenly body to the Earth and the brightest object in the night sky. Venus is never more than 48° from the Sun, which means that it's most easily visible in the early morning and in the evening. For this reason the planet has been called both the Morning Star and the Evening Star. Its beautiful, soft yet brilliant aspect at these liminal times of day has since the earliest times evoked the artistic inspiration of writers and poets who have praised its charm. The aesthetic visual appeal of the planet's physical appearance no doubt influenced its projected embodiment of the common human feeling for beauty and attraction, thus becoming in mythology the goddess of love—the divine personification of this fundamental life principle or urge.

To the ancient Greeks she was *Aphrodite* (from where we derive the word 'aphrodisiac', meaning a love-potion), to the Romans, Venus (from where we derive the term 'venereal' meaning 'of or relating to sexual desire'), in both cases being the goddess of love, beauty and sexual attraction. In the Roman tradition Venus was also seen in a wider sense to embody the principle that unites the opposites of male and female in mutual affection.[85] In western art and culture Aphrodite-Venus has been seen as the paragon or exemplar of female beauty, allure and attractiveness.

The astrological symbol for Venus is a circle set above a smaller cross (Figure 12). The glyph has been described as representing the divinity of spirit (the circle) taking precedence above grosser matter (the cross).[86] The symbolic component that usually betokens the mind, the half-circle, is absent, which can perhaps be taken to signify that the human urge of attraction and love is not one of logical thought, but primarily a motivation of the feelings.

---

[84] Mayo, 1964

[85] Varro, 1938

[86] Mayo, 1972

The symbol taken as a whole has also been seen as a necklace adorning Venus (the neck being associated with Taurus, one of the two signs associated with the planet),[87] or as the hand-mirror in which she surveys her beauty.[88] The symbol is widely used in biological, medical and scientific notation to denote the feminine principle generally.

In developed astrology Venus represents the urge for harmony; this can be harmony with other people by attracting them into close ties, relationships and co-operative partnerships, as well as the urge for harmony in the sense of aesthetics or beauty. It represents the urge and need to judge and value experience through sympathetic feelings; the desire for relatedness, for the uniting of opposites, for peace and the smoothing out of roughness and discordance through charm, affection, partnership, beauty and art. It also relates to the capacity to attract, acquire, possess and enjoy pleasant material things. Venus represents the feminine principle in any sex.

Venus is physiologically associated with the ears (closely connected to our sense of balance), nose, neck and throat (centres of olfaction or smell and gustation or taste, both intimately concerned with what we find attractive, pleasant or 'tasteful'). It is also associated with the kidneys and the venous veins.[89] In traditional astrology Venus is particularly associated with (or 'rules') the zodiac signs Taurus and Libra. The metal traditionally associated with Venus is copper.

Mars

Astronomically Mars is the fourth planet from the Sun in the solar system, after Mercury, Venus and Earth. The most striking aspect of its appearance in the night sky is its distinctive reddish colour. The colour red is universally perceived by humans as a sign of potential danger, most probably from its obvious association with blood. Blood in turn is linked to heightened emotional passions such as lust

Figure 13. The Astrological Symbol for Mars

and anger, as well as to fighting and injury. We speak of blood in terms of anger when we say *"He made my blood boil,"* or *"His blood was up."* Red is also the approximate colour of fire, whose dangerous nature is closely related to the hazards of anger, as when we speak of a 'heated' argument. The planet's conspicuous red colour was therefore a primary reason for its identification with human functions that are evocative of passion and danger.

In mythology Mars thus became a projected symbol of humankind's more martial and passionate functions and urges (the word 'martial' itself derives from the Latin term for the planet or god Mars). Babylonian astronomers knew the

---

[87] Society for the Diffusion of Useful Knowledge, 1839
[88] Mattison, 1872
[89] Mayo, 1964

40

planet as *Nergal,* a god of war, destruction and fire.[90] In old Chinese and other Eastern Asian cultures Mars was known as the 'fire star', being associated with war and killing.[91] In ancient Greece he was *Ares,* the god of war, and particularly of the more merciless and wanton aspects of conflict. Even Zeus, the ruler of the gods in the Greek pantheon, complained to Ares that he was *"of all the gods ... the most odious to me, for you enjoy nothing but strife, war and battles."*[92] To the Romans, Mars was also the god of war, though in that culture he possessed a more dignified and less savage reputation than the Greek Ares, being seen more as a military guardian of the Roman state and people.

The astrological symbol for Mars is a circle with an arrow projecting upwards from its right side at a forcefully elevated angle of about 45° (Figure 13). This glyph has been described as matter (the cross-like arrow) taking precedence over spirit (the circle), suggesting a primarily physical or sensory function,[93] in keeping with Mars's highly corporeal theme in mythology. Forty-five degrees is the angle from which a projectile such as a spear may be thrown the farthest; the angle may thus be seen as a representation of the threatening and powerful thrust of a martial weapon and of the virile strength of the Martian quality. The Mars glyph has also been seen as a depiction of a shield and a spear.[94] The thrusting, 'gravity-defying' angle of the projecting arrow or weapon is also suggestive of a phallus—a martial image.

In biology the symbol signifies the male sex, while in alchemy and chemistry it denotes iron, the oxide form of which is, coincidentally, the substance that covers the planet Mars and which gives it its distinctive red colour. The symbol was first used to denote the planet Mars in the middle ages.[95] As in many astrological planetary glyphs, the meaning of the planet-function seems to converge in the symbol from different possible sources.

In developed astrological symbolism Mars represents the urge for effortful activity, activation, energetic expression, heat, initiatory force, initiative, self-assertion, self-projection, physical strength, working ability, courage, enterprise, sexual energy or potency, and the ability to face challenges, compete, fight and pioneer. Mars represents the masculine principle in any sex. Physiologically Mars is associated with the muscles, the urogenital system, the sex and adrenal glands and the red blood cells.[96] In traditional astrology Mars is particularly associated with (or 'rules') the zodiac signs Aries (and in older traditions, Scorpio). The metal traditionally associated with Mars is iron.[97]

---

[90] Sheehan, 1996

[91] Cochrane, 1997

[92] Powell, 2013

[93] Mayo, 1972

[94] Mattison, 1872; Maunder, 1934; Stearn, 1962

[95] Evans, 1998

[96] Mayo, 1972

[97] Curiously a dietary deficiency of iron can cause the blood to lack adequate healthy red blood cells, often resulting in extreme fatigue—a lack of the 'energy for action' which is so closely associated with the planet's function.

Jupiter

Figure 14. The Astrological Symbol for Jupiter

Astronomically Jupiter is the fifth planet from the Sun and by far the largest in our solar system, possessing more than twice the mass of all the other planets combined. Comprised mostly of gases, this truly giant planet features on its surface a storm (the 'Great Red Spot') that is twice the size of the Earth and which has been raging for more than a hundred years. Jupiter has an exalted appearance, being the brightest object in the night sky after the Moon and Venus. It is bright enough to be seen even in the daytime under favourable conditions. The planet may have a role in protecting the inner planets of the solar system—including the Earth—from an overly high frequency of potentially dangerous impacts from comets and asteroids, by virtue of its enormous gravitational attraction.[98]

In mythology the planet Jupiter is associated with the Greek *Zeus* (Ζεύς) or *Dias* (Δίας), the god of thunder, law and justice, the greatest of the deities in the Greek pantheon. The name 'Zeus' stems from *Diēus*, a god of the heavens,[99] from the Proto-Indo-European root '*dyeu-' ('to shine'), cognate with the Latin *Deus* ('god'), the English 'deity' and the French *Dieu* ('God'). To the Romans he was *Iuppiter* (Jupiter), which word derives from the Indo-European vocative compound *Dyēu-pəter ('Sky-god Father'),[100] and is cognate with the Latin *Deus Pater* ('god father'), the Greco-Roman *Zeus pater* ('Father Zeus') and the Sanskrit 'Dyáuṣ Pitṛ́' ('father of heaven'). The English form 'Jove' originated from the old Latin *Iovis*, from the same Proto-Indo-European root '*dyēu-' as above.[101] It is from this contraction that we obtain the adjective 'Jovian' meaning 'pertaining to Jupiter', and 'jovial' meaning 'merry' (expansive good humour being one of the god-function's typical attributes in mythology and symbolism).

Jupiter is closely associated with the Hindu god *Indra* and the Norse god *Thor*, both of whom have thematic attributes similar to their Greek and Roman counterparts. The core symbolism of these closely allied mythological figures is that of a deity who is supreme amongst the extra-solar planetary gods, being especially associated with thunder, the responsible law of the state, and justice.

The astrological symbol or glyph for Jupiter is a large half-circle to the left of, and slightly above, a cross shape (Figure 14). This symbol has been seen as an orthographic variant of the Greek letter Zeta (Z or ζ), standing for Zeus (Ζεύς).[102] In more specifically astrological sources the symbol has been seen as the mind (the half-circle) above, or rather expanding out of, the level of matter (the cross).

---

[98] Holley, 2006
[99] Beekes, 2016
[100] Watkins, 1969
[101] Online Etymology Dictionary, 2019a
[102] Mattison, 1872

This symbolic representation has been interpreted as the need for the mind or consciousness to expand, extend and develop beyond and out of, the horizon of the immediate physical environment.[103] This accords with the astrological symbolism of the planet, which signifies the urge to grow, expand, prosper and preserve the life (both materially and mentally through understanding), through opportunity, extensive travel over distant horizons, deeper study and broadened experience generally.

The Jupiter 'deity function' represents the person's aptitude for well-being, and the tendency towards cheerful, jovial, optimistic, expansive ways; the person's ability for scope and compensation for inadequacies elsewhere; for healing, growth, and the way in which the person will fortuitously benefit from good luck or success.[104] It is also seen to embody a person's conscience and sense of justice with mercy; their sense of law, order and morals, sometimes in the context of formal religious convictions. Jupiter's function is to expand auspiciously into maturity and fulfilment.

Physiologically Jupiter is associated with organs and processes that are concerned with healing and preserving—the physical correlates or equivalents of Jupiter's psychological functions. These have been identified primarily as the liver, the largest organ in the body (as Jupiter is the largest planet in the solar system) whose function is concerned with detoxification and healing and which is the only organ capable of compensatory growth, such functions curiously mirroring the keyword functions mentioned above; the deposition of fats and the posterior lobe of the pituitary gland.[105] The metal traditionally associated with Jupiter is tin.

Saturn

Astronomically Saturn is the sixth planet from the Sun, and the second largest after Jupiter. The planet's most famous feature is its impressive system of equatorial rings, though since these are not visible to the naked eye they were unknown until they could be observed with the use of a telescope, by Galileo in 1610 and more extensively by the Dutch astronomer Christiaan Huygens in 1659. From the Earth, Saturn does not generally appear as bright as some other planets that are visible to the naked eye such as Venus or Jupiter, though it can appear

Figure 15. The Astrological Symbol for Saturn

brighter than Mars and Mercury. To the unaided eye it presents a somewhat austere appearance with a pale, yellowish colour. Saturn marks the limit or boundary of planets in the solar system that can be seen without optical instru-

---

[103] Mayo, 1972

[104] Jupiter's deific symbolism as healer, compensator and provider of good fortune is curiously in accordance with the planet's astronomical role in protecting the Earth from a dangerously high frequency of asteroidal or cometary impacts, as mentioned above (see Holley, 2006).

[105] Mayo, 1972

ments. Saturn was considered and taught to be the most distant planet from Earth even before the heliocentric nature of planetary orbits was understood.[106]

Saturn has a significant place in mythology, being commonly associated with deities that concern important and somewhat stern and sober societal themes such as *"time-cycles, reaping, darkness, strife, agriculture and social order."*[107] Babylonian astronomers carefully observed the planet's movements and identified it as the god *Ninurta*, originally a deity of agriculture, whose civilising influence freed humans from the sickness of hunger. To the Romans he was *Saturnus*, a god of agriculture, and moreover a mythical king who was said to have ruled all Italy in a supposed Golden Age of lawful behaviour and an absence of any need for toil. Saturnus was considered to be the original founder of all Roman civilisation and the bringer of social order out of chaos.[108] The name 'Saturn', both of the planet and of the Roman god, is probably derived from the Latin *satus*, being the past participle of *serere*, 'to sow' (seed).[109] An alternative origin has been proposed as being from *Satre*, the name of an Etruscan god who has been identified with Saturn, though this etymology remains unclear.[110]

The Romans identified their god Saturn with the earlier Greek deity *Cronus* (alternatively *Cronos*, or *Kronos*), god of time and time-cycles,[111] especially those related to the harvest.[112] Like the Roman Saturn, Cronus was also said to have presided over a 'golden age', free of labour and thus of slavery. Cronus-Saturn is often depicted wielding a scythe, and was closely connected with the commencement of the new year. In Greek mythology Cronus devoured his children, ostensibly because he had learned from a prophecy that one of them would kill him, though the story perhaps originated from an ancient allegory of the collective understanding that time (as Cronus) eventually destroys all he creates. Cronus's sixth child Zeus (Jupiter) was however spared this fate.

The astrological symbol for Saturn is somewhat like a reversed and inverted version of that for Jupiter, being a cross to the left of and above a half circle (Figure 15). The pattern of its components has been described as the mind (the half circle) below the level of matter (the cross), implying a state where physical necessities have precedence over, or impose limits on, the mind.[113] The symbol also has a certain resemblance to the scythe which Saturn is frequently portrayed as wielding. In developed astrology Saturn represents a person's need and tendency for caution, restraint, limitation, discipline, inhibition, self-consciousness and self-control in life; the power for sustained, laborious and monotonous work, requiring patience and a sense of duty.

---

[106] By the Alexandrian astronomer Ptolemy (c. 100 — c. 170 CE).

[107] Mayo, 1972

[108] *Ibid.*

[109] Varro, 1938

[110] Versnel, 1992

[111] Whence we derive time-related words such as 'chronology', 'chronometer', 'chronic', 'anachronism' and 'chronicle'.

[112] Cicero, 1933; Plutarch, 2011

[113] Mayo, 1972

These abilities and attitudes, along with respectfulness (especially for authority) are those that frequently aim for and enable ambition, aspiration and career advancement. It shows a person's need and capacity for serious and sober attitudes, and the realistic and responsible handling of affairs. Where Jupiter is seen to represent expansion, Saturn rather stands for a person's tendency towards restriction, formativeness and rigidity; the need to accept structure and the ties of necessity in life, to bear the weight of responsibility and to keep within necessary bounds.

In a related way Saturn also represents a person's disposition to feel insufficiency in life, to endure and overcome difficulties, often of a chronic nature, and the manner in which the person will be limited, controlled, frustrated or delayed, either physically or emotionally, by what may seem to be the sternness of fate. Saturn has perhaps had an unduly negative symbolic connotation, being seen merely as indicative of things that are simply unfortunate or malevolent (even being known traditionally as 'the great malefic'), but this is a superficial view which misrepresents Saturn's embodiment as the essential human function or urge for necessary order and structure in life.

In its astrologically symbolic or thematic sense Saturn does seem to be something of a mirror-image of the optimistic and expansive function represented by Jupiter, which even appears to be reflected in the horizontal and vertical reversal of the two planets' symbols. It seems fitting that Saturn's symbolic emphasis on limitation and boundaries is coincidentally echoed in the physical planet's visible system of 'bounding' rings. Physiologically, Saturn is associated with the body's skeletal system and the skin, which are symbolic of the structural, formative and limiting characteristic of the planet's theme. Saturn is representative of processes that typically take long periods of time to function and develop, as is the case with the skeleton and the bony system. The planet is also said to be related to the anterior lobe of the pituitary gland.[114] The metal associated in traditional astrological symbolism with Saturn is lead.

Uranus

Figure 16. The Astrological Symbol for Uranus

Astronomically Uranus is the seventh planet from the Sun. Classified as an 'ice giant', it is comprised of comparatively large amounts of frozen water, ammonia and methane, and has the coldest atmosphere of any planet in the solar system. To astronomers Uranus presents as an unusual planet in that, unique in the solar system, the axis of its rotation is tilted almost 90° away from the plane of its orbit around the Sun. This striking phenomenon is thought to have been caused by a collision with a planet-sized object in the early part of the solar

---

[114] Mayo, 1972

system's original formation.[115] Uranus is not one of the 'classical' planets of ancient astrology, since it was only discovered to *be* a planet in 1781 by Sir William Herschel. It had indeed been observed in the heavens before this date, possibly as early as the second century BCE by the Greek astronomer Hipparchus, though it had been presumed to be just another star. This may not be surprising, as Uranus takes 84 years to orbit the Sun; thus its 'wandering' across the night sky relative to the backdrop of the fixed stars—the telltale mark of a planet—was too slow to have been noted. Herschel himself did not name the newly-discovered planet 'Uranus', but suggested that it be called *Georgium Sidus* (Latin for 'George's Star') as a tribute to his patron, the ruling monarch of Britain, King George the Third. Some astronomers had earlier simply referred to the planet as 'Herschel' after its discoverer.

Neither Herschel's appellation *Georgium Sidus* nor his surname proved to be the most popular denomination for the planet, however. In 1782 the German astronomer Johann Bode proposed the name Uranus, which seemed appropriate, since in Greek mythology, just as Saturn (Cronus) was the father of Jupiter (Zeus), who was in turn the father of Mars (Ares), Venus (Aphrodite) and Mercury (Hermes), so the new and next more distant planet should, by following such a mythological hereditary scheme, be named after the father of Saturn, who was Uranus (Greek: Οὐρανός). This designation became the preferred name, and was made universal in 1850 when the UK's HM Nautical Almanac Office, the pre-eminent source for astronomical data and nomenclature, officially recognised and adopted it. The planet has been referred to as Uranus ever since.

In Greek mythology Uranus was the father god of the sky, being one of the 'primordial deities', or the first gods to be born from the void of Chaos. Uranus (sky) mated with *Gaia* (the mother earth),[116] who subsequently gave birth to the first divine generation, known as the Titans. Two of these, Cronus (Saturn) and *Rhea*, united to give birth to Zeus (Jupiter). The prime component in the mythological story of Uranus is that his son, Cronus (Saturn), envied his father's power and, encouraged by Gaia (who had harboured a resentment towards Uranus for hiding away some of their children), castrated his father, flinging his mutilated genitals into the sea. Following his castration, the supreme reign of Uranus supposedly came to an end and he remained as an embodiment of the sky. The name 'Uranus' may derive from Greek, Sanskrit and Indo-European forms which carry the meaning 'rain-maker'. [117] Uranus has been associated with the Roman *Caelus*, and the Mesopotamian god *Anu*, both being gods who also personified the sky. There do not seem to be any especial personality or behavioural characteristics of Uranus in mythology however, other than the themes of his being god of the sky, the antipathy of his offspring and his eventual castration by one of them.

There appear to be two symbols that represent the planet Uranus. The first is a circle surmounted by a capital letter "H" joined by a vertical line extending

---

[115] Bergstralh *et al.*, 1991

[116] In some accounts, Uranus was also the son of Gaia; see Hesiod & Evelyn-White (2006).

[117] Beekes, 2016

from the top of the circle (Figure 16). This symbol was pro-posed by the French astronomer Jérôme Lalande in 1784. Herschel took Lalande's suggested glyph as containing the capital 'H' of his own surname.[118] Modern astrologers often modify the two vertical bars of the capital 'H' into two outward-facing curves or semicircular arcs (Figure 17).[119] The second symbol that is used to denote Uranus is a circle with a central dot (as in the symbol for the Sun) surmounted by a vertically-pointing arrow (Figure 18). This alternative glyph

Figure 17. The 'Splayed Sides' Astrological Symbol for Uranus

has been somewhat vaguely interpreted as comprising *"combined devices indicating the Sun plus the spear of Mars, as Uranus was the personification of heaven in Greek mythology, dominated by the light of the Sun and the power of Mars."*[120]

Figure 18. The Alternative Astrological Symbol for Uranus

Due to the fact that Uranus, like the other 'extra-Saturnian' planets (i.e., those beyond the orbit of Saturn) was only comparatively recently observable as a planet, it did not feature in ancient classical astrology, though modern astrologers do indeed view it as symbolically representing a common human function. In developed astrological symbolism Uranus is seen as signifying a person's urge towards freedom and deviation from the normal; their power to exert a free, rebellious, independent and often unconventional spirit, even if that flies in the face of authority or prevailing social norms. It embodies a person's capacity for originality; for revolutionary ideas; for the espousal of (often abrupt) changes in a social and humanitarian context, even to the point of revolt and anarchy; for sudden and dramatic insight, and the wholly new creative inventiveness of genius; for unorthodox and reformative thought, especially in the realms of science, technology or social issues; for disruption and drastic change.

Physiologically Uranus is said to be associated with the sympathetic nervous system, the pineal gland and the sex gonads.[121] Uranus's keyword associations also suggest the natural abrupt and random process of mutation, which introduces completely new structures or processes in a species that may prove to have value in solving old problems and which will be thus selected for inheritance, looking forward to new possibilities in the future. Uranus's theme of 'deviation from the normal' seems coincidentally physically symbolised by the astronomical planet's unique and dramatic tilted axis of rotation, as well as by its being the first planet beyond the orbit of Saturn, which latter represents apparently inflexible boundaries and which is the last of the 'classical' or 'old order' of planets; in this sense it could be said to represent a breakaway from Saturn's characteristically 'rigid conventions'.

---

[118] Herschel, 1917
[119] Mayo, 1972
[120] NASA, 2018
[121] Mayo, 1972

The human functions or urges represented by the 'extra-Saturnian' planets are often seen by astrologers to be related to the major societal changes and social themes that occurred around the times of their discoveries. In the case of Uranus, it's notable that the American War of Independence—a movement certainly directed towards social freedom and the breaking away from old structures, in keeping with the associations of Uranus described above—was effectively decided in favour of the revolutionaries in 1781 (the year of Uranus's discovery), when a combined American and French force inflicted a decisive defeat upon the English army at Yorktown. Another revolution of a different kind but no less momentous, the Industrial Revolution, with its radical and innovative shift to mechanised production in factories, was establishing itself in Great Britain. It's also worthy of note that the era which saw the discovery of Uranus coincided with the social conditions which foreshadowed that other great rebellion and overthrow of existing authority, the French Revolution, which was around that time fomenting and which began in full earnest only a few years later.

Neptune

Astronomically Neptune is the eighth planet from the Sun in the solar system. So far away is it from its parent star that it takes about 165 Earth-years to make one full orbit. Neptune was unknown to the ancients as its great distance renders it invisible to the naked eye. Indeed, the planet was not discovered by direct observation, but indirectly through mathematical infer- ence. The French astronomer Alexis Bouvard had suspected that perturbations in the orbit of Uranus were the result of gravita- tional attraction by a hitherto unknown planet. The English astronomer John Adams in 1845, and later Bouvard's compatriot

Figure 19. The Astrological Symbol for Neptune

Urbain Le Verrier in 1846, predicted the co-ordinates where the unknown planet should be located. Adams's calculations however did not come to light until after Le Verrier had announced his results. Le Verrier sent his calculations to the German astronomer Johann Gottfried Galle who, with his student assistant Heinrich d'Arrest, looked in the area of sky indicated, and on 23 September 1846 found a body which was not listed on the star map. The next day the body was observed to have moved against the background of stars and to possess a disc, and was thus revealed to be a new planet.

The discovery of Neptune is thus characterised by some confusion and it is difficult to say with certainty who can be said to have discovered the planet: was it Adams, Le Verrier, the observer Galle, or Galle's student assistant d'Arrest (who was the one who announced that the observed object was not on the star map)? The planet's naming was also the subject of confusion—and some deception. Galle suggested the name Janus in a letter to Le Verrier, but Le Verrier replied to say that his own preferred name was 'Neptune' (possibly because of the planet's distinctively vivid dark blue appearance and thus its redolence of the ocean, of which the ancient god Neptune was the divine personification). Le Verrier furthermore added in his reply to Galle that the name 'Neptune' had in any case already been ratified by the French Bureau of Longitudes. This however was not true; indeed the Bureau had no function to name astronomical bodies. Shortly after this, it appears that Le Verrier changed his mind and instead began to believe that the planet should be named after himself. But the international astronomical community had already begun to use the name 'Neptune' and it was this appellation that stuck.[122]

In Roman mythology the god Neptune (Latin Neptunus), after which Le Verrier named the planet, was a deity of water, both of freshwaters and the sea. The name probably derives from the Proto-Indo-European root '*nebh-' meaning 'cloud', which is the cognate source of the Latin 'nebula' meaning 'fog', 'mist' or 'cloud', via a sense of 'moist' or 'wet'.[123] The ancient Roman Neptune was originally a god of springs, rivers and lakes before being identified closely with the Greek god Poseidon—more specifically a god of the sea. Neptune was frequently portrayed as having a turbulent, chaotic character, reflecting the tempestuous and unpredictable nature of the ocean. He is typically depicted as a bearded man wielding a trident, often travelling across the sea in a horse-drawn chariot. Neptune was also worshipped as 'Neptune Equester', patron of horse riding. In the post-Roman western world, however, Neptune as a deity has become almost synonymous with the spirit of the ocean.

The astrological glyph for Neptune is a semi-circle directly above a cross, the vertical bar of which extends upwards, into or beyond the top of the semi-circle. The glyph's geometry seems an apt representation of Neptune's trident (see Figure 19). The symbol has been described astrologically as the mind (the half-circle) being dominant over, though arising out of, matter (the cross),[124] which is in keeping with the central astrological interpretation of the function of Neptune as being one of transcendence (see below). As we've noted, due to its immense distance, Neptune was not observable as a planet to the ancients, and therefore did not feature in classical astrology. Modern astrologers have nevertheless proposed that the planet does represent a common human function, namely, that of the urge for the transcendence or abnegation of the mundane, material self. In developed astrology Neptune represents a person's urge for the non-material or the spiritual; the yearning to seek experience *"beyond and detached from all material form and structure,"*[125] towards subtlety of spirit; to impressionability, immateriality and nebulousness. It is the desire to use the imagination and, from the subtlest and *"most sensitive perceptive faculties"* to have contact with the hidden or the non-material and the intangible.[126]

---

[122] Littmann, 2004
[123] Online Etymology Dictionary, 2019b
[124] Mayo, 1972
[125] Mayo, 1964
[126] *Ibid.*

It is a person's idealistic desire for spiritual refinement and the dissolving of the bounds of the material world, through self-abnegation and self-sacrifice, which can be manifest in mystical experience or trance, in psychic or artistic inspiration and visions, in content from the semi-conscious or the unconscious, in sleep and dreams, day-dreams and unworldliness, as well as in practical self-sacrifice through an impressionable and empathic response to others' needs. If the function is poorly expressed, however, it manifests as mere escapism in the cruder forms of self-dissolution: the 'poor man's transcendence' of getting 'out of oneself' through alcohol, drugs or other poisons; in deception or self-deception, or muddled, impractical and chaotic thinking, vagueness, fantasy and illusion.

Perhaps at best Neptune represents the self-transcendence inherent in spirituality; at worst, a baser physical or mental dissolution towards intoxication, incoherence, derangement, illusion, insanity, hysteria, instability, or even the most extreme and negative form of self-abnegation, that of suicide or near-suicidal behaviour. Neptune is traditionally associated with gases, and an attraction to, or love of, the sea. Physiologically Neptune is said to be associated with the *"thalamus, the spinal canal and the nervous and mental processes generally."*[127]

As was noted in the case of Uranus, the human functions or urges associated with the 'extra-Saturnian' planets are seen by astrologers to be related to identifiable societal changes that occurred at the times of their discovery. The genesis of Neptune's discovery, through indirect, 'non-material' inferential means, may be seen to be coincidentally correlative with the planet's astrological function as embodying an 'extra-material' urge, and the confusion surrounding its discoverers is also suggestive of Neptune's themes of disorganisation, muddle and chaos. Neptune's naming may seem to have been a merely fortuitous following of the tradition of naming planets after ancient mythological gods, though it's nevertheless interesting to note the apparently coincidental parallels between the god Neptune's primary connection with the ocean and the astrological themes of attachment to the sea, as well as the related emphasis on the chaotic and the nebulous. Moreover, many activities of a distinctly transcendent 'Neptunian' nature were indeed in evidence at the time of the planet's discovery. The Spiritualist movement was born in the 1840s, with its typically 'Neptunian' mixture of other-worldliness—as well as of fraud and deception.

In this period the trance states of Mesmerism, with its connections to the Spiritualist movement, saw a surge in popularity, while the consciousness-dissolving practice variously known as 'Neurohypnology' or 'Neurypnology", later referred to more simply as 'hypnosis', began to be explored. In addition, the first surgical procedures under consciousness-transcending anaesthetic (ether) were performed in the 1840s.[128]

---

[127] Mayo, 1964; Mayo, 1972
[128] Fenster, 2001; Long, 1849

Pluto

Figure 20. The
European Astrological
Symbol for the Planet
Pluto

Astronomically, Pluto was for a long time considered the ninth and farthest planet from the Sun, as well as the smallest, though in 2006 its official status amongst astronomers was 'demoted' to that of a 'dwarf planet' residing in the Kuiper belt—a vast ring of small bodies circling the Sun beyond the orbit of Neptune.[129] Pluto is so far away from its parent star that it takes 248 years to complete one orbit, which is highly elliptical, so that the planet comes much closer to the Sun at some times than at others; indeed at times its orbit is within that of Neptune. Pluto's orbit is also dramatically inclined by 17° to the ecliptic, which means that, from the point of view of the Earth, Pluto seems to go to extremes, sometimes appearing very high above the path of the Sun, yet at other times very far below it.

Pluto's discovery was prompted, like that of Neptune, by mathematical inference. Some perturbations in the orbit of Uranus remained unexplained by the existence of Neptune, and some astronomers, notably the extremely wealthy Percival Lowell, set about the search for 'Planet X' at his own observatory at the beginning of the 20th century.[130] The subsequent observations did in fact capture two faint photographic images of Pluto in 1915, but Lowell remained unconscious of their identity with the planet and he died the next year. Lowell's death was followed by a turbulent decade for his observatory, due to vehement efforts on the part of his emotionally intense widow Constance in pursuing a protracted legal battle to prevent her late husband's vast fortune from continuing to provide funding, possibly arising from feelings of revenge and jealousy concerning Lowell's ex-partner. So extreme did Constance's feelings become that she suffered from the psychological conversion disorder of hysterical blindness.[131] The search continued however, under the observatory's new directorship of Vesto Melvin Slipher, who gave the practical task to the young astronomer Clyde Tombaugh. On the 18th February 1930, after nearly a year of exhaustive photographic surveys, Tombaugh discovered a new object which moved independently from the backdrop of stars, and so declared itself to be a planet.

Many names for the new planet were suggested to the members of the Lowell observatory. The name 'Pluto' was said to have been proposed by Venetia Burney, an 11-year-old schoolgirl from Oxford, England, on 14 March 1930. When Venetia's grandfather, Falconer Madan, a retired librarian at the Bodleian Library at Oxford university, happened to read to his granddaughter a newspaper article about the discovery of the new planet, mentioning to her that it still remained unnamed, Venetia, who had an interest in mythology, suggested the name Pluto,

---

[129] International Astronomical Union, 2006
[130] Tombaugh, 1946
[131] Byers, 2011; Byers, 2009

god of the underworld, since the name of that mythological deity had not been used to name a planet. Madan was impressed by his granddaughter's proposed name and communicated it to his friend Herbert Hall Turner, professor of astronomy at the university of Oxford. Turner forwarded Venetia's suggestion to the Lowell Observatory, whose members unanimously agreed upon the name in a vote.

It is notable, however, that many other people had in fact put forward the name 'Pluto' (amongst other suggestions) for the new planet,[132] and that particular or undue credit may have been given to Venetia Burney's choice since her great-uncle, Henry Madan, had been the one to propose the names *Phobos* and *Deimos* for the moons of Mars.[133] In an interview with NASA in 2006, the then-octogenarian Venetia Phair (née Burney) stated that, although she had indeed possessed an early interest in Greek and Roman myths and legends, she wasn't sure whether the specific characteristics of the mythological deity Pluto had influenced her choice.[134] Others had written to the observatory suggesting the name Pluto, either because, alone amongst his mythical brothers Jupiter and Neptune, he had not had a planet named for him, or because the mythical Pluto's association as 'dark', 'unseen' and 'mysterious' seemed appropriate for the remote planet. One correspondent reasoned that *"as Pluto was Lord of the dark region of the dead, so this planet so far from the source of light should receive his name."* It may be worth mentioning that another suggested the name *Electra* since the world was living in 'the age of electricity'.[135]

Whoever may correctly be said to be the originator of the name for the planet, its appropriateness may have been bolstered by the fact that its first two letters, 'PL', are coincidentally the initials of Percival Lowell, whose seminal efforts had set about the search for the new planet, and whose shared resources in the form of his observatory had been instrumental to its discovery. Indeed the symbol first proposed for the planet was a glyph basically comprising these two letters fused into a monogram (Figure 20).[136] The German astrologer Fritz Brunhübner wrote that the symbol for Pluto that is commonly in use today, being the fused monograph of the letters 'P' and 'L' (Figure 20) was first proposed by Frhr. von

Figure 21. The American Astrological Symbol for the Planet Pluto

Kloeckler in his magazine *Sterne und Mensch*.[137] Astrologers in the USA have used an alternative symbol, being comprised of a circle poised above an upturned semi-circle, with both in turn being set above a cross (Figure 21). This alternative

---

[132] Byers, 2015
[133] Byers, 2010
[134] NASA, 2006
[135] plutovian, 2015
[136] Slipher, 1930
[137] Brunhübner, 1934

symbol has been described by the astrologer Marc Edmund Jones as 'soul creating spirit out of matter'.[138]

In mythology the Roman god Pluto originated from the Greek deity *Hades*, the god who ruled the underworld, the dead (since they are buried underground) and wealth, though the name Hades later came to signify the underworld as a place or realm. Hades was the son of Cronus (Saturn) and his consort Rhea. Together with his brothers Zeus (Jupiter) and Poseidon (Neptune), he defeated his father's rule of the heavens. Each brother received a portion of the world to rule. While Zeus-Jupiter was awarded the heavens and Poseidon-Neptune the sea, Hades received rulership over the unseen underworld. The Greek name Hades probably derived from a Proto-Greek form *Awides*, meaning 'unseen'.[139] Perhaps due to an aversion from speaking his proper name and so attracting the attention of this fearsome god of the dead, Hades later came to be referred to as Ploútōn (Greek Πλούτων), meaning 'wealthy', since much wealth and riches, such as fertile crops, precious metals, valuable minerals and jewels come from underground. This name then later became Latinised by the Romans as Pluto, god of the underworld, the dead, and of extreme wealth and riches. Hades-Pluto may also perhaps be understood as a personification of the riches that come from the dead substance in the earth, which brings forth new life through seasonal regeneration.[140]

The principal factor in the mythological figure of Hades-Pluto is his abduction and rape of his consort *Persephone* (Roman *Proserpina*), daughter of Zeus (Jupiter). Proserpina-Persephone was also known as *Kore* (Greek: Κόρη or 'maiden'), a goddess of vegetation and fertility, and Hades-Pluto's rape of Persephone may be an understanding in collectively unconscious myth of the often disquieting but necessary processes of seasonal transformation and regeneration that take place in the fertile earth.[141]

Being at such an immense distance, the planet Pluto was unknown to ancient astrologers and therefore does not feature in classical astrology. Modern astrologers have nevertheless identified a common human function that the planet is said to represent, which may be summarised as the need for *renewal, through expulsion, elimination or transformation*. The function is a person's need at critical times for renewal, by urgently disclosing, unearthing, bringing to light and facing hitherto hidden, deep-seated matters or urges, which have come to such extremes that they have become burdensome and can no longer be contained or allowed to remain as they are, and must be eliminated or transformed. It is important to note that much of Pluto's astrological function is recapitulated in the sign-theme Scorpio which it 'rules', and this section on Pluto should ideally be read in tandem with that on Scorpio.

---

[138] Mayo, 1972
[139] Dixon-Kennedy, 1998b
[140] Cicero, 1933
[141] Athanassakis, 2004; Hansen & Hansen, 2005

Such hidden yet disruptive matters or urges are seen to bring about exigent trouble for the whole system which thus needs to effect a formidable catharsis, through expulsion, elimination or transformation. If left in their suppressed state, they give rise to systemic discomfort and dysfunction. The function can therefore be characterised as the system as a whole marshalling powerful, fundamental forces in response to an extreme aspect of itself which it can no longer tolerate in its current form. It is the urgent need at critical times for the system to delve deep inside and deal with normally hidden or 'covered up' yet potentially disturbing matters which are normally seen as unclean, unsightly, shameful or taboo; as in sexual behaviour, defecation and waste-processing, or matters surrounding birth, decay and death. Upon the necessary renewal through expulsion, elimination or transformation, the function brings about the inevitable endings of old phases and the beginnings of completely new ones.

There are intriguing correspondences between the Plutonian themes of sex and death. Frequently it is only when we attain puberty and begin to be aroused by sexual desire that we become seriously aware of death. One's expressions during the intensely pleasurable climax of the sex act, either facial or vocal, frequently resemble those that occur during intense pain or death. The loss of self-consciousness in the intensity of sexual orgasm has been recognised as a form of 'dying' and is even referred to in French as *la petite mort,* meaning 'the little death'. There is a more fundamental link between sex and death which reflects the connection that has collectively emerged in astrological symbolism. One might simply and reasonably ask: why is there a universal social or public attitude of shamefulness towards sex? Why should such a natural, common and indeed necessary human function be seen as taboo, shocking or sordid in nature?

The answer may be that sex reminds humans of the unpleasant fact of death, and indeed some empirical research has shown that this may well be the case. Psychologists have tested the relationship between ideation about sex and that of death in a number of studies. They found that when people (especially neurotic individuals) had been thinking about their own death, they showed aversion towards physical aspects of sex. The researchers also found that thoughts about sex increased the accessibility of death-related words.[142] It is interesting to reflect that non-human animals do not appear to harbour any such attitudes of shame towards sex, and the research may therefore point to the fact that this is probably because it is only humans who are fully aware of the prospect of dying and who can thus be reminded (even unconsciously) of its necessity, which is reflected in sex and procreation. As the anthropologist Ernest Becker put it, *"sex and death are twins ... animals who procreate die",*[143] and sex reminds us of this unpleasant fact which threatens the integrity of what we perceive to be our selves. Death itself, like sex, is often a somewhat 'taboo' subject, especially in modern western cultures.

The subtle evocation of death as the psycho-social origin of shamefulness or aversion towards matters surrounding sex may explain the Judaeo-Christian Old

---

[142] Goldenberg *et al.,* 1999

[143] Becker, 1973

Testament's account of 'the fall' in the book of Genesis, where the purported first humans, Adam and Eve, instantly felt shame on becoming aware of their 'nakedness' (exposed sexual organs) after they had 'eaten of the forbidden fruit' (knowledge). This may be an allegory of the collectively unconscious awareness of the necessity for sex and therefore death. This knowledge was furthermore revealed to them by a serpent—a reptilian animal closely resembling the venomous nature of creatures that are commonly associated with Scorpio, the sign 'ruled' by Pluto and, like Pluto, characterised by matters surrounding death.

In many ways Sigmund Freud's psychoanalytic theory recapitulates the Pluto function in the psychological realm: powerful and extreme desires which are natural but nevertheless felt to be shameful or taboo are theorised to be hidden or repressed into the unconscious, resulting in neuroses or obsessions. The resolution, elimination or transformation of such disorders is seen to lie in the uncovering and expulsion into consciousness of such matters in the form of a therapeutic catharsis. Significantly, Freud theorised that much of the content of psychological repression was sexual in nature.[144] The Pluto function is thus closely associated with fundamental, powerful and potentially destructive *emotional* forces which have become repressed or which have become too extreme, such as lust, jealousy or vengefulness, or pathological mental intensity.

Pluto is intimately concerned with functions and resources that are *shared in common*, either genetically in sexual matters and blood relationships, or in transmutable assets, including money, taxes, shares, death-legacies and inheritances. Money and 'currency' (including shared funds like stocks) is a powerful generic commodity which is commonly shared by all, the nature and value of which are transmuted from one exchange, transaction or transformation to another. Money is also somewhat taboo and has been nicknamed 'filthy lucre'. Money, like other Pluto-associated activities such as birth, sex and death, is something of which we all partake, though we'd often rather not mention its necessity or how it relates to us personally. It is also a thing that, like sex, is gone the moment it is used.[145] Money—and especially lust or obsession for money— is also of course frequently associated with the callousness and brutality of extreme criminal activities.

Thieving, rape and murder—the non-consensual appropriation of others' possessions, their bodies, or their lives—are examples of the extremely negative side of Pluto-Scorpio, and are all bad or 'lower' manifestations of the associated life-areas of money, sex and death. Defecation is an everyday activity which is associated with Pluto and Scorpio; it is a commonly experienced expulsive activity, whose product is the fertiliser which impersonally enables the transformation of

---

[144] It is a curious coincidence that Freud, who perhaps over-emphasised the sexual urge in his account of the unconscious, himself suffered from a neurotic *Todesangst* or death-anxiety.

[145] See Schopenhauer's discussion of the way that sensual gratification (i.e., sexual orgasm) is a struggle "*ceasing the moment its aim is attained*" (Schopenhauer, 1937).

life into new growth. It is, however, like sex, commonly a taboo and hidden subject, seen as 'dirty' or 'bad'.

Birth, sex and death can be subsumed under the concepts of 'commonality' and 'regeneration' in so far as they are the great 'levellers': things which happen to every person, regardless of the artificial social distinctions of rank or degree, and which are intimately bound up with the commonly shared life-force which is transmuted in these critical periods of regeneration, when an individual shares or merges his or her energies and experiences with those of others. They are not facets of individuality, but transformations of the basic life-stuff that is commonly shared by everyone. These events possess the quality of being 'crisis-like' and are associated with expulsion, the momentum of which is intense and passionate, but which ceases—often violently or in an extreme manner—the moment that it is consummated.

The intense, extreme, transformative and often violent functions of birth, sex and death are necessary in order to allow a new generation to be born, so that life can ultimately continue. Individuals cannot live forever, but life, in an impersonal sense, is allowed to continue—is indeed enabled—by being transformed and renewed through birth, sexual reproduction and death. It is in the Pluto-Scorpio themes of birth, sex and death that we see how we are all made of the same flesh and substance; all part of the same striving of the species against the force of entropy to continue, beyond the individual experience; how we are all required to take part in the commonality of physical transformation that enables such an evolving persistence. In religious literature and philosophy there is frequently a sort of legend or myth which tells us that it is because we have sex that we have to die (e.g., Adam and Eve's 'fall' into the revelation of their sexuality and thus their mortality). This resonates with the fact that most organisms necessarily die to allow survival through sexual reproduction.

The theme of the Pluto function is particularly concerned with extremes—of emotion, force, power and wealth. It is also frequently manifest in hidden factors which are shared on a mass social level; in the criminal underworld, or in the forces which initiate huge financial enterprises or economic crises; or in mass hysteria, mass movements, mob lynchings, political dictatorships or the blood-purges of elements that are perceived as insufferable. The Pluto function is particularly connected to *fundamental* forces and their *transformation*, whether they are highly charged sexual-psychological urges, or the nuclear forces of physics and their transmutation of matter into extreme energy.

Pluto-Scorpio's themes often seem negative in aspect,[146] dealing as they do with powerful fundamental urges and processes which often appear primal or even unsightly. The theme does however have what might be called a 'higher' aspect, which rises above such issues as physical birth, sex and death. This is reflected in the fact that the sign ruled by Pluto—Scorpio—has two symbols, the scorpion *and* the eagle. The scorpion is often seen to symbolise those aspects of

---

[146] Pluto's principles are so similar to those of the sign Scorpio (q.v.) that it seems correct at this point to refer to the principle generally as the 'Pluto-Scorpio' theme.

the sign's theme that manifest on physical or psychological levels; the eagle however can be seen as a token of the functioning of the theme on what may be called a spiritual or mystical level.

The themes of death and transformation remind each one of us of mortality, and often cause us to be dissatisfied with the superficial, and to seek passionately for a deeper meaning in life. Thus the Pluto-Scorpio theme can be manifest, in its 'higher' interpretation, with the intense, one-pointed fervour of the profoundest spiritual quest—the determined effort towards a true mystical experience, in contrast to the blander rites of conventional partisan religion, which contain only vestigial aspects of it, such as in the ostensible experience of commonality, sharing, mystery and transcendence supposedly inherent in the Christian 'communion' observance (though we might do well to remember that the Christian ritual of communion in fact involves the drinking and eating of symbolic communal blood and flesh, which acts, we may tend to forget in modern times through familiarity, starkly bespeak a Pluto-Scorpio theme.) Pluto-Scorpio's theme can therefore be manifested in positive ways (as in mystical union) or in negative ways (as in the basest criminality); but in both cases it involves a passionate intensity. In his introduction to the mysticism of the Neoplatonic philosopher *Pseudo-Dionysius the Areopagite*, the British scholar and translator Rolt refers to this point:

> The same psychic material may take either of two opposite forms, for the highest experiences and the lowest are both made of the same spiritual stuff ... A storm of passion may produce a Sonata of Beethoven or it may produce an act of murder. All depends on the quality and direction of the storm ... There is a higher merging of the self and a lower merging of it. The one is above the level of personality, the other beneath it; the one is religious the other hedonistic; the one results from spiritual concentration and the other from spiritual dissipation.[147]

It may be said that mysticism is to religion what sex is to the mundane life. Being mystically inclined is like being sexually aroused spiritually. It is a determined, one-pointed drive to the ecstasy of spiritual union, just as sex is the determined drive towards the orgasmic ecstasy of physical union. The spiritual pinnacle of the mystical goal of union is achieved by a single-minded obsession, as is the sexual climax, and both are experiences of a closeness to, or even a union with, a common source that we all share, one on a spiritual level and the other on a physical. The Christian mystic Ruysbroeck used the metaphor of sex to describe the mystical union, describing it as 'the coming of our Bridegroom' and 'the dark silence in which all lovers lose themselves.'[148] The Christ figure describes himself in a similar manner when he says to his apostles, *"Can the children of the*

---

[147] Dionysius the Areopagite, 1920
[148] Ruysbroeck, 1916

bridechamber fast, while the bridegroom is with them?"[149] The mystic Jacob Böhme advised those who wish to attain the mystic goal to *"Be always ready, expecting the Bridegroom."*[150] The Christian Bible translated into English refers to sex as 'knowing'. The choice of this translational euphemism may unconsciously reflect the fact that sex, like mysticism, is a 'gnosis', a 'knowing' of that which is intensely sought after by the complete immersion of the self in the thing sought (sex being the physical correlate of such a mystical process).

Ruysbroeck also uses another Plutonian-Scorpionic term, namely birth, to describe the undifferentiated unity of the mystical experience, calling it a *"new birth and a new enlightenment without interruption."*[151] The great German mystic Eckhart referred to the mystical experience of union as the 'birth of Christ in the soul.'[152] The mystical experience can thus also be seen as thematically coextensive with the Pluto-Scorpio function as a birth or rebirth.

Physiologically Pluto is associated with expulsive reflexes such as in vomiting or defecation, and the regenerative forces in the body, such as in cell formation or in sexual reproduction.[153] Just as the deity is associated with the 'lower regions' in a spiritual-cosmic sense, so it is associated with the 'lower regions' in a physiological sense. Pluto is also associated with viruses and cancerous illness.

As was noted in the case of Uranus and Neptune, the human functions or urges associated with the 'extra-Saturnian' planets are often seen by astrologers to be related to identifiable societal changes which occurred at the times of their discovery. Pluto's discovery, as described, was accompanied by themes of extreme wealth and vengeful jealousy surrounding intimate partners and shared financial resources, which are strangely redolent of the Pluto function: Lowell was extremely *wealthy*; he remained *unconscious* that the faint photographic images he captured were those of Pluto and *died* soon afterwards. After Lowell's death his widow pursued a protracted legal battle over her late husband's inordinate *wealth* and suffered from much *vengeful sexual jealousy* over his ex-partner, feelings so *extreme* as to cause a psychological *conversion* disorder of hysterical *blindness* (denial of conscious facts). The period in which the planet was discovered was characterised by the severest economic depression, the era of 'underworld' gangsterism, intimidation and violent crime in the USA, the birth of dictatorships in Europe, and the serious development of nuclear power, all of which possess 'Plutonian' themes as have been described.[154]

---

[149] Mark 2:19

[150] Böhme, 1650

[151] Ruysbroeck, 1916

[152] Blakney, 1941

[153] Mayo, 1972

[154] The use of *plutonium* in nuclear powered weaponry is notable.

The Planets in Retrospect — The Seven 'Classical' Planets

We have examined how natural psychological cognitive processes projected humankind's fundamental urges, principles or functions onto the planets of the solar system as deified personalities.[155] For the seven 'classical' planets (those that can be seen with the naked eye, namely, the Sun, the Moon, Mercury, Venus, Mars, Jupiter and Saturn), this identification was developed and refined over millennia, firmly establishing their physical presences as 'gods' in the heavens, as well as idealised 'gods' in the sense of symbolic representational aspects of human nature.

It's notable that the number seven seems to have a distinct popularity in ancient myth, scriptural motifs and culture. In the Christian Bible's Book of Revelation, there are references to seven churches, seven spirits, seven golden candlesticks, seven stars, seven lamps, seven seals, seven eyes, seven angels, seven trumpets, seven thunders, seven crowns, seven heads, seven golden vials, seven mountains and seven kings. The Bible's Book of Amos exhorts Israel to *"seek him that maketh the seven stars and Orion"*,[156] while the Book of Proverbs famously tells us that *"wisdom hath builded her house, she hath hewn out her seven pillars."*[157]

The very names of the seven days of the week that we use to this day are derived from the names of the seven classical planets. Monday derives from the Old English *Mōnandæg* meaning 'Moon's Day'. The name Tuesday derives from Old English *Tīwesdæg* meaning 'Tiw's day', or the day honouring the combative and warlike Germanic god Tiw (Norse Týr), interpreted or identified by the Romans as Mars. Wednesday derives from the Old English *Wōdnesdæg* meaning 'the day of Woden' a Germanic god (also known as Odin) identified by the Romans with Mercury. Thursday derives from the Old English *Þūnresdæg* and the Old Norse *Þorsdagr* meaning 'Thor's Day', or the day of Thor, a Germanic god identified by the Romans with Jupiter. Friday derives from the Old English *Frīgedæg* meaning the day of the Anglo-Saxon goddess Fríge (Norse: Frigg), a Germanic god identified by the Romans with Venus. Saturday derives from the Anglo-Saxon *Sæturnesdæg*, which name was borrowed directly by the West Germanic people from the Roman Saturn. Sunday derives from the Old English *Sunnandæg* meaning 'Sun's day', based on the Old English 'sunne' for Sun—a translation of the Roman *dies Solis*, 'day of the Sun'. Similar etymological connections of the names of days of the week to the corresponding seven classical planets are to be found in other languages and cultures.

It seems almost certain that the renowned English poet and playwright William Shakespeare was recapitulating the symbolic functions of the seven

---

[155] As noted before, in astrological terminology, the Sun and the Moon are classified as 'planets'.

[156] Amos 5:8

[157] Proverbs 9:1

classical planets, in a sequential or human-developmental sense, in a famous monologue from Act II Scene VII of his pastoral comedy *As You Like It*:[158]

All the world's a stage,
And all the men and women merely players;
They have their exits and their entrances,
And one man in his time plays many parts,
His acts being seven ages. At first, the infant,
Mewling and puking in the nurse's arms.
Then the whining schoolboy, with his satchel
And shining morning face, creeping like snail
Unwillingly to school. And then the lover,
Sighing like furnace, with a woeful ballad
Made to his mistress' eyebrow. Then a soldier,
Full of strange oaths and bearded like the pard,
Jealous in honour, sudden and quick in quarrel,
Seeking the bubble reputation
Even in the cannon's mouth. And then the justice,
In fair round belly with good capon lined,
With eyes severe and beard of formal cut,
Full of wise saws and modern instances;
And so he plays his part. The sixth age shifts
Into the lean and slippered pantaloon,
With spectacles on nose and pouch on side;
His youthful hose, well saved, a world too wide
For his shrunk shank, and his big manly voice,
Turning again toward childish treble, pipes
And whistles in his sound. Last scene of all,
That ends this strange eventful history,
Is second childishness and mere oblivion,
Sans teeth, sans eyes, sans taste, sans everything.

Although the general function embodied by the Sun is omitted, we see the Moon's principle of early infancy and maternity in the 'mewling and puking' infant, Mercury's incipient intellectual development in the schoolboy, Venus's function of love and attraction in the lover, Mars's combative aspect in the soldier, Jupiter's 'professional', mature and wise aspect in the expansive (and expanded) justice, and the restricting and limiting principle of Saturn in the aged 'lean and slippered pantaloon'. Interestingly, Shakespeare appears to anticipate the dissolution and immateriality of Neptune's principle in the forgetfulness and 'mere oblivion" of his 'last scene of all', despite there having been no contemporary knowledge of this 'step' in the developmental succession of planets.

---

[158] It has been suggested that Shakespeare obtained the germ of this astrological-developmental notion from the *Zodiacus Vitae*, a text written by the 16th century Italian author *Palingenius*, which the young playwright probably studied at Stratford grammar school (see Baldwin, 1944), though the evidence is not conclusive.

The Planets in Retrospect — The 'Modern' Extra-Saturnian Planets

As we've noted, although the three 'extra-Saturnian' planets Uranus, Neptune and Pluto were discovered in comparatively recent times and were thus unknown to the ancients, they have nevertheless in modern astrology also been accorded correspondences to what appear to be identifiable, meaningful human principles. We might ask: how did the principle associated with each of these 'modern' planets emerge? How were they discovered or decided upon? We said of the seven 'classical' planets that their associated human principles were psychologically projected onto them, according to the way their appearance and behaviour reminded man of some basic facet of his nature, such as how the swiftness of Mercury's movement was reminiscent of the swiftness of his own thought and communication, or how Mars's fiery red colour reminded man of his own martial and combative nature. We also said that this process most probably coalesced into a common recognition over a long period of time in the collective human unconscious.

Such a process seems plausible in the case of the seven classical planets, whose observable characteristics have been contemplated for millennia, but it may seem less certain for the three 'extra-Saturnian' planets. Although the developed astrological associations of these 'modern' planets do appear to reflect real, common human functions or principles, the celestial bodies were only discovered comparatively recently—scarcely time, we would think, for their symbolic identifications to have been consolidated through a process of common or collectively unconscious assimilation. Being so very far from the Earth, these planets have not been open to general public perusal, but have rather been subjects of study for a smaller class of expert astronomers with specialised equipment. Furthermore, although astronomers named these planets,[159] it was *astrologers* in particular who settled on their associated human principles—an even smaller group to 'represent' the possibilities of human psychological projection. But exactly how did these astrologers derive the themes or principles of these 'modern' planets?

One potential answer is that they simply extrapolated the characteristics of the ancient mythological deity after which each extra-Saturnian planet was named, and used those to formulate the theme of the purported human principles involved. This cannot be a satisfactory explanation however, at least as far as the planet Uranus is concerned, since the ancient deity of that name had no substantive 'functional' themes attached to its myth. Furthermore, in the case of all the 'extra-Saturnian' planets, although there may be intriguing and close correspondences between the named mythological deities and the associated principles, there is typically not enough material in the myths to fully account for them. A more likely possibility is that the associated human principles or functions of

---

[159] The naming of Pluto was somewhat more complex; see the previous section on Pluto.

these planets were derived, either consciously or unconsciously, from significant or salient social themes and world events that were prevalent at the time of their discovery. The choice of a mythological deity-name on the part of the astronomers might also conceivably have been similarly influenced by an unconscious acknowledgement of prominent current conditions, though perhaps not as profoundly as the full-blown human principle that the planet represented to astrologers.

It seems reasonable at any rate to suppose that the planets' discoverers and the astrologers who assessed them symbolically may well have unconsciously attached attributes to the newly found planets (perhaps sometimes including their names) with thematic reference to what were felt to be momentous contemporary factors. No doubt these astronomers and astrologers would have been persons who were intellectual and 'modern' enough in outlook to be aware of and influenced by 'new' ideas, practices, movements and social undercurrents. One may suppose that the astronomers may have wished to associate the dramatic thrust of their great discoveries with names of some significance. Even when the names were fixed upon in strangely tangential ways (as with Venetia Burney's 'Pluto') the naming seems to us to have reflected salient contemporary themes. Generally, the idea that important contemporary social trends, movements, innovations in discovery and the like influenced the astrological-symbolic 'meaning' of the new extra-Saturnian planets seems conformant with our 'projection' hypothesis.

Of course, early astrological commentators typically claimed that they had determined the planets' symbolic themes through their supposedly 'empirical' divinatory studies (working with horoscopes or birth-charts). However, and as we shall see, the astrologers who first described the planets' principles—which descriptions were often strikingly similar to those we recognise today—did so often very soon after the planets' discoveries, when there had not been sufficient time to compare horoscopes of people with the planets in different signs. Furthermore, these astrologers' 'empirical' work, as we shall also see, was often of a frankly ridiculous nature when compared to the scientific method. It is not beyond reason to propose however that these early astrologers' 'empirical' work was in fact a type of confirmation bias at work, but with this important addition: that what was being unconsciously 'confirmed' was at least sometimes itself the tenor of contemporary social trends—being thus projection in another form, with the many and varied symbols in the 'language' of astrology at its disposal. The 'astrological empirical' work may have been yielding meaningful themes, though not through astrological divination, but because it was yet another outlet for the projection of the essence or gist of currently emerging social factors. This process may have been facilitated if the planet's name had already been influenced by contemporary themes.

Modern astrologers sometimes now look back with the benefit of hindsight to a clearer, overall historical characterisation of major social or world events at the time of the 'modern' planets' discoveries and find to their surprise and delight that there were indeed identifiable associations between the planets' (now traditional) astrological principles and the themes that inhered in social or world events at the time of their discovery—not realising that these themes may well have been the projected *result* of those contemporary historical motifs. Here we see an illusory 'divinatory astrology' falsely 'explaining' a phenomenon that had its origin yet again in unconscious psychological projection. In the case of the development of the astrological symbolism for the planet Pluto, as we shall see, such biased retrospective selection or emphasis of certain contemporary events rather than others seems to have played a major role in projecting a symbolic principle that appears to have been originally fixed upon by what appear to be purely chance factors.

The Planets in Retrospect — Uranus

In the case of Uranus, we understand its developed principle or human function to be that of the urge or need for freedom, deviation, unconventionality, inventiveness, independence, sudden and drastic change, rebellion, scientific and humanitarian aims. Quite early on, Uranus was quite unmistakably being astrologically connected with this theme or principle. For instance, the astrologer Robert Cross Smith, writing under the pen-name 'Raphael' in his *Manual Of Astrology* in 1828—a mere 47 years after the planet's discovery—describes Uranus as having its effects *"in a peculiarly strange, unaccountable, and totally unexpected manner"*; that those born under its influence are *"of a very eccentric and original disposition ... unsettled, addicted to change, and searchers after novelty ... searchers after nature's secrets, excellent chymists* [sic], *and usually profound in the more secret sciences,"* having desires for *"pursuits or discoveries out of the 'track of custom'"*.[160]

That Smith's description is an accurate recapitulation of the developed theme for Uranus is beyond doubt. We cannot suspect that this planet's astrological-symbolic principle was derived from characteristics of the mythological god Uranus, since in the case of that ancient deity there are no substantial personality-based themes to be extrapolated. If we are to look, alternatively, for early astrologers' 'empirical' work in establishing the functional theme of Uranus, we might take note that David McCann, a researcher into the history of astrology, has remarked that, *"Earlier astrologers did not rely on the mythological associations of the name to determine the nature of Uranus. When John Varley and John Corfield did that at the beginning of the nineteenth century, it was by observing its effects in nativities."*[161] But such early 'empirical astrological work' seems to have had a bizarre, indeed at times positively farcical nature.

The English painter and astrologer John Varley (1778—1842) was the first to have claimed to have come to believe in the 'suddenness' of Uranus's theme in an apparently 'empirical' manner: he seemingly observed some 'evil aspects' in his

---

[160] Smith, 1828
[161] McCann, 2000

horoscope for a certain day which involved what he saw as a malign influence from Uranus and which would incur a 'sudden accident', though he was unable to interpret the influence properly because the planet was still relatively poorly understood from an astrological point of view. Later on that day, just as he was beginning to think that he might have escaped the evil portent, his house was (presumably 'suddenly') burned to the ground. If the frank absurdity in this isolated but ostensibly significant example of 'astrological empirical work' apparently establishing the 'suddenness' that inheres in Uranus's principle was not plain enough, we go on to learn that the unfortunate Varley had no less than three times suffered the ill-luck of his house being burned down by fire.[162]

So far then, in the case of Uranus at least, the astrological principle of the planet does not appear to have been taken from themes in the mythology of the named deity, since there are no substantive characteristics that could be used as source material. In addition, the available record appears to indicate that the planet's theme was not derived by any method which we could reasonably call 'empirical'. Uranus's principle or theme is, however, certainly related to major world events prevalent at the time of its discovery: the decisive establishment of American independence, the growth of science and the industrial revolution, and the fomenting of the French Revolution, are pretty well correlated with its themes of rebellion and radical change. Of course we think it unlikely that, in the first few years following the discovery of Uranus, astrologers jointly and severally set themselves quite deliberately to fix the planet's astrological principle from some careful, overarching synthesis of global current events; but it is nevertheless possible that, in assigning what they saw as important thematic correspondences to a new and exciting planet, they may well have been subconsciously influenced by the rebellious and disruptive spirit of the times in which they lived. These astrologers were not being influenced by the saliency of the seasons, as had been the case for the ancient Babylonians in the projective picturing of individual signs, but by the saliency of the *times*, in the appraisal of a momentous new discovery in an era of significantly progressive, revolutionary and reforming change.

There are therefore indications that astrologers such as Smith and Varley appear fairly early on to have begun to attribute to Uranus what we now under-stand to be the recognisable outline of its now-familiar developed theme. They appear to have credited this to their own somewhat dubious 'empirical' means, but we rather suspect that these astrologers may well have been unconsciously influenced by the current 'radical' social *zeitgeist* at the time of their writing, and that it was this which influenced their thematic interpretation of the new planet (even if they consciously believed that they were guided by their 'empirical' divinatory work). This indeed could be seen as the collective unconscious influencing what was 'meant' by the new planet.

We favour this conclusion over McCann's more questionable assertion that the Uranus function, principle or theme was simply developed by astrologers in the

---

[162] Farnell, 2005; Varley, 1916

course of their work *"observing its effects in nativities"* since, apart from questioning the validity of such 'empirical work' itself (and we have seen a little of what such 'empirical work' actually involved), there had in any case been far too little time: it would have taken at least 84 years to have compared horoscopes of people with Uranus in all the zodiacal signs. We feel we might reasonably conclude therefore that the characteristics of Uranus's principle were formed by a subtle influencing of astrological theorising by the unconscious assimilation of major contemporary social issues and themes in the era surrounding the planet's discovery.

The Planets in Retrospect — Neptune

In the case of Neptune, we understand its developed principle or human function to be that of the abnegation, denial, dissolution or transcendence of the mundane self; the urge to seek experience beyond the material senses and to embrace the unworldly or the spiritual; the urge towards subtleness, impression-ability, nebulousness, the intangible, the imagination, dreams, visions, the semi-conscious or unconscious. The first ascriptions of astrological themes to Neptune seem to have been those put forward 44 years after the planet's discovery by John Story in his 1890 reprint of the *Complete Arcana of Astral Philosophy*, being a republishing of a work by W. J. Simmonite.[163] The author admits that giving an astrological-symbolical description of Neptune is difficult because of the recency of its discovery, and appears merely to hazard a guess that it is *"very much after the nature of the planet Herschel* [Uranus], *and to have a controlling influence over the minds of those who have to do much with persons who believe in the Art and Science of Astrology, dreams, inspirations, etc"* and *"much after the nature of Herschel's* [Uranus's] *influence, but slower in bringing things to pass, and in a milder way"*.

The inclusion of 'dreams' and 'inspirations' may seem significant to Neptune's developed principle, but the author certainly appears to be casting around somewhat ambiguously as to the astrological significance of the new planet, and to be reiterating the characteristics of Uranus when he includes *"inventions and discoveries of new lights in arts and sciences"*. A letter to the author included at the end of the book, cited as from 'Prof. J. A.' and believed to be from John Ackroyd,[164] describes Neptune's associations in terms which seem somewhat more in agreement with our present understanding of the planet's developed principle. In the letter the writer asserts that the planet:

> appears to have a continuous influence over the minds of spiritu-alists, mediums, prophets, seers, magicians, clarvoyants [sic], enthusiasts, and persons who believe in inspiration, oracles, and futurity. In certain classes it induces to a faith in dreams, spirits and ghosts, tales of wonder and enchantment, witching, charming, necromacy [sic], and fortune-telling in various ways, as

---

[163] Simmonite, 1890
[164] McCann, 2000

> card shuffling, palmistry, geomancy, moles, and other kinds of superstitious craft and artful practices to[o] numerous to name.

Ackroyd's prototypical description certainly seems more reminiscent of the developed Neptune principle as we understand it today. However, he goes on to assert that a person influenced by Neptune may be:

> close, reserved, careful, crafty, ingenious and inventive, studious and clever in mechanical arts, chemistry, etc., a person silent, not of many words, greedy after money and property, selfish and indifferent towards others, of a gloomy, lowering aspect, private and anti-social, careless about dress, personal appearance, forms and fashions, curious, odd and retiring in manners, therefore not much adapted for social life and company.

These latter attributions only vaguely accord with the planet's theme. It is as if the authors and correspondents are for the most part guessing but nevertheless have a presentiment of the Neptune theme knocking on the door of their consciousness and seeking admittance. This is what one might expect if they were, as astrologers, harking back to memories of the discovery of Uranus but also beginning to unconsciously assimilate interests in the emerging 'consciousness-transcending' trends such as spiritualism and hypnotism.

These astrologers of course knew that the mythological deity Neptune was the god of the sea, and the chaos, nebulosity and dissolution involved in Neptune's principle is now easily imagined in a context of the formless and all-dissolving oceans. But this is seeing Neptune's function with the benefit of hindsight and with a refinement of understanding that has taken place over many years. Certainly no references to the mythological deity Neptune seem to have been adduced in the aforementioned early sources. David McCann notes that *"The first published account of its influence by John Ackroyd (in the 1890 reprint of W. J. Simmonite's Complete Arcana of Astral Philosophy) makes no reference to mythology; his conclusions were based purely on the study of the planet in nativities."*[165]

We cannot help but wonder however, how much of the interpretation of Neptune's astrological principle involved in the 'empirical' work of these nativities (horoscopes or birth-charts) was influenced by the 'Neptunian' spirit of the times. It seems clear enough at any rate that Neptune's principle did not grow out of a simple connection with an association with the mythological water-god of the ancients. In addition—and as was the case with Uranus—there was not nearly enough time to compare Neptune's placement in different zodiacal signs in people's horoscopes during the few years following the planet's discovery, which comparison would actually have taken at least 165 years (and this criticism is in addition to our scepticism over the value of such 'nativities' in the first place).

---

[165] McCann, 2000

We can be reasonably certain that we are not employing a confirmation bias of our own when we say that the time of Neptune's discovery was indeed a time of events and trends which relate to what we understand today as the planet's astrological human principle or function. The genesis of spiritualism, hypnosis and anaesthetics, roughly contemporary with the planet's discovery,[166] all stand out as stellar examples of typically Neptunian 'extra-sensory' theme. As was the case for Uranus, it doesn't appear at first blush that astrologers such as Story and Ackroyd were methodically or deliberately deriving the theme of the planet from such current events, but as was also the case for Uranus, we might well suspect that the 'spirit of the times' was nevertheless *unconsciously* percolating into these astrologers' considerations of what the planet 'meant'.

We feel we might therefore conclude that the astrological principle established for the new planet Neptune was, as was the case for Uranus, formed by the subtle and unconscious infusing of new and significant innovations and movements of the era around the time of the planet's discovery (in the case of Neptune, particularly of the 'psychic' or 'non-material' vogue) into astrologers' rudimentary interpretations, influencing the results of their 'empirical work' and consolidating the theme of the newly-discovered planet. We are obliged to note the presence of apparently unexplained coincidences which seem related to its astrological theme, such as the markedly confused nature of the planet's discovery, and the link to the deity of the formless and chaotic ocean,[167] though this may reflect our own bolstering of the projection of the principle through the benefit of hindsight. We suggest that the collective unconscious was able, in apposite times, to articulate a descriptive concept of the characteristics of this particular human function or principle in a coherent way; the excitement accompanying the newly discovered planet once again being an apparently strong enough stimulus to do so (and our biased retrospective perceptions only reinforcing it).

The Planets in Retrospect — Pluto

In the case of Pluto, we understand its developed astrological symbolic principle or function to be the need, at critical times, for renewal, through the disclosing and facing of normally hidden or repressed yet powerful and potentially violent matters or urges, which are often seen as ugly, repugnant or too taboo to be dealt with, but which have nevertheless grown to such extremes or intensity as to have become burdensome or intolerable in their current state, to which the entire system revolts, and which thus urgently need *renewal* in the form of *confrontation, expulsion and elimination or transformation* for normal functioning to be allowed to continue. The more pressing the urge without the much-needed renewal, the more such matters give rise to serious dysfunction to the whole

---

[166] See the separate section on Neptune.

[167] It could of course be said that Le Verrier's preferred choice of name was itself unconsciously influenced by the 'transcendent' trend of the times.

system. The successful achievement of renewal marks the ending of an old phase and the beginning of a completely new one. Manifestations of the Pluto function are said to be apparent in atomic-nuclear and genetic processes; in the personal human processes of defecation, birth, sex and death; pathologically in virus infections, cancerous growths, obsessions and neuroses; and in the social arena as crises in the shared resources of finance and wealth, in serious and violent crime, and in mass socio-political extremes.

Astrological interpretations of the symbolism of the planet Pluto appeared surprisingly quickly after its discovery. Notably, the German astrologer Fritz Brunhübner wrote an entire book in 1934 (just four years after the planet's discovery) devoted to an exposition of its likely symbolism.[168] The preface to Brunhübner's book by the German astrologer Alexander Bethor (1876—1938) states that, in providing an astrological interpretation of the planet, any influence from the name of the mythological deity given to the planet *"should be omitted"*, because *"such naming is done by modern astronomers who have no desire to know anything of the psycho-physical influence of the stars and who (frequently) have only scorn and ridicule for the assumption that such an influence exists"*. In fact, and as we have seen, the name Pluto was proposed by 11-year-old Venetia Burney and a number of others, none of whom were astronomers (though astronomers had the final vote), but Brunhübner's prefatory admonition against deriving the nature of the planet's principle from mythological characteristics of the classical deity is at any rate clear enough.

Brunhübner nevertheless promptly disregards the advice of his own book's preface and begins with an overview of the deity Pluto in mythology, even remarking that the astrological 'meanings' of the visible 'classical' planets were *"taken from the characters of the ancient gods whose names they bear."* We have of course argued that, in the case of the classical planets, their 'meanings' were the result of basic human functions or principles psychologically projected onto them, and that these principles became idealised as deities in myth, seen as supernaturally residing or embodied in the planet in 'the heavens'. One might wonder whether Brunhübner was possibly implying such a process, though this seems unlikely, considering the mentioning of *"the psycho-physical influence of the stars"*.

Brunhübner goes on to remark that mythology can furnish *"a few useful points and facts for the astrological praxis"* but that it *"should be used cautiously"*, and that only *"careful observation in a great number of horoscopes will show what the astrologer can use from the characteristics of the ancient god, Pluto. It would not be proper, however, to turn entirely away from mythology as the names of the celestial bodies were not given merely by chance."* Even this tentative and somewhat ambivalent consideration of the characteristics of the 'ancient god' on Brunhübner's part seems at odds with the book's prefatory injunction to 'omit' influences from mythology, and more

---

[168] Brunhübner, 1934

especially in light of the fact that he acknowledges the apparently fortuitous naming of the planet by the child Venetia Burney.

If Brunhübner is not subscribing to anything like our projection hypothesis, but rather something involving 'influences from the stars', then it is not clear what he might have meant by the naming of the planets as being 'not by chance'—unless it is of the form of an extremely simplistic view such as of celestial bodies 'influencing' the naming process. But Brunhübner offers no explicit account as to how the co-option, evocation or merely fortuitous application of the name of an ancient mythological deity for the new planet might relate to its human principle and thus its astrological symbolism. Only in more recent times has it become apparent that in fact a number of people suggested the name Pluto, which may possibly incline us to credit some collectively unconscious projective process in the planet's naming.

We get the impression that, in settling on a symbolic theme for Pluto, Brunhübner was anxious to appear to do so as a traditional, 'technical' astrologer of horoscopes, but was nevertheless willing to allow some conflation of mythological factors with such 'empirical' work, and in truth reluctant to dismiss the connection with the named ancient deity. If this reluctance stemmed from some suspicion of a psychological process akin to our projection hypothesis, then he doesn't elucidate such an idea (and in fact implicitly brushes it aside in his talk of 'influences'). Perhaps all we can surmise is that Brunhübner vaguely credited some unspecified supernatural process which brought about the choice of the ancient god's name, and that the deity's mythological motifs would thus somehow be mysteriously appropriate for an emerging astrological symbolic theme for Pluto. Characteristics of the mythological Hades-Pluto do indeed recapitulate elements of the now-developed astrological principle of the planet, but Brunhübner was in any case unwilling to assert that the planet's astrological-symbolic principle was simply derived from the named deity.

Despite his somewhat ambivalent introduction, Brunhübner makes a lengthy case for the newly discovered planet Pluto to be the 'ruler' of the death-related sign Scorpio, which it is to this day, the theme of the planet and that of the sign being very similar. He does so by way of somewhat dense and recondite theoretical arguments of planetary sequence, as well as from considerations of mythology. It's clear therefore that Brunhübner did incorporate associations of the mythological deity Hades-Pluto into his view of Pluto's astrological theme, despite his warnings against doing so and his exhortation to discover the principle through 'empirical' astrological methods. Thus he writes, *"Mythology provides us with additional clues. It is well known that Pluto is the lord of the underworld and of the realm of the dead. There is nothing more reasonable than to assign the sign Scorpio to him."* He nevertheless then proceeds once more to de-emphasise any influence from mythology (disingenuously or not) with the assurance that, *"All my numerous investigations on horoscopes confirm the Scorpio characteristics of Pluto."*

As was the case with claims of 'empirical' astrological work done very soon after the discoveries of Uranus and Neptune, it is difficult or indeed impossible to see how the examination of horoscopes could possibly have been carried out in the mere four years that intervened between the discovery of Pluto and Brunhübner's published conclusions. Even setting aside for the moment the question of the validity of birth-charts, the planet is so slow-moving in its solar orbit that, at the time of Brunhübner's writing, it had not yet been observed in its 'ruled' sign Scorpio in the birth-chart of any living person—or indeed in any zodiacal sign other than Cancer, in which it resided at the date of its discovery. We could perhaps be charitable enough to think that Brunhübner may have been referring to something like the investigation of birth-charts of well-known historical figures from history (still a stupendous project for calculation), but he does not mention any such thing, and in any case this seems most unlikely. Brunhübner's account of his 'investigations' therefore seems wholly based on his own intuitive opinion, perhaps heavily influenced by clues from characteristics of the mythological deity Hades-Pluto.

Brunhübner's exposition of Pluto's symbolic astrological principle (from whatever source) is, nevertheless, quite remarkable. Writing in Germany in the mid 1930s, Brunhübner predicted that "*Pluto will ... bring colossal revolutionary changes in all of life's activities, resulting in conflict, strife and unrest.*" Such a comment is descriptively well in accord with Pluto's developed principle and moreover eerily adumbrates events of exactly such a nature within just a few years in Brunhübner's own country, and indeed in the world at large. The evil that was Nazism in Germany can well be characterised in 'Plutonian' terms as a pathological geopolitical force which the whole world needed to face and expel, at a staggering price in terms of death and destruction.

It's possible that there may have been enough pertinent description of contemporary conditions in Brunhübner's exposition of the symbolism of the new planet to unsettle the Nazi regime. On 30 October 1940 the German physicist Josef Wimmer wrote to Reinhard Heydrich, the notorious Nazi SS officer and chief architect of the Holocaust, recommending the seizure of Brunhübner's book from his publisher, accusing the author of "*arbitrarily singling out random coincidences of calculated Pluto constellations and the hour of birth of a politician, scientist or sports personality along with particular traits of character, lifestyle and accomplishments and inversely believing in a causal relationship with the current position of Pluto.*"[169] One might suppose that this veto was motivated by a sober and sceptical scientific outlook, were it not for the fact that Wimmer himself had earlier recommended books to the Nazi authorities which endorsed his own interests in *dowsing*.

Brunhübner is at pains to distinguish between two aspects of Pluto—the 'common', 'serpent' or 'snake' type, and the 'ennobled', 'Janus' or 'eagle' type. This could be understood today as the commonly upheld distinction in Pluto-Scorpio symbolism between the baser tendency to follow or amass the powerful,

---

[169] Wimmer, 1940

raw force of the principle in a selfish or lustful manner as the 'common' type on the one hand, and the propensity to 'rise above' this form of expression and to transform the principle into a more spiritual direction as the 'eagle' type on the other.[170] It seems that Brunhübner's opinion was that the latter aspect is aware of the qualitative distinction between the higher and lower forms and can thus be characterised as *Janus*, the double-headed Roman deity who sees back to the past as well as forward into the future. Indeed, Brunhübner favoured an interpretation of this dual aspect of the Pluto principle to the point where he suggested that 'Janus' would have been a more suitable name for the planet.

Brunhübner prefaces his main chapter on what he sees as the symbolic characteristics of Pluto with a repeated assertion that his investigations of the planet's principle are based upon 'empirical' observations (birth charts or horoscopes). We have already noted that there had been too little time between the planet's discovery and Brunhübner's investigations to allow for the adequate comparison of horoscopes, even if such would have had any value. However, whatever the true source of his conclusions, Brunhübner portrayed the Pluto principle or function pretty much as astrologers describe it today. He describes the planet's symbolic association or function as *"seeking union"*; as having the nature of *"death and rebirth"*; a principle that *"kills or destroys but builds out of the elements of the destroyed"*. Brunhübner saw Pluto as being indicative of *"transformations"* and *"transmutation"*; *"the end and at the same time the beginning"*; a force resulting in *"revolutionary upheavals"*; it is *"renewing"*, *"bringing forth the new"*, *"breaking open"*, *"up-rooting"*, *"eruptive"*, *"revealing"*, bringing forth *"that which has been developed under cover, in secret (underground) into daylight, when the time is ripe ... like a volcano which bubbles and seethes inside until it erupts with elementary force."* Although Brunhübner does go on to ascribe to Pluto some other more 'spiritualistic' themes, it's nevertheless clear that the gist of these key words and phrases, written a mere four years after the planet's discovery, virtually restates the astrological Pluto principle as it is understood today.

If we are sceptical of Brunhübner's claim to 'empirical' work as the source of his conclusions as to the themes for Pluto, then we may wonder—how did he arrive at them? The obvious answer would be that Brunhübner derived his account of the Pluto's astrological symbolism from the characteristics of the ancient mythological deity which bears the planet's given name, despite his claim to have done so from 'empirical' work. The theme of the mythological Hades-Pluto is basically an unconscious acknowledgement of, or 'coming to terms' with, the necessity of sexual reproduction and death for the regeneration of the species. This is couched in the myth as the violent eruption from the unseen underworld or realm of the dead of its ruler or personification, the deity Hades-Pluto, who proceeds to impregnate (abduct and rape) a maiden goddess of the fertile earth (Persephone-Proserpina). This act has long been a primary mythological trope, often in the context of the 'fall' of the year at the Scorpio period in autumn, which

---

[170] It may be worthwhile repeating here that the eagle has long been an alternative symbol for Pluto's ruled sign Scorpio.

highlights sexual procreation as necessary for new life in the face of death. The irrevocable inter-relationship between sex and death are thus intertwined in the myth, which serves as a re-telling of the regeneration that takes place seasonally in the earth, and in parallel, a psychologically cathartic palliative to the uncomfortable prospect of individual death.

The myth thus contains the basic elements of an unseen or invisible underworld of the dead, the eruption of a personification of its powerful force, sex, death and regeneration. It also incorporates a representation of great wealth or riches, as the wealth of vegetable nourishment which grows from decomposed matter under the earth, thus showing the connection of the 'great wealth' aspect of its theme to the central motif of regeneration through death. The gist of these themes permeate Brunhübner's account of the astrological symbolism of Pluto, and he explores them in various aspects of the world around him. Brunhübner plainly writes that *"Pluto is the planet of death"* and he assigns the rulership of the planet to the autumnal or death sign Scorpio. Brunhübner also maintains that Pluto rules what he calls *"the sex sign"* Scorpio. He describes the 'Plutonic force' as *"arousing"* and includes procreation as a 'Pluto characteristic'. He also refers to the inferior Pluto type as *"of a low sexual or sadistic nature"*. It is possible that Brunhübner may have wished to associate Pluto more plainly with sexual regeneration *per se*, but was inhibited from doing so, as overt discussions of sexuality as a natural human urge were still generally thought of as unfit subjects for general public consumption in 1934.

Brunhübner also evokes an association of the planet with wealth. He writes, *"Whatever Pluto gives, he gives in great measure"*, and is ready to predict great wealth when the planet is positioned at birth in favourable ways. Generally we get the impression that Brunhübner was aware of the mythological deity's association with extremes of riches, and he vaguely incorporated this concept into his assessment of Pluto's astrological symbolism. It would therefore appear to us to be a reasonable conclusion that Brunhübner developed his account of the planet's astrological symbolism from the named ancient mythological deity, regardless of his book's prefatory injunction not to heed mythology and his avowed adherence to 'empirical' work. The themes of death, an 'erupting force', and renewal or regeneration are in particular included in his exposition, and all of these are easily derived from the deity's characteristics.

When we come to consider the times in which Brunhübner's wrote, we cannot help but think back to the origins of the principles or functions of the first two 'extra-Saturnian' planets, Uranus and Neptune, which we have attributed to a coalescing consciousness of new social conditions and ideas emerging around the times of their discovery. In a like manner it would at first seem possible to include Pluto in such an 'origin from the zeitgeist' scheme. The discovery of Uranus came at a time characterised by the planet's symbolic theme of dramatic change, most notably in the Industrial revolution, the American revolution and the conditions which foreshadowed the French revolution. The discovery of

Neptune came at a time when its transcendent or non-material theme seemed strikingly writ large in the world, in the development of spiritualism, hypnotism and anaesthesia. In the same way it certainly seems as if Pluto's discovery came at a time when its theme appeared to be reflected in the times: the great magnitude of death on an unprecedented scale in the colossal global conflict of World War II, the apogee of psychoanalysis with its taboo-breaking emphasis on the eruption of a veiled but powerful psychic force in the context of the unconscious sexual urge,[171] the similar eruption of a vast power from a hidden realm in the case of nuclear power, and the theme of extremes of wealth in the Great Depression, all reflected the principle of Pluto as we have surveyed it.

Thus, as in the cases of Uranus and Neptune, the astrological symbolism for Pluto seems to be related to social, ideological and technological conditions around the time of discovery. However, unlike Uranus and Neptune, Pluto's symbolism is, as we have seen, plainly very closely connected to the characteristics of the ancient mythological deity of the name that was given. Should we say that Brunhübner was influenced by the mythological account of the ancient deity Hades-Pluto, or by the tenor of developments in the world around him? The notion that Brunhübner was influenced by the characteristic of the ancient deity seems straightforward enough: as we have seen, Brunhübner virtually restates those characteristics in his account of the symbolism. If we were to say that he was rather influenced by a multiplicity of contemporary trends, all related by the same 'Plutonian theme', then we wouldn't be able to explain how the planet came to be named after a deity whose characteristics were mirrored in such contemporary conditions. If we were to propose that Brunhübner was influenced by both the characteristics of the mythological deity *and* the prevailing zeitgeist of the world around him, then we would have to explain why the mythological deity name given to the new planet and the social conditions of the time both involved aspects which prominently corresponded to the same recognisable theme.

Let's first consider the possibility that Brunhübner's source was the given name of the deity Hades-Pluto. As we have discussed, this certainly would seem to have been the case. Brunhübner's symbolism is, like the developed modern astrological principle, very closely allied with the characteristics of the ancient mythological god. It seems to us perfectly possible that it was upon the deity's characteristics that Brunhübner based the larger part of his symbolism, notwithstanding his claims to have derived it from 'empirical' work with birth-charts. Thus it seems reasonable to suppose that Brunhübner's account of Pluto's astrological symbolism—the first of its kind, and the one that has largely continued to today—had its origins in the characteristics of the ancient mythological deity. In consideration of the unusual coalescence of 'Plutonian' themes in the times around Brunhübner's writing, we have to return to the other possibility mentioned above, that Brunhübner might have been influenced by the characteristics of the deity *and* by the themes apparent in the world around him, and

---

[171] In 1930 Sigmund Freud was awarded the prestigious Goethe Prize in recognition of his contributions to psychology and to German literary culture.

therefore in turn to the question of why the ancient deity after which the planet was named and Brunhübner's contemporary zeitgeist shared such similar themes.

However it appears to us unlikely that Brunhübner was influenced by social trends around him which seem to be associated with the deity and thus the 'Plutonian' theme as we know it—e.g., death, sex via psychoanalysis, eruptive nuclear power, and the extremes of wealth that were consequent upon the Great Depression. It is true that Brunhübner may have sensed the inevitability of imminent conflict and death, steeped as he was in the rise of German Nazism. Indeed it's hard to ignore a certain distasteful fascistic fervour on Brunhübner's part when he writes that *"Pluto is struggle, a struggle until purification is reached"*; that *"Pluto can be called the cosmic aspect originating the third Reich"*; that the emergence of the Pluto principle shows that *"the liberalistic-democratic era dies in order to make room for the 'leader' principle"*; that *"whatever is decayed has to be trodden down"*; that *"This new [Plutonian] era will have to give birth to a new and better human being"*; and that *"under the influence of Pluto the old and decayed will be broken up to make space for the new and coming"*. At times one feels that Brunhübner, although on the face of it evoking the 'Pluto principle' much as we do today, is almost co-opting its essence for a vindication of the vengeful, grudge-bearing Nazi cause that seethed in Germany in the 1930s. But whatever the truth of this might be, it seems plain that Brunhübner was not writing of the 'death' aspect of Pluto's symbolism with reference to a positive certainty of an imminent global conflict. Furthermore he could not have known in advance of the scale of the death in the second world war.

It is difficult to adjudicate Brunhübner's possible intellectual awareness of psychoanalysis. Freud's theory maintained that neurotic illnesses are consequent upon the repression of the sexual urge, and their alleviation comes from the uprooting of such repression by bringing to the light of consciousness ('catharsis') this hitherto hidden and inhibited regenerative impulse. Freud also developed the notion of a 'death drive' (or 'death instinct') which he saw as a natural counterbalance to the sexual drive. We may note the fact that Brunhübner wrote that *"human beings under the influence of Pluto will proclaim and bring to light that which has rested long in the subconsciousness"* and that *"Pluto brings only that which has been developed under cover, in secret (underground) into daylight, when the time is ripe"*. In psychoanalysis the unconscious is seen to be a hidden or unseen and often feared realm or 'underworld' which harbours powerful and untameable forces, and psychoanalysis aims at the deliberate eruption of its pathologically repressed contents. Brunhübner refers to *"Pluto's invisible, concealed and subter-ranean, hidden activities"* and notes that these are *"typically Scorpio characteristics"*.

From these thematic similarities it would be engaging to posit that Brun-hübner in some way sensed the closely related theme of the catharsis of sexual matters in psychoanalysis as a correlating facet of the zeitgeist which was concerned to bring to light dark matters that had long been veiled from public view, but there is no indication that Brunhübner was sufficiently aware of Freud's psychoanalytic theory for it to have seemed to him as associable with the sexual-regeneration theme of the deity. If he had been so aware, he would arguably have made more explicit use of it in his formulation of Pluto's symbolism, but we do not get any such impression from his book. It is of course possible that Brunhübner may have deliberately chosen not to mention matters to do with psychoanalysis, since Freud's theories may well have been seen as 'degenerate' and his Jewish heritage would have been despised by the Nazi regime; Brunhübner may have feared going against such official opinions—or may even have subscribed to them. But this is mere speculation, and there is no clear evidence that Brunhübner was significantly influenced by Freud's theories.

Like the powerful urge to sex, the release of nuclear energy is also the eruption of 'a powerful force residing in a hidden or unseen realm', and it was around the time of Pluto's discovery and Brunhübner's analysis that, in the application of new physics, there was the successful transformation of fundamental nuclear forces of nature and the ability to discharge tremendous amounts of energy, leading ultimately to the atomic bomb, later argued by some as ultimately the necessary release of a hugely powerful force in order for normal functioning or peace to resume. An understanding of atomic physics was of course unknown to the ancients, though as we have seen, the concept of 'the release of great force from an unseen underworld' is central to the mythological theme of the deity Hades-Pluto, as applied to sexual energy. Was Brunhübner so aware of the 'unseen potential' of nuclear fission for it to be associable with the unseen realm of the deity? Brunhübner did indeed mention *the smashing of the atom* and its liberation of tremendous amounts of energy as one of the developments that *Pluto will bring to fruition*. Brunhübner's inclusion of the release of nuclear energy in his writings on Pluto's symbolism is thus intriguing, considering its thematic connection with the libidinal theme of 'powerful eruption' in the deific myth. It seems possible therefore that Brunhübner might just have noted the connection between the 'erupting' deity and the thematically similar contemporary technological development of nuclear power, though he did not appear to treat it as a foundational exemplar of Pluto's symbolic principle.

The concept of 'extremes' seems to be generally associated with the Pluto principle, including extremes of wealth. The deity Hades-Pluto was of course the god of extreme wealth or riches (particularly of those hidden underground). Many point to the fact that the times surrounding Pluto's discovery and Brunhübner's assessment of its symbolism was also characterised by conditions which shortly brought about the greatest economic recession the world had ever seen, resulting in extremes of states of wealth, as well as the spread of gangsterism and the unseen yet powerful and feared elements of the criminal 'underworld' erupting into the common light of day in the United States. It might also be noted that the instigator of the planet's discovery, Percival Lowell, was himself extremely wealthy. However it cannot be that Brunhübner specifically associated this aspect of the planet's astrological representation with his own era's collapse into extreme economic plight, since these economic conditions only came to full force after he wrote his book. As for Percival Lowell's extreme wealth, Brunhübner unsurprisingly made no mention of it, nor is there any indication that anyone other than modern astrologers connect such an abstruse and only vaguely associating factor with the Pluto principle.

We can see that the major motifs that Brunhübner puts forward certainly seem to be apparent in the characteristics of the mythological Hades-Pluto deity (of which he was undoubtedly aware). It does not seem to be the case however that he also derived or even underlined such characteristics of the planet's symbolism from coincidentally thematically related aspects of the world around him, since those aspects that are commonly cited as being related were largely unknown to him when he wrote his account. Although it certainly appears that such thematic connections did exist between contemporary conditions and Brunhübner's account (and ostensibly to a degree that might seem greater than we would expect by chance), a 'zeitgeist influence' for Brunhübner's assessment nevertheless seems improbable. He wrote before the enormity of death that resulted from the second world war occurred, and before the full impact of the extremes of wealth which resulted from the Great Depression were felt. There is neither any indication that Brunhübner was particularly intellectually absorbed in the subject of psychoanalysis for it to be an influence. These factors were indeed thematically related, and focally in the general period, but they don't seem to have influenced Brunhübner's account. Generally, the possibility that Brunhübner was influenced by Pluto-like themes in the world around him seems improbable.

Since we nevertheless cannot help but see 'Plutonian' themes in the period of the planet's discovery, we are forced to consider the possibility that the very naming of Pluto after the mythological deity might have been influenced by such social themes (which thus, in turn, might have influenced Brunhübner to propound the principle on the basis of the deity's characteristics). As we have seen, the name was proposed by the 11-year-old Venetia Burney. Considering her tender age at the time, it seems unlikely that she named the planet after such deep factors as sex or death, or their associated developments in the contemporary world. In the interview with NASA in 2006 Burney stated, *"I was fairly familiar with Greek and Roman legends from books that I had read, and of course I did know about the solar system and the names the other planets had, and I suppose I just thought that this was a name that hadn't been used."*[172]

Burney claimed she didn't think that she had been so 'subtle' as to name it specifically after the god of the underworld, but rather because it was a mythological deity name that hadn't been used. It is true that several people suggested the name 'Pluto', the god of the underworld, but this seems on the most part to have been motivated by the traditional scheme of naming planets after ancient

---

[172] NASA, 2006

deities, Pluto being an offspring of Saturn that had not had its name used for a major or minor planet. In addition, like the deity, the planet was far away in a 'gloomy' region and had long been invisible. The idea that the use of the bleak name of the mythological god of the underworld was in particular favoured, either individually or collectively, because of the similarly dark and foreboding spirit of the times, seems improbable. Indeed, the more than 200 names that were proposed to the Lowell observatory included *Pax* (Latin for 'peace', apparently to reflect the fact that the 1930s was a decade of peace) and even 'Utopia'. Some suggested naming it after the aviator Charles Lindbergh, who had flown across the Atlantic a few years previously, but this was not a suggestion that could be said to have been a 'summing-up' of the spirit of the times.[173] Ultimately therefore the planet seems to have been named to fit with a mythological genealogy with respect to the other planets, rather than to reflect a worrisome reflection of gloomy world events.[174]

It would therefore appear that Pluto was indeed named quite fortuitously after an ancient mythological deity, and not from the spirit of the times as had rather been the case for Uranus and Neptune. Furthermore, it seems that Brunhübner's account of its astrological symbolism was neither derived from the conditions of the world around him, but from the theme of this ancient deity, and that this description of its symbolism continued, to become what in essence is understood to be the planet's principle today. If Pluto was thus named quite unpremeditatedly after the ancient mythological deity, then the 'Pluto principle' of human nature would appear to have its seed in that chance beginning, for it seems that the symbolic principle grew out of the characteristics of that ancient deity.

We are nevertheless left wondering at the seeming coincidence that the deity corresponding to the chosen name appears to share the same themes as the character of the times surrounding its discovery. To us, those times seem to reverberate with the characteristics of the mythological deity Hades-Pluto, in the dark and vengefully seething geopolitical tensions which lead to war and wholesale death (emanating from Brunhübner's Germany), the closely related themes of psychoanalysis at its zenith of acceptance (which resonated very much with the deity's themes of the necessity of an eruptive power towards regeneration), the emerging technology of nuclear power (which, although of course not derived plainly from the mythological account, agrees very much with the Pluto theme of 'an eruptive power from an unseen realm'), and the extremes of wealth that were beginning to be apparent in the Great Depression and the German banking crisis of 1931.

A likely explanation for the apparent abundance of contemporary themes around the time of the planet's discovery is that they are *only* apparent; that modern astrologers look back and unconsciously employ 'confirmation bias' to 'see' contemporary social developments and conditions which share the deity's

---

[173] Or, we might add, one that would have flown itself.
[174] Schindler, 2022

theme—contemporary factors of which Brunhübner was however completely unaware and which thus didn't feature in his account. We believe that this is the correct interpretation and we must therefore conclude that the entire elucidation of Pluto's astrological symbolism and thus the 'Pluto principle' was not derived from the spirit of the times, as seems to have been the case for Uranus and Neptune, but from the characteristics of the deity fortuitously named by Venetia Burney; that the characteristics or themes of this ancient god influenced Brunhübner's account and were subsequently amplified by confirmation bias on the part of modern astrologers to see it in the spirit of those times. We cannot help but marvel at the power of such confirmation bias to cause us to perceive an apparent coalescence of related, 'Pluto-like' themes around the time of its discovery. The apparent multiplicity or amalgamation of contemporary themes that seem to be thematically related to the chance-named deity still seems hugely compelling, and leaves us in something of an epistemological dilemma.

On the one hand we look back and see so many inter-related 'Plutonian' themes in the world around the time of the planet's discovery—a number that appears greater than we might expect by chance. The erupting threat of conflict and death in the world war that was fomenting; the virtual identity of the principle with the tenets of psychoanalysis which was at its height; the tantalisingly similar processes in the newly developing technology of nuclear energy; the extremes of wealth and violence associated with the Great Depression; Lowell's vast wealth and later his widow's vengeful sexual jealousy affecting his death-legacy so strongly—all these cannot help but make one stop and wonder at their thematic similarity and temporal contiguity, let alone their undoubted connection with or restatement of the Pluto principle itself. As if such apparent coincidences of inter-related 'Plutonian' themes weren't enough, in 1978 the American astronomer Jim Christy discovered Pluto's largest moon and named it 'Charon', from 'Char', his nickname for his wife Charlene, plus the suffix '-*on*' from his interests in subatomic particles (such as prot*ons* and electr*ons*), only later to discover that 'Charon' was the name of the ferryman in mythology who transported the souls of the dead to Hades-Pluto's realm of the underworld.[175]

On the other hand, one plainly wonders just how the apparently 'Pluto principle related' contemporary trends could possibly have 'appeared' around the time of the discovery of a planet that was incidentally given the name of a deity which mirrors those trends. However, we are mindful of the study by Van Rooij (1999) mentioned earlier, which showed how those with close knowledge of astrological symbolism have a powerful tendency to accept or perceive apparent exemplars of that symbolism. Such confirmation bias has a tendency to cause us to perceive what we subconsciously expect to see.

Although we conclude that the entire elucidation of Pluto's astrological symbolism seems to have been derived from the ancient deity fortuitously named by Venetia Burney, elaborated or fleshed out by Brunhübner and later amplified

---

[175] Schindler, 2022

by astrologers' confirmation bias, there remains the question of *why* people seem to feel the great need to perceive this theme at all. We suggest that the answer is that such a propensity for confirmation bias on the part of modern astrologers (and even on Brunhübner's part) is itself a form of projection that is identifying a real human principle. We say this because the 'Pluto principle' appears to be a real human principle or function, operating on personal, physiological, psychological and social-geopolitical levels. Thus *the confirmation bias itself may be said to be a form of projection.*

The themes of the planets were projected by humans because they stand for real human urges, functions or principles. For what is a 'human principle or function' (like 'the respiratory system' or the 'cardiovascular system') other than an abstract characterisation that we 'see' by a sort of projection or patterned perceptual imposition of closely related functions? Basic human principles or functions are, after all, posited constructs, hypothesised by something that one might sensibly see as selectively biased projection. The mechanisms of perception, confirmation bias and projection are subtle, and we might conclude that the ancient thematic characteristics of the mythological Hades-Pluto deity comprised a rough rendering of what has become the modern, more clarified or refined account of what we now perceive as the human Pluto principle. The 'confirmation bias' can therefore be thought of as one more way in which we project identifiable facets of the human psyche. *The confirmation bias is the projection*, just as it was for those early humans who gazed at the beauty of Venus and 'saw' the human principle of attractiveness, love and affection.

Our deconstruction here shows that there is no supernatural process at work; rather it reveals the way we are projecting what we take to be (and therefore which, for us, is) a discernible human function, projected in an age more complex than that in which surrounded ancient peoples. For there does seem to be a genuine human principle involved in the need, at critical times, for renewal, by urgently disclosing, unearthing, bringing to light and facing hitherto hidden, deep-seated matters or urges, which have come to such extremes that they have become systemically burdensome and can no longer be contained or allowed to remain as they are, and must be eliminated or transformed. The function certainly seems to make sense and to be applicable to human processes on different levels, such as in personal physical elimination (defecation), in the need for psychological catharsis as a result of repressive neurosis, in the regenerative processes of sex and death, and in very similar processes operating at a societal level. In particular, the often hidden yet powerful and erupting urge for sexual reproduction and the similarly hidden and often 'taboo' natural requirement for death seem the most fundamental aspects of the 'Plutonian' human urge or principle, which enables the genetic pattern of life—humanity's true wealth—to continue.

The Planets in Retrospect — A Summary

Each of the seven 'classical' planets gained its associated function by the resonance of its visible aspect to a recognisable major human function or principle: the central principle of creative life and vitality in the Sun, by way of its powerfully 'alive' physical appearance; the principle of changeable, fluctuating moods and emotions in the Moon, by way of its ebbing and flowing behaviour; the principle of rapid, nervous communication in Mercury, by way of its swift motion across the heavens; the principle of aesthetics and harmony in Venus, by way of its softly beautiful physical aspect; the active and combative principle in Mars, by way of its blood-like, martial red appearance; the principle of optimism and opportunity in Jupiter, by way of its exalted and lordly presence; and the limiting, restricting or formative principle in Saturn by way of its austere appearance and its marking of the distant limits of planetary visibility.[176]

We have seen in the separate sections above that each planet's corresponding human function operates on both physiological and psychological levels, whilst retaining the same essential principle. The Sun indicates the physical heart or core index of the organised system that governs the health of the whole organism, just as it indicates the whole, creative self or spirit psychologically. The Moon's physiological functions are virtually indistinguishable from its psychological aspects, both being concerned with sleep, memory, habits, emotions and the subconscious instincts which guard over nurturance and security. Mercury's physiological aspects in the brain and nervous systems show the physiological basis for its psychological functions of cognition and communication. Venus's physiological areas of the ears, nose and throat, mechanisms concerned with balance, olfaction (smell) and gustation (taste) are intimately connected to the way we determine what is harmonious, pleasant and 'tasteful'. Mars's physiological areas of the muscles, the sex glands and the red blood cells are obvious physical correlates or bases of its psychological functions of martial action, energetic initiative and life combat. Jupiter represents a beneficial, compensatory or healing function, both on a physiological level, corresponding to the healing and detoxifying action of its organ the liver, as well as on a psychological level, in a person's propensity for humour, optimism, growth and prosperity. Saturn's physiological aspects in the skeletal or bony system and skin are symbolic correlates of its long-term, structural, formative and limiting psychological functional characteristics.

The physiological correlates of the (often social) psychological processes of the three 'extra-Saturnian' planets are not so clear. However, cell mutation, which plays a part in evolution by natural selection, seems implicated in Uranus's function of 'sudden and radical change'. The thalamus, which relays sensory information in the brain and which plays a role in governing consciousness, seems to be associated with Neptune's function of consciousness-transcendence

---

[176] The Alexandrian astronomer Ptolemy (c. 100 — c. 170 CE) taught that Saturn, even within the then-extant geocentric model, was the most distant planet from Earth.

and anaesthesia. Finally, expulsive reflexes such as defecation and sexual ejaculation, and the regenerative or transformative functions of the body such as in cell formation and sexual reproduction, are obvious physiological correlates of Pluto's association with psychological elimination, transformation, regeneration or abreaction (as described by psychoanalytic theory) and with the broader generational functions of birth, sexual reproduction and death.

The planets' functions are reflected in their respective physical organs, which together make up the whole body as a system; they are similarly reflected in their psychological faculties, which together make up the whole psyche as a system. Regardless of the level of perspective—body or mind—the underlying planet-principle is the same. These principles, projected onto the planets, can be seen as human archetypes—'memes' or constructs of humankind's most basic functions, produced by the collective unconscious of all mankind over millennia. The 'classical' planets have thus over millennia been the celestial recipients of humankind's psychological projection of his most fundamental functions. In the case of the 'extra-Saturnian' planets, we seem to see a similar projection of fundamental or archetypal human functions. In the case of Uranus and Neptune, this was influenced by the characteristics of the mundane conditions occurring around the time of discovery. These planets appear to have derived their astrological themes by way of the unconscious projection, by those involved in its discovery and subsequent study, of important aspects of the contemporary spirit of the times—the prevailing zeitgeist.

We nevertheless admit that this may not be an adequate account in the case of Pluto. There does indeed *seem* to be a multiplicity of related themes around the time of Pluto's discovery, in the realms of major social and geopolitical trends, and even trivial events and astronomical factors, all apparently coincidentally associated with the ancient Hades-Pluto deity—thematically related but causally unrelated, and perhaps more numerous than might be expected by chance. But we feel reasonably sure that this apparently non-random agglomeration of interconnected motifs is *only* apparent, being the result of a confirmation bias on the part of astrologers and others who look back with the benefit of hindsight to 'see' a common theme. We would also suggest, however, that the motivation behind this confirmation bias is nevertheless yet another collective urge to project a real human principle or function, operating on physiological, psychological and social levels—the 'Pluto' principle, as we have described it.

3

The Characterisation of the Signs

We have seen how in ancient times the important reckoning of the year-cycle lead to the distinction of twelve equal seasonal periods or segments of the year, and how the salient characteristics of each of these were psychologically projected as fancied pictorial representations onto the random star-patterns that happened to lie in the Sun's path at those times of year. Thus the themes of the twelve 'signs' of the zodiac were created—not from the stars, but psychologically 'painted' *onto* the patterns of the stars (those that lay in the path of the Sun)—by way of an unconscious mental projection of the principal characteristics of the current time of the year.

We can now review the composition and structure of the tropical zodiac, in terms of how the constituent signs are comprised and how they relate to one another. The developed zodiac, being a collective projection of fundamental aspects of the human psyche refined over many thousands of years, is now so internally coherent and so comprehensive a picture of humankind's nature and experience that it appears to be an integrated whole—a holistic system. To comprehend this whole one needs to understand each of its necessary, component parts—that is to say, each sign; but since each sign takes an integral aspect of its nature from its place amidst all of the others, it might seem impossible to fully interpret any one without understanding its relationship to all the others.

One might therefore pessimistically conclude that the task of comprehending every sign in relationship to every other would be hopeless; that one may never comprehend the whole that is the zodiac. We nevertheless believe that, with a thorough study of the signs, both as discrete archetypes and as inter-related aspects or integrants of the whole, an awareness of that whole arises, and that it is indeed possible to grasp the holistic nature of the zodiac. This may be best approached by looking firstly at the nature and structural coherence of the primary components that each sign possesses. These basic components are known as polarity, quality (or 'quadruplicity') and element (or 'triplicity').

Polarity

The first way in which the signs are constituted is by the component known as 'polarity'. Each sign is either positive (being typically active, expressive and spontaneous) or negative (being more typically passive and receptive). The first sign, Aries, is positive; the next sign, Taurus, is negative. The alternation of positive and negative polarities thereafter continues sequentially through the signs to Pisces, thus yielding six positive and six negative signs. The polarities of the twelve signs are shown in Table 1.

Table 1: The Polarities of the Signs of the Zodiac

POSITIVE SIGNS *(active, expressive and spontaneous)*	NEGATIVE SIGNS *(passive and receptive)*
♈ Aries	♉ Taurus
♊ Gemini	♋ Cancer
♌ Leo	♍ Virgo
♎ Libra	♏ Scorpio
♐ Sagittarius	♑ Capricorn
♒ Aquarius	♓ Pisces

Quality (or 'Quadruplicity')

The second way in which the signs are comprised is by the component known as 'quality' (sometimes referred to as 'quadruplicity'). There are three such qualities, namely, 'cardinal', 'fixed' and 'mutable'. The first sign Aries is cardinal; the next, Taurus, is fixed; the next, Gemini, is mutable. The qualities thereafter repeat in the same sequence through the twelve signs, such that there are four signs of each quality (Table 2).

Cardinal signs are typically *outgoing and enterprising.* Each cardinal sign ushers in the 'beginning phase' of a new season. Aries marks the beginning of spring, Cancer marks the beginning of summer, Libra marks the beginning of autumn, and Capricorn marks the beginning of winter. The periods of the year which correspond to the cardinal signs are therefore indicators of initiation, enterprise and new beginnings.

Fixed signs are rather characteristically *intense, steadfast and resistant to change.* Each fixed sign marks an 'in progress' phase of a season. Taurus marks the progression of spring, Leo marks the progression of summer, Scorpio marks the progression of autumn, and Aquarius marks the progression of winter. The periods of the year which correspond to the fixed signs are therefore indicators of settled or established attitudes.

Mutable signs are typically *adaptable, variable and open to change.* Each mutable sign marks an ending or 'completion' phase of a season. Gemini marks an ending to spring, Virgo marks an ending to to summer, Sagittarius marks an ending to to autumn, and Pisces marks an ending to to winter. The periods of the year which correspond to the mutable signs are in this way indicators of endings to current conditions and an openness to forthcoming change and to necessary adaptation.

Table 2: The Qualities (or 'Quadruplicities') of the Signs of the Zodiac

CARDINAL SIGNS (outgoing and enterprising: a seasonal 'beginning' phase)	FIXED SIGNS (intense, steadfast and resistant to change: a seasonal 'in progress' phase)	MUTABLE SIGNS (adaptable, variable and open to change: a seasonal 'ending or completion' phase)
♈ Aries	♉ Taurus	♊ Gemini
♋ Cancer	♌ Leo	♍ Virgo
♎ Libra	♏ Scorpio	♐ Sagittarius
♑ Capricorn	♒ Aquarius	♓ Pisces

Element (or 'Triplicity')

The third and final way in which the signs are comprised is by 'element'. The four elements, fire, earth, air and water, are divided equally amongst the twelve signs and, as was the case with polarity and quality, are repeated in sequence through the zodiac. The first sign, Aries, is a fire sign; the second, Taurus, is earth; the third, Gemini, is air; the fourth, Cancer, is water. The elements continue their assignment in this order through the twelve signs (Table 3). Fire signs are *ardent, keen, energetic and assertive*. Earth signs are *practical, cautious and restrained*. Air signs are *intellectual, communicative and mentally active*. Water signs are *emotional, sensitive and intuitive*.

Table 3: The Elements (or 'Triplicities') of the Signs of the Zodiac

FIRE SIGNS (ardent, keen, energetic and assertive)	EARTH SIGNS (practical, cautious and restrained)	AIR SIGNS (intellectual, communicative and mentally active)	WATER SIGNS (emotional, sensitive and intuitive)
♈ Aries	♉ Taurus	♊ Gemini	♋ Cancer
♌ Leo	♍ Virgo	♎ Libra	♏ Scorpio
♐ Sagittarius	♑ Capricorn	♒ Aquarius	♓ Pisces

Each sign's characteristic theme can be thought of as an emergent property of its unique combination of polarity, quality and element. A summary of the composition of all the signs in these terms is shown in Table 4.

Table 4: The Polarities, Qualities & Elements of the Signs of the Zodiac

SIGN	COMPOSITION ACCORDING TO POLARITY, QUALITY & ELEMENT
♈ Aries	Positive (active, expressive and spontaneous) Cardinal (outgoing and enterprising) Fire (ardent, keen, energetic and assertive)
♉ Taurus	Negative (passive and receptive) Fixed (intense, steadfast and resistant to change) Earth (practical, cautious and restrained)
♊ Gemini	Positive (active, expressive and spontaneous) Mutable (adaptable, variable and open to change) Air (intellectual, communicative and mentally active)
♋ Cancer	Negative (passive and receptive) Cardinal (outgoing and enterprising) Water (emotional, sensitive and intuitive)
♌ Leo	Positive (active, expressive and spontaneous) Fixed (intense, steadfast and resistant to change) Fire (ardent, keen, energetic and assertive)
♍ Virgo	Negative (passive and receptive) Mutable (adaptable, variable and open to change) Earth (practical, cautious and restrained)
♎ Libra	Positive (active, expressive and spontaneous) Cardinal (outgoing and enterprising) Air (intellectual, communicative and mentally active)
♏ Scorpio	Negative (passive and receptive) Fixed (intense, steadfast and resistant to change) Water (emotional, sensitive and intuitive)
♐ Sagittarius	Positive (active, expressive and spontaneous) Mutable (adaptable, variable and open to change) Fire (ardent, keen, energetic and assertive)
♑ Capricorn	Negative (passive and receptive) Cardinal (outgoing and enterprising) Earth (practical, cautious and restrained)
♒ Aquarius	Positive (active, expressive and spontaneous) Fixed (intense, steadfast and resistant to change) Air (intellectual, communicative and mentally active)
♓ Pisces	Negative (passive and receptive) Mutable (adaptable, variable and open to change) Water (emotional, sensitive and intuitive)

The signs of the zodiac are thus integrated by a regularly sequential ordering of the factors or components of polarity (positive and negative), of quality or 'quadruplicity' (cardinal, fixed and mutable) and of element (fire, earth, air and water). Each of the twelve signs is characterised by a unique combination of these three constituents. The tabular representation of the signs' components above is comprehensive but doesn't afford a simple view of them, or of their relationships. We therefore also present Figure 22 which exhibits these components and their relationships for all the signs, in an 'at a glance' form, displaying the common view of the developed tropical zodiac in its traditional circular form, showing (from the outside of the circle moving inwards), each sign's symbol or glyph, its numerical sequence, its generally corresponding seasonal year 'segment' (in the northern hemisphere), its quality (or 'quadruplicity'), its element (or 'triplicity') and its polarity.

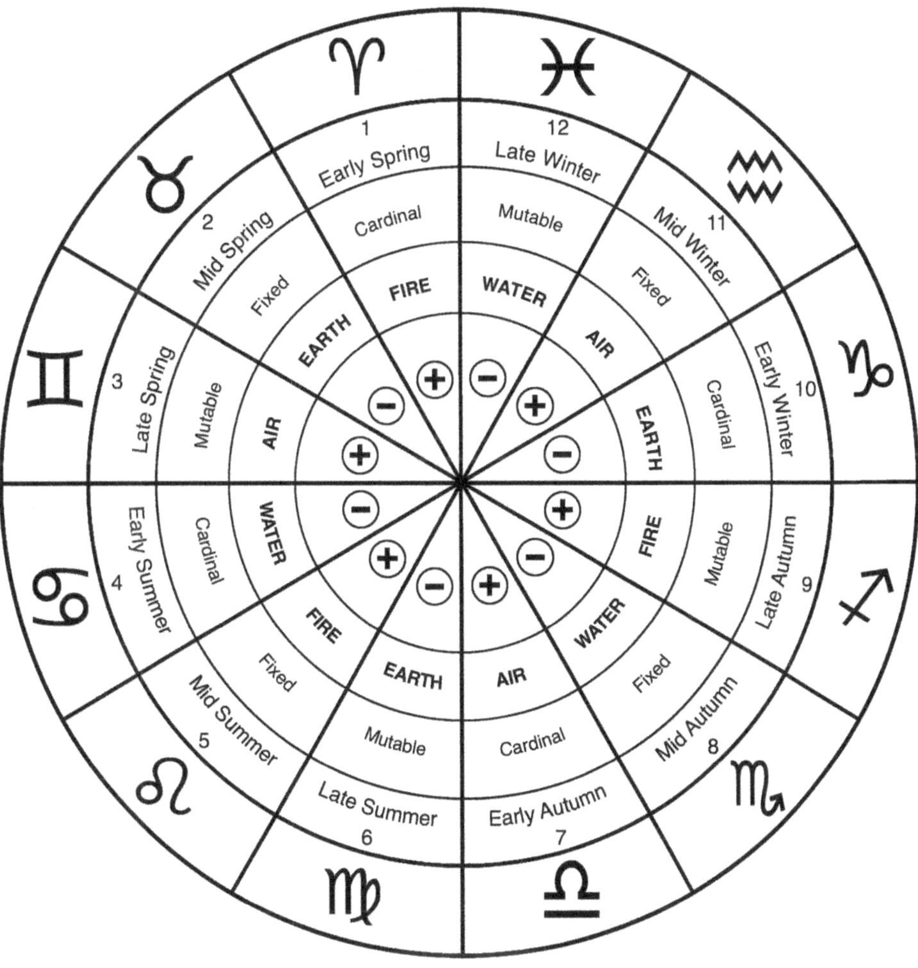

Figure 22. The Twelve Signs of the Developed Tropical Zodiac

We can now proceed to examine the developed characteristics of each sign in more detail, as unique combinations of these components. We can also note how they relate to one another—most especially by comparing each of the signs' characteristics with those of the signs adjacent and opposite to them, as we find that these particular comparisons seem to be the most helpful in revealing the place of each sign in the zodiac as a whole.

It should be remembered that we will be reviewing the signs of the zodiac as they pertain to the twelve fixed and equal periods of the *tropical* zodiac which always begins at the spring equinox, and *not* as they relate to the constellations or star-patterns which have been given the same names and which were once used as markers of these times. This will be the general rule for the names of the signs, except where associations of the named star-constellations would be of interest, where such will be indicated.

For each sign, as we shall now proceed to review them, we will first show a section summarising its early Babylonian origin. This is followed by a section on the sign's composition, including its season, its symbol or glyph, its polarity, quality and element, and its traditional astrological symbolic theme or significance in a summary 'key phrase' form (a short adjectival description). We also show a similar summary 'key phrase' meaning of the 'house' with which the sign is traditional associated (the 'house key phrase' is essentially a reiteration of the theme of the 'sign key phrase', but couched in terms of 'spheres of life' or 'life activities', often used for astrological divinatory purposes, but employed here as a useful and often revealing way to view each sign-theme).

In the case of the last six signs, from Libra to Pisces inclusive, we add a note describing the way in which each of these signs seem curiously to be thematic 'extensions' of their opposite sign in the first six; that is, from a 'personal' theme (in the case of the first six signs) to a more social or 'other related' theme (in the case of the corresponding last six signs). We then proceed to note each sign's 'ruling' planet (the planet most associated with the sign). Thereafter follow sections detailing each sign's traditional physiological associations, a description of each sign's stereotyped psychological 'personality' or 'type', a more detailed account of the time of year to which the sign roughly corresponds in the northern hemisphere, and finally an examination of the sign's association with, and applicability to, various forms of mythology, religion, folklore and custom.

The entire sequence of the twelve signs taken as a whole—the zodiac—of course reflects the complete seasonal pattern of the solar year, the overall characteristics of which we will discuss in Chapter 4, *A Return to the Sun: The Year*.

The Characterisation of the Signs — Aries

In the early Babylonian star-map known as the *Mul.Apin*, written in cuneiform on clay tablets and dating to around 1,000 BCE, the *constellation* that we now know as Aries was referred to as the 'Hired Man' (Babylonian *Mul Lu-Hun-ga*). It is situated close to the constellations the 'Plough' (Babylonian *Mul Giš-Apin*, the modern *Triangulum* and *Gamma Andromedae*) and the 'Field' (Babylonian *Mul Aš Gan*, the modern Square of Pegasus). Its heliacal rising is listed in the Mul.Apin as occur-

Figure 23. Aries — the First Sign of the Zodiac

ring on the first day of the first month,[177] roughly corresponding to the spring equinox, being the time of *hiring men* to *plough* in the *fields* for spring sowing.[178] Thus in these very ancient records it seems possible to discern the projection of salient characteristics of this seasonal time of the year onto the star-patterns that were seen to be in the path of the Sun.

It has been proposed however that the Babylonian name Mul Lu-Hun-ga may in fact have carried the meaning (or have carried the additional, possibly punning meaning) of 'sheep (or lamb or ram) of appeasement', since the cuneiform sign *Lu* is a homophone for both the meanings 'man' and 'sheep' (or 'lamb' or 'ram'),[179] and the sign *Hun-ga* can also signify the meaning 'to appease' or 'to placate'. The 'Hired Man' constellation of stars is indeed written plainly as 'the ram' (Babylonian *Mul Udu-Nita*) in later Babylonian texts,[180] where the cuneiform component *Udu*, signifying 'sheep' (or 'lamb' or 'ram') is represented by a cross inside a circle, which may have been a signification of the four quarters of the year, of which the spring equinox is perhaps the most principal component, marking as it does the beginning of the zodiacal year and the rebirth of life in the natural world.[181] It is difficult therefore to determine with certainty whether the Babylonian name for the constellation Aries signified a projection of a 'hired man ploughing in the field', or more simply a spring 'sheep (or lamb or ram) of appeasement', or indeed both. Nevertheless we can see that specifically vernal themes certainly surface in the Babylonian name of the constellation that has its heliacal rising around the time of the spring equinox, supporting our projection hypothesis.

---

[177] The time of a star's heliacal rising is that time in the year when a terrestrial observer can see that the star (especially a star in the ecliptic—perhaps the leading star of a zodiacal constellation) is rising very close to the Sun. The star is briefly seen to rise on the eastern horizon just before the sunrise, before the Sun's rays obliterate its visibility. It is a useful indicator with which to infer the time of year when a star or its parent constellation actually lies behind the Sun.

[178] Hartner, 1965; White, 2014

[179] A homophone is a word that is pronounced the same as another word but which has a different meaning to that other word, such as 'rose' as the past tense of 'to rise' and 'rose' as the flower.

[180] White, 2014

[181] Interestingly this shape or glyph frequently accompanies depictions of Jesus when specifically portrayed as the 'lamb of God' in a possibly Aries-like context (see below).

White (2014) suggests that in ancient Babylonia the constellation known as the 'Hired Man' (or the 'sheep' or 'lamb' or 'ram' of appeasement) was amongst a group of stars and constellations including Taurus the bull and *Capella* the 'goat-kid', which were *"a succession of springtime images"* created sequentially to mark the position of the spring equinox against the stellar backdrop as that point changed over time due to precession. White has described how they were *"created in successive epochs to mark the ever-westward shift of the spring equinox through the stars"* and that *"these star-figures are essentially similar in nature as they all embody the same seasonal symbolism"*. In time the 'vernal constellation' that we now know as Aries the ram or lamb seems to have come to mark the spring equinox possibly around the 3rd millennium BCE, and certainly by the middle of the 2nd millennium BCE.[182,183] Following the subsequent establishment of the tropical zodiac, whose beginning is fixed at the spring equinox and thus remains forever unaffected by precession, Aries became and thereafter remained the first of the twelve signs (see below).

Aries — Composition

Season: beginning of spring.

Symbol: ♈ The horns of the ram; the head, as seen from the front; the male genitals.

Polarity: Positive (active, self-expressive and spontaneous).

Quality: Cardinal (outgoing, enterprising; the beginning of a new season).

Element: Fire (ardent, keen, energetic, assertive).

Sign Key Phrase: The positive, cardinal, fire sign is: self-assertive, self-promoting, forward-looking, urgent, frank, straightforward, direct, go-getting, forceful, impulsive, restless, bold, uninhibited, fearless, courageous, pioneering; shows initiative, enterprise; seeks adventure and challenge; seeks quick, concrete results; needs to project into life actively, energetically, competitively and combatively.

House key phrase: Activities and matters to do with and which promote the separate, individual, particular person; spheres of life that are a person's own, special, self-centred interests, by which the individual expresses separateness of being and personality, and by which the person approaches, views or appears to the world, via a mask or persona.

Ruling planet: Mars. The particular association with Mars is appropriate, as the self-assertive, contentious attributes of Aries are evocative of the similarly active, energetic and forceful mythological attributes of the red planet. The name of the month of March, within which the sign Aries begins at the spring equinox, is derived from *Martius*, the Latin name for Mars. Martius was the first month in the old Roman calendar and, significantly for the combative sign Aries, marked the beginning of the season for waging war.

---

[182] White, 2014

[183] See Figure 8.

Aries — Physiological

Aries's traditional physiological association is with the head as a whole, and sometimes the face particularly. The associations seem appropriate, since Aries is the 'head' of the zodiac, and the sign's go-getting and pioneering characteristics reflect a desire to be 'at the head of things'. The head and face are evidenced in colloquial expressions commonly used to indicate the 'persona', as in the 'wearing a particular hat', and 'showing one's face to the world' as indicative of one's outward-facing aspect or demeanour. Physiologically, Aries indeed recapitulates its theme of the way we 'face' the world and 'head out' into it.

The Aries 'Personality' in Astrology

We may examine how the 'personality' of the zodiac's first sign Aries has been constructed and epitomised in developed symbolic astrology. We can imagine the Aries 'character' as decisive, particularly with regard to matters promoting the self; urgent in manner, actively projecting into life, self-assertive, uninhibited, frank, direct, straightforward, energetic, forward-looking, pioneering, competitive, combative and impulsive; welcoming a challenge and seeking quick, concrete results; being particularly concerned with matters to do with self-promotion and with the projection to the world of their appearance ('persona') and of their own separate, individual and self-centred interests. The motto of the Aries 'personality' might be "Go for it!" The common expression, to 'think of Number One', meaning to be primarily concerned with one's own interests, would also aptly apply to the Aries type and reflects the primacy of the first, leading place in the zodiac.

At best, the personality appears as bold, fearless, courageous, showing initiative, go-getting, enterprising and adventurous—perhaps as a brave and incisive leader or pioneer. At worst it appears as self-centred, over-impulsive, too direct, forceful, reckless, brusque, crude, rude, contrary, quick-tempered, angry, argumentative and aggressive, insensitive to others and bullying, over-optimistic, thoughtless and foolhardy, conceiving the start and end of an enterprise but being too quick, impatient or restless to consider the finer points or pitfalls that may lay in between.[184] However, it's possible to see how one might view the 'Aries type' as being a variable locus along a gradation between such 'best' and 'worse' extremes, whilst retaining the sign's essential characteristics. We could say that the Aries sign-theme teaches us to be brave, active, incisive and initiatory when circumstances demand it—without being merely impulsive or overlooking alternative views, the finer points or the longer-term consequences of our actions.

---

[184] Many bold and apparently fearless actions leave us wondering if their hallmark was bravery or stupidity.

Aries — Season

The keyword descriptions of Aries typify a portrayal of the rebirth of nature at the beginning of spring. The start of this season is marked by the spring or vernal equinox (also known as '0 degrees Aries'), roughly around which point in time the Sun rises exactly in the east and the days and nights are of equal length throughout the world.[185] In many ways this point marks the beginning of the year for the living, natural world in the northern hemisphere.[186] From this time onwards the days finally begin to get longer than the nights, and winter's advantage of darkness is at last overcome. At this time of increasing light and warmth, nature finally emerges from the seeming dissolution of winter into a joyous time of rebirth, and is now intent on survival, thus taking on an urgent, forward-looking, 'me first' attitude. With increased sunlight and warmth there is new growth for vegetation and an increasing availability of food. Animals in hibernation wake to the call of new life, and most creatures become more active.

Away from the tropics or subtropics where there is little seasonal variation in climate, biological mechanisms in plants and animals perceive the marked change in the length of the day and stimulate their reproductive behaviour accordingly. Small animals with short gestation periods (such as birds) mate in the spring, giving birth to their offspring before the end of summer. Larger animals with longer gestation periods (such a sheep) mate in the autumn in order to be able to give birth in the spring—thus the appearance of lambs and the activity of 'lambing', appropriately for the sign of Aries the ram or lamb. In this way the offspring of both types are able to grow when the climate is moderate and food is more abundant.[187]

Many animals have therefore evolved to take advantage of the climatic circumstances of early spring in order to mate and give birth, and in this season the urge for life ardently asserts itself. Seeds for vegetable crops are also planted. Birds begin their song in the early mornings, to attract mates and to warn rivals away. The life of nature takes on the characteristic of the aggressive and combative initiator, the bold pioneer, showing independent action and a sense of personal identity. What exactly lies in the future is not as important as energetically originating the actual move towards it, and meeting the pressing need for survival.

---

[185] The spring equinox technically refers to the precise point in time at the beginning of spring when the tilt of the Earth's axis is inclined neither away from nor towards the Sun, the centre of the Sun being in the same plane as the Earth's equator. The word 'equinox' comes from the Latin meaning 'equal nights', since it is around this point that the day and night are equal around the world (technically, the 'equilux'), though this occurrence may not occur exactly on the day of the equinox. The term 'equinox' however was in antiquity (and still is) often used for convenience to refer to the actual equilux—that day when light and dark are of equal length.

[186] The identification of the sign-themes throughout are with the seasons of the northern hemisphere, since it has been predominantly in the populations inhabiting that region of the globe that the greater part of this cultural perception has been made.

[187] Shinomiya *et al.*, 2014

Aries — Mythology, Religion, Folklore & Custom

The general theme of new life and rebirth at this time of the year is marked appropriately in many ways by various myth-telling traditions, folklore and customs.

Aries — Ancient Egypt

For the ancient Egyptians, if the symbol of a ram as depicting the assertive beginning of life in spring wasn't projected into the stars, it certainly was present in religious ceremonial. The great deity *Amon* was portrayed as a vigorous man with the head of a ram, and was associated with the return of spring at the vernal equinox. Amon's most important symbol was the ram's horns, the 'horns of Amon' (from whence the distinctive rams' horn-like shape of *ammonite* shells take their name). In conjunction with the Sun he was known as *Amon-Ra,* his temple being approached by an avenue of massive statues with rams' heads.[188] At the full moon nearest the spring equinox, the Egyptians prepared his great celebration, carrying his ram's-headed statue in procession. The observance reached its climax on the fourteenth day of that moon when *"all Egypt was in joy over the dominion of the Ram."*[189] The marking of the halfway point into the first moon-period after the spring equinox with a celebration involving the symbol of a ram foreshadows the same choice of time and symbolism in the analogous Jewish celebration of the 'Passover' with its lamb, to which we now turn.

Aries — Jewish Tradition: the Passover

The Jewish spring equinox Passover festival, in which a male lamb (a ram) was traditionally sacrificed, is popularly seen as a yearly commemoration of the sparing of the Israelites from God's destruction of the first-born in Egypt, as described in the Judaeo-Christian Old Testament texts.[190] The origins of the festival are however much older than these purported events, and it is now believed that the festival was developed from ancient spring seasonal feasts, becoming later subsumed into the Biblical story.[191] The yearly festival is celebrated for a week starting on the 15th day of the Hebrew month of *Nisan,* which corresponds to the night of the first full moon following the spring equinox.[192] Thus we see that the Jewish Passover is, like the Christian Easter, a festival wholly tied to the spring equinox or the beginning of Aries. The history, symbolism, myth and etymology of the Passover festival is interesting though at times complex, and the reader is referred to Appendix 2: *The Judaeo-Christian Passover* for a fuller account.

---

[188] Olcott, 1911

[189] *Ibid.*

[190] Exodus 12

[191] Tigay, 2004

[192] Due to calendrical variations it is sometimes the *second* full moon after the spring equinox.

Aries — Christianity

It is interesting that part of the preparation for the traditional Jewish spring equinox festival of Passover, the sacrifice of a ram, involved a particularly thorough inspection of the animal to ensure that it had no 'blemishes'. Aries represents 'completely fresh new beginnings' after the completion of the heavily karmic theme of Pisces at the end of the zodiac, and the insistence of the 'unblemished' aspect of the spring lamb in these traditions is reminiscent of the need for a decisive transition from the blame-oriented sign of Pisces to the completely fresh, 'karma-free' sign of Aries. The eating of unleavened bread in the Judaeo-Christian tradition at the spring equinox may also recapitulate this transition, where the emphasis is on eradicating any residual karma from the previous cycle—symbolised here by the absence of fermenting yeast or leaven.

The Christian figure of Peter encapsulates this symbolism when he says, *"Purge out therefore the old leaven, that ye may be a new lump, as ye are unleavened. For even Christ our Passover is sacrificed for us."* Peter continues the exhortation to be 'karma-free' in the context of the spring equinox rituals by recommending us to be *"not with old leaven, neither with the leaven of malice and wickedness; but with the unleavened bread of sincerity and truth."*[193] In the same spirit, the spring equinox marks the end of Lent in Christianity—the conclusion of a karma-cleansing period of self-abnegation that is represented by the Pisces sign-theme.[194] Aries therefore represents a successful 'passing beyond' of the karma of the previous year-cycle: all was paid for in Pisces, so the world can begin anew in Aries without the burden of karmic consequences.

Christianity celebrates 'Easter', the most important 'feast' in its calendar, on a date which is fixed to the spring equinox by being, for convenience, placed on the first Sunday after the first full moon following the day of the spring equinox. It's interesting to note that the Christian year calendar is therefore wholly determined by the zodiac, since the date of Easter, tied as it is to the beginning point of Aries, begins and governs the entire cycle of moveable feasts in its liturgical year.[195] For Christians the time of Easter marks that time in the New Testament story when Jesus supposedly resurrected from the dead, three days after being buried following his crucifixion[196]—a theme of rebirth wholly in keeping with the sign-theme of Aries. That the date of the Christian Easter is emphatically connected to the spring equinox and the beginning of Aries is evident in the disparaging comments made by certain early Christians concerning others who had thought of celebrating the festival before that time. Anatolius of Laodicea for example wrote in the 3rd century CE that *"Those who place* [Easter and the beginning of Aries] *in* [Pisces] *and fix* [it] *accordingly, make a great and indeed an extraordinary mistake."*[197]

---

[193] 1 Corinthians 5:7
[194] See *Pisces* in this chapter.
[195] With the exception of Advent.
[196] 1 Peter 1:3; Romans, 6:4
[197] Eusebius & Williamson, 1989

The term 'Easter' developed from the name of the pre-Christian Germanic spring deity *Ēostre* or *Ostara*,[198] and associations with symbols of fertility and new life at the beginning of spring such as with eggs or rabbits (the 'Easter bunny') or hares is still remembered today. The names of these Germanic spring deities may have derived from the earlier Babylonian and Assyrian goddess *Ishtar* (or *Ištar*), the Phoenician *Astarte* and the Egyptian *Isis*, divinities associated with spring.[199] At the spring equinox the Sun rises exactly due east, and the terms for Easter, Ēostre and Ostara are etymologically cognate with the word 'east',[200] illustrating the original association with the Sun's rising precisely in the east, marking the subsequent and welcome prospect of more sunlight than darkness during the day.

The Christian story of Easter has parallels with other myths which also describe the resurrection of a god-man occurring around the spring equinox. The ancient deity *Adonis* was worshipped by the Semitic peoples of Syria, his myth being later borrowed by the Greeks at least as early as the fifth century BCE. Although unfortunately killed by a wild boar in his youth, Adonis was said to have been resurrected back to life in the spring.[201] The Phrygian deity *Attis*, who like Jesus was apparently conceived of a virgin, was also mythologised in ritual to have suffered death (his effigy being affixed to a sacred pine tree) and to have then resurrected three days later at the spring equinox.[202]

Clearly the Christian Easter celebration of Jesus's resurrection has a strong thematic resemblance to the resurrection of life that occurs in the natural world at the spring equinox. Christians either believe that it was sheer coincidence that Jesus was resurrected from the dead at the beginning of spring—also the time of rebirth in the natural world—or that the real time of year of his resurrection is unknown, and that a date fixed close to the spring equinox was deliberately chosen in order to supplant (or possibly echo) pre-existing traditions and customs which reflected nature's own theme of new life and resurrection at this time. Those who see the Jesus story as a fragmented allegory of the progression of the solar year view the Christian Easter tradition as the theme of 'resurrection of new life at the spring equinox in the natural world' being given a part in a story—the Jesus story. In this view, Jesus is not 'the Son of God' but the Sun itself, and the story of his resurrection at the Easter equinox is a social re-telling or fable, in collective myth, of the reawakening of the return of the Sun's power in the spring, a widespread story prompted since time out of mind by changes in the natural world.

In the text of the Christian New Testament, the vernal equinox also corresponds roughly to the date of Jesus's conception, celebrated in Christianity as the ancient 'Feast of the Annunciation' (Latin: *Conceptio Christi*) on the 25th of March,

---

[198] Bede, 1999; Holtzmann, 1874
[199] Hislop, 1862
[200] Watkins, 2000
[201] Frazer, 1894
[202] *Ibid.*

nine months before the traditional birthday of Jesus on the 25th of December.[203] The feast was alluded to as early as the year 656 at the Council of Toledo.[204] For those who see the Jesus story as a solar year myth, Jesus, representing the Sun, is 'conceived' at the beginning of the solar year (the vernal equinox) and is thus 'born' nine months later, just after the winter solstice or Christmas (when the Sun is 'reborn' in so far as the increase of its light and power again becomes discernible).

In the gospel of Luke we read that Jesus's conception at the vernal equinox occurred 'in the sixth month' of Elisabeth's pregnancy with John the Baptist, the latter being therefore conceived at the autumn equinox and thus born at the summer solstice.[205] In the 'solar year myth' interpretation of the Jesus story therefore, John the Baptist, being conceived at the autumnal equinox and so born at the summer solstice (the time of the final height of the Sun's power), was a representation of the 'descending' Sun, while in contrast, Jesus, conceived at the spring equinox and born on the winter solstice (the time of the emerging strength of the Sun), was a representation of the 'ascending' Sun. Indeed in the Christian Bible, John the Baptist remarks of Jesus that *'He must increase, but I must decrease.'*[206]

Continuing the interpretation of the Jesus story as a solar myth in the context of the sign Aries, we read that John the Baptist hails the Jesus Sun-figure, saying, *"Behold the Lamb of God, which taketh away the sin of the world."*[207] The 'sin' or 'bad time' of the world being represented here can be interpreted as the Sun's time in the darker and colder half of the year in autumn and winter; thus when the Sun enters the spring equinox at the beginning of the sign of Aries the ram or lamb, and the days begin to get longer than the nights, that 'evil time' is taken away. The Sun (represented by Jesus) has triumphed over the darkness of winter, thus 'taking away the sins of the world'.

A lamb which is victoriously resurrected after being slain might at first appear to be an odd motif to illustrate a supposedly authoritative spiritual text, though scholars have pointed out that the Jewish spring equinox Passover observance, where a young lamb is sacrificed, developed from older rituals of the semi-nomadic past of the Israelites, where the sacrificial animal represented a deity which was expected to resurrect.[208] The same theme also appears many times in the Christian 'Book of Revelation', the lamb of this text being also described as having 'twelve apostles',[209] evocative of the twelve zodiacal signs which begin at the lamb's own time of Aries. This ancient symbolic theme of the 'death and resurrection of the Sun' at the spring equinox, involving the ritual sacrifice and subsequent resurrection of a lamb, clearly accords closely with the

---

[203] Irenaeus, 1885
[204] Baynes, 1878
[205] Luke 1:36
[206] John 3:30
[207] John 1:29; John 1:35
[208] Mowinckel, 1922; Prosic, 2004
[209] Revelation 21:14

Christian story when viewed as myth, as well as with the recurring representation of a 'triumphant lamb' in Christian iconography from its earliest times.

Many early churches, such as the *Santi Cosma e Damiano* in Rome, feature ancient mosaics depicting the *Agnus Dei* (Latin for 'lamb of God'), some of whom include a row of twelve rams, reminiscent of the 'avenue of rams' heads' in the rituals of the Egyptian Amon-Ra, described above. Since the Middle Ages numerous depictions of Jesus as a lamb have appeared, often significantly featuring a cross within a circle—a visual symbol identical to the Babylonian cuneiform *Udu* sign for 'sheep', 'lamb' or 'ram', which also marked the principal cardinal point of the spring equinox (see above); the symbol is thus ancient in this connection, and may represent an acknowledgement, either consciously or in a collectively unconscious sense, of the basic solar year-cycle as the four main quarters of the year.

Aries — Other Associations

The theme of 'resurrection of life', which so closely recapitulates a description of the natural world in spring at the vernal equinox, has been symbolised by eggs since ancient times. This long association may not seem surprising, since both eggs and the spring are obviously indicative of new life. In modern times Easter eggs are usually chocolate confectioneries, commercially supplied and bought as treats, though there is an Easter tradition of decoratively painting real birds' eggs. The marking of the spring equinox by decorating eggs dates back to long before Christianity. We learn that, *"During the spring cycle of festivals, ancient pre-Christian peoples used decorated eggs to welcome the Sun and to help ensure the fertility of the fields, river, herds, and ultimately man."*[210]

In early Indian Vedic tradition, the spirit who created the 'world egg' often reincarnated or resurrected from it in different forms.[211] The egg as a symbol of newborn life, regeneration and resurrection also existed in pre-dynastic ancient Egypt; here, representations of Osiris, the ancient Egyptian deity of the dying and resurrecting cycle of agriculture, depict him being resurrected from the shell of a broken egg.[212] Also in ancient Egypt, both real and artificial eggs, decorated with geometric patterns in gold and silver, were placed into tombs with the dead. These were not funerary food offerings, as they had been pierced at one end and their contents removed; they were thus purely symbolic. Zettler *et al.* (1998) inform us that *"the practice of furnishing graves with ostrich eggs or ostrich egg vessels was probably widespread in third-millennium BCE Sumer,"*[213] and that *"the egg iconography passed into Christian and even Islamic art; the idea of the egg associated with new life remains with us today in the symbolism of Easter."* Other researchers tell us how *"early cultural associations of the eggs and feathers were with death/resurrection*

---

[210] Grobman, 1981
[211] Newall, 1971
[212] *Ibid.*
[213] Zettler *et al.*, 1998

and kingship respectively, a symbolism that was passed on into early Christian and Muslim usage."[214]

Despite these ancient associations of eggs with the spring, death and resurrection, Christianity has nevertheless attempted, sometimes by way of decidedly unconvincing artifices, to appropriate the 'new life' symbolism of eggs at Easter wholly to itself, for instance by affirming that the tradition of dealing with eggs at Easter somehow represents Jesus's empty tomb after his resurrection.[215] It has even been somewhat less than joyously proposed that the game of 'Easter egg cracking', where eggs are cracked competitively together, *"symbolizes a wish to break away from the bonds of sin and misery and enter the new life issuing from Christ's resurrection"*.[216] In addition to egg-cracking, there are other quite energetic egg-games practiced at equinox-Easter, such as egg-rolling, egg-hunting and egg-racing. Even these have been appropriated as supposedly Christian remembrances: in the case of the egg-hunt, for instance, it has been suggested that the finding of the egg is in fact some way reminiscent of the joy of *not* finding Jesus in his tomb.[217] It is somewhat difficult to believe however that the many enthusiastic egg-based spring rituals throughout the world owe their origin to a solemn remembrance of the Christian Easter story. Indeed, given the ancient origin and the widespread heritage of the practice, we see that the egg is not a solely Christian symbol, but a collective, human emblem of rebirth, particularly and appropriately commemorated at the time of the rebirth of life in the natural world at the spring equinox.

In Great Britain and other countries there is a custom at Easter of eating 'hot cross buns', being small circular cakes marked with a cross, reminiscent (as are the crossed circles often accompanying Christian representations of Jesus as the 'lamb of God') of the four quarters of the 'cross of the year'—particularly significant at the spring equinox. The cakes have been regarded as having a positive, Aries-like apotropaic power and were often kept all year to ward off evil. The 'hot' epithet of the confectionary is not usually present at the time of eating, yet the name, redolent of the characteristically 'hot' Aries, remains. There seems to be some contention as to how old this practice might be. The ancient Egyptians baked cakes marked with a pair of horns which they offered to the goddess of the moon.[218] The ancient Greeks offered to their own deities similarly marked cakes made from flour and honey, calling them *bous* after the symbol of the ox stamped upon them. Although the etymology of the English word 'bun' is subject to dispute, it's possible that it may have derived from the accusative form of this Greek word, being *boun*.[219] The Greeks later marked such cakes with a cross, either to make their breaking easier, or as a representation of the four quarters of the moon, or of the year. The Romans continued the tradition of eating cross-marked buns at

---

[214] Green, 2006

[215] Jordan, 2000

[216] Geddes & Griffiths, 2002

[217] Glass, 2014

[218] Britannica, 1911

[219] *Ibid*; Thompson, 2000

sacrifices. When archaeologists excavated the town of Herculaneum, devastated in 79 CE by the volcanic eruption which also destroyed Pompeii, they found small bun-sized loaves marked with crosses.[220] In the chancel of the Byzantine church of *San Vitale* in Ravenna, a 6th century CE mosaic depicting Abraham's feast shows crossed cakes or buns being served to guests, who are seated close to a scene portraying the biblical story of the attempted sacrifice of Abraham's son Isaac, and perhaps significantly, the ram that was sacrificed instead.[221] A similar mosaic of the 5th century CE depicting Abraham offering crossed cakes or buns can be seen in the church of *Santa Maria Maggiore* in Rome. The pagan traditions of the Saxons are also said to have included the baking of loaves or buns marked with crosses to honour the divinity of spring.[222]

The long association of the spring equinox/Easter period with hares or rabbits (the 'Easter bunny') has been the subject of some rather confused debate recently.[223] Such debate seems on closer inspection to be based upon a doubt as to whether hares or rabbits particularly were associated with the spring Germanic goddess Ēostre or Ostara, citing the fact that the oldest reference to such a connection seems to date back only as far as the writings of the 19th century philologist Adolf Holtzmann.[224] Indeed the debate seemed to include an implication that there may never have been such a Germanic goddess as Eostre-Ostara, taking as its reason that the only significant surviving historical allusion to such a deity was that of the 7th century mediaeval English Benedictine monk, writer, linguist and translator Bede.[225] However, other scholars have considered that the Christian Bede is unlikely to have invented a Pagan goddess.[226] Other folklore which associated Eostre-Ostara with hares and eggs, in a fanciful legend of how the hare was originally a bird, but which was changed into a hare by Eostre-Ostara and which went on to lay eggs in the spring, has been the subject of similar discussion.[227] The historical recency of sources which attest to the association of Eostre-Ostara with hares (or indeed, with egg-laying hares) seems no criticism however of an association of the spring with hares or rabbits generally, and as the folklorist Billson has noted, *"there are good grounds for believing that the sacredness of* [the hare] *reaches back into an age still more remote, when it probably played a very important part at the great spring Festival of the prehistoric inhabitants of* [Great Britain]."[228]

---

[220] Thompson, 2000

[221] The story of Abraham's near-sacrifice of his son and the actual sacrifice of a ram instead is thematically suggestive of both the later tradition of Jesus's 'sacrifice' at Easter and other ancient traditions of a spring lamb-sacrifice (see Genesis 22).

[222] Guardian, 2019; Guardian, 2011

[223] Winick, 2016

[224] Holtzmann, 1874

[225] Bede, 1999

[226] Billson, 1892

[227] *Ibid*; Walsh & Walsh, 1889

[228] Billson, 1892

The Characterisation of the Signs — Taurus

*Figure 24. Taurus —
the Second Sign of
the Zodiac*

The constellation that we know as Taurus has been identified as a bull for an extremely long time—perhaps as far back as 15,000 BCE or even earlier.[229] Taurus marked the time of the spring equinox from about 1,500 BCE to 4,000 BCE (see Figure 8), though the dates are necessarily uncertain due to the large size of the constellation and the uncertainty as to which of its stars may at any time have been constituents of the fancied image. Certainly the bright star Aldebaran and the highly visible Pleiades (or the 'Seven Sisters', a cluster of prominent stars in the constellation) would in all likelihood always have been conspicuous components.[230]

It has been estimated that the constellation Taurus, known to the Babylonians as the *Bull of Heaven* (*Mul Gu-An-na*), marked the spring equinox between the 5th millennium BCE and the latter half of the 4th millennium BCE. Though the constellation Taurus as we understand it did not lie behind the Sun at the spring equinox until just before the 4th millennium BCE (see Figure 8), its observation before sunrise by its *heliacal rising* (before inference of the time of its asctual rising behind the Sun, which would have been unlikely at this very early time), *would* have marked the equinox, for a period of time before the beginning of the 4th millennium BCE. Thus the heliacal rising of the constellation as the Bull of Heaven, before as well as after the 4th millennium BCE, could have projectively characterised the beginning of spring, by virtue of that season's thematic association with the important cattle calving season which typically commenced at springtime. With the gradual progress of the precession of the equinoxes however, the spring equinox came to be marked by Aries, known in Babylonia as the Hired Man or the Ram (or possibly both by way of word-play; see the preceding discussion on Aries).[231] By the time the Hellenic tropical zodiac was established, the sign Taurus marked the later, more established mid-spring period, irrespective of the sidereal position of the constellation that bears the name, and much of its projective interpretation has since been concerned with the seasonal conditions of this somewhat later period of the year, as is set out below.

Taurus — Composition

Season: Mid spring.

Symbol: ♉ The face and horns of a bull.

Polarity: Negative (passive, self-repressive, receptive).

---

[229] Sparavigna, 2008; Whitehouse, 2000

[230] As was pointed out in Chapter 1, in around 4,400-2,200 BCE, the four prominent stars of Aldebaran in Taurus, Regulus in Leo, Antares in Scorpio and Fomalhaut in Aquarius approximately but conveniently marked the four important cardinal points of the year, becoming known as the 'royal stars' later in Persia.

[231] Hartner, 1965; White, 2014

Quality: Fixed (intense, steadfast, resistant to change; the established progress of a season).

Element: Earth (practical, cautious, restrained).

Sign Key Phrase: The negative, fixed, earth sign is: sensible of the need for the common-sense, practical, material values of sustenance, support, security, comfort and beauty; disposed to strong feelings; organically related; stolid, down-to-earth; productive, industrious, possessive, cautious, withholding, conservative, sensible; immovable, with fixed ways and opinions; sceptical, peace-loving, steadfast, reliable, enduring, patient, stubborn.

House key phrase: Activities and matters to do with personal material values and security; possessions, resources, comfort and feelings. Matters connected with concrete, organic, material relatedness, such as food, property, money, beauty, adornment and things that make life more pleasant to the senses generally.

Ruling planet: Venus. There is an affinity between the principle of the planet Venus, with its focus on the evaluation of pleasant experience through the feelings, well-being, peace and aesthetic harmony, and Taurus, which is similarly associated with material security, comfort and beauty.

Taurus — Physiological

The traditional physiological association of Taurus is with the nose, ears, throat and neck—generally, the 'ear, nose and throat' areas. It's notable that the bull, which symbolises Taurus, has a particularly prominent and powerfully developed neck, and is appropriately often seen with a ring through its nose. In many cultures, the bodily areas of the ears, nose and throat are those which are likely to be adorned by expensive jewellery, whose function of augmenting aesthetic appearance resonates well with the Taurus themes of wealth and beauty.

The Taurus 'Personality' in Astrology

We can assess how the 'personality' of the zodiac's second sign of Taurus has been developed in divinatory astrology. We see the Taurus 'character' as cautious, withholding and possessive; motivated by strong values and feelings, particularly of a concrete, materially-oriented or organically-related nature. The personality is particularly concerned with sustenance, support and security. Down-to-earth values are prized, such as those concerned with material resources like food, property, money, comfort, beauty and peacefulness—all things that make life more agreeable to the senses. The Taurus 'character' is sensible, patient and pragmatic, setting great store by the practical, reliable, enduring and common-sense virtues of industriousness and tangible productivity. Stolid and steadfast, the Taurus personality is essentially conservative and sceptical, with a tendency to immovable, fixed ways and opinions.

At its best, the Taurus personality is a defender of the realistic need for material nourishment; of the necessary ground and support in life; for the sensible valuing of peace and stability; for the common-sense practicalities of subsistence which must be met before we can engage in more abstract, let alone spiritual activities. At worst, the character is one who is too materialistic, too sensuous, self-indulgent, over-possessive and grasping; one who is 'stuck in a rut', stubborn, resentful of contradiction, and whose thoughts follow apparently reliable but often dull, boring and unoriginal patterns. As is the case with all the zodiac signs however, it may be more helpful to view the 'Taurus personality type' as a potentiality along a range between such extremes, whilst retaining the sign's essential characteristics. From this construction of the Taurus 'personality' we might say that the Taurus sign-theme teaches us to value the material security and subsequent comfort and peacefulness which comes from common-sense and practical endeavours, without being over-materialistic or unwilling to embrace more intellectual concerns or necessary change.

Taurus — Season

The key descriptions of Taurus recollect a depiction of nature in mid-spring. After the urgent, 'survivalist' period of Aries which started at the spring equinox and which marked the rebirth of life in the natural year, the living world in the northern hemisphere now seeks to consolidate and secure its position by conservatively seeking valuable material assets; by the possession and defence of attractive, stable, comfortable and safe environments which meet its need for food and strength. The emphasis is on sensible, down-to-earth productivity and the possession of material wealth and security, in terms of sustenance and also in terms of territory, both of which lay a stable ground for future life, growth and the rearing of offspring.

Feelings, sensations and physical gratifications are now important, and the senses rightly delight in concrete, tangible pleasures, as well as in the attractive adornment of the environment to be seen in leaves, flowers and all growing things. The keywords of the Taurus sign-theme manifestly reflect the qualities of the natural world in the corresponding seasonal period, when the initial energy of spring is directed into a material-oriented and sensuous abundance.

Taurus — Mythology, Religion, Folklore & Custom

The middle or heart of the Taurus period, at the beginning of the month of May, marks one of the four 'cross-quarter points', a point midway between an equinox and a solstice (in this case, between the spring equinox and the summer solstice), and a number of cultural celebrations of the characteristics of this seasonal period have traditionally taken place at this particular time, the midpoint of the first quarter of the year, when the days are still lengthening. There is a great fecundity in nature at this time, an emphasis on material growth, and the natural world revels in blossom and fertility. These characteristics have been appropriately marked by various folk celebrations.

The Roman festival of *Floralia*, held around the beginning of May, was dedicated to and personified by *Flora*, the Roman goddess of flowers. It celebrated the renewal of organic growth and was marked by dances, drinking and the wearing of colourful clothing to match the appearance of the new blossoms. *Beltane* is the Gaelic name for May and also for the seasonal rituals at the beginning of that month in Ireland, Scotland and the Isle of Man. In the Celtic period, Beltane celebrated the fertility that came with the increasing power of the Sun, which was symbolised by the lighting of outdoor fires (the name 'Beltane' derives from a term meaning 'bright fire'). Appropriately enough for the period of Taurus the bull, cattle and other livestock were traditionally driven past the fires and from there to their summer pastures. The may bush (hawthorn) was decorated with ribbons, and sprigs or boughs of the tree were hung up on doors and windows.

The eve of the first day of May has been celebrated with similar fire festivals in many parts of Europe. Following the introduction of Christianity the festival has commonly been given the name *Walpurgis Night* (or local variants) after being associated with the English missionary Saint Walburga, who was canonised on 1st May around the year 870. In Wales the festival is known as *Calan Mai*. As well the lighting of fires and the decoration of houses with flowers, Calan Mai features mock battles between characters dressed to symbolise winter and summer. Appropriately the summer character wins the conflict, whereupon a May King and Queen are crowned, followed by feasting, drinking, dancing and games. Many elements of the pagan fertility celebrations at the beginning of May have survived the Christianisation of the year calendar. The modern celebrations of May Day are perhaps best known for the traditional dancing around the maypole (a phallic symbol of fertility) and the crowning of the May Queen with flowers. The May Day's symbolising of the key motifs of the Taurus sign-theme—fertility in particular—is well evidenced by the prudish reactions of the sixteenth century Puritan Philip Stubbes upon witnessing the celebrations:

> They have twenty or forty yoke of oxen, every ox having a sweet nosegay of flowers tied on the tip of his horns, and these oxen draw home this Maypole (this stinking idol rather) which is covered all over with flowers ... they leap and dance about it as the Heathen people did at the dedication of their idols, whereof this is a perfect pattern, or rather the thing itself.[232]

---

[232] Stubbes, 2010

The Characterisation of the Signs — Gemini

In ancient Babylonia the constellation we know as Gemini was known as the *Great Twins* (Babylonian *Mul Maš-tab-ba-gal-gal)*. These Babylonian twins, named *Lugal-irra* and *Meslamta-ea*, like their Greek mythological counterparts Castor and Pollux (see below), were considered powerful warriors, and at least one, also in a similar fashion to their Greek parallels, was seen as regularly journeying to and from the underworld or the

Figure 25. Gemini — the Third Sign of the Zodiac

realm of the dead (the name *Meslamta-ea* means 'he who comes forth from the Meslam', the place of the underworld).[233] These peregrinations to and from the underworld also mirror those of the later Greek god Hermes (the equivalent of the Roman Mercury and planet 'ruler' of the sign Gemini) in his role as *Hermes Psychopompus*, the guide of souls to the underworld,[234] and as a frequent emissary to Hades, the land of the dead.

The Great Twins were seen as powerful guardians of doorways or entrances, and had an important role in watching over one of the two Babylonian entrances to the underworld—namely, the one at the summer solstice, that time of year being considered in ancient Mesopotamia a gateway to the underworld, since unlike in milder European locations, it marked a relentlessly hot and parched period of the year when most vegetation died.[235] Thus the Babylonian constellation the Great Twins can be seen as a representation of spirits who anticipate the deathly time of the summer solstice. When the Greek tropical zodiac became later established the sign Gemini marked this early summer period leading up to Cancer, but with more temperate seasonal associations and with more developed themes of communication, as described below.

Gemini — Composition

Season: Late spring.
Symbol: ♊ The twins, stylised as the duality in the Roman numeral II.
Polarity: Positive (active, self-expressive and spontaneous).
Quality: Mutable (adaptable, variable; open to seasonal change).
Element: Air (intellectual, communicative, mentally active).
Sign Key Phrase: The positive, mutable, air sign is perceptive, inquisitive; inclined to relate and adjust to the immediate environment; given to seek out information, to intellectualise, to ratiocinate, to reason; intelligent; well disposed to manipulate abstract concepts logically and to communicate the apprehension and awareness of them alertly with others; highly communicative; mediating, interpreta-

---

[233] Black & Green, 1992
[234] See Chapter 2.
[235] White, 2014

104

tive; adaptive, adaptable, versatile, variable; witty; restless; desiring variety and change; nervously active.

House key phrase: Activities and matters to do with mental and intellectual occupations and interests, thought processes, communications (in the sense of communicative journeying as well as of transmitting and receiving information); speech, writing; learning and education (especially early or formative learning in youth and the early environment); close mental contacts such as that with siblings (especially brothers), other near relatives, neighbours, immediate acquaintances; the general cognitive relating and adjustment of the self to the immediate environment.

Ruling planet: Mercury. This planet's emphasis on the nervous system, learning, mentality and communication corresponds appropriately with the intellectual aspect of the Gemini sign-theme.

Gemini — Physiological

The traditional physiological areas and systems associated with the sign Gemini are the hands, the lungs and the respiratory system, as well as the nervous system generally. The hands are especially associated with Gemini; significantly, we shake hands when we greet each other 'as brothers'—brothers being also closely associated with the sign-theme. The hands are also the bodily instruments of the communicative activities of writing and indicating. The dual branching of the hands and lungs are reminiscent of the essential duality that is characteristic of Gemini and which is stylised in its symbol. The sign is traditionally said to confer or denote a lasting youthful appearance in those of its nativity.

The Gemini 'Personality' in Astrology

From the foregoing we can see how the 'personality' of the sign-theme Gemini has been constructed and epitomised in traditional divinatory astrology. We see the Geminian 'character' as nervously active and intelligent, inquisitive, at home with abstract ideas, communicative, versatile and ready to interpret and adapt to the immediate environment.

At best the personality is a bright intellectual, adept at manipulating and organising abstract concepts, and fluent at interpreting and communicating them. However, Gemini has to be careful to avoid being only fairly good at doing too many things, or being extraordinarily good at doing trivial things. At worst, the personality is superficial, inconsistent, without continuity and diffuse; merely clever or cunning rather than intellectual; dissipating nervous energy, and given to nervous disorder. However, as with all the zodiac signs, it is more helpful to view the 'Gemini personality type' as a potentiality along a gradation between such extremes, whilst retaining the sign's essential characteristics. From this construction of the Gemini 'personality' we might say that the Gemini sign-theme teaches us the value of learning, adaptive intelligence, clarity of abstract thought, and of clear communication in such faculties as speech and writing, without allowing such mental intelligence to become merely clever, superficial, diffuse or dissipated, or persuading us to deal with symbols alone.

Gemini — Season

The key-phrase descriptions of Gemini in some ways recapitulate a portrayal of the natural world in late spring. After the security-oriented 'consolidation' time of Taurus, the year moves on to Gemini, which, like all signs of the 'mutable' quality, characterises the end-phase of one season and the anticipation of the next. Gemini marks the end of spring, and looks forward to the change to summer. In the Gemini period, the 'looking ahead' is positive in nature, as it looks forward to the better days of the year. The natural world begins to adjust to environmental changes or cues which herald the promise of that imminent transition. It has to prepare and adapt intelligently, to think of the possibilities ahead. In the Geminian period, the weather is typically at last improving; the power of the Sun is at a culminating phase of its increasing strength in terms of day-length. At the end of Gemini, on the summer solstice, this continuing increase of daylight will come to an end when days are at their longest; after that time, the power of the Sun will start to decline.

The days of the better weather in Gemini see people more able engage in outdoor activities and to communicate with each other. It is the season to be curious as to what may be 'out there'. The beginning of Gemini is perhaps not quite summer; rather, it develops ideas of what to expect and how to prepare for summer. Many young animals and newly-fledged birds now engage in vital early learning, to adapt in order to be able to survive on their own; they begin to make short journeys away from their homes and nests into their immediate environment. It is a time of learning, adaptation and a positive anticipation of summer.

Gemini — Mythology, Religion, Folklore & Custom

There don't appear to be any especial folkloric customs which specifically reflect the Gemini theme in late spring. Celebrations of the improving climate and the subsequent fecundity of nature seem to have already been observed in the earlier May time of Taurus. The sign Gemini 'the twins' does however make a surprising appearance in the Christian New Testament, as represented by the figures of the disciples James and his brother John. These two apostles are described as the sons of *Zebedee*, and curiously nicknamed by Jesus as *Boanerges*, which is interpreted in the text as *"sons of thunder"*.[236] Regarding the etymology of the Greek inscription 'Boanerges' (Βοανηργες) from Hebrew, we know that the Hebrew root *B'ne* indicates 'sons of', though there seems to be no Hebrew word that corresponds to the suffix *-erges*. However, as some scholars have observed, the Hebrew word for 'thunder' is *re'em*, whose middle phoneme *ayem* is often

---

[236] Mark 3:17

substituted in translation to Greek by 'g' (making *regem*), and an error could very easily have been made in transliterating the final consonant, so as to produce *B'ne-reges* or 'Boanerges'.[237]

But why are James and his brother John referred to as the 'sons of thunder'? In Greek mythology, Zeus is the god of thunder, and the sons of this thunder god were Castor and Pollux (the latter being sometimes known as *Polydeuces*), identified and deified as the brightest stars in the constellation of Gemini. These two stars are enshrined in Greek myth as the *Dioscuri*, from the Greek *Dioskouroi* (Διόσκουροι), from *dios*, 'god' or genitive form of 'Zeus', and *kouroi*, 'boy-son'; thus 'the sons of God' (i.e., of Zeus, the principal god of the Greeks). The Dioscuri have many of the characteristics of the sign Gemini. Their depictions emphasise duality and both are considered to be exceptionally youthful in appearance.

In a popular version of their myth, while both were understood to be the sons of Leda (mother of Helen of Troy and queen of Sparta), Pollux was seen to be fathered by the divine Zeus, while Castor's father was said to be Tyndareus, king of Sparta. This form of their legend recounts that when the mortal Castor was on the point of dying, Pollux begged Zeus to let his dear brother share his own immortality in order that they could stay together. Zeus agreed, and they were transformed into the eternal constellation Gemini. The agreement was however made upon the condition that Pollux should give half of his immortality to his mortal brother Castor,[238] thus enabling the two to alternate between the heaven of Olympus and the underworld of Hades together (which alternation may possibly have symbolised the fact that constellation Gemini is visible for only six months of the year).

Accounts of the parenthood of the Dioscuri are however very often confused and contrary. They have always been seen as twins, even in the legend which tells of them as having different fathers. It is possible that Tyndareus's name may have been interposed in the 'different fathers' myth in order to interpret their archaic name *Tindaridai* in Spartan inscriptions and other literature, causing confused accounts of their parentage.[239] Other accounts in myth of Castor and Pollux frankly assert that both were fathered by Zeus: "*Hesiod in giving their descent makes them* [Castor and Pollux] *both sons of Zeus*,"[240] and "*According to another version* [of their myth], *Castor and Polydeuces were both sons of Zeus, and this is the meaning of their name 'Dioscuri'.*"[241] Zeus, as we have noted, is the god of thunder, and Castor and Pollux, the Dioscuri, were therefore the sons of the thunder god Zeus.

Thus we see that James and John, called the 'sons of thunder', are readily identifiable with the Dioscuri—Castor and Pollux—the 'sons of the thunder god Zeus' and the mythological identities of the two principal stars in the constellation Gemini. It has been pointed out that other evidence from many diverse

---

[237] Harris, 1913; Hodum, 2012
[238] Britannica, 2023
[239] Burkert, 1985
[240] Evelyn-White, 1914
[241] Grant & Hazel, 2001

world sources shows a widespread custom of nicknaming twin brothers as the 'sons of thunder', occurring in cultures as disparate as East Africa, Greece, Scandinavia and Peru.[242]

There is further evidence to suppose that the disciples James and John were representations of the Dioscuri, sons of Zeus, and thus in turn representations of Gemini. In mythology the Dioscuri twins joined Jason on the 'Argonauts' expedition, during which a fierce storm was eventually placated by a prayer, followed by the descending of lightning-like flames or stars upon the heads of the two Dioscuri. This was the mythical explanation of 'St. Elmo's Fire', the electrical discharge which creates a glow about the mast-head and rigging of ships, which to this day is said to herald to sailors the end of a storm.

A vestige of this legend of the Dioscuri's ability, like their father Zeus, to call fire from heaven, is retold in the New Testament narrative in a passage when Jesus was refused entry into a Samaritan village; the brothers James and John (representing the Gemini twins) ask him, *"Lord, do you want us to call fire down from heaven and destroy them?"*[243] Jesus reprimands their tempers, but the passage assumes that the brothers have these powers, which reiterates those of the Dioscuri in the Argonaut legend. If it were not for this mythical connection it would be surprising, to say the least, to suppose that these two apparently simple fishermen had such powers, which are not alluded to anywhere else in the New Testament. Indeed we find that the legend of the Dioscuri in the context of James and John is told yet again in the text: the brothers ask to sit on either side of Jesus on the heavenly throne and share his glory[244]—a restatement of the Greek mythical tradition that Castor and Pollux were granted a special place in heaven by Zeus.

If the foregoing mythical explications were not enough, we read that James and John were, in the Bible narrative, apparently the sons of *Zebedee*. Now the name 'Zeus' became Romanised to 'Jupiter' by way of *Zeus-pater* ('Zeus the father'), the 's' being dropped from 'Zeus', to form 'Jupiter', whose primary syllabic structure is phonologically equivalent to Zebedee. In support of the notion that the name 'Zebedee' is cognate with 'Jupiter', Harris (1913) remarks, *"It might be suggested that the awkward and unnatural expression, 'the mother of Zebedee's children,' which occurs twice in the Gospel of Matthew, would be perfectly lucid, if 'Zebedee's children' were equivalent to the Dioscuri or 'Zeus's boys'."*[245,246] Significantly, in the first of these passages referred to by Harris, when, as is suggested, there are reasonable grounds for interpreting 'Zebedee's children' as the Dioscuri, we once more find the request to Jesus (this time from their mother) that her sons *"may sit, the one on thy right hand, and the other on the left, in thy kingdom,"* again recalling Castor and Pollux being granted a prominent place in heaven by Zeus.[247]

---

[242] Harris, 1913

[243] Luke 9:54

[244] Mark 10:37

[245] Harris, 1913

[246] Matthew 20:20, 27:56

[247] Matthew 20:20

Taken together, these careful interpretations of the Christian New Testament's 'James and John the sons of Zebedee', nicknamed the 'sons of thunder', show them to be none other than Castor and Pollux, the Dioscuri, the sons of the thunder god Zeus and the mythological identities of the principal stars in the constellation Gemini.

The Characterisation of the Signs — Cancer

Figure 26. Cancer — the Fourth Sign of the Zodiac

In ancient Babylonia the stars of the constellation that we know as Cancer the Crab (Babylonian *Mul Al-lul*) had their heliacal rising, as they do now, around about the time of the summer solstice. In Mesopotamia however this period of the year was marked by conditions of heat and drought so extreme as to cause most vegetation to wither and die; the constellation was thus closely associated with death and the underworld. A lack of monumental iconography of a divine crab in Mesopotamia may be explained by its alternative representation as a turtle (Babylonian *Kušu* or 'water creature'), which was frequently represented.[248] The figure of the crab-turtle (Cancer) was notably depicted in combination with those of the goat-fish (Capricorn) and the ram-headed staff (Aries), which together underline their significance as representations of three of the cardinal points of the year (the solstices and equinoxes).

The Crab constellation lies close to another, known as the Serpent, which is a manifestation of the many-headed Hydra or 'water-snake' of Greek myth. The Hydra was seen as restraining the egress of waters from the underworld,[249] thus giving an allegorical explanation in myth for the drought that lay upon the earth at the season of the summer solstice. The Crab and the Hydra were both seen as guardians to the entrance of the subterranean realm of the dead. When Heracles, the great hero of Greek myth, fought and killed the Hydra as one of his twelve 'labours', the creature was assisted by a monstrous crab which emerged from nearby in the watery swamp where they fought, nipping Heracles's foot.[250] It was for some time assumed that the part of the myth involving the crab was 'grafted onto' the myth of Heracles' labours by astrologers merely to ensure a full compliment of twelve signs of the zodiac;[251] however it has more recently been pointed out that the narrative does in fact have parallels with much earlier Mesopotamian myths concerning the deity Ninurta, which themselves probably gave rise to the Greek legend.[252]

It is believed that the Babylonian Crab constellation's projected association of death was largely inherited from the adjacent Serpent constellation in order to

---

[248] White, 2014
[249] *Ibid.*
[250] Graves, 2017
[251] *Ibid.*
[252] White, 2014

accommodate the effects of precession: the 'underworld' associations of the Serpent were transplanted to the Crab as it gradually became the latter which rose at the appropriate time of the deadly hot summer solstice period.[253] This may account for the pertinacious projection of such an important seasonal theme into what is in fact a very faint star-pattern. When the Greek tropical zodiac became later established, the beginning of the *sign* Cancer of course still marked this summer solstice period, but with themes which reflected the more temperate European climate, and developing more appropriate seasonal motifs of the natural world concerning gestation, nurturing of the young and the emotional domestic sphere generally— though still with distinct references to the Sun's 'height' at the inceptive point of the summer solstice; these more well-known post-Hellenic associations are described below.

Cancer — Composition

Season: The summer solstice, into early summer.

Symbol: ♋ The crab's claws; the human breasts.

Polarity: Negative (passive, self-repressive, receptive).

Quality: Cardinal (outgoing, enterprising; the beginning of a new season).

Element: Water (emotional, sensitive, intuitive).

Sign Key Phrase: The negative, cardinal water sign is: reflective, emotional, instinctive; defensive, sensitive; oriented to security, both internal (in terms of physical and emotional security) and external (in terms of the security of a domestic shelter or home); loyal, protective, nurturing and nourishing; mothering; oriented to habitual behaviour; tenacious, resourceful; subject to a conflict between an instinctive outgoing urge (the cardinal quality) and an emotional and indrawn disposition (the negative polarity and the water element), resulting in a periodic, rhythmic withdrawing into the security of a womb-like shelter (either physical or psychological) in order to restore the self-confidence and stability required for subsequent egress into the external world and the expression of the outgoing nature; thus vulnerable, withdrawing, defensive and easily hurt, but externally giving the appearance of inviolable self-possession and resistance; oriented to domesticity, family, kin, land or country; patriotic; sympathetic, tender, imaginative, sentimental, introspective, moody, reserved, withholding; oriented to rhythms, memory, collecting (especially of perceived resources but also emotion-laden paraphernalia).

House key phrase: Activities and matters to do with the home or the domestic sphere, as the base for the self and the containing arena of one's gathered resources, for nurturing, protection and survival; family life and intimate relatives; race, clan, local area and country; the womb and the grave; emotions, inner feelings, intimate imagination, fantasies.

---

[253] White, 2014

Ruling planet: the Moon. There is an affinity between the maternal-feminine, emotionally nurturing, protective and family-oriented principle of the 'planet' the Moon and the zodiac sign Cancer, which recapitulates many of the same themes.[254]

Cancer — Physiological

Cancer's traditional physiological associations are with the chest, the female breasts and lactation, menstruation and the female reproductive system, and the stomach and alimentary system generally. Cancer's traditional glyph or symbol is said to resemble the shape of the female breasts, or the crab's claws protecting its chest, which symbols recapitulate the sign's themes of nourishment and protection.

The Cancer 'Personality' in Astrology

From the sign's composition and keyword descriptions we may understand how the 'personality' of the sign-theme Cancer has been constructed and epitomised in traditional divinatory astrology. We see the Cancerian 'personality' as being emotionally sensitive, tender and sympathetic; sentimental, reflective, introspective and imaginative; loyal, instinctive, nurturing and nourishing; oriented to domesticity, family, kin and land or country; thus patriotic; needing internal security (in terms of emotions) and external security (in terms of a physical home or shelter); oriented to habitual rhythms between the outer world and the inner life.

The Cancerian type is seen as constantly needing to deal with the emotional conflict involved between the outgoing and inward sides or urges of its nature— much like the light and dark sides of the Moon, its ruling 'planet'. The type is seen to be oriented to the past and memory; given to collecting (of perceived assets and of objects to which it is emotionally attached); resourceful, protective, defensive, tenacious and withholding. In traditional astrology, the unrestrained expression of the Cancerian type is said to result in almost obsessional collecting or hoarding—an exaggeration of Cancer's natural impulse to stock the domestic sphere with resources, in case they may be of use for the purposes of nurturing, protection and family survival.

At best, the Cancerian 'personality' is a tenaciously loyal parent or care-giver, identifying constructively with family, clan or country; protecting and nourishing those under his or her charge, and given to a rich imaginative life. At worst, the type is excessively sensitive, too moody, emotionally unstable, too reserved, over-protective, over-clannish and over-withholding. As with all the zodiac signs, however, it's probably best to see the 'Cancerian type' as a potentiality along a range between such extremes, whilst retaining the sign's basic characteristics. From this construction of the Cancer 'personality' we might say that the Cancer

---

[254] In traditional astrology the Sun and the Moon are referred to as 'planets'.

sign-theme teaches us the need for a secure inner life, both of the emotions and the imagination, and for a safe and stable external life in terms of the home or base, together with the importance of cherishing those close to us whose care is in our charge or who are otherwise dear to us.

Cancer — Season

The foregoing key-phrase descriptions thematically recapitulate that 'slice' of the solar year that corresponds to the sign Cancer, which begins on one of the four great pillars or 'cardinal points'—the Summer solstice in the northern hemisphere, when the light of day from the Sun is at its longest duration and straightaway begins to get shorter. The sign Cancer is therefore characterised both by an outgoing expression but also by a concurrent 'retreating' of the Sun in terms of the length of light it gives to the day. The Cancerian 'conflict', touched on above in the Cancerian 'personality', between an outward-facing and an inward-facing nature, is perhaps echoed in the contradiction inherent the summer solstice itself—the 'highest' time of the light of the Sun, yet at the same time, the point of its falling.

Immediately after moving into Cancer, the Sun appears to progress back-wards along the zodiacal arc, in a manner that has been likened to the 'sideways' or 'retreating' motion of a crab—reminiscent of the timid, retreating aspect of the sign-theme. The key descriptions of Cancer given above may be said to typify certain aspects of the natural world at this time of year, which for many creatures are concerned with inwards-looking matters concerning the home or the nest, the related activities of protecting, nurturing, nourishing and rearing of their young, and the security of the family and the 'home patch' generally. The sign-theme reflects the necessarily tender, emotional and more introspective quality of these activities, and moreover the possibility of emotional insecurity when they are threatened, either externally by predatory danger, or internally by discord or disloyalty.

Cancer — Mythology, Religion, Folklore & Custom

The Christian church celebrates the feast of St. John the Baptist ('St. John's Day') on 24th June, approximately at the summer solstice. The commemoration of his nativity is one of the oldest feasts in the Catholic calendar, being listed by the Council of Agde in the year 506. The feast is unique in the Catholic calendar in that it is the only saint's feast to commemorate a birth rather than a death. In the New Testament, John the Baptist was reported to have been born six months before Jesus. Jesus's mother Mary was told by an angel at the 'annunciation' that she had conceived, and that her relative Elisabeth—John the Baptist's mother—was at the same time six months' pregnant, making John the Baptist six months older than Jesus.[255] If we accept the traditional account that Jesus was born at the winter solstice, then according to this information John the Baptist was born at the summer solstice. John the Baptist was therefore 'born' six months before Jesus as a 'forerunner' or 'herald' of Jesus 'to announce his arrival'. This also places John the Baptist's date of conception to be around 24th September or approximately at the autumnal equinox, and indeed the Catholic Feast of the Conception of John the Baptist takes place on that date.

In the 'solar year myth' interpretation of the Jesus story, John the Baptist, 'born' at the summer solstice, may be seen therefore, like Jesus, to be a representation of the Sun in its journey through the zodiac, but specifically a representation of the Sun as it *declines* from the summer solstice (as daylight lessens), whilst Jesus is a representation of the Sun as it *ascends* from the winter solstice (as daylight increases). This is spelled out in the New Testament. The gospel of John reports that while Jesus's disciples were baptising a debate broke out between some of the disciples of John and another Jew concerning purification. In this debate John argued that Jesus *"must become greater,"* while he (John) *"must become less".*[256] John the Baptist, a representation of the Sun at the summer solstice or the beginning of Cancer (when the days begin to *decrease* in length), refers to Jesus as a representation of the Sun at the winter solstice (when the days begin to *increase* in length).

This myth, metaphor or analogy of the Sun through half of the year is also evidenced in the story when Jesus describes John as *"a burning and shining lamp, and you were willing to rejoice for a while in his light";*[257] here Jesus, the Sun at the winter solstice, is referring to the memory of the earlier bright and shining Sun of the summer solstice, in whose light the people, for a time, were glad to rejoice. Significantly, John the Baptist is commonly represented in Christian iconography as holding a cross within a circle—the symbol of the four great points of the year (the solstices and the equinoxes), which underlines the symbolism of a process of the year cycle.

As well as alluding to the summer solstice at the beginning of the sign Cancer, the Christian New Testament story refers more specifically to the *constellation* Cancer, albeit quite cryptically. We read a curious account of Jesus riding into Jerusalem, impossibly upon two animals at once—a colt *and* an ass.[258] As in so many of the stories of the New Testament, the passage is nonsensical if taken literally, but becomes comprehensible when understood as a symbolic representation of the Sun's journey through the ecliptic. In this passage, the animals referred to are symbols of the two stars in the constellation of the sign Cancer: *Asellus Australis*, the 'southern ass-colt or donkey' (now known as *delta Cancri*), and another called *Asellus Borealis*, the 'northern ass-colt or donkey' (now known as *gamma Cancri*). In the Jesus story of the Sun's journey through the zodiac of the year, the Sun's passing though the sign Cancer and the joyous time of summer,

---

[255] Luke 1:36
[256] John 3:30
[257] John 5:35
[258] Matthew 21:7

with the bright, warm weather and the prospect of the harvest to come, is symbolised by Jesus's 'triumphal' or happy entry into Jerusalem, 'riding' these two most conspicuous stars in the constellation Cancer, both of which have names of asses, colts or donkeys.

In terms of thinking about 'the height of the Sun's power' in the course of the year there can easily be something of a conflation of the summer solstice and the later summer period. The Sun's power in terms of length of daylight is certainly at its greatest *at* the summer solstice, yet in meteorological terms the 'height of the Sun's power' is generally in the later and often hotter days of summer. With this observation in mind, it may be argued that, although Jesus's 'transfiguration' (where his face 'did shine as the Sun' up a 'high mountain') may fittingly mark the *astronomical* high point of the summer solstice at the beginning of Cancer,[259] it may seem more appropriate in a *meteorological* sense to place this part of a potential solar-year myth element in Leo.[260]

Although the sign Cancer denotes that time of year when the Sun's power begins to diminish in terms of daylight, many traditions have naturally felt the need to celebrate the Sun's culmination of power at the beginning of the sign—the summer solstice—though often also with a symbolic reference to its subsequent 'fall'. It is hard to imagine just how one might go about ritually recreating the symbolism of the Sun attaining the peak of its glory at the summer solstice *and* then immediately 'falling away' to successively decreasing hours of daylight, but the people of Europe and Great Britain have in times past managed to do just that, and in a strikingly appropriate way. An old tradition for St. John's Eve—the night before the feast of St John the Baptist on 24th June (the approximate time of the summer solstice)—has been the rolling of a flaming wheel down a hill. A Gloucestershire monk in the 14th century described the ritual as being practiced as early as the 4th century in France, while other records show that it was common in northern Europe by the 16th century.[261] The custom was recorded as taking place in Wales in the early 19th century, when wheels 'swathed with straw' were set alight and sent rolling down a hill.[262]

A belief was said to be held that if the fire went out before the wheel reached the bottom, a poor harvest was indicated, but that if it stayed alight, a prosperous harvest-time was ensured—an almost one-to-one symbolic correspondence between the relative ripening power of the Sun and its effects on the yield of crops. One can hardly think of a more apt or ingenious way of representing the Sun at the height or turning point of its annual power on the summer solstice, and then straight away 'falling' towards the later part of the year and autumn, than a flaming wheel or bundle placed high on the summit of a hill, and set immediately to roll down—just as the imminent diminishing light of the Sun will immediately cause the days to shorten.

---

[259] Matthew 17:1-2
[260] See the separate section on Leo.
[261] Hutton, 1996
[262] Trevelyan, 2014

Many other celebrations are recorded both in mainland Europe and Britain involving the communal lighting of fires and lamps on Midsummer's Eve, in the countryside, in town streets, and even in royal palaces, with much merry-making and feasting, to mark the Sun's seasonal zenith on St. John's Eve, the evening before the summer solstice. Indeed, by the 16th century the Midsummer Eve revels had become so elaborate and riotous that official 'watches' were required to police the celebrations, and even these turned into hugely exuberant processions of pageantry.[263] The rituals petered out when the deprecations of Protestantism linked the practice with what was seen as 'popery', and when the governing authorities began to fear a potential danger of rebellion in such mass congregations of unruly crowds. The summer solstice at the beginning of the sign Cancer was also symbolised in a remarkable and somewhat esoteric zodiacal allegory of the year cycle, in the 12th century Welsh prose epic the *Mabinogion*, which we shall explore more fully in Chapter 4.

The Characterisation of the Signs — Leo

The group of stars that we know as Leo was one of the earliest fancied constellations, being pictured as a lion from at least as early as 4,000 BCE.[264] As we pointed out in Chapter 1, from around 4,400 BCE to 2,200 BCE, the four prominent stars of Aldebaran (in Taurus), Regulus (in Leo), Antares (in Scorpio) and Fomalhaut (in Aquarius) approximately marked the four important 'cardinal' points of the year—the spring equinox, the summer solstice, the autumn equinox and the winter solstice, respectively.[265] From some of the earliest times of the psychological projection of seasonal themes onto star-patterns therefore, the constellation 'the lion' marked the time of the 'great triumph of the Sun' in terms of its brightest manifestation in the year—the period beginning at the longest day at the summer solstice.

Figure 27. Leo — the Fifth Sign of the Zodiac

In ancient Babylonia the constellation was known as the 'Great Lion' (Babylonian *Mul Ur-Gu-la*). The male adult lion with its majestic appearance, its corona-like mane and its naturally dignified but ferocious demeanour seems innately appropriate for a visual representation of the Sun, especially at the year's solstitial 'high point'. The iconographic projection of a fierce lion for the time of the summer solstice was also *climatically* apposite in Mesopotamia, as this period of the year was a time of intensely ferocious heat and drought. The constellation of the lion was in addition, from very early times, closely associated with the king and the king's relationship to the realm. The principal star of the constellation, *Regulus* ('little king' in Latin) was known in Mesopotamia as *Sharru* or 'the

---

[263] Hutton, 1996
[264] Pasachoff, 1992
[265] By virtue of their heliacal rising at those times in the year.

king'.[266] The lion as a fierce carnivorous predator (the *king* of the beasts') was also an apt representation of the king as a warrior. When the post-Hellenic tropical zodiac became later established, the *sign* Leo forever marked the height of the Sun's meteorological power in mid-summer,[267] retaining many of the old associations of power and kingship from its early Mesopotamian origins, but also emphasising notions of creativity and recreation, as set out below.

Leo — Composition

Season: Mid summer.

Symbol: ♌ A lion's mane or tail; the corona of the Sun.

Polarity: Positive (active, self-expressive and spontaneous).

Quality: Fixed (intense, steadfast, resistant to change; the established progress of a season).

Element: Fire (ardent, keen, energetic, assertive).

Sign Key Phrase: The positive, fixed, fire sign is given to a characteristically powerful, joyful and creative attitude; to a sense of authority, mastery, command and influence; is impressive, dramatic, proud, dignified; sincere; enthusiastic; desires self-expression, self-assertion; is self-assured, outspoken; broad-minded, gregarious, generous, warm-hearted; oriented to overall organisation and integration of the whole.

House key phrase: Activities and matters to do with self-expression, creativity, joy, pleasures, love affairs, children, sports, games, entertainment, risks, gambling and speculation; recreation and exposition of the self; one's need for expressions of creativeness and happiness; the display of one's power and prowess; the organising and integrating of the broad spectrum of one's talents and qualities into an impressive and powerful projection of one's own unique image; the offspring of one's mind (i.e., ideas) as well as one's physical offspring.

Ruling planet: the Sun. There is a natural thematic kinship between the masculine and fatherly principle of the Sun and the authoritative and imposing characteristics of Leo, which will become more evident as the sign is described. One can see the function of the Sun in Leo's composition: in the spontaneous and expressive positive polarity, the static nature of the fixed quality, and the energy-laden nature of the fire element. Thus to our Earth-bound perception, the Sun, although apparently fixed and unchanging, at the same time incessantly pours forth vital energy. Much of the following description of the sign Leo should be read in conjunction with the notes on the 'planet' the Sun.

Leo — Physiological

Leo's traditional physiological association is with the heart, corresponding to the 'authoritative' index of the whole organism (see the section on Leo's planetary ruler, the Sun), the cardiovascular system generally, and the spine or back.

---

[266] Rogers, 1998; White, 2014

[267] In the northern hemisphere.

The Leo 'Personality' in Astrology

From a synthesis of Leo's composition and keywords we can see how the 'personality' of the sign-theme Leo has been constructed and epitomised in traditional divinatory astrology. The Leo 'mode of expression' can be seen as proud and dignified, with a distinct reluctance to brook mockery; as impressive and wishing to demonstrate prominence, authority and command; as seeking the broad picture and naturally wanting to orchestrate, integrate and organise matters overall and to be managerial; as self-expressing and demonstrative, with a general urge to display; as magnanimous, gregarious; joyful, humorous, sunny and optimistic; creative, recreational and dramatic.

Leo can be thought of as the 'king' or 'father' amongst the signs, often seeing the other signs as its own 'subjects'. It is the notion of 'the all in the one and the one in the all'. Like the Sun, Leo is associated with royalty. The monarch, despite being only a single individual, traditionally refers to him or herself as 'we', which may reflect the fact that Leo sees itself as the all-inclusive, integrating 'centre stage' authority, speaking for everyone. The monarch belongs to the people, as much as the people belong to the monarch. It is the correlate in society of the heart in the body. It is the unifying principle of society (at least in monarchical societies); the people identify with the monarch, which is often more particularly associated (superficially at least) with the male king rather than the female queen. The monarch is the organising principle or symbol that typifies or expresses the nature of, and thus gives coherence to, the realm, and whose all-inclusive aspect prevents any one particular part of the societal body from becoming too singularly emphasised. The physical crown that the monarch wears symbolises the Sun with its corona (Latin for 'crown'); visually the crown is indeed the stylised picture of the Sun as seen from above.[268]

Drama and humour are quintessentially 'Leonian' qualities, and they may be seen as a readiness to embrace and even caricature all the ways and types of the world, good and bad, fair and foul, tragic and comic. Drama and humour bespeak each and all of Leo's 'subject' signs, somewhat as an actor or conductor 'plays' or registers the whole range of characters or instruments. Drama 'acts-out' all the various signs or 'agents' of the whole. To be an actor is to attempt to represent the whole experience, the whole gamut of impressions, of all the various aspects of human life.

If one wishes to imagine a portrait of the Leo 'personality' in one's mind's eye then one can hardly do better than to imagine an impressive-looking, authoritative but generous and kindly father figure in the summer sunshine, joyfully and proudly beholding his children, his own creation, as they play and happily indulge in recreation; encouraging them with a humorous paternal eye and bestowing upon them a sunny generosity; not afraid to order, command and organise their lives, even sternly at times, but also sincere and enthusiastic in his

---

[268] See *The Sun* in Chapter 2.

love for them. This picture is incidentally also instantly reminiscent of the common notion of God as the ultimate father figure, and the Leo sign-theme is the archetypal attitude of both the familial father and 'God the father'. It's also an image that's coextensive with the archetypal characterisation of the Sun.

At best Leo embodies such an ideal picture; at worst, the type is overly 'egoistic', proud, conceited, pompous, patronising, intolerant of criticism, autocratic, being too fixed in opinions, exaggerative, too inclined to wish to outdo or outshine others, overbearing, domineering, and lacking the humbler senses of self-deprecation or irony. Leo loves to be (or at least loves to be thought of as being) an authority on subjects and an 'authority' generally, and this trait may be immodestly overstated. As with all the signs, however, it is perhaps more accurate to see the 'Leo type' as a potentiality along a gradation between such extremes, whilst retaining the sign's essential characteristics. We might say that Leo teaches us to see the 'big picture' or the whole, and when necessary, to take command and direct, in order to integrate matters and our lives holistically, without allowing such a need to manifest itself as merely gratuitous autocracy, intolerance or domination.

Leo — Season

The foregoing key-phrase descriptions of Leo recapitulate a portrayal of the natural world in the impressive days of mid-summer, the sunniest time of the year, when the weather is at its best and people are most able to indulge in joyful, recreational activities. In summer everything is in full bloom, young animals play, and life is for living. The season is the vindication and happy achievement of all the striving and preparation that has been undertaken since spring emerged from winter. The first rewards of natural fruition and of hard-earned cultivation begin to appear and there is a great anticipation of the bounties of produce.

Leo — Mythology, Religion, Folklore & Custom

The theme of joyous living in mid-summer has been appropriately marked by various cultural festivals. The middle or heart of the Leo sign period, around the beginning of August, marks one of the four 'cross-quarter points' mid-way between a solstice and an equinox (in this case, between the summer solstice and the autumn equinox) and has been celebrated in folklore and myth. The Gaelic festival known as *Lughnasadh* is celebrated in this period, usually around the 1st August, being squarely athwart the sign Leo. It marks the very earliest beginnings of the harvest, or the 'first fruits' of the year. Lughnasadh historically involved large assemblies of people, often gathering at the tops of hills, with recreation in the form of athletic games and trade. The name of the festival derives from the name of the Irish deity *Lugh*, and the Old Irish *násad* ('an assembly of people'). The festival has given its name to the modern Irish word for the month of August, which is *Lúnasa*. Some have argued that the deity Lugh is not a deity of the Sun,[269] for the same linguistic reasons that we should apparently not suppose the Welsh *Lleu Llaw Gyffes* to be so;[270] yet it is nevertheless widely accepted that Lleu Llaw Gyffes is almost certainly Lugh's Welsh counterpart in myth. Lugh's epithet *Lámfada*, meaning 'long arm', likely referring to his skill with arms,[271] closely resembles Lleu's expanded name ('Llaw Gyffes'), meaning 'with the steady (or skilful) hand'. Moreover, an analysis of symbolism in the Welsh Mabinogion shows that Lleu is undoubtedly a representation of the light of the Sun (see Chapter 4), which of course makes us suspect that Lugh, as the Welsh Lleu's Irish counterpart, has similar solar associations, despite the linguistic objections. Lugh is described in the Irish epic myth *Táin Bó Cúalnge* as 'with a great head of curly yellow hair',[272] which accords with the eponymous epithet given to the Welsh Lleu by his mother *Arianrhod*, namely, 'the fair-haired one (of the steady hand)'.[273] These descriptors of flowing blonde hair are themselves suggestive of the Sun with its radiating golden corona. Since ancient times hair was frequently associated with the Sun's corona, such as in the appearance of the Sun-god Apollo *"with the sun's rays in the form of spikes coming out of his head"*.[274]

There are also attributes of the Lughnasadh festival itself that are distinctly appropriate to the characteristics of the sign Leo. Lughnasadh was marked by the eminently 'Leonian' themes of recreational games and horse racing, such as the *Tailteann* Games in Ireland, reputed to have been inaugurated by the deity Lugh himself. The festival also involved 'trial' love matches or affairs—a traditional 'Leonian' association. The ritual of climbing to the top of hills or mountains at the time of Lughnasadh has been observed for over 1,500 years, and is still practiced today, albeit within a Christianised ethos, on 'Reek Sunday' or 'Garland Sunday', where pilgrims walk 'sunwise' around the mountain *Croagh Patrick* in County Mayo.[275] This rite is suggestive of an apparent urge to experience the 'high point' of the Sun in summer, similar to the rituals observed for the summer solstice in the preceding sign Cancer.

As we mentioned in the previous section on the sign Cancer, when one thinks in terms of the 'height of the Sun's power' in summer, one can think of it in terms of the greatest length of *daylight* on the summer solstice at the beginning of Cancer, or more *climatically* as the later and often hotter days of 'real summer' in the time of Leo. The Sun often typically has its greatest climatic effect in the seasonal part of the year corresponding to the sign Leo, and we note that in traditional astrology it is Leo which 'rules' (has a particular affinity with) the Sun. The period of Leo is certainly that which more recognisably marks the time of the first tangible proofs

---

[269] Hutton, 1996

[270] See Chapter 4: *A Return to the Sun: the Year.*

[271] Koch, 2006

[272] O'Rahilly, 2019

[273] It may also be noted that the Welsh name for 'lion' is Llew, phonologically almost identical to 'Lleu'.

[274] Roberts, 2013

[275] Harbison, 1995; Monaghan, 2009

of the Sun's agricultural blessings, and the rituals of Lughnasadh embody this maturer aspect more emphatically. Indeed the deific mythology of the cultural ritual of Lughnasadh in Leo appears most fundamentally to celebrate the Sun in its role as the happy giver of the bounty of the very earliest fruits of harvest. The folklorist Máire MacNeill has described how the ritual involved a symbolic cutting of the first of the corn, with thanks being given to the deity.[276]

Ritual dramatic plays (another Leonian theme) were performed at the summits of hills, where actors would represent the gods and other forces involved, particularly the triumph of Lugh over the powers of blight and other factors that threaten control of the grain, the latter being represented by a female mythological figure known as *Eithne*. Such rituals may have had ancient antecedents, for example in the similar representation found in the myth of the ancient Greek god Hades (the Roman Pluto), who attempts to abduct the grain-goddess Persephone (the Roman Proserpina), but who is forced to allow her to return from his underworld prison in time for the harvest to begin.[277] The equivalent of Lughnasadh in English-speaking countries is known as *Lammas*, the first harvest festival of the year, especially of wheat. The name derives from the Anglo-Saxon *hlaf-mas* or 'loaf-mass'. A special celebratory loaf was often made from this first cereal harvest and was reputed to have protective, apotropaic powers, especially if crumbled into the four corners of a barn.[278]

In the 'solar year myth' interpretation of the Jesus story, the height of the Sun's influence in the summer part of the year is represented by his 'transfiguration', where he is shown at his 'highest point', 'up a high mountain', where his face "*did shine as the sun*".[279] The actual 'transfiguration' element of the story seems to be solely though dramatically comprised of a period when an effulgence of very bright light emanated from Jesus. We have already noted how 'the height of the Sun's influence' can in the one 'maximum daylight' sense correspond to the period of Cancer, and in another sense of the meteorological or climatic height of summer, correspond to that of Leo.

When viewing the Jesus story as a myth of the solar year, that part telling of his 'transfiguration' certainly seems to represent this seasonal theme of the 'height of the Sun's influence', though it might be difficult to know whether to place the event symbolically at the summer solstice at the beginning of Cancer, or in Leo. Certainly the tradition of the Catholic Christian church places the 'feast' of the transfiguration squarely in Leo, on 6th August. This date was fixed by Pope Callixtus III, ostensibly to commemorate the raising of the Siege of Belgrade in 1456.

---

[276] MacNeill, 1962

[277] See *Pluto* in Chapter 2.

[278] It's not known why precisely four pieces were chosen, though it may be speculated that the choice of four parts for four 'corners' was a collectively unconscious gesture to the four 'corners' or cardinal points of the year.

[279] Matthew 17:1-2

However we suspect that collectively unconscious resonances with the year-story may have influenced this dating (it would have seemed entirely wrong, for instance, had that pontiff fixed the date to commemorate Jesus's 'shining like the Sun' in the depths of autumn or winter). Significantly, just before the point of this transfiguration, Jesus nevertheless predicts his death—a reminder that although the Sun (symbolised by Jesus) is now attaining the peak of its influence, it will inevitably head southwards as it descends towards the 'dying' part of the year in autumn and winter.[280]

Figure 28. Virgo — the Sixth Sign of the Zodiac

The Characterisation of the Signs — Virgo

In ancient Babylonia the constellation that we know today as Virgo was then known as the Furrow (Babylonian *Mul Ab-sin* or *Mul Ki-hal*). The Furrow was pictured as the goddess *Šala* holding an ear of barley, in a similar way to the later representation of Virgo the virgin (see below). Like Virgo, Šala symbolised the early autumn fields, ready to receive the life-engendering seed, so to produce the vital harvest of the year. The modern constellation Virgo is in fact an amalgam of the Babylonian Furrow and another Mesopotamian constellation, the Frond. Whilst the figure in the Furrow was depicted holding an ear of barley cereal, the figure in the Frond held a date-palm frond.[281] When the Greek tropical zodiac became established, the *sign* Virgo retained the barley stalk, and occasionally also the palm frond, despite the fact that these crops did not figure in the wheat and olive based Greek harvest. Interestingly Mercury was often represented close to representations of the goddess Šala, prefiguring the modern association of the planet with the sign Virgo.

Virgo — Composition

Season: Late Summer.

Symbol: ♍ A maiden (virgin) holding an ear of corn; three ears of corn; the hymen or female pudendum; the legs of a human female, crossed in a pose of modesty; the intestines; the Roman letters 'M' and 'V' combined as 'Maria Virgo'.

Polarity: Negative (passive, self-repressive, receptive).

Quality: Mutable (adaptable, variable; open to seasonal change).

Element: Earth: (practical, cautious, restrained).

Sign Key Phrase: The negative, mutable earth sign is analytical, critical and discriminating; has an urge to sift detail, to take to pieces, to disassemble; is apt to evaluate life by facts and logic; practical; inclined to an urge to work methodically towards efficiency and perfection; precise; thorough; reserved, modest, unassuming; conscientious, helpful; predisposed to an attention to purity, hygiene and cleanliness.

---

[280] Matthew 16:21
[281] White, 2014

House key phrase: Activities and matters to do with work, particularly in service, and of a detailed, thorough and practical nature; practical responsibilities; mundane but necessary tasks; conformity and useful service and duty to the community as a necessary and interdependent part of the whole; relationships with employers, employees and coworkers; health, fitness, efficiency and hygiene.

Ruling planet: Mercury. Both the signs Gemini and Virgo are 'ruled' by (have a close affinity with) the planet Mercury, whose function is fundamentally one of mentality, nervous transmission and thought. In the case of Gemini, which is an air sign and thus typically intellectual, communicative and mentally active, the affinity is with the more abstract and logical nature of the planet's intellectual function. In Virgo, which is an earth sign and therefore more practical, cautious and restrained, the thinking function of Mercury is applied more particularly to pragmatic, serviceable and utilitarian matters; to the attitudes and activities that require close mental discrimination and attention to detail.

Virgo — Physiological

Virgo's traditional physiological association is with the digestive system, particularly the small intestine and, in keeping with the key themes of the sign as described above, with its function of discrimination; of separating out, retaining and absorbing what is good, and discarding what is unwanted waste. The connection of this physiological aspect of Virgo and the nervous nature of its 'ruling' planet Mercury is reflected in the fact that the functioning of the gastrointestinal tract is governed by its own nervous system—the 'enteric nervous system'. Sometimes described as a 'second brain', the enteric nervous system can operate autonomously, though it communicates closely with the central nervous system (which governs 'higher' mental processes) through what has become known as the 'gut-brain axis'. As an example of this communication between the two systems at a basic level, the mere sight or smell of food generates gastric secretions in readiness for digestion.[282] More subtly, undue anxiety in the higher central nervous system can cause disorders in the digestive tract through its effects upon the enteric nervous system—and vice versa.[283] This is in keeping with the traditional astrological description of the Virgo sign-theme as one prone to worry or fretting, with resultant intestinal disorders. The connection is reflected in common parlance, as for instance when we remark that we have a 'gut feeling' about something which causes us a certain apprehension.

The Virgo 'Personality' in Astrology

From the foregoing we can see how the 'personality' of the sign-theme Virgo has been constructed and epitomised in traditional divinatory astrology. The

---

[282] Filaretova & Bagaeva, 2016
[283] Myers & Greenwood-Van Meerveld, 2009; Liu *et al.*, 2011

Virgoan 'type' can be seen as one who is analytical, critical, attentive to detail and methodical; modest, reserved, conscientious and helpful, particularly in work and service; one who perhaps pays especial attention to thoroughness in health, efficiency and hygiene. At best, the personality appears as one who takes responsible duties seriously, as say, a policeman, serving the community in a position of 'purity' and probity, whilst sifting factual details; or as a nurse, serving in a valuable health and hygiene oriented community capacity; or as a quality-control officer, aiming for thorough standards and efficiency, through meticulous discrimination; as an unassuming, quiet and methodical 'back-room boffin'; or as an assiduous butler or other servant. At worst, the personality may be merely hypercritical, pedantic, carping, over-fastidious, given to unnecessary fretting and worry; narrow, specialising too much, obsessed with detail and perhaps also with hygiene; over-modest, too diffident, prudish, suppressing emotional outlets. However, as with the other sign-themes, it is probably best to view the Virgo 'type' as a potentiality along a spectrum between such extremes, whilst retaining the sign's essential characteristics. We might say that Virgo teaches us, when necessary, to be discriminating, conscientious, attentive to detail, modest and cognisant of health and efficiency, without allowing this to become a tendency to be hypercritical, prudish or obsessed with worrisome detail.

Virgo — Season

The foregoing key-phrase descriptions of Virgo recapitulate a portrayal of the natural world in the period of the harvest time, in late August and September. The fundamental 'attitude' both of the sign-theme and of the seasonal harvest-time activity which it represents has been ably described as an *"unconsciously motivated process of grinding and separating material into assimilative, digestible particles, that only the pure essence shall become part of themselves".*[284] This description emphasises *discrimination*, in both the activity of the harvest, where careful discernment is required to separate the wheat from the chaff in order to prepare grain for flour, and in the attitude of its symbol the maiden or virgin (frequently depicted holding an ear of corn), who discriminates to seek the best of all the candidates for her procreation, and thus for the best possible future ('harvest') for her genes.

Virgo the virgin or maiden perhaps more specifically symbolises the *potential* or expectation of the harvest—'the essence of fertility'. Virgo therefore has an emphasis on good health and purity, as the maiden must be in good health and pure to be worthy of the coupling and sexual union to come; the passing on of good genetic material. The attractiveness of a maiden is after all to a great degree the appearance of good health.

Other facets of the sign's keywords show its representation of the harvest: essential practical work, service and duty are the needful qualities for this

---

[284] Mayo, 1964

important activity of the year. Attention to detail is particularly necessary in order to discriminate good fruit from that which is unwanted—a seasonal 'process of digestion' which corresponds with Virgo's physiological associations as described above. The harvest of course follows the sowing of the springtime and the fructification of the summer months, and thus Virgo, the time of the harvest, is a karmic time to reap what was sown. Virgo, like all signs of the mutable quality, brings an end to one season (in this case, summer) and looks forward to a change to come (here, to the prospect of autumn and a practical preparation for the decline of the year).

Virgo — Mythology, Religion, Folklore & Custom

The Christian church celebrates the feast of the nativity of the virgin Mary on 8th September, in the middle of the Virgo sign-theme period. This festival celebrates the birth of Mary, the mother of Jesus in the Christian New Testament story, who reputedly gave birth to Jesus despite being a virgin.[285] Up to the 17th century it was traditional to depict Mary with a star on her shoulder, which most likely represents *Spica* (*α Virginis*),[286] the brightest and most prominent star in the *constellation* Virgo, whose name, *Spica Virginis* means 'Virgo's ear (or spike) of grain' in Latin, restating the association of the Virgo sign-theme with fertility and the time of the harvest. Part of this constellation was known as 'the Furrow' in ancient Babylonia, and was represented by a goddess with an ear of grain. Both names are in keeping with the theme of fertility. Many other images of the virgin Mary depict her either holding an ear of corn or in close proximity to decorative motifs of ears of corn.[287] Virgo is sometimes also depicted holding a palm branch in her other hand, which is an ancient symbol of triumph and rejoicing. In the case of Virgo it may be seen as symbolising the joy of the expectation of a harvest time to come, whether literal or spiritual. The Christian tradition views the virgin Mary as the paragon of purity—a central Virgoan trait. It seems therefore that an association of the principles of the astrological sign-theme of Virgo with the biblical virgin Mary became more vigorously apparent *after* the New Testament narrative texts had been composed. Stephen Benko has described the popularity of great fertility goddesses from Syria to Libya and Rome around the second century CE which were all considered to be images of a celestial virgin:

> The Roman soldier and the Christian visionary both see a woman
> appearing in the sky, and for both she is a divine and royal figure.
> This is not just a coincidence. The concept of the constellation
> Virgo was destined to play an unusual role in Christian theology
> just about the time when the inscription of *Donatianus* was

---

[285] Matthew 1:18; Luke 1:26-31
[286] Goodman, 1990
[287] *Ibid.*

written.[288] Around the middle of the second century, Christians began to return to their pagan intellectual origins, referring to and quoting Greek and Roman authors.[289]

Benko recounts how a poem of one of these rediscovered classical authors, that of the Fourth Eclogue by Virgil in 40 BCE, tells of *"the birth of a child whose coming will usher in a new age, free of every sort of wickedness which thus far has hung over mankind as an evil curse"* and which runs *"Now returns the virgin"*. The context of this revived poetic myth makes it clear that the virgin being referred to is the constellation Virgo. Benko goes on:

> It was, of course, not difficult for Christians to put the emphasis upon the meaning of the word Virgo, Virgin. While this was legitimate for pagans as well, the Virgin par excellence for Christians was the mother of Jesus. And so in Christian interpretation Virgil's poetic line became a reference to Mary ... The rest of Virgil's poem underwent a similar allegorisation and eventually Virgil himself was regarded as a prophet who foretold the birth of Christ. But παρθένος, or Virgo, in Greco-Roman religious usage can also mean any one of the 'virgin' goddesses — Demeter, Juno, Isis, *Atargatis, Caelestis,* and Aphrodite, to name a few. The question is, then, could Christians interpret Virgil's poem as a reference to Mary if some form of mental association between the image of a virgin goddess and Mary had not already taken place? Whatever the answer to this question may be, the fact remains that in this case there is a direct overlapping of the pagan Virgo and the Christian Mary. In other words, it was in the interpretation of the Fourth Eclogue that Christians openly identified Mary with the celestial virgin goddess of paganism.[290,291]

In medieval Europe a female figure, sometimes depicted with an ear of grain in one hand and a date palm in the other, was identified with the Virgin Mary.[292] In later developments of Christianity, although St Augustine had quite sensibly argued in his *De Trinitate* that one could not possibly know the actual appearance of the mother of Christ, it wasn't long before an inevitable plethora of theological

---

[288] Donatianus was a Roman soldier who left a poem, known as the 'Carvoran Inscription', which was a paean of praise to the virgin goddess, in Hadrian's wall around the 3rd century CE.

[289] Benko, 2004

[290] *Ibid.*

[291] In the Mabinogion, a collection of 12th century Welsh prose stories which originated from much older oral traditions, a female figure symbolising the vegetative fecundity of the harvest time, *Blodeuwedd,* appears to have arisen quite independently of Christian influence (see Chapter 4).

[292] O'Neil, 1976

disquisitions over the subject of holy images, together with a sheer human fascination for the archetype of the fertile figure of the virgin, conspired to ascribe concrete characteristics to Mary. In the 16th century Johannes Molanus (1533-1585), professor of theology at Louvain, described the personal appearance of the Virgin Mary in his *De Historia Sanctarum Imaginum et Picturarum* as having a complexion that *"reminded one of wheat"* and of an individual character *"cultivating a surpassing humility"*, which descriptions were apparently derived from the *Life of the Virgin* as set down by the Greek monk *Epiphanius* in the ninth century.[293] The reference to wheat is obviously redolent of some sort of harvest, in keeping with the associated seasonal period of the Virgo sign-theme. It may be thought that Molanus's description went further than might have been considered theologically seemly, as it incorporated descriptions that could almost be described as positively aroused, when he continued to propose that the virgin *"was blonde, her eyes sharp, tawny, with olive-coloured pupils. Her eyebrows were charmingly curved, [and] black, her nose somewhat long, her lips rosy and filled with the sweetness of words, her face not round or sharp."*[294] These are basic contemporary descriptions of an attractive maiden and recapitulate the sense of the sign's aspect as a pure and fertile maiden, promisingly ripe for a fecund harvest.

The key associated themes of Virgo as described above are also prevalent in much art and iconography of the virgin Mary. The 15th century painter Antonello depicted her *"as a young woman, with her hands crossed in front of her in the gesture of humility"*,[295] a characterisation highly evocative of one interpretation of the Virgo sign glyph, as described above. The virgin Mary has also frequently been depicted in devotional art as wearing a dress decorated with ears of wheat—a clear association with the themes of agricultural fertility and an expected harvest. The first of these 'ear of wheat dress' depictions appears to have been a statue erected at Milan Cathedral in the late 14th century which was destroyed and replaced by a painting in 1465. Other works depicting the virgin Mary in a dress decorated with ears of wheat include a German woodcut of around 1470, *Maria im Ährenkleid* ('Madonna in the Robe of Wheat Ears'), now in the National Museum in Copenhagen, and several others from 15th-century Germany, Switzerland and Austria.[296]

The 'ear of wheat dress' representation has been piously interpreted in conventionally religious metaphors, such as *"the Blessed Virgin as fertile soil and untilled field of God called to bear fruit"*,[297] although to those who see much of the Christian New Testament story and its iconographic sequelae themselves as mythological allegories for the solar year, the meaning of the image becomes more specifically a characterisation of the virgin field which is to bear the actual agricultural harvest. It is important to note however that a truly spiritual sense

---

[293] Winston, 2002
[294] *Ibid.*
[295] *Ibid.*
[296] Nagel & Wood, 2010
[297] Peters, 2020

may nevertheless be apparent if one is prepared to embrace the myth itself as spiritual. A hymn to the Virgin Mary, even if understood as deriving from the myth of the seasonal part of the year, does not detract from the sublime beauty of its essence. If Jesus is seen as a representation of 'the Sun as God', then Mary the virgin, who had the ability to give birth and so bring forth his spirit, symbolises the apotheosised virgin fecundity or promise of the 'mother earth' which is endowed with the ability to bear the fruits of the harvest which have been engendered or impregnated by the summer Sun-god.[298]

It is perhaps worth reiterating that, as Stephen Benko and others have described, the iconographic and symbolic association between the virgin and images of the harvest, such as of wheat and bread, has spiritual-mythological antecedents which are much older than the Christian story, such as that of Demeter, the ancient Greek goddess of the harvest. Demeter's attribute was an ear of wheat, symbolising fertility, her Roman counterpart being *Ceres* (from Proto-Italic **kerēs*, meaning 'grain' and etymologically cognate with 'cereal'). In the ancient Greek festival of *Haloa* in Athens, bread from the new harvest was dedicated in thanks to Demeter.[299] In Christian iconography a dove appears as a herald of Mary's virginal conception of Jesus—for example, in the annunciation as depicted by Fra Angelico, Van Eyck, and the 16th century French *Book of Hours*—and the dove has figured as a major symbol in ancient myth-stories of virgin births. Furthermore, the ancient Greeks in turn identified doves with the Pleiades constellation, whose heliacal rising was at the time of the approaching harvest.[300] Benko describes the 'extension' of such ancient virgin fertility divinities, harvest festivals and their symbols into the Christian era:

> In its veneration of the Virgin Mary, not only did Roman Catholic Christianity absorb many elements of the cults of Greek and Roman goddesses, but Mary in effect replaced these deities and continued them in a Christian form ... there is a direct line, unbroken and clearly discernible, from the goddess-cults of the ancients to the reverence paid and eventually the cult accorded to the Virgin Mary.

Benko concludes that the ancient female virgin fertility deity, whose symbolic foundation was the fertile earth which is impregnated by the Sun to produce the harvest, was adopted by or extended into Christianity as the virgin Mary who *"received the role of the bride, as the 'virgin earth' who was impregnated by the word of God, as the symbol of the church, the bride of Christ."*[301]

---

[298] In the New Testament we read of the virgin Mary's 'annunciation', when the angel Gabriel appeared to her, saying, *"The Holy Ghost shall come upon thee"* (Luke 1:35).

[299] Benko, 2004; Peters, 2020

[300] Rigoglioso, 2009

[301] Benko, 2004

The Characterisation of the Signs — Libra

In ancient Babylonia the stars which comprise the constellation that we now know as Libra the Scales were in fact part of the constellation Scorpio the Scorpion—specifically, the claws of the scorpion. Over time, the two bright stars *α Librae* and *β Librae*, once the southern claw and the northern claw of Scorpio respectively, became part of a separate constellation, the 'scales' or 'balance'—the modern Libra (being the Latin plural form of the word meaning 'weighing scales'). In the cuneiform Babylonian star-map known as

Figure 29. Libra — the Seventh Sign of the Zodiac

the *Mul.Apin*, dating to around 1,000 BCE, the star-pattern Libra was listed as '*the Scales, the horn of the Scorpion*' (Babylonian *Mul.Zibanu* or *Mul.Zi-ba-an-na*), showing its emergence from the Scorpion constellation. Even the later Greek astronomers referred to stars in Libra as 'the claws of the scorpion'.[302] It has been suggested that this transformation of part of the constellation of the Scorpion into a separate star-pattern known as Libra the Scales was due to an adjustment made in order to accommodate the precession of the autumnal equinox.[303] Where that point in the year was once unequivocally marked by the body of the group of stars long known as the Scorpion, the effects of precession shifted the point to the stars at the very periphery of the constellation (*α Librae* and *β Librae*).

The fancied pictorial projection of the autumnal equinox by this much smaller group of stars was subtler and more abstract than the 'death of the year' in the scorpion's sting. The Scales still carried the sense of the autumn and the fall of the season, but in terms of a more considered and astronomically advanced marking of the 'balance' of the two halves of the year. The scales are incidentally also reminiscent of the physical instrument used in the autumn to weigh the produce of the harvest—the tangible result of this first half of the year from the viewpoint of the annual cycle of life. It's interesting to note that the emergent constellation 'the Scales' was sacred to the Babylonian Sun god *Šamaš*—especially in his role as judge, assessor and arbiter of disputes, which themes are very much consonant with the developed symbolism of Libra as the 'evaluation of two sides'. The association of the constellation 'the Scales' with Šamaš therefore reflects this more conceptual representation of the autumnal equinox: there is a developing emphasis on the abstract appreciation of the concept of 'balancing' generally, that has its genesis in the consideration of the 'balanced' view of the two halves of the year—the fecund fruits of the first half and a consequent consideration of the prospects of the second.

---

[302] Rogers, 1998; White, 2014
[303] White, 2014

Libra — Composition

Season: Autumn equinox, into early autumn.

Symbol: ♎ The scales or balances.

Polarity: Positive (active, self-expressive and spontaneous).

Quality: Cardinal (outgoing, enterprising; the beginning of a new season).

Element: Air (intellectual, communicative, mentally active).

Sign Key Phrase: The positive, cardinal, air sign is oriented to an attitude of relatedness, seeking relationship; therefore co-operative; disposed to evaluation and impartial judgement, especially of harmony, beauty, art, balance and form; charming, kind, affectionate; seeks peace, calm; averse to discord and conflict; easy-going; oriented to an urge for unity with others; diplomatic, tolerant; apparently indecisive (often through an unwillingness to be against the ideas of any one party).

House key phrase: Activities and matters to do with the seeking of balance and harmony, and therefore wholeness of the self through the identification and unity of the self with significant others, on a personal level and on equal terms; close associations and connections with others, especially those with which one wishes to unite oneself; partnerships, in personal relationships, marriage, business or other joint endeavours; contracts.

Sign as 'Extension': Libra conforms to the curious and ubiquitous pattern where the last six signs of the zodiac seem to be 'extensions', thematically, of the first six—extensions from themes to do with the 'individual' (in the case of the first six) to those same themes applied more widely, extensively and typically to do with 'others' (in the case of the latter six). The Aries-Libra polarity exemplifies this pattern of 'wider extension to others' perhaps more simply than any other, being the first such to be traced in the zodiac sequence. As we saw, Aries emphasises the viewpoint of 'the self', whereas the 'extended' opposite sign to Aries, Libra, emphasises a viewpoint of 'relation to others' generally. As Aries was a person's expression of his or her self and singularity, so the opposite 'extension' of Aries, Libra, is a person's expression of unison and partnership with others.

Ruling planet: Venus. Libra is 'ruled' by (has a close affinity with) the planet Venus. Both the planet Venus as a human urge, function or principle, and the sign Libra as a mode of expression, concern relatedness and harmony, in terms of the need to achieve relatedness and harmony in relationships with others, as well as in terms of the need for relatedness and harmony in aesthetics or beauty.

Libra — Physiological

Libra is traditionally associated physiologically with the lumbar region generally and the kidneys in particular. Libra's key themes of evaluation and balance are echoed in some prime functions of the kidneys. One such function is to evaluate, for regulation, the body's 'acid–base balance', or the pH value of extracellular fluid, including the blood plasma. These organs also evaluate and balance factors that govern the long-term regulation of blood-pressure, as well as water and salt levels. The health of the muscles in the lumbar region (the 'lumbar extensors') has been found to be crucial for whole-body postural *balance*.[304]

The Libra 'Personality' in Astrology

From the foregoing we can see how the 'personality' of the sign-theme Libra has been constructed and epitomised in traditional divinatory astrology. We might envisage the 'Libran personality' as easy-going, charming, co-operative, tolerant, diplomatic and able to see both sides of issues; apparently indecisive, due to the characteristic impulse to appreciate the viewpoints of opposing parties and both sides of an issue; desiring rapport, agreement, peace and harmony, averse to conflict or discord; evaluative, a good judge, appreciating harmony and beauty in art. Libra is sympathetic to what is 'fair' in both senses of the word. At best, the personality shows the archetypal peace-maker, the diplomat who, by virtue of being able to see both sides of an issue and by thus being capable of charming disparate factions into adopting a compromise, can bring about peace and harmony. At worst, the personality may be one who is weakly indecisive, lacking the confidence to make a stand, desiring 'peace at any price', frivolous and squeamish to the harsher realities of life. However, as with all the zodiac signs, it's perhaps more helpful to view the 'Libra personality type' as a potentiality along a gradation between such extremes, whilst retaining the sign's essential characteristics.

Libra — Season

The keyword descriptions of the Libra sign-theme, which emphasise relatedness, balance and evaluation, are recapitulated in the natural world at this time of year. Libra begins at the autumn equinox, when the days and nights are of equal length, and the world is in a natural form of balance. The days and nights were also of equal length at the spring equinox, but that point marked the beginning of life emerging from winter (in the northern hemisphere), whereas the autumnal equinox marks the time when the whole circle of the zodiac is in balance at the year's halfway point: the first half has passed, and the latter half is to come.

This concept of an evaluation of the two 'halves' of the year at the time of Libra is particularly apparent in agriculture. The Libra period is the time when the harvest is evaluated and assessed. Balances or scales are actually used at this time to weigh the fruits of the harvest. The Libran themes of relatedness, balance, comparison and evaluation are evident as one looks back to that which was planted and how it has now come to fruition; how the efforts of the first half of the year relate to the prospects of the second; how the community's earlier efforts will relate to the necessity of coping with the less productive and harsher seasons ahead.

---

[304] Davidson *et al.*, 2004

130

In keeping with the Libran keywords of aesthetic harmony, at this time of the year the leaves of deciduous trees 'turn' to form beautiful displays of colour. The beauty is often seen to be tinged with a certain poignancy, as unconsciously one compares the recent glory of summer to the prospect of the impending 'falling' of the year.

Libra — Mythology, Religion, Folklore & Custom

In the Roman Catholic church, the major feast day around the time of the autumnal equinox and the beginning of the Libra sign-theme is that of *Michaelmas*—the feast of the archangel St Michael. St Michael is an almost perfect emblem or re-statement of the Libra sign-theme. One of his divine functions is to descend propitiously to the soul at the hour of death, to give it a chance to evaluate its state (restating the Libran theme of 'evaluation'). This function can easily be seen as a correlate of the moment at the autumnal equinox when the year begins to fall or 'die' and a similar evaluation takes place. Indeed, St Michael is specifically assigned at this moment with the task of weighing souls, in order to assess the relative amounts of piety and sin, and in this role he is commonly depicted holding scales or balances, just as in the Libran symbol. As one author notes, "*St Michael's decisive role in the* [weighing of souls] *is surprising as there is no scriptural warrant for his exercise of such an office.*"[305]

Here we are reminded that this major representational function of the Christian figure of St Michael, as with many other Christian iconographic and thematic characterisations, developed well past the purportedly historical time of the Jesus figure. Intriguingly, another role of the archangel St Michael was as a warrior, specifically as one to fight a dragon.[306] It may not be too implausible to suppose that the basis of this thematic iconography lay in the contiguity of St Michael-Libra to the adjacent sign Scorpio, which latter has been variously represented as some form of vile, venomous or dangerous creature. In this interpretation, St Michael-Libra is thus an apotropaic representational form which allays the prospective distress of the imminent period of the inherently fearsome Scorpio sign-theme. The New Testament figure known as John the Baptist was conceived on or around the date of the autumnal equinox at the beginning of the sign Libra. The Catholic church duly celebrates the feast of the *Conception of the Precursor* (i.e., of John the Baptist) in Libra, on 23rd September. As we noted in our discussion of the sign-theme Cancer, John the Baptist was conceived at the autumn equinox and so born at the summer solstice at the beginning of the sign Cancer, thus representing by his birth-date the Sun as it *declines* from the summer solstice, whilst Jesus, conceived at the spring equinox and thus born at the winter solstice, is a representation by his birth-date of the Sun as it *ascends* from the winter solstice.[307]

---

[305] Johnson, 2005

[306] Revelation 12:7–9

[307] See the discussion on the 'birth' of John the Baptist nine months before the autumn equinox (the beginning of Libra), at the summer solstice, in the section on the sign Cancer in this chapter.

The autumn equinox at the beginning of Libra, being the mid-point of the 'darker turning' half of the year (between the summer and winter solstices), has been artfully characterised in the mediaeval Welsh body of prose stories known as the Mabinogion, which we discuss more fully in Chapter 4.

The Characterisation of the Signs — Scorpio

Figure 30. Scorpio — the Eighth Sign of the Zodiac

The pattern of stars that we know today as the constellation Scorpio (sometimes called Scorpius) has been projectively imagined as a scorpion since at least as early as the star-maps of ancient Mesopotamia, where its Babylonian name was Mul Gir-tab, meaning '(creature with) a burning sting'. The constellation heliacally marked the autumn equinox between around 4,400 and 2,200 BCE.[308] The gradual effects of precession however caused that cardinal point to shift with respect to the positions of the stars and eventually to become marked only by those stars at the extreme periphery of the star-pattern; these equinox-marking stars at the very edge of the Scorpion eventually came to be seen as a separate constellation, known both as the 'claws of the scorpion' and 'the scales', but understood exclusively today as Libra the scales or balance (see the separate section on Libra). Thus we can see that, although the original, ages-old projection of the autumn equinox as a deadly venomous scorpion had long been an apt projection of the 'sting of death' to the Sun's power and light as the year 'falls' towards its decline, its later projection onto the newly fancied constellation the Scales reflected a still appropriate but somewhat more refined projection of this seasonal time as the 'balance' of the year at its halfway point.

Scorpio — Composition

Season: Mid autumn.

Symbol: ♏ The scorpion; the eagle; the scorpion's sting; a phallus.

Polarity: Negative (passive, self-repressive, receptive).

Quality: Fixed (intense, steadfast, resistant to change; the established progress of a season).

Element: Water (emotional, sensitive, intuitive).

Sign Key Phrase: The negative, fixed, water sign is penetrating, passionate, secretive, subtle, dark, deep, introspective, suspicious, obsessive, intense, one-pointed, wilful, extreme, purposeful, mystical; oriented to identify with the commonly shared source and resources of life; subject to a strong desire to transform, and to uncover or reveal that which is masked, hidden or taboo; oriented to the hidden, fundamental regenerative processes and powers that are inherent in birth, sex and death.

---

[308] Rogers, 1998

House key phrase: Activities and matters to do with feelings, possessions and resources that are shared with, or gained through, others; matters concerning the commonly shared generative and regenerative life-force, evident in birth, sex and death, and the strong emotions that surround these spheres of life (e.g., passionate love or hate, jealousy, betrayal or revenge); wills, inheritance, legacies and bequests; monies and funds that belong to others, in the form of taxes, stocks and shares; deep research and investigation; fundamental life mysteries; non-orthodox spiritual conversion or mystical experience.

Sign as 'Extension': Scorpio adheres to the constant pattern wherein the last six sign-themes are 'extensions', respectively, of the themes of the first six; extensions from themes to do with the 'individual' to those same themes applied to 'others'. As Taurus was centred on *personal* feelings, possessions and resources (in line with the more 'personal' aspect of the first six signs), so its opposite Scorpio is associated with matters concerned with the need to share feelings, possessions and resources with *others* (such as in convertible resources and money), or with the actual sharing or possession *of* others, physically (as in sex). Taurus is connected with 'pleasant indulging' of the more enduring sensations (such as food), while Scorpio is connected with the 'pleasant indulging' of shorter-lived and intense or even ecstatic sensations—especially those that are shared with others or which tap a resource commonly shared with others (such as sex). Taurus was retentive (personally possessive of resources), while Scorpio is expulsive (sharing resources with others).

Ruling planet: Pluto. Before Pluto was discovered in 1930, Mars was the planet that was traditionally said to 'rule' (be particularly associated with) the sign Scorpio. That connection seemed apt, given Scorpio's formidably powerful and aggressive characteristics, though the astrological associations which later developed for Pluto seemed even more suitable for the intense, deep and extreme forcefulness of this sign. Indeed, much of the descriptive nature of the sign Scorpio is a restatement of the principles of Pluto, and these notes on Scorpio should be read in tandem with the section on that planet.

Scorpio — Physiological

Scorpio's physiological associations are with the reproductive system and its organs, and the rectum. The physiological processes associated with these are clearly related to Scorpio's (often taboo-laden) functional sphere of renewal or regeneration, expulsion and elimination.[309] There are physiological correlates of Scorpio's 'extension' of its opposite sign Taurus. Scorpio is associated physiologically with the genitals, which in the case of the male has a morphological likeness to the nose, associated with Taurus. It is also interesting to note that the voice in the throat, physiologically associated with Taurus, typically changes or 'breaks' upon sexual maturity, physiologically associated with Scorpio. Another physio-

---

[309] These themes are closely allied to those of Scorpio's 'ruling planet', Pluto (q.v.).

logical association in the Taurus-Scorpio polarity of opposition is evident in the fact that the nasal lining (associated with Taurus) is made from erectile tissue, of the same type as that found in the organs of sexual arousal (associated with Scorpio), and many associations between the physiology of the nose and that of the genitals or of sexual arousal and behaviour have been documented.[310]

The Scorpio 'Personality' in Astrology

From the sign's composition and keyword descriptions we may see how the 'personality' of the sign-theme Scorpio has been constructed and epitomised in traditional divinatory astrology. We may see the Scorpio 'personality' as being emotionally intense, subtle, introspective, brooding, secretive and suspicious; penetrating, purposeful, single-minded, fervent, determined, deep ('still waters run deep'); passionate, wilful; possessing restrained power, but ready to strike like the scorpion's sting. At best, the 'extreme' quality of the personality shows the emotional dissociation, determined control and penetrative courage of the surgeon,[311] soldier, detective, investigator or mystic. At worst, the extreme quality manifests in ways that are positively obsessive, resentful, jealous, vindictive, vengeful, gratuitously extreme, in an unprincipled or 'low' manner, and capable of cold cruelty and criminality.

It was noted in the section on the sign's ruling planet Pluto that Scorpio has two symbols, the scorpion and the eagle. The scorpion is often seen to symbolise those 'lower' aspects of the sign's theme which can manifest on both physical or psychological levels, whereas the eagle symbolises the 'higher' aspect of the sign's theme on a spiritual or mystical level. However, as with all the zodiac signs, it is perhaps more accurate to view the 'Scorpio personality type' as a potentiality along a spectrum between its extremes, whilst retaining the sign's essential characteristics. We might say that Scorpio teaches us, perhaps especially in times of extreme crisis, to be passionate, single-minded and unswerving in our determination to see things through to the end, without allowing such qualities to cause us to engage in destructive, cruel or mindless obsession.

Scorpio — Season

The middle of the Scorpio period, around the beginning of November, marks one of the four 'cross-quarter points', being those times in the year midway between an equinox and a solstice—in this case, between the autumn equinox and the winter solstice. The foregoing keyword descriptions of Scorpio recapitulate the dramatic and somewhat unwelcome transformation or 'turning' of the season in the northern hemisphere when autumn firmly takes hold. The length of

---

[310] Bhutta, 2007; Bhutta & Maxwell, 2008; Book, 1971; Mazzatenta *et al.*, 2015

[311] It's notable that being a surgeon means parting the surface of another's flesh and gaining entrance to what lies hidden inside—an occupation that is physically commensurate with the 'penetrative' theme of Scorpio.

daylight becomes alarmingly shorter, and the weather begins to turn rough and extreme—even violent, around the time of Scorpio. It seems as if a curse has been put on the land. The year seems to 'turn bad', as if it feels the 'sting of death'. It is as though something bad has happened; as if something has gone wrong.

The season mirrors Scorpio's function 'to remove outer masks, to uncover or reveal', as the landscape is uncovered and revealed, as trees and other growing plants shed their 'clothing' of leaves. The state of the season is reminiscent of the 'fall' of the Judaeo-Christian biblical Genesis, when things are explicitly stated to have 'gone wrong'. Indeed the season is called 'Fall' in the United States, ostensibly as being reminiscent of the falling of leaves, but in a wider collective unconscious sense perhaps also reminiscent of the alternative meaning of 'fall' as of the year 'falling from goodness or grace'.

When the patterns of the stars behind the Sun were first being used to mark the times of the year, and when the most salient meanings concerning those times of the year were being projected onto these patterns, the form of a scorpion was attributed by man's psyche as being appropriate for the time of year that is now called Scorpio, for as the scorpion stings with a kiss of death, so at this time of year something seems to have stung the Sun's journey with a kiss of death: the length of its light in the day dwindles away, the world becomes darker and colder, and once leaf-clad trees become starkly bare. All appears to be 'going wrong'. Nature is beginning the difficult and death-like yearly process of regeneration. Petals and leaves return to the earth to be transformed to the stuff from which new life can be re-created.

Scorpio — Mythology, Religion, Folklore & Custom

The state of this season of the 'fall' of autumn, when things seem to go 'bad', is indeed redolent of Scorpio's keyword themes of death, blood, passion, and extremes, and appropriate cultural embodiments of the period, as celebrations or festivals marking these dark themes, are widespread. The image of the scorpion as an association with death and the underworld is indeed ancient. In tablet nine of *The Epic of Gilgamesh* (c. 2,100 BCE), the eponymous hero, a legendary young god-king of ancient Mesopotamia, grieving for the death of his best friend and now himself fearful of death, journeys to seek the secret of eternal life. At the 'end of the earth' he comes to a tunnel, leading under mountains along the 'path of the Sun', which is the gate to the underworld, and guarded by scorpion people. Gilgamesh passes through the tunnel in complete darkness, and manages the subsequent journey to arrive at a paradisiacal 'garden of the gods' before the Sun 'catches up with him'.[312]

In modern times the ever-popular celebration of Hallowe'en, held on 31st October, with its accent on themes of death and darkness, is celebrated in the time of Scorpio. The festival is a modern interpretation of the Celtic festival of *Samhain*,

---

[312] Dalley, 1989; George, 2003

whose name derives from the Old Irish for 'summer's end'.[313] The festival is a collective response or resonance to the end of the harvest season and the beginning of the 'deathly' part of the year. James Frazer has pointed out that, while Samhain and Beltane (Beltane being at the 'opposite' end of the year to Scorpio, at May Day in Taurus) were of scant interest to agriculturalists, they were very important to cattle herdsmen such as the pastoral Celts: at Beltane, a festival celebrating life, cattle were driven to their pastures, while at Samhain, a time concerned with death, the cattle were rather driven back from these pastures for slaughter.[314]

At Samhain, the door to the underworld of the dead was thought to be opened, whereupon deceased spirits were regarded as being able to enter the world of the living. People attempted to protect themselves from the more malevolent of these ghosts, often by way of disguise—which custom survives to this day in the dressing-up involved in Hallowe'en celebrations. Christianity reinterpreted the Celtic festival with its theme of remembrance of the dead as the celebrations of 'All Souls Day' (or 'The Commemoration of All the Faithful Departed') and 'All Saints' Day' (which honours those more fortunate departed souls who had ascended to heaven and attained a beatific state). It seems clear enough that the festival of Samhain functions collectively as a way to bring the uncomfortable fact of death, whilst current in nature, from the unconscious into the conscious mind, and to come to terms with it in ritual.

In Scorpio's month of November, on the 5th, 'Guy Fawkes Night', otherwise known as 'Bonfire Night', is still celebrated in Great Britain. Given the overarching theme of the 'death' of the year at this time, we might sensibly wonder whether this celebration or observance is really primarily concerned with commemorating the 'Gunpowder Plot' (the failed assassination attempt against King James I) of 1605. Why did the celebration of this particular historical incident become so very popular, elaborate and moreover so persistent? We would suggest that the apparent commemoration of the foiling of the gunpowder plot with its lighting of great outdoor fires may in fact be an unconscious excuse to rail against the dying of the year's light in an emphatic way. The English writer Thomas Hardy, describing the time of lighting bonfires in early November in his novel *The Return Of The Native* wrote:

> Indeed, it is pretty well known that such blazes ... are rather the lineal descendants from jumbled Druidical rites and Saxon ceremonies than the invention of popular feeling about the Gunpowder Plot. Moreover to light a fire is the instinctive and resistant act of man when, at the winter ingress, the curfew is sounded throughout Nature. It indicates a spontaneous, Promethean rebelliousness against that fiat that this recurrent season shall bring foul times, cold darkness, misery and death.

---

[313] Rogers, 2003
[314] Frazer, 1894

The fire and fireworks ritual resonates with and acknowledges the urge of the Scorpio period of the year—to release a deep collective need to express violent shows of execution, to see fires outdoors, to hear the intensity of powerful explosions, to express the dark, passionate and extreme feelings towards death which is inherent in the season. Some writers have touched upon this notion to a degree, arguing that, just as the earlier Catholic church in Britain 'took over' ancient pagan year festivals, so did the emerging Protestant church *"acquire their own rituals, adapting older forms or providing substitutes for them."*[315] It has been asserted that there's nothing to link Samhain and 'Bonfire Night' in an historical-geographical way,[316] but our contention is that the link is not historical-geographical, but psychological, and specifically in a collective sense, where peoples unconnected by place or culture spontaneously respond in similar ways to the 'death season' of the year.

In old England, November, the Scorpio month, was the 'blood month'. The growing season came to an end, food stores were strictly limited, and non-breeding cattle were brought back from summer pasture and slaughtered so that the people could *share meat* (an activity almost perfectly 'Scorpionic' in symbolism). When the remaining meat had been preserved, the fat rendered and the hides treated for later use, the carcasses that were left were converted into ground fertiliser by their incineration in a 'bone fire', the latter term being later shortened to 'bonfire'. As the persistence of the name suggests, the fires that apparently commemorate the burning of Guy Fawkes are likely to be a collective-unconscious association with the 'bone fires' that were a distillation of the heightened consciousness of death in this 'falling' time of the year. The period of Scorpio is generally a popular time for 'carnivals' and the lighting of fires out-doors; significantly, the word 'carnival' means 'time of eating of meat,' resonant with the Scorpio theme of the sharing of a common physical substratum.

In November people in the United Kingdom also remember the dead of the two world wars, and a special service of commemoration is held on 'Remembrance Sunday'—the Sunday closest to the 11th of November, which is the date of 'Armistice Day', the anniversary of the end of the conflict of the First World War in 1918. That date is itself marked with a similar commemoration by many allied nations, such as 'Veterans' Day' in the USA. In many places, the remembrance of the dead is accompanied by a brief period of silence. Although the remembrance of the dead of the world wars is supposedly tied to 'Armistice Day', it is indeed an odd 'coincidence' that such a time of remembrance of the dead should be observed in this time of Scorpio, when so many others festivals and commemorations of the dead take place, with their roots in the dying seasonal aspect of the year. Although the armistice to end World War I was indeed signed on that date in 1918, hostilities continued in many parts of the world, and the date does not coincide with the end of the later and more destructive conflict of World War II. It seems quite possible that, like 'Guy Fawkes Day', the date has been favoured by

---

[315] Underdown, 1985
[316] Hutton, 1996

an ancient and unconscious need to mark the death of the year (and thus death generally) at this particular time.

It might seem fantastical to suppose that humans might be unconsciously impelled to recapitulate the theme of Scorpio in the midst of this time of year so openly as to affix an emblem of a blood-red wound to the Sun's place on the body—the heart—and to associate it with death, violence and war, thus simulating the appearance of a 'wound to the heart' which symbolises so exactly Scorpio's 'wound' to the Sun as it sinks away in autumn. Yet this is precisely what people do. The symbol of 'Remembrance Sunday', which honours the dead of the two world wars, the poppy, though reminiscent of those which grew on the battlefields of Flanders, does not flower in November, and is, significantly, of a blood-red colour, and thus extremely resonant with death and the general themes of Scorpio. The heaps of poppy wreaths that are laid upon the ground on 'Remembrance Sunday' can easily be seen as 'shared blood'—an essential Scorpio concept. The peculiar endurance of this observance since its original innovation at the close of the First World War by Moina Belle Michael and Anna Guérin,[317] and moreover the striking correspondence of the emblems of its ritual to the symbolic themes of the Scorpio time of year, are certainly intriguing, to say the least. Notions of coincidence or causality seem impossible to fathom, yet the custom of wearing a blood-red mark next to one's heart at this 'deathly' time of the Sun's journey through the year certainly presents as an ideal representation of a collectively unconscious urge to identify with the 'dying' of the annual cycle and thus of death generally.

A 'Festival of the Dead', generally held after the harvest and around Scorpio's time of the year, has been observed since ancient times by many world cultures and peoples, including the Peruvians, the Pacific Islanders, the people of the Tonga Islands, the ancient Persians, the ancient Romans, as well as by the northern nations of Europe.[318] In the ancient Inca religion the whole month of November was known as *Ayamarca*, which means 'Festival of the Dead'. The *Día de los Muertos*, or Day of the Dead, is celebrated in Mexico on 2nd November and has similar associations with Samhain. In Finnish, November is called *marraskuu*, meaning 'month of the dead'. To those who see the Christian story of Jesus Christ as a fragmented allegory of the Sun's journey through the year, the figure of Judas most aptly represents Scorpio: it is Judas as the 'fall' of the autumn who 'betrays' Jesus (the Sun) with the 'kiss of death'. The scorpion has been a symbol of Judas in Christian iconography,[319] and was depicted on the shield of Roman soldiers at the crucifixion, as in Luini's fresco *The Crucifixion* in *Santa Maria degli Angeli*, Lugano.[320]

---

[317] Johnson, 2015; Michael, 1941
[318] Smyth, 1867
[319] Ferguson, 1977
[320] Hastings, 2004

If one would seek to explain the existence of many festivals of death in different cultures around the world as merely coincidentally occurring during the Scorpio period, then a moment's reflection upon the essential aspects of the season may modify such a conclusion. In November in the northern hemisphere, when one looks upon trees with their leaves shed in scattered heaps upon the ground and their limbs bare like bones; when one sees the Sun showing weakly and low over the horizon, its light a mere shadow of what it was in the glorious days of summer, the length of the day thus horribly shortened, and darkness now all too quick to fall; when one sees the natural world in this apparently decayed state, then it is certainly difficult to imagine these festivals of death and dying being naturally celebrated at any other time of the year.

As we noted in the section on the Scorpio's 'ruling planet' Pluto, there are important connections between the themes of sex and death, which are both closely associated with the planet Pluto and the sign Scorpio. Like many organisms, humans have evolved sexual reproduction in order to continue the species, but this necessitates the death of the individual. Thus death and sex are intimately bound up in humankind's collective unconscious, so much so that, for humans—who, unlike other animals, are aware of this fact—the sexual act has become a 'taboo' subject, most likely because it reminds people of the unpleasant necessity of death.[321]

The violent and transformational natures of the Pluto- and Scorpio-associated processes of birth, sex and death means that such matters are frequently feared and even suppressed as things not to be mentioned or discussed in an everyday way. They are often 'locked away' in the unconscious mind. The autumn celebrations which bring these themes (especially death) out into the open enable us to come to terms with them. In this way they can be seen as almost psychoanalytic cathartic processes, acting on a societal level.

The Characterisation of the Signs — Sagittarius

The origins of the sign Sagittarius are somewhat complex and obscure. In ancient Babylonia the *constellation* that we know today as Sagittarius the centaur was identified as *Pabilsag* (Babylonian *Mul Pa-bil-sag*). Though depicted as a hunter armed with a bow and arrow, Pabilsag was not however fancied exactly in the form of a centaur—the figure with the upper body of a human and the lower body and legs of a horse—as was the later Hellenic representation which gained much traction in Greek myth and which eventually became the symbol for the zodiac *sign* Sagittarius. The Babylonian Pabilsag was rather

Figure 31. Sagittarius — the Ninth Sign of the Zodiac

variously depicted with a number of physical attributes in different combinations, sometimes sporting wings, sometimes with the tail of a scorpion, sometimes with

---

[321] Becker, 1973; Goldenberg *et al.*, 1999

a dog's head (as well as a human's), sometimes with the feet of a bird. What seemed to be common to all was that the upper body was that of an archer (that is, a figure, usually a man, armed with a bow and arrow), and the lower body was comprised of various animal body components.

The concept of the centaur has been said to have arisen from the first reactions of peoples who did not ride horses to the sight of roving nomads who did, instilling a belief in the former of a terrifying half-horse, half-man creature. This notion is given some credulity in light of the fact that, at the time of the Spanish conquest of south America, the native people reportedly saw the mounted *conquistadors* as similarly composite creatures.[322] The image of the hunting centaur appears on the carved boundary stones of the late second millennium BCE Kassite peoples of ancient Babylonia, though the name of the constellation Pabilsag can be found in much older Babylonian records.

Modern scholarship has suggested that the name of the Babylonian hunter deity and constellation *Pa-bil-sag* carries the meaning 'chief ancestor' or 'forefather', and that the figure was a representation of an ancestral warrior-being who guarded the souls of the dead on their journey to the underworld, by hunting down demons who threatened these recently departed spirits.[323] Certainly the figure of Pabilsag presents as a 'wild hunter'. Given these mythical antecedents, we may consider the time of the year in which the constellation is seen to be in the path of the Sun: it is the month that leads to the darkest part of the year (in terms of length of daylight), before the slow return of the Sun's light after the winter solstice. It is the season when the days are getting dramatically shorter and shorter, and the world seems darker and darker. It may not be difficult therefore to conceive of a projection, in the darkest and most threatening time of year, of an untamed ancestral hero, a powerful and lustful hunter who is able to protect the human spirit in the forbidding and wild world of such gloomy and baleful times.

Sagittarius — Composition

Season: Late autumn; the period leading up to the winter solstice.

Symbol: ♐ The centaur's bow and arrow pointed towards the horizon. The less stylised form of a complete centaur figure is sometimes depicted holding a spear.

Polarity: Positive (active, self-expressive and spontaneous).

Quality: Mutable (adaptable, variable; open to seasonal change).

Element: Fire (ardent, keen, energetic, assertive).

Sign Key Phrase: The positive, mutable, fire sign is predisposed to a wide, extensive, broad, free-ranging, explorative and deep perspective; given to seek freedom, space, opportunity and adventure; inclined to seek meaning, understanding, new experience and new horizons beyond the immediate or commonplace environment; foresighted, adventurous and ambitious, both physically and

---

[322] Lawrence, 1994
[323] White, 2014

mentally; broad-minded, open-minded, philosophical, moralistic; optimistic, jovial; generous, humorous, benevolent; sincere, frank.

House key phrase: Activities and matters to do with the projection of the self beyond the commonplace to new horizons, in extensive, wide-ranging and deep communications and journeyings, either physically as in adventure, exploration or foreign travels, or mentally as in higher education and profound study such as of philosophy, law, justice, 'social morality' or religion; traditionally also relatives who are not of one's own blood, such as in-laws.

Sign as 'Extension': Sagittarius conforms to the pattern where the last six sign-themes of the zodiac appear to be 'extensions' of the corresponding themes of the first six—extensions of themes to do with the 'individual' (in the case of the first six) to those same themes applied more widely, extensively and typically to do with 'others' (in the case of the latter six). As Gemini was centred on personal intellectual pursuits, purely abstract, logical relations and close communications to do with the immediate environment, Sagittarius centres on more socially-oriented, wider and deeper mental matters, such as in philosophy, law and morality, and in more extensive communications and journeys to more distant horizons (e.g., to foreign countries).

Ruling planet: Jupiter. Jupiter's function to grow, expand, prosper and extend the life through wider and deeper understanding (whether materially by travel, or mentally by understanding) accords well with the above keyword descriptions of the Sagittarius sign-theme.

Sagittarius — Physiological

Sagittarius's traditional physiological association is with the liver, and the hips and thighs or upper parts of the legs. The liver has healing, compensatory and detoxification functions which enable growth, while the thighs are the 'drivers' of ambulation and hence may be seen as a token of travel or exploration. These physiological functions recapitulate the Sagittarian keywords as described above. As a physiological correlate of the sign's status as an 'extension' of Gemini, Sagittarius's association with the legs and thighs (the limbs which carry the body to explore 'farther afield') appears as an extensional 'magnification' of Gemini's association with the arms and hands (the limbs which typically explore the immediate environment).

The Sagittarius 'Personality' in Astrology

From the foregoing we can see how the 'personality' of the sign-theme Leo has been constructed and epitomised in traditional divinatory astrology. We might envisage the Sagittarian 'character' as possessing a wide, deep, extensive, expansive, free-ranging and explorative attitude, in either physical or mental pursuits, or both; perhaps one involved in higher education (especially philosophy), or in a profession such as law; an ambitious and foresighted type who seeks space, freedom, opportunity, adventure, meaning and understanding; who looks for new experience and new horizons beyond the immediate or commonplace environment; philosophical and moralistic, yet open-minded and broad-minded; often sporty and sportive; optimistic, jovial, generous, benevolent, sincere and frank.

At best the personality is an adventurer, explorer or a philosophical seeker after wider and deeper meaning. At worst the character is over-enthusiastic, extremist, extravagant, tactless, boastful, inconsiderate, exaggerating, careless, too moralising and restless. However, as with all the zodiac signs, it's more helpful to view the 'Sagittarius personality type' as a potentiality along a gradation between such extremes, whilst retaining the sign's essential characteristics. We might say that Sagittarius teaches us to go beyond the commonplace and to explore the wider and deeper aspects of life; to grasp opportunity when it arises, and when the time is propitious to set our sights optimistically upon the horizon for adventurous and worthwhile goals which broaden our experience and understanding—without allowing such impulses to cause us to be over-optimistic, gratuitously extravagant or too concerned with overly inflated ideas or exploits.

Sagittarius — Season

In the northern hemisphere the period of Sagittarius takes place at the very latter part of autumn, the last part of the solar year in which the light of the day is continuing to shorten towards its briefest duration. In ancient times a readiness for far-ranging exploration and hunting may have frequently been required in order to find sufficient sustenance during this period, and in anticipation of the even harsher time of winter on the horizon, as there was little or no food to be had from cultivation. Such hunting exploration, undertaken in small groups or even alone, would have brought about a sense of freedom, as well as a more 'philosophical' frame of mind fostered by the knowledge that little more can be done to prepare for the dark season ahead. Ultimately however such an adventurous and explorative state of mind would have also engendered a certain optimism for the prospect of the returning light at the coming winter solstice.

Like all mutable signs, Sagittarius brings an end to one season—in this case, the darkening autumn—and looks forward to a change to come. The change that is looked forward to in the case of Sagittarius is the winter solstice, which marks the start of a completely new solar cycle, along with an end to the gloomy shortening of the days and the prospect of increasing hours of daylight. The return of the sun's light is an horizon to be welcomed, but in Sagittarius it is just that—on the horizon, so the prevailing sense is one of optimistic far-sightedness.

Sagittarius — Mythology, Religion, Folklore & Custom

The characteristically Sagittarian theme of forward-looking, philosophical optimism is clearly in accord with what was seen in ancient times as the impending prospect of the return of light at the solstice, but which in the modern era has become, for a great part of the world, the characteristically extravagant 'festive season' of the advent into the Christmas period. It is true that Christmas Day itself occurs shortly *after* the winter Solstice, in the succeeding sign-period Capricorn, but it seems reasonable enough to assert that the greater part of what we understand today as 'Christmas' is in reality the inordinately long period of its preparation throughout the time of Sagittarius. This period of the year certainly reflects Sagittarian themes: there is generosity in the buying of gifts, and merriment is supposedly a distinctive feature of the season. Sagittarius is associated with alcohol and the convivial mood of joviality that it induces. The sign's 'ruling' planet, Jupiter, is associated with expansiveness and excess, both of which may be said to be frequent hallmarks of over-indulgence in the Christmas season. Jupiter's traditional physiological association is with the liver, which is especially vulnerable to the over-intoxication of alcohol that takes place during the long Christmas period.

The latter part of the time of the sign-theme Sagittarius corresponds to the time of the ancient Roman celebration of *Saturnalia,* which shares some characteristics with the modern Christmas. The nature and origin of the ancient Saturnalia festival is however difficult to fathom, and the reader is directed to Appendix 3, *Saturnalia and Kronia.* For those who see in the Christian story of Jesus an allegory of the Sun's path through the year, the time of Sagittarius corresponds to Jesus being brought before the local representative of the law, judgement and justice, in the figure of the Roman governor Pilate, whose name means 'armed with a spear', which phrase is descriptive of the constellation Sagittarius the centaur, which was frequently symbolised as a centaur wielding, not an arrow, but a spear.[324]

The Characterisation of the Signs — Capricorn

Figure 32. Capricorn — the Tenth Sign of the Zodiac

The constellation that we know today as Capricorn (or more correctly, *Capricornus,* being Latin for 'the horns of a goat') was originally known as the Goat-Fish (Babylonian *Mul Suhur-Maš-Ku),* being a composite creature with the head and front legs of a goat and the tail of a fish. The first known pictorial portrayal of the Goat-Fish in ancient Mesopotamia was from the later part of the 3rd millennium BCE, in the form of a being closely associated with *Enki,* the deity of the life-giving waters.[325] That the Goat-Fish was being depicted specifically as a constellation is

---

[324] Bagdasarov, 2001
[325] Reade, 1997; White, 2014

clear from its appearance on many carved boundary stones which include celestial allusions, as well as from astrological predictions concerning the ominous portents of planetary bodies that might be found to appear in the star-pattern. The portrayal of the constellation passed into later Greek accounts without much alteration, though the Greeks augmented the Goat-Fish figure with further mythical tales.[326]

It has been argued that the Goat-Fish constellation was likely created (projected pictorially) in the mid to late 3rd millennium BCE, when the stars which comprised its head and horns would have had their heliacal rising at the time of the important winter solstice, its fishy tail rising some time later during the following month. Thus the symbolism of the constellation was likely to have been intimately bound up with the 'rebirth' of the Sun after the solstice. It has been further suggested that the constellation drew its nature from the fusion of two separate constellations, the Stag and the Fish, where the Stag was an ancient constellation which rose at the time of solar rebirth at the midwinter solstice, while the rising of the Fish constellation symbolised the 'rescuer' of the Sun in its incipient ascendancy from the *"watery depths of winter"* in order to *"guide it safely towards dry land"*.[327] Capricornus or the Goat-Fish is the faintest constellation after that of Cancer, so there must have been a great impetus for it to have been projectively fancied as a meaningful pictorial figure. The important rebirth of the Sun at the winter solstice and its struggle for continued ascendancy towards spring would have been just such a fitting motivation for a star-picture to be 'seen' at that cardinal point.

Capricorn — Composition

Season: Early winter; the period following the winter solstice.

Symbol: ♑ The Goat (a stylised depiction, including the looped fish's tail on the right).

Polarity: Negative (passive, self-repressive, receptive).

Quality: Cardinal (outgoing, enterprising; the beginning of a new season).

Element: Earth: (practical, cautious, restrained).

Sign Key Phrase: The negative, cardinal, earth sign is cool, calculating, rational, deliberate; cautious, prudent; sober, serious, responsible, disciplined, inclined and ready to bear limitation, hardship and frustration; conforming, conventional; conscientious, dutiful, industrious, punctilious, concentrating, assiduous; practical, resourceful, methodical, given to careful planning; patient, persevering; aspiring, ambitious; self-contained, oriented to the solitude and control required for personal integrity, advancement and the building of the necessary securing boundaries and formative structures which promote achievement.

---

[326] Olcott, 1911

[327] White, 2014

House key phrase: Activities and matters to do with practical, ambitious, security-making matters beyond the narrow protective circle of the home; worldly attainment; the establishment of oneself in the wider community; role, social stature, status, prestige, reputation, attainment and career; necessary material responsibilities; toil; things which take a long time and which require patience and forbearance to achieve.

Sign as 'Extension': Capricorn follows the pattern where the last six sign-themes of the zodiac appear to be 'extensions' of the corresponding themes of the first six—extensions of themes to do with the 'individual' (in the case of the first six) to those same themes applied more widely, extensively and typically to do with 'others' (in the case of the latter six). Where Cancer centres on security, role, status, standing and responsibilities in personal, domestic, family and home affairs, Capricorn centres on security, role, status, standing and responsibilities *outside* the home, in the outer social world of career, in the public gaze and amidst the appraisal of *others*.

Ruling planet: Saturn. There is clearly an affinity between the principle of the planet Saturn, whose function is to bring about necessary formativeness, discipline, limitation, restraint and self-control, and the keyword descriptions of the Capricorn sign-theme.

Capricorn — Physiological

The traditional physiological association of Capricorn is to the skin, the skeletal structure in general and the knees in particular. The skin is symbolic of the 'limiting' aspect of Capricorn, while the skeletal structure is symbolic of its structural or formative characteristic.

The Capricorn 'Personality' in Astrology

We can see how the 'personality' of the zodiac's tenth sign of Capricorn has been constructed or epitomised in developed divinatory astrology. One might imagine a Capricorn 'type' as one who is sober, serious, industrious, hard-working and disciplined; conservative and conventional in outlook; not afraid to undertake long-term tasks with patience and responsibility, however arduous, wearisome or limiting the effort, in order to achieve respect and status. At best the personality may be seen as one who is able to endure long-term restriction and adversity for the achievement of worthwhile goals. At worst the character might be looked upon as one who is too severe, rigid, exacting, cold, pessimistic, narrow-minded and over-conventional. As with all the zodiac signs, it is however more helpful to view the 'Capricorn personality type' as a potentiality along a range between such extremes, whilst retaining the sign's essential characteristics. We might say that Capricorn teaches us, when the time is appropriate, to maintain the discipline and the serious and responsible attitude—even to bear long-term hardship where necessary—in order for us to advance, often through difficult times, without letting such traits cause us to be cold, rigid, over-conventional or too austere.

Capricorn — Season

The keyword descriptions of Capricorn recapitulate the harsh, sober realities of the beginning of winter, once the festivities associated with Sagittarius and the expectation of the winter solstice have ended. At the winter solstice, the Sun appears at its lowest altitude above the horizon, and (in the northern hemisphere) it is at its southernmost point in the sky. The shortest day of the year has passed, it is true, and the Sun deity has indeed been 'reborn' in terms of its light, but the days take a long time to lengthen, and night and day are frequently accompanied by cold and even severe weather. It remains a gloomy prospect. As the days slowly begin to get longer, the emphasis is on the beginning of a long and difficult ascent, an arduous climb back up to better seasonal conditions. In nature the emphasis is on austerity; the world appears barren and is characterised by harshness, dearth and insufficiency. There is a promise of gains far ahead, but these have to be worked hard for, with diligence, control, and sober, realistic determination. Limitations, difficulties and privation must be endured.

Capricorn — Mythology, Religion, Folklore & Custom

When, thousands of years ago, humans began to change from the hunter-gatherer lifestyle to one of agriculture and settlement, the determining of the year cycle became of huge importance for the practices of sowing and reaping of crops, the management of livestock and the conservation of food resources during the unforgiving winter. Thus in these Neolithic times people erected firm, solid structures, such as at Stonehenge in Britain and Newgrange in Ireland, with which to align the rising and setting Sun and thus reliably mark the 'cardinal' times or points of the winter solstice, the spring equinox, the summer solstice and the autumnal equinox. The winter solstice in particular has been marked around the world by various celebrations and mythologies which highlight and reflect the theme of the beginning of the new solar year, when the power of the Sun appears to grow once more as the daylight at last begins to lengthen. Many such observances have specifically taken the form of a symbolic rebirth of a heroic deity which represents the Sun in its yearly course. The Jesus story begins roughly at the winter solstice. Although the Christian New Testament texts do not mention a date in the year for his birth, the 25th of December was chosen from very early times.

Hippolytus of Rome (170–236) wrote early in the 3rd century that the birth of Jesus took place on 25th December.[328] The *Chronography* of 354 CE documents evidence of the celebration, on 25th December, of a formal Christian liturgical feast of the birth of Jesus. For those who regard the Jesus story as a solar year myth, Jesus, as an allegorical personification of the Sun, is 'born' roughly three days after the winter solstice, at the point when the lengthening days first become positively discernible to the careful observer.

---

[328] Hippolytus, 204

As well as directly marking the 're-birth' of the Sun, other myths and customs associated with the Capricorn sign period, both ancient and modern, also tend to reflect the somewhat grim and serious character of this winter period.[329] The tradition of making 'New Year's resolutions' shortly after the beginning of the new solar year in this period, most often of a self-controlling nature, is clearly in accord with the Capricorn-Saturn theme of the need or urge for serious responsibility and self-discipline in order to achieve desired goals. The period just before the winter solstice, though strictly within the preceding sign Sagittarius, was associated in ancient Rome with Saturn, the 'ruling planet' of Capricorn, in the observance of the festival of *Saturnalia*. The nature and origin of the ancient Saturnalia festival is complex and difficult to interpret, and the reader is directed to Appendix 3, *Saturnalia and Kronia*. The winter solstice at the beginning of the sign Capricorn was characterised in a remarkable zodiacal allegory of the year cycle, in the mediaeval Welsh prose epic the Mabinogion, which we explore more fully in Chapter 4.

The Characterisation of the Signs — Aquarius

The constellation that we know today as Aquarius had its origins in the star-pattern known to the Babylonians as The Great One (Babylonian *Mul Gu-la*). The image fancied in the Great One was that of a gigantic male figure, towering over mountains and pouring water from a pitcher held in each hand. The figure projectively symbolised the conspicuous conditions of the natural world in the late winter season of the year when this constellation was in the path of the Sun, namely, the life-

Figure 33. Aquarius — the Eleventh Sign of the Zodiac

giving rains which began at this time and which enabled the irrigation for a hopefully rich barley crop.[330] The Babylonian Great One was strongly identified with Enki, the god of wisdom and water. It seems to us entirely possible that Enki's association with wisdom sprang at least in part from the technical inventiveness necessary for the practice of efficient irrigation. When the Greek tropical zodiac became later adopted, the *sign* Aquarius forever marked the period of mid to late winter, and became more closely associated with the sense of hopefulness in the anticipation of spring on the horizon. The 'inventive' theme of the tropical sign may nevertheless be seen as a direct successor of the technological 'inventiveness' of irrigation, also in hope of better times to come after winter.

Aquarius — Composition

Season: Mid Winter.
Symbol: ≈ The water-carrier, stylised as ripples or waves of conducted energy.[331]

---

[329] In the northern hemisphere.
[330] White, 2014
[331] It's notable that it is not the conducting material, such as water, that is actually moving forward in a wave, but energy.

Polarity: Positive (active, self-expressive and spontaneous).

Quality: Fixed (intense, steadfast, resistant to change; the established progress of a season).

Element: Air (intellectual, communicative, mentally active).

Sign Key Phrase: The positive, fixed, air sign is erratic, unpredictable; unusual, unorthodox, unconventional, progressive, revolutionary; detached, scientific, truth-seeking; original, creative, inventive; idealistic, friendly, humanitarian; dogmatic; community-oriented; optimistic; oriented to objectives, hopes and wishes (especially social).

House key phrase: Activities and matters to do with detached, non-intimate contacts; friendships and acquaintances, especially those made in social groups with common objectives; friends and social connections that help and influence; clubs, groups, societies, organisations, associations; the identification with and achievement of creative interests and objectives that are for the benefit of a group or community, as distinct from personal aims and ambitions; traditionally one's 'hopes and wishes'; dealing with the future; horizons, goals, objectives, shared ideals, causes; unconventional, technological, scientific, humanitarian and reformative enterprises or activities.

Sign as 'Extension': Aquarius adheres to the pattern where the last six sign-themes of the zodiac appear to be 'extensions' of the corresponding themes of the first six—extensions of themes to do with the 'individual' (in the case of the first six) to those same themes applied more widely, extensively and typically to do with 'others' (in the case of the latter six). Where Leo centres on organisation and creativeness in personal matters (e.g., in personal recreation, one's family, etc), Aquarius centres on organisation and creativeness with others (e.g., in community groups, scientific concerns, etc).

Ruling planet: Uranus. The common human function or urge represented by the planet Uranus has been characterised as that of the natural impulse towards freedom, deviation from the normal, unconventionality and a questioning of authority or of orthodox modes of behaviour and thinking. This accords well with the keyword descriptions of Aquarius's inventive, progressive and reformative outlook.

Aquarius — Physiological

The traditional physiological areas associated with Aquarius are with the calves of the leg, the ankles, and the circulatory system. Curiously enough, the calf muscle has been considered as part of the circulatory system, and is even referred to as a 'second heart' as it functions to pump blood vertically back up through the body, which the heart cannot do alone.[332] These physiological associations seem in accord with Aquarius as the opposite or 'extending' sign to Leo, whose ruling planet, the Sun, is closely associated with the heart and the

---

[332] Uhl & Gillot, 2015

circulatory system. The process of mutation, so necessary at times for evolutionary diversity and hence species survival, may also be seen as an Aquarian-Uranian element in the evolution of the physiological system, recapitulating as it does the theme of 'drastic deviation' or unconventionality.

The Aquarius 'Personality' in Astrology

From the foregoing we can see how the 'personality' of the sign-theme Aquarius has been constructed and epitomised in traditional divinatory astrology. We might imagine the 'Aquarian' character as a person who is friendly, though dispassionately so and not in an intimate sense, but rather one who identifies with like-minded acquaintances in wider social groups of people (the 'cells' of the body politic), especially those who share common (often progressive) creative ideals, either in scientific and technological innovation, politics, social reform or humanitarian objectives. The Aquarian 'personality' can be seen as one who places great value on freedom and independent, original and inventive thought, thus being frequently seen as erratic, unpredictable, unconventional, unusual, different or even plain 'mad'.

At best the Aquarian personality is one who is not afraid to shake off what are perceived as outmoded patterns of thought, and to embrace new ideas, ideals and technologies, often for the benefit of a community as a whole. At worst the personality is one who is gratuitously 'different' and too detached, being rebellious for the sake of rebellion; explosively unconventional, unpredictable and wayward in a psychopathological sense ('mad' in the worst sense of the term). As with all the zodiac signs, it is however more helpful to view the 'Aquarian personality type' as a potentiality along a gradation between these extremes, whilst retaining the sign's essential characteristics. We can see how Aquarius teaches us to entertain completely new and even radical ideas and practices when these become necessary and useful to society, without allowing such an impulse to degenerate into mere perversity or freakishness.

Aquarius — Season

The keyword descriptions of Aquarius, particularly those that emphasis the theme of communal hopes and wishes, recapitulate aspects of the season of midwinter in the northern hemisphere. In this time of year one looks hopefully for promising signs of future changes; for the appearance of the first magical inklings of spring. One begins to entertain expectations and aspirations for the better weather and a new life that is to come. Such hopes and wishes may seem too 'progressive' to others, but they're prompted by a definite change in the revolution of the year. As the weather becomes ever so slightly warmer, the rains come, rivers flood, and the earliest flowering plants appear.

Aquarius is the time for the first crazy hopes which some people have the temerity to entertain that things might change for the better. The period has been appropriately marked by widespread celebrations and rituals which underscore a theme of hopefulness for a change in the climate and which often involve seemingly far-fetched methods of divination of early signs of the spring.

Aquarius — Mythology, Religion, Folklore & Custom

Chief among the seasonal celebrations which recapitulate the theme of Aquarius is *Imbolc* (also called *Saint Brighid's Day*), which is a Gaelic-Celtic festival held on 31st January to 1st February. Imbolc is one of the four 'cross quarter' days; that is, one placed midway between a solstice and an equinox—in this case, between the winter solstice and the spring equinox. Its basic theme is the marking of an optimistic hope for the first anticipated signs of spring. The name 'Imbolc' stems from the old Irish '*i mbolg*' meaning 'in the womb', referring to the nascent growth of spring, such as that of pregnant ewes, with their new life still hidden. Celebrations often included the lighting of candles and fires to symbolise the increasing power of the Sun. The time of Imbolc has been a focal point of such ritual seasonal observation from as early as Neolithic times, and some megalithic monuments from this era, such as the *Mound of the Hostages* on the Hill of Tara in Ireland, are aligned with the rising sun on this day.[333]

Variations of the Imbolc festival with its basic theme of hopes and wishes for the return of the Sun's light have been held in many Celtic lands, such as Scotland, Ireland and the Isle of Man, and also in Wales where it is known as *Gŵyl Fair y Canhwyllau*. The festival was associated with the Celtic-Irish goddess Brighid long before the emergence of Christianity. The influence of the pagan Brighid was so strong that the early Celtic Christian church in Britain felt obliged to assimilate her as 'Saint Brigid'. The figure of Brighid was associated with the return of the lighter half of the year. She was reputed to visit one's house at Imbolc, and it was considered good luck to leave her food, drink and even a bed to sleep on. 'Brighid's crosses', reminders of the four parts of the year demarcated by cross-quarter points such as Imbolc, were made from rushes; a figure of the deity was similarly fashioned and carried from house to house. Items of clothing would also be left outside on Imbolc for the goddess to bless, to be used later for healing and protection.

In keeping with Aquarius's key description of the community's 'hopes and wishes', Imbolc was considered a good time for groups to gather and engage in various forms of weather divination—to look forward hopefully to the future for signs of the coming spring. A favourite form of such weather divination was to see if animals such as badgers or snakes would come out of their winter dens. This practice is a forerunner of the more modern North American tradition of 'Groundhog Day', a social event where people look for the emergence from its burrow of the groundhog, whose choice of movements traditionally determines whether spring will come early or late. Imbolc is virtually contemporaneous each

---

[333] mythicalireland.com, 2019; newgrange.com, 2020

year with the Christian festival of *Candlemas*, a term which traditionally referred to the blessing of candles by a priest, which practice may originally have been connected symbolically in the collective consciousness, like that of Imbolc, with the return of the Sun's light and power.

In the interpretation of the story of Jesus in the Christian New Testament as the remnants of an allegory of the Sun in its journey through the year, there is an interesting part to play for the sign Aquarius, when Jesus meets a figure called 'John the Baptist'. Aquarius begins roughly thirty days after the winter solstice, when Jesus as the Sun is 'born' as the solar year is reborn. The period of thirty days between the winter solstice and the time of Aquarius can be seen as being allegorised in the Christian texts as the interim before Jesus began his ministry at the 'age of thirty'.[334] In this interpretation Jesus therefore begins this ministry in Aquarius, the rainy season when rivers flood, by visiting 'John the Baptist',[335] whose practice of baptism exactly recapitulates the ancient Aquarian symbol of a man pouring water from a pitcher, being thus a personification of the Sun at Aquarius. The sign Aquarius had in addition long been symbolised by an 'angelic man' figure; thus the symbolising of Aquarius in the New Testament by a very spiritual man is appropriate.

John the Baptist rather wildly prophesies a good thing coming in the near future, just as the rituals of the time of Aquarius prophesy the coming of spring. As the season which corresponds to the time of year of the sign Aquarius 'looks forward' to better times to come in the Sun's journey, so in the New Testament, John the Baptist looks forward to the 'better man' to come—that is, Jesus, *"whose shoes* [he was] *not worthy to stoop down and unloose"*.[336] John declares that he baptises with water, but that the coming Jesus figure will rather baptise with fire,[337] representing the return of the Sun's influence. In any interpretation of the Christian New Testament story, John the Baptist does present as a somewhat strange, slightly maniacal or even crazy figure,[338] which is in keeping with the theme of 'unconventionality' in the Aquarius period of the year.

A little later in the New Testament story after this meeting we read another passage that seems to symbolise an astronomical event, also concerning the Aquarius time of the year. At the beginning of this period, the *constellation* Aquarius originally marked this seasonal time by lying behind or 'in the path of' the Sun (inferred to be as such, as we have noted, by observation at sunrise or sunset). The constellation in this period may thus be seen just above the western horizon at sunset. As the year slowly progresses, and as the Sun moves further through the Aquarius sign-period, these stars become progressively lower and lower on the horizon at dusk, until finally they disappear below it at sunset

---

[334] Luke 3:23

[335] Mark 1:9; Matthew 3:13; Luke 3:21

[336] Mark 1:7

[337] Matthew 3:11

[338] John is represented as wearing clothing made of camels' hair and a leather loin-girdle, and as sustaining himself on locusts and wild honey.

around 9th February (in the latter part of the Aquarius sign-period). This astronomical fact seems allegorised in the New Testament by a reference to John the Baptist (representing the Sun in Aquarius) being 'put in prison';[339] that is, being put below the horizon into the darkness.

This allegory of the astronomical event is augmented further in the story. We read in the gospel of Mark that Herod, the Roman-appointed governor of Judaea, heard of Jesus and wondered if he was John the Baptist, whom he had apparently ordered to be beheaded, saying, *"It is John, whom I beheaded."*[340] The text goes on to give an account of how Herod had been persuaded to behead John the Baptist by his sister-in-law *Herodias*, who had apparently danced so well at a supper that Herod agreed to give her anything she wanted—which was John the Baptist's head on a plate. Both Mark and Matthew are at pains to record that John was beheaded *"in the prison"*.[341] Despite the narrative drama of John the Baptist being beheaded in prison on the orders of Herod's dancing sister-in-law, the 'beheading' may allegorically refer to the mere tip of the constellation Aquarius (John's 'head') being just visible above the darkness below the horizon (the 'prison'), as the time of the sign Aquarius (then marked by that constellation) progresses to its end, and before it disappears.[342]

In a curious coda to the apparently dramatic events in the gospels concerning John the Baptist's beheading, we read in Matthew that, *"When Jesus heard that John had been put in prison, he withdrew to Galilee."*[343] This seems to make little sense if taken literally. Why would Jesus show no concern for his beloved and innocent cousin's imprisonment and subsequent execution by beheading? Jesus apparently says and does nothing concerning this sorry event, but merely continues on his way. The passage does makes sense however if it is understood as an allegory of the astronomical event of the constellation Aquarius (represented in the story by John the Baptist) moving lower and lower in the sky at sunset throughout the Aquarius sign period, until it is finally 'put in prison' and 'beheaded' (moved all but entirely below the horizon). Following these events, Jesus (the Sun) simply continues his travels 'into Galilee', which Greek word of Hebrew origin גליל means 'circuit' and can be understood as the circuit of the zodiac.

---

[339] Matthew 14:3

[340] Mark 6:16

[341] Mark 6:27; Matthew 14:10

[342] The Catholic *Feast of the Decollation* (an extremely ancient celebration) which commemorates John the Baptist's beheading (or 'decollation') is held on 29th August—not in the time of Aquarius, but roughly six months later in Aquarius's opposite sign Leo, when the constellation Aquarius becomes visible again above the eastern horizon at sunset.

[343] Matthew 4:12

This otherwise enigmatic passage in the New Testament thus becomes clear in an allegorical interpretation: towards the end of the Aquarius period of the year, the constellation of Aquarius (characterised in astrological symbolism as a 'spiritual man' figure pouring water from a pitcher, and in the case of the New Testament, by the spiritual John the Baptist who baptises with water in exactly the same manner) moves almost completely below the darkness of the horizon (is 'put into prison'), a few remaining stars still just visible (giving it a 'beheaded' appearance), whereupon the Sun (Jesus) continues on his way through the zodiac ('into Galilee').

The Characterisation of the Signs — Pisces

Figure 34. Pisces — the Twelfth Sign of the Zodiac

The constellation that we recognise today as Pisces emerged as a composite of two separate but celestially contiguous and thematically linked Babylonian star-patterns. The first of these was *Anunitum*, which roughly corresponds to the more northern fish of the modern Pisces, pointing up towards the constellation Andromeda. The name Anunitum means 'goddess of heaven' and can be seen as a variant name of the goddess of lust and power *Inana*, who was given that same epithet, and whose seasonally-symbolic journey to the underworld we shall encounter in Chapter 4. The constellation Anunitum was however represented as a fish: plain depictions of a fish with reference to the constellation are seen in ancient Mesopotamian seals,[344] and it's notable that a form of the older Akkadian name for 'fish', *nūnu* (as *nuni*), is embedded in the curiously syllabic written construction of the name *A-nu-ni-tum*.

The second Babylonian constellation which, conjoined with Anunitum, has played its part in making up the modern Pisces, is the Swallow. The Swallow is represented as joined to Anunitum by a cord, which motif has survived in many modern depictions of Pisces, where the two fishes are frequently shown as similarly joined together. The constellations Anunitum and the Swallow seem to have been considered as virtually one and the same for astrological purposes in ancient Babylonia. The Akkadian name for the Swallow, *Šinūnūtu*, like that of Anunitum, contains the root name for 'fish', nūnu. In addition, certain Babylonian astrological prognostications or omens reveal that Anunitum and the Swallow could both be understood as 'fish'. As has been remarked of the impact of this essentially 'dual' Babylonian fish-bird constellation, *"We can see that the modern image of Pisces as a pair of fish is, in effect, concealed within the Babylonian symbol of the fish and bird."*[345] It has been speculated that the fish-bird symbol reflected the fruitfulness of the waterways and marshlands of ancient Mesopotamia, which, thoroughly irrigated by the time of late winter when the fish-bird constellation

---

[344] Wallenfels, 1993; White, 2014
[345] White, 2014

lay behind the Sun, were home to both of these notably edible species.[346] When the Greek tropical zodiac became later adopted in other parts of the world with different environmental conditions, the *sign* Pisces forever marked the often sparse and other-worldly period of late winter (see below).

Pisces — Composition

Season: Late Winter; traditionally, the fasting period of Lent.

Symbol: ♓ The fishes.

Polarity: Negative (passive, self-repressive, receptive).

Quality: Mutable (adaptable, variable; open to seasonal change).

Element: Water (emotional, sensitive, intuitive).

Sign Key Phrase: The negative, mutable, water sign is self-denying, self-abnegating; extremely impressionable and emotionally sensitive to others; receptive, intuitive, imaginative; sympathetic, kindly, compassionate, easy-going, generous; nebulous, formless, fluid, intangible, indistinct, chaotic; obscure, unworldly, other-worldly, seemingly psychic; oriented to surrender, escapism and a need to transcend the everyday, the material, and the self.

House key phrase: Activities and matters to do with self-abnegation, self-disintegration, self-sacrifice; selfless deeds (often prompted by the conscience as amendment for past wrongs); karma, guilt and penance; disassociation or dissolution of the personality (sometimes apparent as 'madness'); forgetting; escape from the everyday; withdrawal, retreat, surrender, seclusion, retirement from society; incarceration or confinement (e.g., in prison, through chronic ill-health in hospital, or enclosure in a religious house); confusion, enigmas; deception; mysterious matters and hidden problems (from unseen causes) as well as hidden resources; fantasy; the hidden life of the subconscious, unconscious or 'psychic' realm; service (to the 'absolute' or God); transcendence, spirituality and mysticism.

Sign as 'Extension': Pisces conforms to the pattern where the last six sign-themes of the zodiac appear to be 'extensions' of the corresponding themes of the first six—extensions of themes to do with the 'individual' (in the case of the first six) to those same themes applied more widely, extensively and typically to do with 'others' (in the case of the latter six). As Virgo was centred on self-effacing *personal* practical service, so its opposite sign Pisces concerns self-effacing spiritual service to *others* and to the 'absolute' or God.

Ruling planet: Neptune. The fundamental human function or urge for self-abnegation, self-dissolution, the withdrawal from and the transcendence of mundane reality and everyday experience, as represented by Neptune, is recapitulated in many of the above keyword associations of Pisces. There are some particularly interesting physiological connections between the human function represented by Neptune and the keyword associations of Pisces, which are discussed below.

---

[346] White, 2014

Pisces — Physiological

The traditional physiological association of Pisces is primarily with the feet. In keeping with the self-disregarding, spiritual aspect of Pisces, the feet are in a sense the humblest part of the body: they surrender to, and take the burden of, everything else. In certain religious and cultural practices the feet are often suggestive of the self-abnegation or humility that is the hallmark of the Pisces theme. The practice of washing another's feet is widely seen as the quintessential act of humility in an avowed servant or subordinate. In the Christian New Testament the figure of Jesus exemplified and recommended to his followers the practice of self-abnegation and humility by washing the feet of his disciples just before his last supper with them and his subsequent execution.[347] That self-effacing practice (centred upon the part of the body associated with Pisces) is commemorated and re-enacted by the Catholic Christian church on 'Maundy Thursday' (the Thursday before Easter), when the Pope traditionally washes the feet of twelve people (curiously, the 'feet of twelve people', as Pisces is—physio-logically—the 'feet' of the twelve signs).

Pisces' ruling planet Neptune is associated with analgesia, anaesthesia, and the ingestion of alcohol and drugs generally. The 'numbing' effect of analgesia and anaesthesia is a re-statement of the concept of self-abnegation and self-denial in the realm of the senses, a physiological counterpart to the spiritual or mystic life, which tells us to let go of or deny all self-referential sensory impressions.[348] Interestingly, the physiological *modus operandi* of anaesthesia is—characteristically for the obscure nature of Pisces—still largely a mystery.

Analgesic agents like morphine do not however seem to work in such a way that the pain itself is somehow obliterated, but rather by a process whereby the mind's relationship to it is changed, such that one is no longer concerned by it; as if the mind itself has withdrawn from the pain—in the same way the mind withdraws from or disregards the vicissitudes of mental impressions in spiritual meditation. Pisces is associated with mystery and deceit as well as analgesia, and fittingly, analgesics and anaesthetics may be said to 'deceive' the mind by way of a mysterious, unknown process into withdrawing from the fact of pain, as if in a meditative trance.

Alcohol, the world's most ancient drug, harms the liver especially, which is the organ associated with Jupiter (Pisces's traditional 'ruling planet' before its modern connection with Neptune). Alcohol is the prototypical 'karmic' drug—the 'guilty pleasure' is inevitably offset by the 'payback' of the hangover. Alcoholism and the widespread urge to take drugs can be seen as a crude attempt to respond to the spiritual need for transcendence of the self, but in a harmful and counter-productive manner. This seems consonant with the common reference that drug takers use to 'getting out of it' or 'getting out of one's head': one temporarily has

---

[347] *"If I then, your Lord and Master, have washed your feet; ye also ought to wash one another's feet. For I have given you an example, that ye should do as I have done to you."* (John 13:1-15)

[348] Or, perhaps, the belief in a self-referential nature of sensory impressions.

existence or experience apart from oneself, or apart from the 'particularity' that masquerades as the self. As the English writer and philosopher Aldous Huxley remarked in his *Doors of Perception*:

> Most men and women lead lives at the worst so painful, at the best so monotonous, poor and limited that the urge to escape, the longing to transcend themselves if only for a few moments, is and has always been one of the principal appetites of the soul.[349]

The natural desire for transcendent experience may be sought by the use of drugs or alcohol, but these can be destructive ways to attempt to satisfy the need. Only rarely in the life of an individual do they give a person a true and moreover a safe transcendent experience, and their continued and habitual use can cause harm and distract the user away from natural and safer methods such as in practices of meditation.

It is interesting to note that the organisation devoted to the alleviation of alcoholism, Alcoholics Anonymous, had its origin partly in the insight of the psychologist Carl Jung that, since the craving for alcohol-induced sensory self-dissolution is a crude expression of the innate desire for spiritual transcendence, only true spiritual experience can therefore proffer a cure.[350] Jung wrote to Bill Wilson, later the co-founder of Alcoholics Anonymous, giving his opinion that a patient's craving for alcohol was "*the equivalent on a low level of the spiritual thirst of our being for wholeness, expressed in mediaeval language: the union with God.*"[351] Jung goes on, "*You see, Alcohol in Latin is "spiritus" and you use the same word for the highest religious experience as well as for the most depraving poison. The helpful formula therefore is:* spirituus contra spiritum." The Latin phrase that Jung quoted had the somewhat punning meaning of 'spirit working against spirits', or 'the true form of spirituality taking the place of the cruder or counterfeit form in the alcohol-induced intoxication'.

The point here is that the Pisces sign-theme represents the practice of the dissolution of the self, but that this can be effected in a positive or 'higher' way, by self-denial and transcendence into a spiritual or mystical state of undifferenti-ated unity by way of a practice such as meditation; or it can be attempted in a negative way, where the 'lower' form of self-dissolution involved is in drug-taking or in other negative forms of escapism. Both forms nevertheless have their origin in the basic Piscean urge to dissolve and therefore transcend the perception of self. It is interesting to note, in the anecdote concerning Jung, the coincidence that the root word 'spirit' is used to connote the most basic mind-transcending drug—alcohol—as well as the aim of 'spirituality', both of which are linked to Pisces' theme of transcendence.

---

[349] Huxley, 1954
[350] Levin, 1995
[351] Letter from Carl Jung to Bill Wilson, dated 30 January, 1961.

The Pisces 'Personality' in Astrology

From the sign's composition and keyword descriptions we may see how the 'personality' of the sign-theme Pisces has been constructed and epitomised in traditional divinatory astrology. We may imagine the characteristically 'Piscean' person as one who is inclined to be more imaginative than practical, highly emotionally sensitive to others, being one who sympathises with them in the subtlest ways, being more alive to the states and needs of other people than to their own; one who registers the states (especially the emotional states) of others deep within themselves, and who responds with sympathy and self-sacrificing service. The Piscean 'personality' may be seen as so sympathetic to others that they may often be simply gullible, easily deceived and easily led—a 'soft touch'.

The 'personality' can be seen as one who is so intuitively and imaginatively attuned to the finest and most subtle impressions and cues of others that they appear 'psychic'. The 'type' may also be seen as a 'dreamer', often caught up in the nebulous, emotionally fluid and chaotic 'other world' of their imagination. They may surrender to forms of other-worldly escape to the point of being drawn to retreat, seclusion or isolation, seeking to escape or transcend their own selves altogether. The sign-theme Pisces is therefore very much concerned with the destruction or letting-go of that which claims attachment to, or that which appears to constitute, the self—of the sensations and thoughts that constitute apparent selfhood, and moreover of the suffering that is a corollary of being slavishly attached to identification with material sensation and self-based ideation. This can be seen in a spectrum of Pisces-related endeavours and circumstances, from the use of alcohol and drugs, to selfless work carried out in reward-denying seclusion (or in enforced seclusion), and in its 'highest' form, in the discovery of the spiritual or mystical life.

Pisces may seem to have as its central message 'do for others' but more properly it is 'deny yourself', 'become dead to yourself', or 'forsake the apparent personal "I" with its manifold impressions', in order to surrender any distinction between a personal self and the universal One Self which is uncontaminated with particular objects. The 'doing for others' comes as a natural corollary of self-denial, but the main theme is self-abnegation. The surrendering of the "I" apparent in oneself is the means whereby the personal spirit merges into, or discloses its identity with, the universal spirit, as the waters of a particular river at last merge into the boundless ocean. The ethos of Pisces is that kernel of truth which humanity sees in the fundamental spiritual impulse, unadulterated by religious division, namely, the mystic withdrawal from, and abnegation of, the apparent self, which paradoxically results in the discovery of the one true self.

At best, the Piscean personality is self-abnegating without engaging in gratuitously harmful self-neglect; one who sacrifices or surpasses the personal self in compassionate practical assistance for others; or one who goes beyond self-identification with mundane experience to achieve what may be said to be a spiritual or mystic transcendence. At worst, the personality is 'non-material' by living too much in the imagination and being severely confused, unrealistic and impractical; one who is merely gullible to others and themselves; one who is a prey to hidden, unconscious maladies which are wholly negative; one who loses touch with reality in chaotic self-deception, delusional fantasy, or in the extreme self-dissolution of insanity; one who is self-denying merely by engaging in self-neglect, gravitating towards 'self-transcendence' in its coarser forms, such as in the use of alcohol or drugs ('getting out of themselves'). As with all the zodiac signs, it is however more helpful to view such an idealised 'Piscean personality type' as a potentiality along a spectrum between such extremes, whilst retaining the sign's essential 'self-abnegating' characteristic. Thus we can perhaps say that Pisces teaches us to gain transcendence of our selves through the imagination, through the practice of compassion and practical self-sacrifice to the needs of others, and in the self-abnegation that is inherent in contemplative meditation, without allowing such an impulse to manifest itself in merely delusional escapism, or in the more primitive forms of self-dissolution such as in wholly negative substance-induced delirium.

Pisces — Season

The key descriptions of Pisces, with its accent on self-denial or self-abnegation, are clearly evocative of late winter as embodied in Lent, the sparse time of year in the ancient natural world, when food is almost impossible to be found and material stores have been all but exhausted. It is interesting to note that fish—the symbol of Pisces—is traditionally eaten in the period of Lent. At this time, self-abnegation in nature is a necessity and not an idealised option, though the season's conditions have come to be embodied by religious and folk myth as a time when, apparently coincidentally, the self-abnegating practices of Lent are entered into voluntarily. In this period of the year, the natural world, in a form of limbo between winter and spring, between death and rebirth, appears asleep, as if in a dream, having forgotten its self-preoccupation. The inuring of life to this season's meagre accommodation to bodily needs brings about an other-worldliness, a sense of surrender, and a dissolution of the mundane preoccupations of the self. The idea of renewal seems a supernatural fantasy, but only imagination and a transcendent faith can sustain the spark of life at this time. This description of the natural world at this time of year is a recapitulation of the Piscean keyword ethos.

Pisces, like all mutable signs, brings an end to one season (in this case, winter) and prepares for a change to come. The stern and even terrifying aspect of late winter means the prospect of either death, or rebirth in the spring. Nature prepares to make a commitment to a completely fresh start, the complete destruction of the old and the beginning of a new state that is nevertheless an unknown. If the zodiac is taken as an analogue of life, at the stage of Pisces, the personal commitment is also to an unknown—a fantasy, a dream, perhaps an illusion. Only faith, not logic, can be the guide. The truly spiritual or mystic individual may at this point seek a liberation from the cycle of death and rebirth.

Pisces — Mythology, Religion, Folklore & Custom

The Christian period of Lent is essentially coextensive with the period of Pisces, recapitulating this zodiac sign both seasonally and thematically. Lent begins on Ash Wednesday, which falls forty-six days before Easter Sunday, the latter being the variable Christian 'feast' date which effectively marks the spring equinox and thus the beginning of the next sign Aries and an entirely new cycle of the zodiac. Although Easter Sunday is a 'movable feast' (its date varies from year to year) it falls on the first Sunday after the first full moon following the spring equinox, and is thus irrevocably tied to that cardinal point, the beginning of the zodiacal year. Lent ends roughly around the time of Easter; thus in essence it corresponds with the time of the Pisces sign-theme.

In thematic terms, the purpose of Lent in the Christian liturgical calendar is primarily one of self-abnegation or self-denial, typically involving the 'giving up' or denying oneself of one's usual complement of food or other consumable facets of life that may have given one indulgent pleasure. It may also involve some form of penance, by giving alms for the poor, or by mortifying the flesh, or some similar form of self-sacrifice. It is also seen as a preparation for the renewal inherent in Easter (the marker for the spring equinox—the beginning of Aries and the new zodiac cycle). The thematic correspondence of Lent with the 'self-abnegating' keyword associations of Pisces as described above is clear.

The practices of Lent purportedly commemorate that part of the story in the New Testament when Jesus is said to have fasted in the 'wilderness' for forty days, during which his faith was tempted by the devil. In the interpretation of the Jesus story as a rough allegory of the Sun's journey through the year, it is easy to see the period of Jesus's 'fasting in the wilderness' as an image of one having to endure the dearth inherent in the natural world in the very last part of winter before the renewal of life in spring. One can see that the seasonal time of the Christian period of Lent, its recommended observances, and the part of the Jesus story that it purportedly commemorates, restate the sign-period of Pisces, both seasonally and thematically, and it seems reasonable to suppose that the origin of Lent may lie in a mythologised allegory of the forced 'self-abnegation' that occurs in the lean times of late winter.

There may be other parts of the Christian New Testament story that recapitulate in fragmentary form the sign Pisces, in particular that part of its narrative which follows Jesus's meeting with John the Baptist (the representation of the previous sign Aquarius). Here the Sun would be said to pass out of Aquarius and to enter the sign Pisces, whose symbol is two fishes, and indeed we read that, after his meeting with John the Baptist, and following his fasting vigil in the wilderness, whilst *"walking by the sea of Galilee"* (i.e., continuing on the circuit of the zodiac),[352] Jesus meets with *two fishermen*, Simon and Peter.[353] There then follows a series of sermons given by Jesus which particularly stress the Piscean

---

[352] 'Galilee' or Γαλιλαία in the original Greek means circuit'.
[353] Matthew 4:18

key-phrase of self-abnegation as set out above, as in the moving 'sermon on the mount',[354] with its emphasis upon faith and the karmic consequences of humility and good works, and a little later the quintessential exhortation to self-abnegation:

> Ye have heard that it hath been said, An eye for an eye, and a tooth for a tooth: But I say unto you, That ye resist not evil: but whosoever shall smite thee on thy right cheek, turn to him the other also," and "Ye have heard that it hath been said, Thou shalt love thy neighbour, and hate thine enemy. But I say unto you, Love your enemies, bless them that curse you, do good to them that hate you, and pray for them which despitefully use you, and persecute you.[355]

Shortly after these depictions of the self-abnegating Pisces sign-theme in the New Testament, we also read of Jesus calming a storm at sea,[356] which may be seen to symbolise the Sun (Jesus) in this part of its yearly course meeting calmer and milder weather at this more temperate time of the year, as winter draws to a close.

---

[354] Matthew 5:1-12
[355] Matthew 5:38-44
[356] Matthew 8:23-27

4

A Return to the Sun: The Year

We have examined the twelve signs of the zodiac and seen how each encapsulates themes which correspond to the seasonal characteristics of its period in the year.[357] Taken together, the signs comprise the zodiac—the story of the Sun's journey through the year, a story which has, over millennia, become a prime representation of humankind's basic life concerns. If the planets have been projected essences of humankind's basic principles, functions or urges, then the zodiac of signs is a coherently patterned, truly holistic distillation of man's most fundamental attitudes and modes of expression or behaviour. It's remarkable that, in the heavens, mankind has looked within and from the collective unconscious articulated a framework of archetypal symbolism representing the whole psyche.

In the case of the signs of the zodiac, the story of the *year*, the constantly recurring cycle of Earth's journey around the Sun (or from the geocentric viewpoint upon which the zodiac is based, the apparent journey of the Sun in its annual journey through the seasons), retold and refined for so long in the collective unconscious, has informed the nature of myth, religion and custom. For this is the basis to understanding the signs: that they are the Sun's 'stations', the main periods or 'slices' of the year, each with its own seasonal characteristics.

Since the seasons of the year have had so much symbolic importance to humans, it's worth reminding ourselves why they exist in the first place. The answer lies in the somewhat prosaically simple fact that the rotation of the Earth about its polar axis (and thus its equatorial plane) is obliquely angled, by about 24°, to the plane of its orbit around the Sun. This means that different parts of the Earth's surface receive different amounts of light and warmth from the Sun at different times of the year (Figures 3 and 7).

Thus, for example in the northern hemisphere, the year follows a course from increased daylight and heat in the spring, to maximal light and warmth in summer, to a period of dwindling light and warmth in autumn, and finally to a period of minimal light and warmth in the winter.[358] There is therefore an overarching pattern, of a birth, a flourishing, a decline and a dearth, of light and warmth, in the course of each year—along with life's inevitable response to that pattern.

It may be worthwhile to consider the briefest of astronomical overviews of this cause of the seasons and their course through the repeating cycle of each year. We have attempted to present this visually (Figure 35).

---

[357] Once again it may be worth restating that we are referring to the seasonal characteristics of the more culturally impactful northern hemisphere.

[358] The patterns are of course the same but reversed to each other for the north and south hemispheres, such that when (for instance) summer begins in the northern hemisphere, winter begins in the southern hemisphere, and so-on.

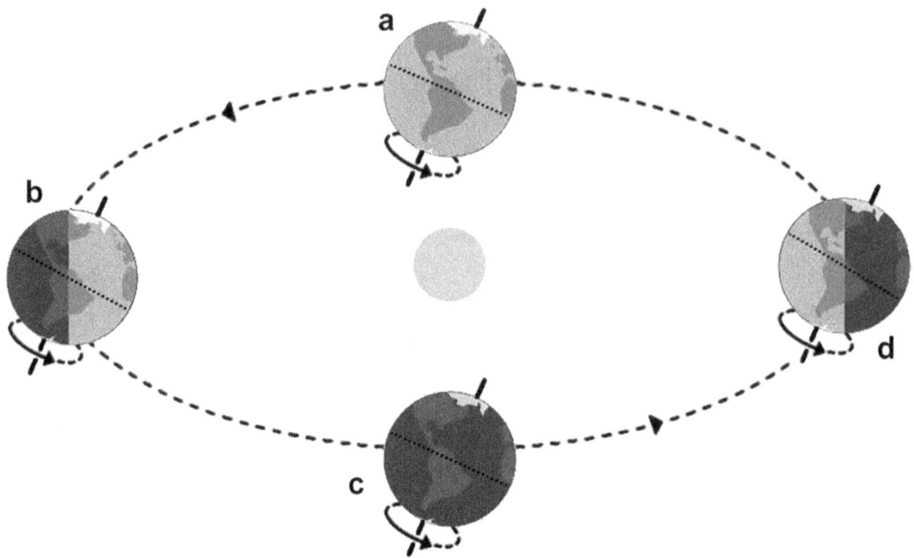

Figure 35. The Earth at Four Stages Along Its Orbit Around the Sun

At each of the points in Figure 35 (not to scale) we see how the Earth's rotational axis is tilted away from the plane of its orbit around the Sun (shown by the wide dashed ellipse). Figure 4 also shows this axial tilt. We thus also see the concomitant tilt of the equator (the dotted line across the globe). Note that the Earth is rotating all the time at each of these stages in Figure 35. At the spring equinox (a) and the autumnal equinox (c) there is an equal amount of daylight and night across the Earth's hemispheres. At stage (b) we see the summer solstice in the northern hemisphere, where that hemisphere tips towards the Sun, receiving more of its light than the southern hemisphere; for the same reason, stage (b) is the winter solstice in the southern hemisphere, which receives less of the Sun's light. At stage (d) we see the winter solstice in the northern hemisphere, where that hemisphere tips away from the Sun, receiving less of its light; for the same reason, stage (d) is the summer solstice in the southern hemisphere, which receives more of the Sun's light.

The year on Earth is therefore most essentially defined by the Sun's course from lighter and warmer to darker and colder days; from the point of view of living organisms, from an 'easier' part of the year to a more 'difficult' part. Life on Earth has adapted both physiologically and behaviourally to this perennial cycle in order to survive and flourish, and humans have been no exception. The seasons may seem so obvious to us as to make us forget their impact upon human life. To the ancients, however, who lived 'closer to nature' than we do in modern societies, the determining and marking of the beginnings and endings of the seasons was of crucial importance, not only psychologically, in terms of marking the Sun's passage from cold and comparative darkness to greater light and warmth, but moreover for the vital planting and sowing of crops—that harnessing of the Sun's energy in the yearly cycle which enabled the procurement of food, and thus survival and continued reproduction. Since it was a life-and-death issue, the importance of this cycle cannot be overemphasised in terms of the way it pervaded every facet of man's view of himself and of the cosmos around him.

To give an example of the way in which the importance of the solar cycle of the year is thoroughly ingrained upon us as living creatures, we might return to the question we posed in Chapter 3—why do we become happier when the Sun shines? The fact of being cheered by sunlight seems so obvious that few might bother to ask why this should be, though the effect has been confirmed by careful research.[359] It's not that it's merely due to increased warmth, since we can feel increased warmth by other means and yet not feel the joy that the Sun brings us; equally we can experience joy at the very sight of sunshine, even if it doesn't bring warmth at all. It must be from an ancestral—if not evolutionary—acknowledgement in our biological memory of the Sun as the primary indicator of the likelihood of better living, and its absence with the death-like aspects of night and winter with their all too real dangers. Such an evolutionary account is in fact likely to be the case, as we now know that we are chemically 'hard-wired' to respond positively to sunlight, the amount and duration of which causes significant changes in the hormones and neurotransmitters that regulate mood.[360]

Thus there has not only been a practical adaptation to the seasons of the Sun along with their various changing qualities, but also and inevitably a deep psychological internalisation of them, which has permeated humankind's self-expression, in cultural metaphors for life, in custom and in primordial allegorical tales of myth and religion. Though by no means absent in the southern hemisphere, this process has occurred most actively in the northern hemisphere, since there has been a greater amount and variety of myth-making there, and it is with descriptions of the archetypes and myths of the year's main seasons in the northern hemisphere that we are here primarily concerned.

Time and again, dramatic stories and allegories of the year-cycle, of the Sun's heroic journey along its path from light to darkness and back to light again, of the vernal period of resurgent growth, of the fruition of summer, followed by its 'tragic fall' into autumn and winter, only to be reborn again triumphantly in spring, have been told, re-formulated and re-characterised, creating some of the most fundamental motifs, patterns and archetypes in the cultural expression of humankind's collective psyche. The great social anthropologist and folklorist James Frazer remarked in his seminal work *The Golden Bough* that for many cultures and myths, the changes of the seasons were *"explained by the life and death of gods"*:

> The spectacle of the great changes which annually pass over the
> face of the earth has powerfully impressed the minds of men in all

---

[359] Harmatz *et al.*, 2000
[360] Lambert *et al.*, 2002

> ages, and stirred them to meditate on the causes of transforma-
> tions so vast and wonderful ... [people] pictured to themselves the
> growth and decay of vegetation, the birth and death of living
> creatures, as effects of the waxing or waning strength of divine
> beings, of gods and goddesses, who were born and died, who
> married and begot children, on the pattern of human life.[361]

We can now review some of these mythological tales which allegorically re-enact the cyclic progress of the year and the major points along the way, emphasising as they do the 'death' of the heroic Sun in the autumn and winter and its 'resurrection' in the spring.

Mesopotamia — Inana (Ištar) and Dumuzid (Tammuz)

Inana (later known as *Ištar*) was the most important female goddess of ancient Mesopotamia, being a deity of sexual procreation, lust and power. Inana was also associated with the planet Venus.[362] The most famous myth associated with Inana is that of her descent and return from the underworld, which is ruled by her sister, the goddess *Ereshkigal*. There are two versions of the myth. The first is the Sumerian, being that of the religion practiced by the people of Sumer, the first literate civilisation of ancient Mesopotamia, emerging between the 6th and 5th millennium BCE. The second, later and briefer, derivative version is that of the religion of the Akkadian empire, emerging after the Sumerian civilisation, around 2,334 BCE. The core features of the myth are however the same in both versions.

The impetuous Inana decides to travel to the underworld and, aware of the potential dangers of such an undertaking, instructs her servant *Ninshubur* to wear her drabbest mourning clothes and to lament for her disappearance ostentatiously, and if she (Inana) does not return within three days, to entreat the gods for help. Inana arrives at the gates of the underworld and vociferously demands of her sister Ereshkigal that she be allowed entry. Annoyed and suspicious, Ereshkigal instructs the gatekeeper of the underworld to weaken Inana by removing her garments and jewellery one by one as she enters through each of the seven gates that lead into the subterranean realm. By the time she reaches her sister, Inana is naked and thus stripped of her power. She nevertheless proceeds to sit on Ereshkigal's throne in an attempt to establish herself as queen of the underworld. However, the *Anuna*, the seven judges of the netherworld, intervene and decide against Inana's plan. The Anuna transform Inana into a corpse and hang her on a meathook. Immediately following Inana's death, all fertility and growing things on the earth perish.[363]

Following these events Inana's servant Ninshubur does as she was commanded and appeals to the gods for help in rescuing her mistress from the

---

[361] Frazer, 1894
[362] Black & Green, 1992
[363] Pryke, 2017; Penglase, 1994

underworld. Only one, called *Enki*, is prepared to help. To do so he creates two androgynous, sexless beings called the *kurgarru* and the *galaturru* from the dirt under his fingernails, who journey to the underworld, where they gain Ereshkigal's favour and revive Inana's lifeless body. The emissaries then conduct Inana back from the underworld, passing the seven gates and retrieving Inana's clothes and jewellery, and thus her power. Ereshkigal however sends demons to follow Inana, who insist that a substitute must be found to take Inana's place in the underworld, or Inana will be dragged back underground. Once back in the world of the living, the demons suggest various of Inana's servants as the substitute, but Inana argues against each choice, pointing out how each has lamented her in a seemly way and so does not deserve the fate. Finally, Inana and the demons come upon Inana's husband *Dumuzid* (also known as *Tammuz*). It is apparent that Dumuzid has not mourned Inana, as he is in a resplendent state and surrounded by slave girls. The demons duly drag Dumuzid down to the underworld as the chosen substitute.

The Sumerian poem called *The Return of Dumuzid* describes how Dumuzid's sister *Geshtinanna*, his mother *Sirtur* and Inana lament intensely for Dumuzid's death, until a fly reveals where he may be found; the three mourners duly find Dumuzid where the fly had directed them. At this point it is agreed that Dumuzid must spend half of the year in the underworld with Ereshkigal; for the other half of the year, Dumuzid is allowed to return whilst his sister Geshtinanna takes his place. Fertility is presumed to return to the earth on Inana's return, certainly in the Akkadian version of the myth.[364]

In the myths of Inana/Ištar and Dumuzid/Tammuz it is impossible not to see an allegory for the annual disappearance and reappearance of the power of the Sun, from winter to summer, to bring about fertility in the land. Inana's gradual denudation reminds us of the progressive 'disrobing' of deciduous trees of their leaves in autumn. The perishing of life in the world following Inana's apparent death mirrors the natural aspect of vegetation in winter, while her re-clothing on her return, along with the subsequent return of life to the world, similarly echo the seasonal return of life in spring.

Mesopotamia — Ningishzida

Dumuzid's sister Geshtinanna was also associated with the male deity *Ningishzida*, possibly being his consort. In the Early Dynastic period of Mesopotamia (2,900–2,350 BCE) the yearly death of vegetation was attributed to Ningishzida's descent to the underworld, which was marked by a procession of lament and visits to the graves of the deceased. When Ningishzida returned in spring he was said to *"break through the earth like fresh grass"*.[365] Here again we see a mythologising of the basic cycle of the primary seasons of the year.

---

[364] Penglase, 1994; Katz, 2015
[365] Wiggermann, 1998

Egypt - Osiris

The myth of *Osiris* is perhaps the most developed and influential of its kind in ancient Egyptian mythology. Osiris, son of the earth-god *Geb* and the sky-god *Nut*, was god of fertility, agriculture, life and vegetation, as well as of the afterlife, the dead and resurrection. Taken together these roles recapitulate in deific form the major facets of the solar year.[366] The earliest known corpus of ancient Egyptian religious writings, known as the *Pyramid Texts*, describe how Osiris, ruler of Egypt and symbol of order and the power of life, is murdered by his brother *Set*, who by contrast is the lord of the barren desert and who represents the negative principles of chaos, violence and disharmony. Following his murder, Osiris's wife Isis mourns her husband and searches for his body. Eventually she finds him and with the help of *Thoth* (an Egyptian deity associated with the Greek Hermes and the Roman Mercury) and *Anubis* (god of embalming and mummification) she restores Osiris's body to life long enough for her to become pregnant by him and to conceive a son, Horus.

A later and more connected account of the myth is told by the Greek historian and philosopher Plutarch (c. 46 CE — c. 119 CE).[367] In this fuller account Set murders Osiris by trapping him inside a chest or coffin which is then thrown into the Nile river. The chest floats out to sea, finally to arrive at the town of Byblos, where a tree grows around it. The king of Byblos has the tree felled and made into a pillar for his palace. Isis extracts the coffin and her husband's body, the tree-pillar being left behind as an object of worship. Set however then dismembers Osiris's corpse, and Isis later buries the dissected pieces.

In the earlier Egyptian accounts Isis gives birth to Horus whilst hiding from Set in a secluded thicket of papyrus on the banks of the Nile.[368] Thereafter Isis finds it necessary to guard her son from various menaces, which often take the form of the stings and bites of venomous scorpions or snakes. To protect Horus from these dangers, Isis pleads with deities such as the earth-god Geb or the sun-god *Ra*. Horus however survives the various perils and achieves adulthood, whereupon he challenges Set for the throne of Egypt. The dispute between Horus and Set takes the form of appeals to the creator gods Ra and Atum, as well as physical confrontations. Horus mutilates or steals Set's testicles, and Set tears out one or both of Horus's eyes—an important act symbolically as Horus's eyes were said to be the embodiments of the Sun and the Moon. Set also sexually violates Horus, though Set's defeat becomes imminent when Horus's seed enters him, to appear on Set's forehead as a 'golden disc'.[369] Horus later retrieves his

---

[366] Frazer, 1894

[367] As Frazer (1894, Vol. VI) has pointed out, *"so numerous are the allusions to* [the myth] *in the* [earlier Egyptian] *Pyramid Texts that by their help we could reconstruct the story in its main outlines even without the narrative of Plutarch."*

[368] It's notable that the Greek word for 'holy scripture' (i.e., made of papyrus) in the sense of 'Bible' is Βίβλος ('byblos') and a confusion of the two terms may have been the origin of the later Greek account of Osiris's body 'floating to Byblos' (see Frazer, 1894).

[369] te Velde, 1967

lost eye, perhaps with the help of other gods, which signifies the restoration of his kingship.

In some accounts Horus simply reinstates the orderly rulership once held by Osiris; in others however that rulership is divided between Horus and Set, Horus ruling over the fertile and life-giving parts of the country, while Set rules over the barren desert. Some interpretations see the latter outcome as Horus and Set ruling over two opposing but natural principles of the world, a little like the Chinese concept of yin and yang: contrasting yet co-existing—even mutually interdependent—aspects of existence.[370]

The accounts of the struggle between Set and Horus tend to be somewhat complex and varied, though many of its main symbolic elements seem suggestive of the archetypal story of the year's major seasonal change. The 'good' part of the year, in terms of the period of the growth and fruition of vegetation, is well symbolised by Osiris, offspring of the earth and sky, ruler of agriculture and the positive power of life, whose rites of death and burial began with a ploughing of the earth and ended with the erection of a tree-like pillar with a cross-bar at the top. Frazer relates how Osiris's *"character as a tree-spirit was represented very graphically in a ceremony described by Firmicus Maternus. A pine-tree was cut down, the centre was hollowed out, and with the wood thus excavated an image of Osiris was made, which was then 'buried' in the hollow of the tree. Here, again, it is hard to imagine how the conception of a tree as tenanted by a personal being could be more plainly expressed."*[371] This ritual association of Osiris with vegetation in the particular form of a tree is in accord with the Greek account of Osiris emerging at death from a tree-coffin.

As Osiris was identified with the positive, life-giving, vegetative part of the year, his consort Isis was given many epithets identifying her specifically with the spirit of the harvest, such as 'she who has given birth to the fruits of the earth', 'mistress of bread', or even more plainly as 'the green corn-field itself, which is personified as a goddess'.[372] As Stephen Benko has put it, *"As wife of Osiris and mother of the sun-god, Horus, [Isis] was deeply connected with the origin of life."*[373] It is not surprising therefore that the Greeks readily associated Osiris's wife Isis with the harvest-goddess Demeter, one of the 'virgin-goddesses' identified by Benko,[374] as well as with Artemis, who fulfilled the commonly seen dual aspect as virgin goddess and source of fertility.[375]

The threatened dominion of Set's overwhelmingly negative characteristics suits a representation of the threatening decay of the year into a more sombre and barren period. But just as the year itself eventually turns away from its gloomier side, so in time Osiris's positive spirit returns once again as Horus. After being divinely protected in the unfavourable environment, Horus's seed finally engen-

---

[370] te Velde, 1967
[371] Frazer, 1894
[372] *Ibid.*
[373] Benko, 2004
[374] *Ibid.*
[375] Heyob, 1975

ders a Sun-like 'golden disc' out of the darker aspect as embodied by Set, further echoing a symbolic representation or allegory of the turning year-cycle. It's notable that when Horus regains the positive principle of the kingship, he 'retrieves his eye', which organ, as we have noted, is likely to have been a representation of the Sun as well as of kingship.[376] In some accounts this is also accompanied by the restoration of Set's mutilated testicles, which may equally represent the re-establishing of the year's regenerative process for the next cycle.[377] The representation of both figures as opposing but mutually inter-dependent natural forces may be seen as an overall, holistic appreciation of the polarised nature of the whole year-cycle. The myth was symbolically instantiated in historical Egyptian kingship, with each new king being seen as renewing the positive aspect of life, just as Horus does in the myth.[378]

The Greek World — Adonis and Aphrodite

Aphrodite is an ancient Greek goddess very similar to (if not mythologically identical to) the Mesopotamian Inana-Ištar and the Phoenician Astarte, being a deity of love, lust, power and procreation.[379] The Roman goddess Venus was a syncretised continuation of Aphrodite, and both were associated with the planet Venus. The myth of Adonis and Aphrodite has very close thematic parallels with that of Inana-Ištar and Dumuzid-Tammuz, as outlined above.[380]

The name Adonis comes from the Greek Ἄδωνις, in turn from the Canaanite 'adōn', meaning 'lord' and is cognate with the Hebrew 'Adonai' "אֲדֹנָי", a title for God. Adonis was a mortal man, often seen as the model of perfect male attraction. Adonis's mother *Myrrha* had boasted that her daughter was more beautiful even than Aphrodite. In jealous retaliation, Aphrodite cursed Myrrha with an over-whelming lust for her (Myrrha's) own father, King Cinyras of Cyprus. Adonis was the issue of the incestuous union that resulted. Aphrodite nevertheless cared enough for the baby Adonis to take it to the underworld, to be reared by the fertility goddess Persephone.

When Adonis reached manhood, Aphrodite saw that he was extremely handsome and coveted him as a lover; Persephone however wanted to keep him for herself. The great Zeus settled the dispute by decreeing that Adonis would spend half the year with Persephone in the underworld and half above with Aphrodite. A different version of the myth tells how, after Adonis is killed by a wild boar whilst hunting, both Aphrodite and Persephone beg Zeus to resurrect him, each wanting to keep him for themselves. In this account Zeus resurrects Adonis before imposing the same seasonal decree. Whichever version we take, it

---

[376] Note the similarity of the basic geometry of an eye, as a near-circle with a central dot-like pupil, and the astrological symbol for the Sun—a dot within a circle—which 'planet' is representative of both the vital power of life and kingship.

[377] te Velde, 1967

[378] Assmann, 2001

[379] Breitenberger, 2007

[380] Cyrino, 2010; Kerényi, 1951; West, 1997

is not difficult to see the myth of Adonis and Aphrodite as another example of a beautiful male dying and resurrecting solar figure, disappearing to the 'underworld' for half the year, once more bearing witness to a collective projection in myth of the world's primary seasonal contrast.

The Greek World — Attis

Attis was a deity in the mythology of the ancient Phrygians, an Indo-European speaking people related to the Greeks, whose kingdom, Phrygia, lay in the west central part of Anatolia (modern Turkey). The cult of Attis began in that region around 1,250 BCE and continued throughout the ancient Greek world, becoming a solar deific myth in the Roman empire in the 2nd century CE. The myths of these ancient peoples tell how the Olympian gods feared the hermaphroditic 'mother nature' deity *Agdistis* (also known as *Cybele*) and so cut off the latter's genitals. From the blood that issued from this mutilation an almond (or pomegranate) tree grew, from which the river nymph *Nana* took a seed, hiding it in her bosom. This seed caused the virgin Nana to become pregnant with the baby Attis, whom she later abandoned. Attis was reared by a 'he-goat' and grew to be exceptionally beautiful—so much so that Agdistis-Cybele fell in love with him.

In one version of the story which echoes a part of one version of the story of Adonis and Aphrodite, Attis was killed by a wild boar. In another version, Attis was sent by his foster parents to Pessinos in Asia Minor to wed the king's daughter; however, at the marriage ceremony, the jealous Agdistis-Cybele appeared in full radiant glory, causing Attis to become mad and castrate himself on a tree. Flowers (particularly violets) were said to have grown from Attis's spilled blood. According to the ancient Greek traveller and geographer Pausanias (c. 110 BCE—180 BCE) in his *Description of Greece*, Agdistis-Cybele begged Zeus to resurrect Attis, but Zeus only ensured that his body did not decompose. In Ovid's account of the myth, following his death, Attis is said to have been changed into a pine tree.[381]

An annual festival was held to commemorate the story of Attis. At the spring equinox a tree was cut and brought into the sanctuary of Agdistis-Cybele. Attis's effigy was placed in the tree which was adorned with violets in commemoration of the flowers which were said to have sprung up from his blood. On the third day after the placing of the effigy, the *Day of Blood* took place, when the high priest would draw blood from his own arm as an offering. On the fourth day the *Festival of Joy* ('Hilaria') took place to celebrate Attis's resurrection. Attis's effigy was kept for a year and then burned.[382]

The myth of Attis is very similar to that of Adonis and Aphrodite. Indeed as James Frazer remarked, "*The legends and rites of the two gods were so much alike that*

---

[381] Ovid, 8
[382] Frazer, 1894

the ancients themselves sometimes identified them."[383] The story of Attis is another example in myth of a beautiful male solar figure who annually dies (or lies dormant) but resurrects, again representing in the human psyche the overarching seasonal fact of the year—the annual cycle of the death and rebirth of vegetation—via symbolical legend, social custom and ritual. The self-infliction aspect of Attis's death may in particular represent the apparent self-infliction of vegetative life in its spontaneous 'death' at autumn and winter, prior to its resurrection in spring.

The Greek World — Demeter and the Eleusinian Mysteries

One ancient myth of the year-cycle concerns Demeter, the ancient Greek goddess of agriculture and the harvest.[384] Demeter, as we saw when reviewing the zodiac signs, is very closely associated in a thematic sense with the sign Virgo, particularly in its representation of wheat and the harvest-time. In Greek mythology Demeter became—by her own brother Zeus—the mother of Persephone (also known as 'Kore', meaning 'maiden'), another fertility goddess.[385] The Greek myths tell how Persephone, whilst tending the flowers of the earth, was abducted by Hades, the god of the underworld (the originator and thematic equivalent of the Roman Pluto) and forcibly taken to his subterranean realm.[386] Persephone's mother Demeter subsequently abandoned her usual superintendence of the fertility of the earth in order to search for her daughter, causing dearth and drought in the land, and subsequent suffering and death amongst the people.

The mighty Zeus did not however want such a state of affairs to continue, and sent his messenger Hermes (Mercury) to order Hades to return Persephone to the earth and her mother. The fates however had long before decreed that anyone who ate or drank whilst in the underworld would be forced to spend eternity there, and Hades had tricked Persephone whilst she was in his subterranean realm into eating four or six pomegranate seeds. Caught between the ruling of the fates and Zeus's decree, Persephone was obliged to reside in the underworld with Hades for four or six months of the year (one for each pomegranate seed eaten), whilst for the remaining time she was allowed to live on the earth. Thus every year during the winter months when Persephone was absent, Demeter grieved for her daughter and would not tend the earth, which became barren; once Persephone returned in spring, Demeter rejoiced at her daughter's reappearance and allowed growth to take place again.

---

[383] Frazer, 1894

[384] The virtually exact equivalent of Demeter in the ancient Roman world was known as the goddess Ceres.

[385] The ancient Roman equivalent of Persephone was known as Proserpina.

[386] The 'abduction' of Persephone by Hades seems to us most likely to be a euphemism for forced impregnation—rape—by the agency which powerfully demands and initiates the regeneration of life (represented by Hades-Pluto) and in doing so necessitates death (see the section on Pluto in Chapter 2 and that on Scorpio in Chapter 3).

Demeter's response to her daughter Persephone's seasonally alternating disappearance to, and reappearance from, the underworld, in the form of neglecting the growth of vegetation in winter and then promoting it again in spring respectively, symbolises the cycle of vegetative decay, death and rebirth in the annual seasonal change from the 'descent' of the Sun's light and warmth in autumn, the passage through the dark, cold winter and the return of light and warmth again in the spring. So important was this symbolism in the myth that it became a major festival or cult during the Hellenistic period, as well as later in Rome, being embellished and re-enacted with secret rites and ceremonies, to which only a select few were initiated.[387]

The cult of the basic seasonal story became known as the *Eleusinian Mysteries*, and appears to have been an important cultural contemplation of the way the year reflects the constant cycle of growth, fruitfulness, decay, death, and the notion of a resurrection to a rebirth or afterlife, in both nature and humankind. A sort of holistic contemplation of the entire process, the *épopteia* (Greek: ἐποπτεία) was seen as the highest attainment of the rites. It is quite extraordinary that such a sublime and refined meditation upon the year's cycle and its analogous kinship to human life became so important in this ancient and longstanding contemplative ritual. It has been suggested that aspects of the original Eleusinian cult survive even into modern times, as some of its rites have been associated with the figure of Saint Demetrius of Thessaloniki, venerated as a patron saint of agriculture and fertility.[388]

Jesus Christ

In the four texts which in the first century CE came to be chosen out of many candidates to be the accepted canon of the Christian 'New Testament', the collated story of the life of Jesus Christ,[389] there is a discernible overall narrative structure that certainly appears to resemble an allegory of the Sun's journey through the year, with Jesus as the central, heroic solar figure. To illustrate this, we can firstly summarise the 'overall' or major points of the seasonal story of the year-cycle in the natural world, at the four cardinal points of the solstices and the equinoxes. These begin with the 'birth' of the Sun's light (in terms of the return to an increase in daylight) amidst the darkness of winter, shortly after the winter solstice. The next major point is the seemingly miraculous rebirth of new life and growth at the spring equinox. Then comes the joyful and radiant summer, the 'crowning point' of which may be seen *astronomically* as when the Sun is at its highest at the summer solstice, and *meteorologically* as continuing on to the rest of the fructifying days of summer. Finally there is the decay after the autumn equinox as the year 'turns' towards the death-like winter.

---

[387] Nilsson, 1940
[388] Kloft, 2010
[389] Keeler, 1888

These principal points of the natural year-cycle are directly comparable to corresponding episodes in a similarly overall view of the life of Jesus. Firstly there is the birth of Jesus in a dark cave or farm building, shortly after the winter solstice.[390] Another major event is the miraculous resurrection or rebirth of Jesus shortly after the Passover (the spring equinox).[391] We can also identify the dramatic culmination of Jesus's life in his 'transfiguration' when he appeared engulfed in effulgent light and his countenance shone 'like the Sun' at a 'high place'.[392,393] Finally we can distinguish Jesus's betrayal by his disciple Judas,[394] and his subsequent death by execution.

These four major episodic themes thus appear in both the seasonal progression of the year and in the Jesus story, with obviously similar thematic correspondences. Their chronological sequence in the Jesus story is not exactly the same as in the course of a single year-cycle, since Jesus's resurrection at the spring equinox could not have sensibly fitted the story narrative as occurring between the time of his birth and that of his flourishing. However, it's notable that the traditional 'feast days' of the Christian liturgical calendar which annually mark the principal parts of the Jesus story *do* in fact follow the corresponding sequence of the year chronology, as if such a living calendrical timeline was ultimately more important than the various fragmentary textual narratives that were originally gathered together and collated to comprise the corpus that became the officially accepted canon.[395]

At this juncture it's nevertheless important to ask: might a general parallel exist between the progression of the year and the trajectory of *any* person's life, in the sense of a developmental sequence? If such a general parallel were the case, then clearly it would be nonsensical to point to an especial correspondence between the sequence of the year and the life of Jesus in particular, more than for any other individual (assuming for the moment a non-mythical status for Jesus). Later on we explore this possibility and we argue that there is indeed a discernible 'overall' parallel or metaphor between the seasonal sequence of the year and that of human life (of birth, growth, decay and death).[396] However, this general or overall parallel does not contain the recognisably distinct and particular correspondences of points in the year-cycle as does the outline story of Jesus that we describe above.

---

[390] The traditional day of Jesus's birth is the 'feast' of Christmas, which has been observed on 25 December—three days after the winter solstice—since at least as early as the 3rd century CE (see Hippolytus, 204).

[391] The Christian texts describe how Jesus was crucified around the date of the Passover or spring equinox (John 19:14) and was miraculously resurrected from the dead 'on the third day' afterwards (1 Corinthians 15:3–7). The Christian 'feast' day that commemorates the resurrection of Jesus is Easter, which is the first Sunday after the first full moon following the spring equinox.

[392] Matthew 17:1-2

[393] The 'feast of the transfiguration' is traditionally held in the days of summer in August.

[394] Matthew 26:14

[395] Keeler, 1888

[396] See Chapter 4.

172

We are not all, like Jesus in the story, born shortly after the winter solstice, as the solar year may be said to be. We do not all experience the apex of our lives by being visibly exalted in effulgent light whilst at a high place, whereas the parallel between the 'transfiguration' of Jesus with his face 'shining like the Sun' and the actual Sun at the height of summer is clearly a close analogy. Do we all become 'betrayed' by an agent of death, as the year is 'betrayed' by the arrival of the decaying time of Scorpio (i.e., late autumn), leading into winter? One might say so, though one might also say that Jesus's betrayal by Judas is certainly a better and more dramatic parallel with the seeming 'betrayal into death' of the year than the average person's encounter with old age and decease. Certainly we do not all become resurrected at the spring equinox (except perhaps psychologically), but in the case of the Jesus story we are to understand that Jesus was indeed physically resurrected, and just at that time of the year that marks the physical rebirth of life. We might therefore say that the Jesus story looks more like an allegory or metaphor of the progression of the year than does the life of an average person.

Furthermore, and unlike some of the other more general or overall 'year myths' that we discuss, there are not only these dramatic scene-like correspondences between the broad, major points of the year's progression and the Jesus story. Correspondences of many quite specific and identifiable images, events and astronomical phenomena, over and above the four main points mentioned above, are in fact referenced appositely, either in the earliest texts or in later traditions, to the point where they amount to a re-telling of the succession of the zodiacal signs. We might therefore proceed through a descriptive account, not only of the four major points as mentioned above, but also through these more specific elements of similarity, one by one, and note the quite comprehensive correspondence, analogy or parallel between the course of the year and the story of Jesus, which together they constitute.

Jesus was born on Christmas Day[397]—three days after the winter solstice (the beginning of the sign Capricorn), when the returning (lengthening) daylight can begin to be discerned. This theme of 'the birth of the Sun' or 'the birth of the light' seems to be emphasised in the story (rather than the specific thematic keywords of the sign Capricorn) and seems appropriate when we consider that Jesus asserted that he was *the light of the world*.[398] Following this representative nativity, Jesus reputedly began his 'ministry' thirty days later,[399] symbolically corresponding to the thirty days of this first sign, bringing him thence to the sign Aquarius. At this point he meets the somewhat unconventional character of John the Baptist (he wore camels' hair and ate only locusts and wild honey),[400] whose practice of baptism virtually restates the Aquarian symbol of a man pouring water from a pitcher. Furthermore, just as the season which corresponds to the

---

[397] Hippolytus, 204
[398] John 8:12, 9:5
[399] Luke 3:23
[400] Matthew 3:4; Mark 1:6

time of year of the sign Aquarius 'looks forward' to better times to come, so John the Baptist expressly looks forward to the 'better man' to come, that is, Jesus.[401]

Not long after Jesus's meeting with John the Baptist, an odd thing happens in the gospel narrative: John the Baptist is 'put into prison', though this is recorded quite blandly and draws no comment from Jesus, who merely continues on his way to Galilee.[402] This part of the story, devoid of any explanatory embellishment, may be an allegory of the *constellation* Aquarius, representing John the Baptist, which at this sign's time of year appears lower and lower in the sky at sunset until, at the end of the sign Aquarius, it disappears under the horizon (is 'put into prison'), to be replaced in the Sun's path by the constellation Pisces. Jesus, as the Sun, does not react, but simply 'goes on his way to Galilee'. As we have noted, the word 'Galilee' in Greek ('Γαλιλαία') means 'circuit' or 'circle', and may well have originally been a term representing the annual path or circuit of the Sun (i.e., the ecliptic or zodiac). Thus the allegory of this curious episode in the story may simply be that the constellation Aquarius ('John the Baptist') becomes occluded by the horizon at the observing time of sunset at this time of year ('put in prison') and thereafter the Sun ('Jesus') carries on its way through the circuit of the zodiac ('Galilee').

This would bring the Jesus narrative to the sign Pisces, and at this point, the story involves decidedly Piscean themes. Remembering that the Piscean time of the year reflects the fasting period of 'Lent' when food stocks are low and self-abnegation is imposed by nature, we read that Jesus spends a prolonged time fasting in the desert, being in his extreme hunger tormented by tempting visions from the devil.[403] Recalling also that Pisces is symbolised by two fishes, we note that Jesus then happens upon *two fishermen*, Simon and Peter.[404] Jesus then engages in particularly characteristic Piscean self-denial through acts of healing and through the message of the sublimely self-abnegating 'sermon on the mount', being so self-denying as to make the exhortation to "*love your enemies, bless them that curse you, do good to them that hate you, and pray for them which despitefully use you, and persecute you.*"[405]

After Pisces comes Aries, the ram or lamb, associated with the rebirth of life in the natural world at the spring equinox. Jesus's miraculous resurrection is an extremely appropriate allegory of the Sun's revival of life at the spring time of this sign, as are the accounts of the rebirth of other dying-and-rising deities in other solar-year myths. If the resurrection in the New Testament story is taken as a parallel to the sign Aries, then we note that the event does not follow the zodiac sign sequence in the story narrative, to come after the biblical events corresponding to the earlier signs, as described above. Indeed it could not, since doing

---

[401] John the Baptist says, "He that cometh after me is mightier than I, whose shoes I am not worthy to bear." (Matthew 3:11.)

[402] Matthew 4:12; Mark 1:14

[403] Matthew 4:2

[404] Matthew 4:18; Mark 1:16

[405] Matthew 5:44

so would cause it to intervene anachronistically between Jesus's birth (at the winter solstice) and the remainder of his life (through the rest of the year). We may reflect however that, in an allegory of the Sun's journey through the year, while there seems good reason to include a representation of 'birth' at the winter solstice,[406] the theme of the 'miraculous rebirth' of Sun-engendered life in the spring is certainly too compelling to omit, regardless of strict chronological order.

The thematic correspondence of the resurrection to the Aries time of rebirth is unambiguous. Furthermore we have seen that the traditional annual 'feast days' of the church calendar—including that which commemorates the resurrection— do indeed follow the zodiac sequence, with the result that the living celebration of the Jesus story in practice is quite in accordance with the progression of the year with its seasonal-zodiacal themes. The 'Jesus story as year allegory' might, one suppose, have alternatively told of his birth in the spring, but the spring time of year had already long been strongly associated with ancient symbolic rituals of rebirth, such as in the Passover.[407] It is more fitting, then, that the story and the living tradition in the Christian calendar fix upon a winter solstice birth and a spring equinox rebirth. In assessing the life of Jesus as an allegory of the Sun's journey through the year therefore, both a birth at the winter solstice and a rebirth at the spring equinox seem appropriate.

The characterisation of Aries also arises in the gospel of John. We read that John the Baptist hails Jesus, saying, *"Behold the Lamb of God, which taketh away the sin of the world"*.[408] We have already seen how the sign Aries represents the completely fresh, new and 'sin-free' beginning of things, following the karma-cleansing period of self-denial represented by Pisces. Thus John the Baptist's words seem to recapitulate well the theme of Aries as the 'taking away' of sin or karma, as inherent in Jesus as the 'lamb of God'. With this in mind we also note that, at the time of the Jewish spring equinox Passover ritual, which involves verifying that the sacrificial lamb has no faults or blemishes,[409] and shortly before his execution—often seen, as in John the Baptist's remark, as a sacrifice that takes away 'the sins of the world'— Jesus was 'examined' by Pilate and was similarly found to have 'no fault'.[410]

As we noted in Chapter 3 when discussing Aries in the context of the Christian tradition, we may also trace Jesus's *conception* to the beginning of the sign Aries (the spring equinox), by reason of the traditional account of his birth at the winter solstice. A date approximating the spring equinox was indeed officially marked as the 'Feast of the Annunciation' (the occasion of Jesus's conception) by the Christian church at the Council of Toledo in 656.[411,412] Thus the allegory seems to be that Jesus as the Sun is 'conceived' at the spring equinox, 'born' nine months

---

[406] The Sun is 'born' at the time of the winter solstice, in so far as its light in the day at last begins to lengthen after months of apparently waning power.

[407] See Appendix 2: *The Judaeo-Christian Passover.*

[408] John 1:29

[409] See Appendix 2: *The Judaeo-Christian Passover.*

[410] John 18:38, 19:4

[411] Exactly, the 25th of March.

[412] Baynes, 1878

later at the winter solstice or Christmas (the 'birth' of the Sun's light and power) and resurrected or reborn again (typically marked by a sacrifice) at the spring equinox (the time of the Passover).[413]

There appears to be nothing either in the Christian New Testament texts or in later developed traditions of the religion which particularly denotes or otherwise symbolises the theme or characteristics of the sign Taurus. The next sign Gemini however does make an appearance, in the form of a mythological representation of the two main (brightest) stars of its constellation. As we saw in the discussion of the sign Gemini, the two disciples James and his brother John, the sons of Zebedee, are indisputable representations of Castor and Pollux, the Dioscuri of Greek myth and the sons of Zeus (Jupiter). That these disciples are indeed symbols of the Dioscuri is reinforced by the scriptural text's reference to these deities' ability to 'call fire from heaven', as they did in the Greek tale of Jason and the Argonauts, as well as by their request to be seated next to Jesus, as they similarly requested to their father Zeus in the earlier myth.[414]

The periods of the year marking the signs Cancer and Leo both tend to be thought of in terms of 'summer'. It's often difficult to recognise that the days start to become shorter after the summer solstice at the beginning of Cancer as, meteorologically, the weather frequently continues to be 'summery' well into the time of the sign Leo. This common conflation of the signs Cancer and Leo as the year's 'height of the Sun' seems to be reflected in the New Testament texts. There is nevertheless a curious passage in the Jesus story that seems to be tied specifically to the sign Cancer, or at least to the constellation that bears that name. We read that Jesus rides into Jerusalem, impossibly on two animals at the same time—a colt *and* an ass.[415] This passage is nonsensical if read literally, but is comprehensible once it is understood that the two animals are in fact representations of two of the main stars in the constellation Cancer, namely, *Asellus Australis*, the 'southern ass-colt or donkey' (*delta Cancri*), and another called *Asellus Borealis*, the 'northern ass-colt or donkey' (*gamma Cancri*). The sign Cancer's representation of that part of the year following the summer solstice and the joyous time of the summer resonates well with the figure of Jesus, as the Sun, triumphantly entering Jerusalem—the heart of the story's geographical region as much as the heart of the year—by 'riding' the two conspicuous stars of the constellation Cancer at the same time.

The feast of the birth of John the Baptist is placed on 24th June, roughly at the time of the summer solstice, and indeed we may infer his birth to be at that date, since in the New Testament we read that his mother Elisabeth was in the sixth month of her pregnancy when Mary conceived Jesus,[416] which latter date must have been at the spring equinox if we accept that Jesus himself was born at the

---

[413] See Chapter 3 for more on Christian traditions at the time of the spring equinox in Aries.

[414] See Chapter 3 for details of Gemini's Castor and Pollux in the Christian New Testament texts.

[415] Matthew 21:7

[416] Luke 1:36

winter solstice.[417] As was mentioned earlier in the section on the sign Cancer, the significance of John the Baptist being born at the summer solstice when the Sun is at its 'highest point' but immediately about to decline in terms of daylight, is borne out by Jesus describing John as *"a burning and shining lamp, and you were willing to rejoice for a while in his light"*,[418] and by John's statement that Jesus (a representation of the Sun as it *ascends* from the winter solstice) 'must become greater' while he (John, a representation of the Sun as it *declines* from the summer solstice) 'must become less'.[419]

The 'height of the Sun's power' through the signs Cancer and Leo also appears to be represented in the New Testament text by Jesus's 'transfiguration': Jesus (the Sun) climbs to a 'high point' (the Sun in the northern hemisphere is at its highest point in the sky at the summer solstice) and is then 'transfigured' in bright light, while his face 'shone like the Sun'.[420] The Catholic 'Feast of the Transfiguration' is actually observed on 6th August, in the middle of the 'impressive summer' sign Leo. As we noted in the main section on the sign Leo, it is interesting that, just before the transfiguration, Jesus predicts his death, reminding his disciples (or the reader) that, although the Sun is then at the moment of the peak of its influence in terms of daylight and warmth, it will inevitably descend towards the 'dying' part of of the year in autumn and winter.[421] Generally we see that both the signs Cancer and Leo seem to share in the representation of 'the height of the Sun's power' in the Christian New Testament, astronomically and meteorologically, much as they commonly do in the natural world.

From Leo we pass to Virgo, and it seems clear that the prime candidate for a symbolic representation of Virgo is Mary, the famously virgin mother of Jesus. We saw in Chapter 3 that the developed thematic presentation of Mary is an exact restatement of the characteristics of the zodiac sign Virgo: the demure and pure virgin, fitting to bear fruit, whether physical or spiritual. The appearance of Jesus's virgin mother does not follow any obvious chronological sequence in the New Testament narrative which would fit into a simple 'story of the progression of the zodiac'. She does not, for instance, appear directly after the events of the Cancer/Leo transfiguration. The appearance of the virgin Mary as 'mother of God' in the narrative occurs chiefly in the account of Jesus's nativity. Nevertheless we cannot ignore that her later iconography corresponds overwhelmingly to the zodiacal Virgo; like Isis and Demeter in more ancient myth, she appears as a deific aspect of that sign, the virgin fecundity or promise which is able to bring forth the fruits of the solar spirit upon Earth.[422]

---

[417] As we noted earlier, the date of John the Baptist's *conception* was duly placed around the time of the autumnal equinox, and the Catholic 'Feast of the Conception of John the Baptist' takes place approximately at that date, on 24 September.

[418] John 5:35

[419] John 3:30

[420] Matthew 17:1; Mark 9:2; Luke 9:28

[421] Matthew 16:21

[422] See Chapter 3 for a more detailed account of the symbolism of the virgin Mary in the Christian New Testament and later iconography.

Virgo's succeeding sign Libra seems to have no thematic correspondence in the New Testament narrative, though we note that the beginning of this sign—the autumnal equinox—must correspond to the date of John the Baptists's conception, since his mother Elisabeth was recorded to be in her sixth month of pregnancy when Mary conceived,[423] which must in turn have been at the spring equinox if Jesus was born at the winter solstice (and indeed some Christian traditions still honour the 'Feast of the Conception of St John the Baptist' on 23rd September, being roughly the date of the autumnal equinox).

At this point in the story,[424] we read with some puzzlement that Jesus cursed and withered a fig tree when he was hungry and found no fruit on it, despite the text itself describing how it was not the season for such fruit. We have read much dense and recondite material asserting that this act actually somehow represents Jesus's oddly abrupt cursing of Israel and the Jews for their lack of belief in him;[425] or that it is a display of the 'rigours of his justice', showing *"his justice on the sinners who bring forth not the expected fruits of grace";*[426] or even that it represents a stern reference to the tree in the garden of Eden, the apparent misuse of which by Adam and Eve brought bad things into the world.[427] However, it may simply represent the presence of autumn, when the leaves fall off the trees. The episode appears in the correct place, relative to the other events, for such a seasonal reference (for instance in the gospel of Matthew), though it might be hard to decide whether to attribute such a simple autumnal reference to Libra or Scorpio.

After Libra we come to Scorpio, the sign of unmasking, of the transformation of the life-force, and of death. As we've seen, the season of Scorpio represents the 'fall' of the year, the 'unmasking' of trees of their leaves, and figuratively the 'betrayal' of the Sun's light into darkness. It is not difficult to see the symbolic counterpoint of this process in the New Testament's betrayal of Jesus by Judas, representing the ineluctable regenerative force in the time of Scorpio.[428] Judas is the 'one of the twelve' (disciples, signs or months) who betrays Jesus (the Sun) with a kiss (the 'kiss of death'), leading to the latter's death by crucifixion. We have indeed seen how the figure of the scorpion has been used as a symbol of Judas himself.[429]

Following Scorpio we come to Sagittarius, which we might at first think suffers the same fate as Taurus, as there appears to be no obviously discernible allusion to Sagittarius's associated themes in the story of Jesus. However we have seen how Sagittarius is associated with law, judgement and justice, which is precisely what Jesus is forced to confront at this point, in the person of the Roman legal governor Pilate, whose name ('πειλατος', Strong's Greek #4091) means

---

[423] Luke 1:36

[424] Matthew 21:18; Mark 11:12-14, 11:20-26

[425] Burkett, 2002; Dumbrell, 2001

[426] MacEvilly, 2017

[427] Smith, 2023

[428] The ineluctability of this part of the year, as represented in the story, is even alluded to by Jesus, when he says at the 'last supper' that *"one of you shall betray me"* (Matthew 26:21).

[429] See Chapter 3.

'armed with a spear'—descriptive of the constellation Sagittarius, which was frequently symbolised as a centaur wielding a spear rather than a bow and arrow.[430]

After Sagittarius we pass to Capricorn, and we note that this is the sign which corresponds to the time of the year and to the narrative episode in the New Testament where we *began* the story of Jesus, at his birth. This nativity, as the 'birth of the Sun' at the time of Christmas, shortly after the winter solstice at the beginning of Capricorn, when the daylight begins to 'return' (increase in length), can certainly be seen as a symbol of this sign's season, if not of the more specific Capricorn-themed keywords. However, Jesus's story, following his arraignment before the Sagittarian Pilate, is not yet finished, but continues with the account of his death by crucifixion and his subsequent miraculous resurrection—the latter, as we have seen, having being already symbolised by Aries. After Sagittarius then, the themes of Capricorn, Aquarius and Pisces are not repeated in the New Testament narrative; the story instead continues to his death and from there to his resurrection—analogously, straight to Aries.

We therefore see that there is undeniably *some* form of a recognisable metaphor or allegory of the Sun's journey through the year in the story of Jesus. The year's major themes of 'the birth of the Sun' (the beginning of an increase in daylight) at the winter solstice (the Christmas nativity), its 'high point' at the summer solstice (the 'transfiguration'), its 'kiss of death' in the autumn (the betrayal by Judas) leading to its 'death' in the winter and thence to its 'rebirth in spring' (Jesus's resurrection) are, as in other year myths, emphasised *overall* in the narrative, over and above an exact adherence to the sequential enumeration of the zodiac signs. Further allusions to the zodiacal signs—and even sometimes to elements of their original constellations—are however also apparent (and for the most part, in the correct zodiacal sequence), in the depictions of Aquarius as the water-pouring John the Baptist; as Pisces in the Lenten desert-fasting, the fishermen-disciples Simon and Peter and the self-abnegating 'sermon on the mount'; as Aries in Jesus's resurrection and his role as the *"lamb of God, which taketh away the sin of the world"*; as Gemini in the identity of his close disciples James and John as the Dioscuri or that constellation's principle stars Castor and Pollux; as Cancer in that constellation's 'donkey stars' of *Asellus Australis* and *Asellus Borealis* upon both of which he (impossibly) rode in triumph into Jerusalem; as Leo in Jesus's 'transfiguration';[431] as Virgo in the developed description and iconography of his mother the virgin Mary; and as Sagittarius in the figure of Pilate.

Except for Taurus and Libra, each sign of the zodiac is represented in an appropriately thematic way in the Jesus story. Each of these representations takes the form of an incident or image that is relevant to the theme of the sign. They also all derive directly from the early New Testament texts themselves, with the exception of Jesus's birth as being on the winter solstice at Capricorn (which date

---

[430] Bagdasarov, 2001

[431] We note the difficulty in teasing apart the signs Cancer and Leo as indicators of 'the impressive height of the Sun's power in summer'.

of the year was not set until some two hundred years after the purported time of his life) and of his virgin mother as Virgo, whose thematic and iconographic sign-correspondences appear to have derived from continuing traditions developing after the compilation of the various original sources.

Furthermore, taking the comprehensive gospel of Matthew as our main guide, the order in which these representations appears in the text is virtually the same as their order in the zodiac, the only aberrations to or absences of zodiacal sequencing being for the signs Aries, Gemini and Virgo. In the case of Aries, as we discuss above, the placement of Jesus's resurrection at the spring equinox, though thematically exact, is necessarily at variance with a strictly sequential story taken as occurring during the course of one year. John the Baptist certainly hails Jesus in terms which are unequivocally redolent of the theme of Aries, but the account of this (in the gospel of John) appears just *before* Jesus's Piscean encounter with the fishermen Simon and Peter, and not just *after* it, as might be expected if the sequence were to hold precisely at every turn.

In the case of Gemini, there is a definite reference of the disciples James and John to the Dioscuri Castor and Pollux, the stars of the constellation Gemini (in Mark and Luke), but this does not appear just before any Cancerian theme (for instance, just before the reference to the two Cancerian 'donkey-stars' upon which Jesus impossibly rode into Jerusalem). In the case of the sign Virgo, we see that, although the developed descriptions of Jesus's virgin mother Mary perfectly encapsulate the theme of Virgo, there is no episodic allusion to her (nor any other Virgo-like symbolism) in the story where some representation of Virgo might be expected, as for instance just before Judas's Scorpio-like betrayal.[432] Concerning the less than perfect sequence of sign-representations, it should be borne in mind that there are in any case great difficulties in reconciling sequences of events between the gospel texts themselves. In addition we would again draw attention to the fact that the textual sources of the Jesus story were arbitrarily collated from many disparate forms to finally comprise the arrangement which constitutes the current officially received version.[433] It may also be pointed out that there are curious passages in the New Testament which even seem to hint overtly at a zodiacal and astrological-planetary basis for the narrative. In the gospel of Mark the figure of Jesus himself seems to allude to such an allegory when he says to his disciples:

> Having eyes, see ye not? and having ears, hear ye not? and do ye
> not remember? When I brake the five loaves among five thousand,
> how many baskets full of fragments took ye up? They say unto him,
> Twelve. And when the seven among four thousand, how many
> baskets full of fragments took ye up? And they said, Seven. And he
> said unto them, How is it that ye do not understand?[434]

---

[432] There is indeed the parable of the ten *virgins* just at that point, but we feel that this does not adduce a particularly Virgoan theme.

[433] Keeler, 1888

[434] Mark 8:18-21

When we recall the twelve tribes of Hebraic Israel, the 'woman with a crown of twelve stars' and the 'Tree of Life' yielding 'twelve kinds of fruit each month' in the Book of Revelation,[435] and the proliferation of the number seven in other books of the New Testament (see Chapter 2), it would seem positively obtuse for an intelligent modern—or even then-contemporary—reader not to suspect, at least, an allusion to the twelve signs and the seven classical planets in this passage.

We feel that it seems fair to conclude that in the Christian Jesus story, it seems impossible to deny that some sort of allegory of the year and its course, including specific references to individual signs (and those largely in the correct zodiacal sequence) is certainly discernible, and for the most part from the original texts (though in the case of the signs Capricorn and Virgo, from scriptural, religious and cultural developments which post-dated the texts that were collated to be the accepted canon of the New Testament). Was the story of Jesus expressly fabricated, even if over a period of years, to be a deliberate allegorical myth of the Sun's journey through the year? We think it unlikely. However, if Jesus was indeed an historical person, then it is certainly interesting how these familiar and perennial symbols of solar myth accrued to his story and his later iconography. We might perhaps conclude that the overall lineaments of that central solar mythical archetype somehow naturally emerged in humankind's collective unconscious, being ineluctably drawn to form amidst the fragmentary mass of historical account, myth, quasi-spiritual works and folk traditions which were conceived, amalgamated and textually inscribed over prolonged periods of time. The projection here was not onto the scattered stars, but rather into the various cultural and scriptural traditions, scattered over generations. We should not forget however, that even if the story is wholly a myth, it is just as much a potential source of spirituality, as if it were true.

Europe — Yarilo

Yarilo (Cyrillic: Ярило)[436] is a mythic or divine representation of vegetation, fertility, springtime rebirth and the year-cycle generally in Slavic countries. The name derives from a proto-Slavic root roughly corresponding to the meaning 'youthful life-force'. Until as recently as the 19th century, folk festivals celebrating the return of nature's vitality in the spring were celebrated in Slavic countries, with Yarilo as the eponymous deification of that natural regenerative energy. Yarilo was represented in myth as a vigorous youth adorned with a crown of wildflowers and holding a sheaf of wheat. Effigies of the deity were processed through the countryside and stories told of the triumphant return of Yarilo from distant lands. In autumn his effigy was burned after the harvest to ensure the return of his fecundity the following year.[437] A 12th century biography of the

---

[435] Revelation 12:1, 22:2

[436] There are various spellings of this deity, including *Yarilo, Jarilo, Iarilo, Jarylo, Yaryla, Juraj, Jurij* and *Gerovit*.

[437] Dixon-Kennedy, 1998a

German bishop Otto of Bamberg recounts how, in his attempts to convert Slavic pagans, he encountered spring festivals along with other dedicatory emblems in honour of an 'idol' called *Gerovit*, being a German variant appellation of Yarilo.[438] Yarilo was seen as a form of a dying and resurrecting deity representing the life-force of vegetative nature, decaying in the autumn after the harvest and thereafter dwelling in the underworld (in ancient Slavic countries, supposedly located across the sea in a place to where where migratory birds flew), only to return in spring to bring fertility and vigour to the land once more.[439]

Ireland & Scotland — Cailleach and Brighid

In Gaelic myth the two major seasonal halves of the year have been characterised as two goddesses, *Cailleach* and *Brighid*. Cailleach (also known in Scotland as *Beira*) was represented as an old hag, the queen of winter, ruling the months between Samhain (1st November) and Beltane (1st May). Cailleach was associated with snow-capped mountain peaks and was said to carry a staff that would freeze the ground.[440] Legend held that if Cailleach intends a long winter, she makes the weather on Imbolc (1st February) sunny so that she can get about to gather more winter firewood; if however she intends winter to be short, Imbolc will be overcast and dark. Brighid was rather associated with aspects of the year's more benign progress after Imbolc (her feast day) and the beginning of spring, such as healing, protection, domestication and poetry. In the Middle Ages Brighid was syncretised (culturally subsumed in identification) by the Christian church as Saint Brigid, who shared many of the goddess's thematic characteristics. Cailleach and Brighid have been seen as two aspects of a single Gaelic goddess of the year.[441]

Wales — The Mabinogion

The *Mabinogion* is a collection of the earliest prose stories of Britain, compiled in Welsh around the 12th century from much more ancient oral traditions. In the fourth book of the epic, we read a curious tale that, like many myths, makes no sense whatever until it is understood as an allegory of the solar year. The story tells of the adventures of a male hero named Lleu Llaw Gyffes. The hero was sorcerously contrived by the magician *Gwydion* to be born of a virgin named *Arianrhod* or *Aranrhod* (meaning 'silver wheel' in Welsh).[442] The boy was cursed by his mother never to have a name, unless it was one given to him by her, but Gwydion nevertheless tricked Arianrhod into unintentionally naming the boy 'the golden-haired one with the skilful hand' (or sometimes, 'the lion with the

---

[438] Robinson, 1920

[439] Katičić, 2010

[440] Mackenzie, 1917; Briggs, 1967

[441] McNeill, 2013

[442] We note that Lleu, like Jesus Christ and Attis, is born of a virgin, and both have been interpreted as representations of the Sun in its course through year.

steady hand'); thus the boy became named as Lleu Llaw Gyffes, which has that meaning in Welsh. He is often referred to as simply Lleu, sometimes spelled Llew, the Welsh word for 'lion'.

It has been something of received wisdom in recent times to dismiss the notion that Lleu is a deific-heroic representation of the Sun. This has mostly been the result of some fastidious etymological theorising that, firstly, the name Lleu *possibly* derived from the Proto-Celtic "Lugus" (the name of a Celtic deity), and that secondly, *if* that is so, this name could not have derived from the Proto-Indo-European root *leuk* meaning 'light' or 'brightness', since the 'k' consonant suffix could not have developed into a 'g' sound.[443] It seems improbable however that the Proto-Indo-European root *leuk* (from which is derived the Latin 'lux' and the Greek 'λευκός' or *leukós*, both meaning 'light') could *never* have become phonologically altered in the vernacular to 'Lug', 'Lugus', or indeed Lleu. In any case, these etymological quibbles are, as we shall see, comprehensively and finally vitiated by an analysis of the Mabinogion narrative which shows unequivocally that Lleu is indeed a mythical representation of the Sun—particularly the *light* of the Sun, as it increases and decreases with the cycle of the year (the basis of many myths and the adventures of heroes and deities).

In the tale of the Mabinogion, Lleu's mother Arianrhod places another curse on him: that he will never have a human wife; but Gwydion frustrates this curse by magically making a beautiful woman from the sweetest flowers of the countryside. She is named *Blodeuwedd* (meaning 'face of flowers' or 'face of blossoms' in Welsh) and becomes Lleu's bride. But Blodeuwedd falls in love with *Gronw Pebr* (sometimes called *Goronwy*), an evil lord of Penllyn, and invites him into her castle, where they become lovers and set about to discover how they might be able to kill Lleu in order to be together. To this end, Blodeuwedd asks Lleu outright how he may be killed. Lleu replies that the only way he may be killed is by the use of a spear which has been a whole year in the making, and only when he is standing with one foot on a cauldron placed under a roof, and the other foot placed on a young goat. This peculiar tale goes on to tell how Blodeuwedd betrays Lleu by revealing this information to her lover Gronw, who lies in ambush with a spear he has indeed spent a year making, while she persuades Lleu to show her the curious posture in which he may be killed. As soon as Lleu enacts the pose he has described, Gronw fires the spear into his side. After being struck, Lleu is not however killed, but is transformed into an eagle, and flies away. The evil Gronw then takes possession of the land.

This tale appears to be nothing but pregnant nonsense until it is explained as an allegory of the Sun facing its 'demise' in the 'darker' half of the year at the autumn equinox, midway between the summer and winter solstices. Lleu ('the golden-haired one', or 'the lion'—names obviously symbolic of the Sun, the former by description of its corona and the latter through its rulership of the sign Leo) is only 'killed' (his light only fails), when he is betrayed by Blodeuwedd (a

---

[443] Schrijver, 1995

woman who closely resembles the vegetative fecundity of the sign Virgo), into poising or balancing between a cauldron 'placed under a roof' (that is, in the domestic setting of a house, a symbol of the nourishing domestic arena of the sign Cancer) and a goat (the sign Capricorn)—in other words, at the autumn equinox, the time of the year when the Sun is 'balanced' (at Libra, the balance or scales) between the summer solstice at the sign Cancer and the winter solstice at the sign Capricorn; and it is at the autumn equinox at Libra of course that the Sun's light 'fails', in so far as the darkness of night (symbolised by Gronw) becomes longer than the day and so begins to 'rule' the land. It is in this precarious position in the year that the Sun may look towards its eventual 'demise' through autumn and towards winter. Furthermore, following his 'fall', Lleu does not actually die, but turns into an eagle (the 'higher' symbol of the sign Scorpio).

So we see that this otherwise nonsensical tale in the Mabinogion tells us, in the form of a riddle of symbols, that, in his yearly progression, the Sun (Lleu the 'golden-haired one' or the lion) begins to fail or fall (to lose his power of light) when the sign Virgo (Blodeuwedd) 'betrays' him to the sign Libra—the 'balanced position' between the sign Cancer (the domestic cauldron) and the sign Capricorn (the goat), being the point of the autumn equinox when the darkness (Gronw) begins to rule, though the Sun duly goes on to become Scorpio (the eagle). The tale in fact continues with further allegories of the progression of the Sun through the zodiac. After Lleu's transformation into an eagle, the magician Gwydion wanders through the countryside until he comes upon the house of a peasant, who tells Gwydion that his sow goes out every day and disappears, no-one knowing where, *"any more than if she sank into the earth"*. Gwydion tells the peasant that he will watch to see where the sow goes. He does so, and observes that the sow capers off to a valley called *Nantlleu*, which may be translated as 'the valley of Lleu'. He sees the sow feeding off rotten flesh, maggots and other decomposing material. It seems clear that the sow here represents the Sun progressing in its course through the sign of Scorpio ('Lleu's Valley'), with its signature elements of death and decomposition.[444] Above the sow, at the top of a tree, Gwydion sees an eagle. The eagle once again symbolises Scorpio, but here in the traditionally 'higher' or more virtuous aspect of the sign. Gwydion sings to the bird, and gradually it descends from the tree until Gwydion is able to strike him with his magic wand, whereupon it transforms itself back into Lleu. Lleu (as the Sun having experienced the dark and leaner part of the year) appears to Gwydion as a *"piteous sight, for he was nothing but skin and bone"*, but *"before the end of the year he was quite healed"*.

Lleu begins to speak of a recompense for the treachery meted to him by Blodeuwedd and Gronw. Lleu and Gwydion accordingly set off for the land usurped by his betrayers, and they eventually catch up with the pair. Gwydion

---

[444] 'Lleu's Valley' is reminiscent of the tunnel, leading under mountains along the 'path of the Sun' and guarded by 'scorpion people', through which the Mesopotamian hero Gilgamesh had to travel in his journey through the underworld (see the section on Scorpio in Chapter 3).

turns Blodeuwedd into an owl as her punishment, while Lleu demands that Gronw must stand in the same place where he (Lleu) was when Gronw struck him, and Lleu in the place where Gronw was. Despite protests, Gronw is forced to do this, and this time Lleu spears and kills Gronw. Thus in this completion of the allegory, Lleu as the Sun, having passed through to the other, lighter 'side' of the year cycle, now reclaims his former strength and power by seeing Gronw as the darkness standing in the same relation to the zodiac, but this time looking in the reverse direction, to the Spring equinox and the following happier times of sunshine and summer.

The Arthurian Legends

At this point we would like to draw the reader's attention to a possibility that the authors have for long suspected but have not had time to formulate properly. We believe it almost certain that the Arthurian legend, in its overall or outline form, is another rendering of the solar myth, not deliberately set down as such by any one specific writer, but brought into being by the natural accretion of its elements in the collective unconscious from a myriad of sources in Britannic traditions since mediaeval times or earlier. We had once looked upon this conjecture as purely speculative, though as time has passed we have been more and more persuaded of it, and we feel obliged to disclose our suspicions, briefly describe them, and let the reader form his or her own opinion on the matter.

Difficulty has plagued attempts to find an historical Arthur, as it has with attempts to find an historical Jesus. In the case of Arthur, scholarship has come up against a perhaps less culturally sensitive dead-end, ending in somewhat uninspiring identifications of the figure with Romano-British warlords and military leaders, such as *Riothamus*,[445] which rather bland linkages add no further substantive information and amount to little more than a change of name, made more colourless by the absence of anything in the way of explication or even of interest concerning the various features of the actual legends, which, after all, have been the most compelling aspects in the first place. Nothing could be less interesting than an essentially unavailing search for an historical Arthur figure which entirely glosses over the psychological significance of the account as myth or legend.

In a summary of the legend, we see a central hero—a king (Arthur)—attended by a number of equal but subordinate knights with various personalities, who gather about a 'round table'. The number of the 'knights of the round table' varies considerably in the different sources, though it is however curious that if someone is asked, *"How many knights of Arthur's round table were there?"* most people will commonly answer that the number was twelve. The knights are seen as continually on a quest to secure the 'Holy Grail', being a sacred or magical chalice or cup which provides sustenance and healing. The king is taught and

---

[445] Ashe, 1985

advised by a magician (Merlin). The king is betrayed by the sexual union of his queen (Guinevere) and one of his knights (Lancelot). The legend is closely connected to a myth in which a 'fisher king' is charged with the protection of the grail, but who is wounded in the genitals by a lance as a punishment for forbidden love, which injury, since he is the embodiment of his lands, causes his kingdom to wither and become barren (the 'Wasteland') and forces him to bide his time—curiously, as a fisher—until another person, sometimes portrayed as an innocent and naïve young knight, can complete some task and so heal or renew him.

It seems clear that, in its summarised form as set out above, one can discern the components of the solar myth. King Arthur is the Sun (we recall that the Sun has frequently been identified with kingship). Arthur's close teacher and magician-adviser Merlin distinctly resembles the planet-function Mercury. Arthur presides over the signs in the form of his 'knights' who are represented as ranged about the 'round table'—very reminiscent of the zodiac, both in shape and function: a circular place for a set of distinct characters, the structure emphasising the equality of its constituent members. In the 13th century French text component of the legend, *La Queste del Saint Graal* ('The Quest of the Holy Grail'), we read that *"The Round Table was constructed, not without great significance, upon the advice of Merlin. By its name the Round Table is meant to signify the round world and round canopy of the planets and the elements in the firmament, where are to be seen the stars and many other things."*[446,447]

If Arthur is seen as the Sun, then the betrayal in the form of Lancelot and Guinevere's illicit sexual coupling is not dissimilar to the age-old personification of the year's 'betrayal' in the 'fall' of autumn, as told in various embodiments on the themes of sex and the concomitant threat of death, such as in that of Persephone's rape by Hades, and in Blodeuwedd and Gronw Pebr's betrayal of Lleu in the Mabinogion, which instances of 'wickedness' are seen to cause the experience of a barren and deathly 'wasteland' time of winter. This is more credible when viewed together with the interweaving of the 'fisher king' legend, with its account of the wounding to the king's genitals, since the 'wounding' in the case of the year-cycle naturally occurs in the autumnal time of Scorpio which is appropriately associated with sex, the sexual organs and the necessity of death, and which betokens the 'fall' of the year towards apparent death or near decrepitude, to be left only with a faint sense of hope for the future, dependent on an innocent and pure hero of renewal. Here of course we note that the wounded king who awaits the renewal of the land as a *fisher* is easily seen as an embodiment of Pisces the *fish*, the last sign of the year's zodiac, which similarly awaits the renewal of life in the natural world. The theme of cyclical rebirth in the interpretation of the Arthurian legend as solar year myth is supported by certain traditions which assert that Arthur never truly died but will again return, being thus referred to as the 'once and future king'.

---

446 Pauphilet, 1923
447 Comfort, 2000

The Arthurian legends are of course extremely fragmented and diverse. As was the case with other myths of the year-cycle from light to dark and again to light, from life to death and again to life, we do not think that they were consciously written down as deliberate exemplars of such a myth-story of the solar year, but rather that this primal myth naturally coalesced by way of the collective unconscious into the tales, to assume the outline shape that has become so familiar.

The Year-Cycle in Myth: A Summary

We have reviewed some of the world's mythological stories which, in dramatic form, recapture allegorically the primary aspect of the changing seasons on Earth—the 'fall' of the year (in terms of decreased light and warmth, along with the subsequent effects on vegetation and life generally) from autumn, into the deathly 'underworld' of the winter, and the joyous 'rebirth' of light, warmth and life in the spring. These myths often feature a 'solar hero' who embodies the Sun on this annual journey; one who dies or is taken to an underworld but whose spirit resurrects in the spring.

In Mesopotamia, Inana was this spirit of life in the natural world—life which dwindles away while she is 'dead' in the underworld, only to return when she returns. A variant of the story was told where Dumuzid embodies the seasonal change by spending half the year in the 'underworld' and the other half returned to the world of life. The yearly death and rebirth of vegetation is alternatively attributed in Mesopotamian myth to Ningishzida's descent and return to and from the underworld. In Egyptian myth the allegory is repeated when Osiris, personification of the growth, death and rebirth of vegetative life—the very distillation of the year cycle—and whose consort is the harvest goddess Isis, is murdered by Set, lord of barrenness and disharmony, though Osiris's spirit is resurrected as Horus. As we noted, the Egyptian account of the struggle between the positive figures of Osiris, Isis and Horus on the one hand, and the negative figure of Set on the other, was to some degree seen as an innate and natural antagonism in the order of the cosmos (or, we might say, as a polarised but holistic and stable nature of the major halves of the year-cycle).

In the Greek world, the beautiful mortal Adonis is taken to the underworld, to be reared by the fertility goddess Persephone, only to have the latter covet him for herself. Upon Zeus's intervention, Adonis, like the Mesopotamian Dumuzid, must spend half the year in the underworld and half in the realm of the living, once again allegorising the primary seasonal change of the year. In the Greek myth of Attis, the major seasonal theme is mythically alluded to once again when a beautiful male solar figure is changed into an evergreen tree following his death (or dormant state), only to resurrect at the spring equinox. In the Greek Demeter we essentially see Virgo, the fecund maiden, embodiment of the harvest. Her offspring Persephone is also restrained by the spirit of the underworld, causing dearth in the land. Despite Zeus's intervention, Persephone, like Dumuzid and

Adonis, must also spend half the year in the underworld, causing barrenness in the land, and half in the living world, allowing life. The fundamental seasonal allegory in the myth of Demeter and Persephone became so important to the Hellenistic mind that it became the meditative object of an intensely felt ritual— the Eleusinian mystery cult. As one writer remarked, *"Virgo was Demeter in Greece, who was analogous to Ishtar in Babylon and Isis in Egypt. Each of these goddesses travelled to the underworld to rescue a dead loved one - Demeter's daughter Persephone, Ishtar's husband Dumuzi (Tammuz), and Isis' husband/brother Osiris - and this was the mythical origin of autumn and spring."*[448]

A variety of religious texts originating from the first few centuries CE in Judaea were, over some years and for various reasons (often in the interests of powerful church leaders), brought together to describe a biographical account of an individual—Jesus—whose major life events have stark parallels with the age-old story of the Sun's journey through the major seasons of the year (and far more specifically than could be said to be the case for an average human being). This biographical account also contains specific references to zodiacal and other celestial phenomena that deal with the progression of the year, and for the most part in the correct sequence. The religion which was based upon the stories of this miraculous biography of Jesus became Christianity and was to reverberate around the world. It became endorsed by the Roman emperor Constantine around 312 CE and claimed a scriptural basis from a delimited set of the multifarious texts concerning the life and sayings of Jesus and his followers. Many ancient texts concerning Jesus were however excluded by powerful church leaders. As one bible scholar has described, the New Testament *"emerged out of the conflicts among Christian groups"*.[449]

Indeed there is ongoing debate and scholarship, not only regarding the question of what might constitute veridical textual accounts of the life and sayings of Jesus, but concerning the very historicity of the figure himself. The disputations between those who maintain that the stories of the now-canonical New Testament texts are the literal truth and those who see them as a fragmentary collection of mythical tales have been vigorous and trenchant. Those who see the texts as strictly historical accounts have argued extensively, as have those who have pointed to the lack of historical evidence and the mythical aspect of many of the stories.[450]

We do not pass judgement on this debate; we rather wish simply to point out that the life of Jesus certainly *appears* to recapitulate an allegory of the solar year in its major phases, and with many appropriately-placed seasonal and even celestial references. Indeed, the longer the story of Jesus has been officially held, consolidated and promulgated within the Christian church, the more comprehensively it has been set within a framework which admits of an allegory of the

---

[448] Rogers, 1998
[449] Ehrman, 2000
[450] Carrier, 2014; Doherty, 2012; Ehrman, 2012

year.[451] The 'fit' of the Jesus narrative to a solar allegory is bound to be contentious to those who cannot accept anything but the literal truth of the received selection of texts, but the compelling nature of the allegorical correspondence forces us at least to draw attention to it. It may be that Jesus existed historically and that his life, by sheer coincidence, happened to recapitulate the Sun's journey through the year more than could be said to be usual. Or it may be that we ourselves are guilty of an overwhelming confirmation bias that causes us to merely imagine the allegories which we only seem to see. Or it could be that Jesus did not exist and that the story is, at least in part, another allegory, in a long line of solar myths, of the seasons of the year. It will be for the reader to decide for him or herself which of these seems most likely to be correct.

In Europe, the legend of Yarilo in Slavic tradition tells of the year's life-force, symbolised by the spirit of verdant vegetation, dying after the autumn harvest, only to return in triumphal resurrection in the spring. In the Celtic world, the goddesses Cailleach and Brigid represent the two 'halves' of this perennial tale of the year's vital energy, Cailleach representing its absence in the winter and Brigid its return in spring. In the Welsh Mabinogion we find a truly extraordinary and cryptic characterisation of the light of the Sun being 'tricked' and apparently killed by the forces of darkness which manifest at autumn, only to re-emerge in the spring. The tale is remarkable for its colourful symbolism of specific signs of the zodiac in the course of its allegorical year narrative. We suspect there may be other such solar-year myths and symbolic references in the Mabinogion which remain to be unravelled. In the Arthurian legends we also see in outline form the signature symbols and actions of the solar myth, synthesised by the collective unconscious from diverse tales and narrative strands which, joining together as one, assume the shape of the general myth as iron filings form to make a pattern around a magnetic field.

We can see that the fundamental theme of the Sun's descent into a 'deathly' half of the year (of restricted light and warmth), often characterised by an allegorical betrayal or some appropriately negative force, only to be joyously resurrected in the spring, has been internalised as such an important and primordial process in humanity's collective unconscious, that it has been embedded as a core trope into many world myths (more than we have outlined here), each with its own particular form of dramatic characterisation (though sometimes, perhaps necessarily, extremely similar) but all re-telling the basic story of the changing seasons of the year. Having appraised this history of the 'overall' story of the Sun's journey through the year in terms of the mythical representations of the major seasonal changes, we might now turn to a more granular examination of the solar year as it pertains to the developed component zodiac signs, their composition and their relationships to each other as an holistic pattern or whole.

---

[451] We are thinking here of later (post-first-century) Christian traditions such as the setting of the birth of Jesus on Christmas Day, shortly after the 'birth of the Sun' at the winter solstice, and the consolidation of descriptive appurtenances of the virgin Mary to recapitulate the zodiac sign Virgo the virgin, etc.

The Zodiac as a Holistic System

We've seen how the age-old story of the Sun's journey through the seasons and signs of the year has appeared in various allegorical and mythical forms, though perhaps the ultimate symbolic representation of the year's progression is the zodiac of twelve signs. To gain a picture of the zodiac as a whole we must examine how its component signs relate to each other. When we do, we're surprised to find that particular angular relationships between signs always bear the same type of thematic relationship. Adjacent signs will always show one recognisable form of mutual association, signs opposite to one another will always show another, and so-on. This geometric coherence is curious; it bears scrutiny to anyone who cares to examine the structure and therefore seems unlikely to result from the imposition of some sort of confirmation bias. To illustrate, let's examine the relationships of signs 30° apart (adjacent signs), signs 180° apart (opposite signs), signs 90° apart, and signs 120° apart. We'll see that, in every case, for each of these four types of angular relationship, and without exception, a characteristic type of connection is apparent, in ways which apparently emerge from the signs' compositions in terms of polarity, quality and element.

Signs 30° Apart (Adjacent Signs)

Adjacent signs (30° apart) are always different in terms of all components; that is, they have different polarities (either positive or negative), different qualities (either cardinal or fixed or mutable) and different elements (either fire or earth or air or water). In addition, their differing elements are not 'kindred'. By 'kindred' elements we mean those which seem conceptually to go together easily. Fire is kindred with air, and earth is kindred with water. Fire and air signs are always of the positive polarity, and in their physical forms combust well together. Earth and water signs are always of the negative polarity, and physically mix well together. Other, 'non-kindred' pairings of elements (fire-water, fire-earth, air-earth and air-water) do not share polarity and seem antagonistic physically: both water and earth extinguish fire, earth traps air, and air struggles to be free of water.

Adjacent signs therefore seem different in every conceivable way: they share neither polarity, quality nor element; in addition, the difference between their elements is a 'non-kindred' difference. This marked contradistinction between adjacent signs is borne out by a comparison of their keyword natures, as shown below in Table 5. Each row in Table 5 shows signs that are adjacent to each other in the zodiac. A sign in the left column can be compared to its adjacent sign in the right, and vice-versa.

Table 5: Thematic Relationships Between Adjacent Signs of the Zodiac

Aries: self-assertive, survivalist, direct and straightforward, concrete.	*Pisces*: self-sacrificing, nebulous and other-worldly.
Taurus: cautious, security-seeking.	*Aries*: outwardly-projecting, reckless, adventurous.
Gemini: restlessly intellectual, abstract-oriented and inquisitive.	*Taurus*: cautiously & practically material, feelings-oriented, fixed.
Cancer: emotional, intuitive, memory and habit-oriented.	*Gemini*: intellectual, logical, conceptual, abstract-oriented.
Leo: self-expressive, cheerful, comprehensively generous to all, outspoken, self-assured.	*Cancer*: introspective, inward-looking, moody, partisan & protective, reserved, indrawn, shy.
Virgo: attends critically to detail, self-effacing, serving, modest.	*Leo*: generalises and sees the overall 'big picture', dignified, self-expressive, proud.
Libra: looks for relatedness & agreement between things.	*Virgo*: discriminating, looks for differences between things.
Scorpio: one-pointed, single-minded, wishes to uncover and expose a single shared, commonality.	*Libra*: attuned to relatedness, other-oriented, wishes to smooth over, accept and combine differences.
Sagittarius: given to a wide, extensive, open attitude, seeks broad, expansive space to range in, open, candid, frank.	*Scorpio*: given to a one-pointed, single-minded attitude, seeks to penetrate intensely upon a commonly shared single, inner focus, secretive, suspicious.
Capricorn: serious, cautious, prudent, conforming.	*Sagittarius*: jovial, adventurous, explorative, broad-minded.
Aquarius: unconventional, progressive, original, unpredictable.	*Capricorn*: conventional, conservative, methodical, formulaic.
Pisces: emotional, impressionable, compassionate, spiritually-inclined.	*Aquarius*: detached, dogmatic, clinical, scientifically-inclined.

Although it is perhaps not accurate to say that adjacent signs are 'opposites of one another', one can see that they are nevertheless always fundamentally different, this being reflected by the comprehensive difference in polarity, quality and (non-kindred) element. These differences, as they're fleshed out in the descriptions of their themes, are verifiable by anybody who cares to review the traditional summaries of the zodiac signs (see Chapter 3). It's notable that there are no exceptions: there are no two adjacent zodiac signs that do not show these truly contrasting natures. It seems remarkable how this consistently orderly pattern of principled relationships between the signs arose from the zodiac's origin as a seasonal calendrical marker system.

Signs 180° Apart (Opposing Signs)

Signs of the zodiac which are opposite each other (separated by 180°) also have a consistent type of thematic relationship. These opposing signs always share the same polarity and quality, and although they always have different elements, the differing elements are nevertheless always what we have termed 'kindred' or conceptually agreeable, as discussed above (either fire and air, or earth and water pairs). The relationship between opposite signs is not quite one of a 'fundamental difference' as might be said to be the case with adjacent signs; it rather appears to be one of 'complementariness' or 'extension'. Generally, the characteristics of the first six signs deal with themes which apply to 'the self', while the characteristics of the last six deal with virtually those same six themes, but as they are extended, as it were, through being applied to 'others', or beyond the self. An overview of this consistent relationship between all opposing signs of the zodiac is outlined in Table 6 below. Each row in the table shows signs that are opposite to each other in the zodiac. It can be seen that there appear to be no exceptions or deviations to the general thematic pattern here described: all opposing signs of the zodiac partake of the complementary or extended 'self' and 'other' relationship.

Table 6: Thematic Relationships Between Opposing Signs of the Zodiac

Aries	*Libra*
• The sense one has of one's individuality, personhood or singularity. Subjective. Decisive (due to self-orientation).	• The sense one has of one's relatedness to others; of unison and partnership. Relative. Indecisive (due to other-orientation).
Taurus	*Scorpio*
• Personal feelings and possessions, as in the comfort of material possessions and other pleasant material things. • The sensual indulgence in personal enjoyments such as comfort, food, beauty and other pleasant sensations, which are the more enduring pleasures. • The experience of the individual life-force that regenerates life through the sustenance of the personal body, as in food.	• The feelings and possessions of others, those commonly shared with others, and the 'possession of others', as in transformable or convertible currency or money, and in sexual relations. • The 'pleasant sensual indulging' in tastes and sensations with and of others, as in sex, which is intense but short-lived. • The experience of the impersonal life-force that is regenerated through and commonly shared with others, as in birth, sex and death.

Table 6: Thematic Relationships Between Opposing Signs of the Zodiac (Continued)

Gemini	*Sagittarius*
• Personal abstract mental cognition and intellectual pursuits. • Short communications, journeys and interactions in the immediate environment.	• Wider and more socially-oriented mental cognition and pursuits, such as law, philosophy, morality. • Wider and more extensive communications and journeys, such as to foreign countries.
Cancer • One's security, standing and role in personal, domestic, home and local affairs.	*Capricorn* • One's security, standing and role in the outer world of others, as in career and public society.
Leo • Organisation, creativeness and integration in personal matters (e.g., in personally created offspring, in the creative objectives of establishing a family, and in other personal creativity and recreation).	*Aquarius* • Organisation, creativeness and integration with others (e.g., in the creative aims of community groups, in establishing social objectives, scientific concerns, etc).
Virgo • Self-effacing personal practical service, purity and goodness (specifically personal when in terms of health).	*Pisces* • Self-effacing spiritual service, purity and goodness (to others and to the 'absolute' or God).

Signs 90° Apart ('Square' Signs)

If we examine the relationships between zodiac signs that are 90° apart (known in astrological terminology as being in 'square' aspect), we can see that there is also a consistently principled relationship involved in all cases. Signs connected by this 90° square aspect share the same quality ('seasonal phase'), but have different polarities and different elements; in addition, the differing elements are 'non-kindred'. The square relationship has been seen in divinatory astrology as the most difficult relationship. This may not be surprising as the same 'seasonal phase' is thus being expressed in the most different way possible. Once again there are no exceptions to the overall pattern for this association: all signs connected by this square aspect reflect the difficult relationship when their themes are compared, as is shown in Table 7, whose rows detail the signs that are 90° apart from each other in the zodiac.

Table 7: Relationships Between Signs of the Zodiac That Are 90° Apart

Aries—Cancer: Both are outgoing and enterprising (cardinal quality, or 'beginning' seasonal phase), but Aries's fiery nature is blunt, bold, uninhibited and forward-looking, while Cancer's watery nature is sensitive, diffident, emotional, and influenced by the past and memory.
Taurus—Leo: Both are intense, steadfast and resistant to change (fixed quality, or 'in progress' seasonal phase), but Taurus's earthy nature is withholding, conservative and motivated by practical common-sense, while Leo's fiery nature is magnanimous, open-handed, broad-minded, and motivated by a desire to be impressive.
Gemini—Virgo: Both are adaptable and variable (mutable quality, or 'ending or completion' seasonal phase), but Gemini's airy nature is communicative, theoretical, abstract, variable, eclectic, adaptable and changeable, while Virgo's earthy nature is reserved, practical, concrete, analytical, discerning, attentive to detail.
Cancer—Libra: Both are outgoing and enterprising (cardinal quality, or 'beginning' seasonal phase), but Cancer's watery nature is partisan, defensive, instinctive, moody, homely and withdrawing, while Libra's airy nature is unbiased, diplomatic, compromising, rationally evaluative, inclined to seek harmony and avoid discord, and given to open collaboration & relatedness.
Leo—Scorpio: Both are intense, steadfast, resistant to change (fixed quality, or 'in progress' seasonal phase), but Leo's fiery nature is open, sunny and cheerful, broad-minded, magnanimous and generous, while Scorpio's watery nature is introspective, dark, brooding, single-minded, suspicious and jealous.
Virgo—Sagittarius: Both are adaptable and variable (mutable quality, or 'ending or completion' seasonal phase), but Virgo's earthy nature is practical, conscientious, attentive to useful detail, modest and reserved, while Sagittarius's fiery nature is adventurous, freedom-loving, expansive, broad, open, wide-ranging and exploratory.
Libra—Capricorn: Both are outgoing and enterprising (cardinal quality, or 'beginning' seasonal phase), but Libra's airy nature is genial, light-hearted, fair, easy-going, averse to discord and inclined to aesthetic evaluation, while Capricorn's earthy nature is austere, serious, stern, strict, enduring of hardship and inclined to practical and utilitarian industry.
Scorpio—Aquarius: Both are intense, steadfast, resistant to change (fixed quality, or 'in progress' seasonal phase), but Scorpio's watery nature is passionate, secretive, silent, brooding, suspicious, relating to the possessions of others or the possession of others, while Aquarius's airy nature is detached, oriented to open, equal group objectives, outspoken, friendly and humanitarian, relating to ideas, ideals and objectives shared equally with others.
Sagittarius—Pisces: Both are adaptable and variable (mutable quality, or 'ending or completion' seasonal phase), but Sagittarius's fiery nature is philosophically moralising, self-expansive, adventurous and explorative, while Pisces's watery nature apprehends intuitively, is self-sacrificing and inclined to withdraw from the world.

Table 7: Relationships Between Signs of the Zodiac That Are 90° Apart (Continued)

Capricorn—Aries: Both are outgoing and enterprising (cardinal quality, or 'beginning' seasonal phase), but Capricorn's earthy nature is prudent, patient and methodical, while Aries's fiery nature is impulsive, impatient and spontaneous, seeking quick, concrete results
Aquarius—Taurus: Both are intense, steadfast, resistant to change (fixed quality, or 'in progress' seasonal phase), but Aquarius's airy nature is erratic, unconventional, unorthodox, and motivated by original, progressive, revolutionary, abstract ideas, while Taurus's earthy nature is stolid, conservative, sceptical, and motivated by common-sense, tried-and-trusted, practical, material values.
Pisces—Gemini: Both are adaptable and variable (mutable quality, or 'ending or completion' seasonal phase), but Pisces's watery nature is intuitive and emotional, and given to relate to the spiritual, the subconscious or unconscious, while Gemini's airy nature is intellectual, logical, and given to relate consciously and rationally to the environment.

Again, there are no exceptions: all signs of the zodiac that are in 'square' aspect to each other, being 90° apart, partake of this particularly difficult relationship, in having such disparate themes.

Signs 120° Apart ('Trines')

Another consistently principled relationship subsists between signs that are 120° apart (known in astrological terminology as being in 'trine' aspect). This relationship is traditionally characterised as one of 'ease of expression' between the sign-themes involved, which share the same polarity and element, though they have different qualities or 'seasonal phases'. If we refer to the signs connected by this 120° relationship we can see that they do indeed have largely consonant natures, 'agreeing' with each other thematically by virtue of this sharing of polarity and element.

• Aries, Leo and Sagittarius all express themes which share the active, self-expressive and spontaneous nature of the positive polarity, as well as the *ardent, keen, energetic and assertive* nature of the fire element.

• Taurus, Virgo and Capricorn all express themes which share the passive, self-repressive, receptive nature of the negative polarity, as well as the *practical, cautious and restrained* nature of the earth element.

• Gemini, Libra and Aquarius all express themes which share the active, self-expressive and spontaneous nature of the positive polarity, as well as the *intellectual, communicative and mentally active* themes of the air element.

• Cancer, Scorpio and Pisces all express themes which share the passive, self-repressive, receptive nature of the negative polarity, as well as the *emotional, sensitive, intuitive and unstable* nature of the water element.

Consistent Relationships Between the Signs

What is notable from the above is that all these principled relationships, arising from the pattern of the signs as combinations of polarity, quality and element, are consistent and comprehensive throughout the whole pattern of the zodiac. We don't see the descriptive characteristics of any one sign awkwardly not conforming to the overall pattern of relationships. Looking at the signs' keyword themes, we see that all adjacent signs do indeed have the characteristic difference in thematic nature that goes with different polarities, different qualities, and different 'non-kindred' elements. All opposite signs are indeed connected thematically by a relationship of 'complementarity' or 'extension'. All signs 90 degrees apart do have the 'difficult' thematic relationship, while the keywords of all those that are 120 degrees apart are all connected by the 'easy' relationship. The whole system of signs retains these thematic relationships without anomaly. The sequence of signs does not appear to be merely contrived to fit such a structure, and it seems unlikely that we are employing confirmation bias in perceiving such an overall pattern.

It seems extraordinary therefore how the zodiac, a projection of seasonal sign-themes, refined and distilled over millennia, could result in such a complete and systemic structure of human attitudes, with such an unwaveringly consistent internal coherence, from the orderly relationships of polarity, quality and element. When the zodiac developed from the early Mesopotamian year-calendar, we may presume that no-one expressly set out or convened to decide that, somehow, not only should twelve signs characterise the seasons, but that they should also strictly conform to a coherent pattern of components; that the last six should be thematic 'complementary extensions' of the first six, or that any of the other orderly relationships described above should inhere in them, yet these relation-ships nevertheless apply throughout.

Given the remarkably consistent nature of the zodiac as a whole as here described, it seems that the zodiac and its constituent signs have somehow developed to become a holistic representation, in the collective unconscious, of inter-related principles which together formulate a coherent framework of humankind's most fundamental functions and concerns; a refinement of the characterisations of the seasons which acts—metaphorically or otherwise—as a mirror or recapitulation of the most basic concerns of human life. One realises that the signs originally emanated from the arbitrary enough phenomenon of the seasonal segments of the year, along with their attendant conditions and activities; nevertheless the way that these have apparently captured the most basic human behaviours and expressions is quite striking.

The practice of using astrological sign keywords has been seen as a long-established heuristic for characterising and transmitting important seasonal attributes from one generation to the next, before the development of more rigorous scientific methods. As one writer has commented on the origin and evolution of such a general process from the initial establishment of seasonal descriptors:

> To survive, ancient civilizations would have had to convey their seasonal heuristics from one generation to the next. They needed a popular mechanism to transmit essential information about the environment so that it would become part of collective memory. The pervasiveness of astrology across the ancient world speaks to its perceived value and ease of assimilation. Numinous archetypical imagery would have been an effective means of transmitting this information within the culture ... Myths imbued the signs of the zodiac with numinosity, drawing on archetypes projected from the collective unconscious ... As symbols of the myths that accompany them, signs of the zodiac can be located relative to archetypes within a collective unconscious defined by culture.[452]

The development and refinement of the zodiac signs over the ages has, we would assert, created a descriptive repository of the most fundamental or archetypal 'modes of expression' of the human psyche, and furthermore in a curiously meaningful, orderly, coherent, structured and moreover comprehensive manner. Humans are pre-eminent pattern-seekers, and if we ourselves are not here merely seeing chimerical patterns elicited by confirmation bias, then we would propose that the zodiac has been humanity's most profound perceptive projection of an organised, holistic overview of its life and nature, and from a collectively unconscious source.

---

[452] Hamilton, 2015

5

Constructs, Metaphors, Models & Prediction

The different star-patterns seen to be behind the Sun at twelve different seasonal segments of the year provided convenient random stimuli onto which people unconsciously projected symbolic pictures of their most salient life-concerns, typically as these related to those times of the year. These fancied pictures and their associated seasonal themes became the 'signs' of the zodiac. The time-scale involved in the evolution of this process was immense, and the remarkable coherence of the resulting inter-related pattern of the twelve signs as a whole—the zodiac—suggests that, over the ages, the projected symbolism transcended the originally purely practical seasonal concerns and simplified or condensed to embrace and typify the most important and foundational components of human life and experience generally. It therefore seems that, over millennia (and thus projected from a collective unconscious), the signs of the tropical zodiac have evolved to become truly archetypal symbols of human nature.

The theorist who appears to have approached our 'projection hypothesis' of the origin of astrological symbolism most closely seems to have been the Swiss psychiatrist Carl Jung. He remarked:

> The starry vault of heaven is in truth the open book of cosmic projection, in which are reflected the mythologems, i.e., the archetypes ... The collective unconscious—so far as we can say anything about it at all—appears to consist of mythological motifs or primordial images, for which reason the myths of all nations are its real exponents. In fact the whole of mythology could be taken as a sort of projection of the collective unconscious. We can see this most clearly if we look at the heavenly constellations, whose originally chaotic forms are organized through the projection of images. This explains the influence of the stars as asserted by astrologers. These influences are nothing but unconscious, introspective perceptions of the collective unconscious. Just as the constellations were projected into the heavens, similar figures were projected into legends and fairy tales or upon historical persons.[453]

Though Jung here asserts that the 'influences of the stars' described by astrologers are explicable as 'unconscious introspective perceptions of the collective unconscious' (with which assertion we would wholeheartedly agree),

---

[453] Jung, 1969a

he nevertheless also (and contradictorily) seemed to admit the validity of predictive astrological horoscopes or birth charts, and attempted to give an account of their ostensible mechanism by means of evoking the notion of 'synchronicity' or an 'acausal connecting principle'—a non-causal, synchronistic link between terrestrial events and corresponding patterns observed in the heavens. We would argue that Jung's notion of synchronicity, though bold and intriguing, is otiose, since the very notion of natal horoscopes or 'birth charts' has come about because of a misunderstanding of the origin of the signs.

Proponents of divinatory astrology have lost sight of (or have never understood) the simple fact that the thematic correspondences between seasons and constellations (later, signs) came about solely through the pareidolia-like projection of the former onto the latter. The star-constellation (or later, the sign) Scorpio, for instance, does not cause conditions on Earth to be intense and death-related. It is the season that is intense and death-related, because the summer is passing and the year is turning towards its darker half and winter. The constellation Scorpio was originally fancied as a potentially deadly scorpion *because* that was an appropriate or salient fancied characterisation of the seemingly life-threatening terrestrial seasonal condition, projected onto the pattern of the stars that lay behind the Sun at that time of year.

The idea and practice of natal 'Sun signs' ignores the fact that the zodiac signs came about as markers of the seasons, as defined by the Sun (and by no other celestial body), not as causal agents. A lack of understanding of this true origin most likely fostered a notion of an 'influence from the stars' (or a 'synchronistic' principle) to be unnecessarily assumed and conceptually bolted-on to the seasonal correspondence.[454] Worse, the even more egregious extension of this mistaken notion into natal *'planets in signs'* (other than the Sun) not only magnifies that error but also introduces celestial bodies that have nothing whatever to do with the origin of the signs.[455] Given these considerations on the true origin of the signs and its misunderstanding, we find, unsurprisingly, no evidence to suppose that birth horoscopes do in fact predict personality.

Jung's position however is not clear, and with the benefit of hindsight seems somewhat prevaricating (or more charitably, exploratory). He certainly seemed to apprehend the essence of the projection of archetypes onto star-constellations. For, beside his remark, already noted above, that 'influences of the stars' are explicable as 'unconscious introspective perceptions of the collective unconscious', he also wrote:

---

[454] A causal effect of Sun-engendered seasonal conditions, such as climate, upon newborn life, may in principle be possible, to small degrees and in very general ways, but resort to such speculation seems to us to be a tell-tale misunderstanding of the true seasonal origin of the 'Sun-signs', and unsurprisingly there is no evidence to support it.

[455] We remind the reader once again that the Sun is seen in traditional astrology as a 'planet'.

> ... astrology is of particular interest to the psychologist, since it contains a sort of psychological experience which we call "projected"—this means that we find the psychological facts as it were in the constellations. This originally gave rise to the idea that these factors derive from the stars, whereas they are merely in a relation of synchronicity with them.[456]

Yet at the same time Jung *appeared* to propose his notion of synchronicity as a mechanism to account for prediction or delineation of personality. It would seem that Jung did not consider the simpler seasonal cognitive-projective aetiology of the zodiac signs, and apparently could not fully shake off an acceptance of some sort of validity of horoscopes. In Jung's defence it should be added that he evidently also felt uneasy with the lack of empirical evidence, as when he stated, *"What I miss in astrological literature is chiefly the statistical method by which certain fundamental facts could be scientifically established."*[457]

Despite this uncertainty over Jung's acceptance or otherwise of predictive astrological horoscopes, we nevertheless feel that he would have been in agreement with our position that the astrological symbolism of the planets and the signs represents the most well-developed collective representation of archetypal human principles or functions. This being the case, one might expect at least some aspects of the signs, or of their structural components (polarity, quality and element), to be demonstrably relatable to established psychological constructs, metaphors, models or theories, such as those which relate to personality, development and needs, as we understand those concepts today.

In pursuing this question, it is important to note that we are primarily interested just to see whether the signs or their components can be considered as useful constructs in these ways, and not whether they may be predictive with regard to season of birth, as is assumed in divinatory astrology. It would be interesting enough to see if humankind has indeed, by way of collective projection, symbolically embedded in the signs a meaningful and accurate array of descriptors of the fundamental aspects of human nature—perhaps even a comprehensive one. If in addition one did find that some or all of these keyword descriptions were actually *predictable* from the corresponding zodiacal season of birth (for instance in terms of personality measurements later in life), then of course that would be extremely interesting (if not, to us, astonishing). Establishing an ability to predict is not however our main aim, and we must admit that we greatly doubt that such would ever be found to be the case.

We would moreover say this of any potential seasonal predictive possibility: that we could only envisage the characteristics of the sign in which the *Sun* resides at birth as being even theoretically predictable from some seasonal effect. We cannot see how the themes of zodiac signs in which other planets (Venus, Mars, etc.) reside at birth could *possibly* have any correspondence to later human

---

[456] Jung, 1973
[457] *Ibid.*

personality, needs or development, since, as we have pointed out, the zodiac signs derive wholly from salient aspects of the seasons, projected from the collective unconscious, and these are determined by the apparent geocentric position of the *Sun alone*, and by that of no other heavenly body.

To illustrate this point by way of example, we might imagine for the moment that we do indeed find evidence that being born when the Sun is 'in' say, the sign Aries (at the beginning of spring, when the world around is in a state of rebirth of energetic growth) can somehow confer a similar personality (of being energetic and of a forward-looking nature, etc.) upon the human neonate. Whatever the remarkable mechanism responsible for this might turn out to be, it would be wholly due to the course of the *Sun* through the year causing the *season* of spring. However—and crucially—there could be no equivalent potential mechanism which could influence the personality of the newborn from the zodiac-sign placement of *any* of the other planets, since none of these are in a like manner associated whatsoever with the season of birth. Thus, although we of course acknowledge that empirical evidence can be the only ultimate arbiter, we nevertheless view any practice of 'divinatory' astrology which pertains to the geocentric position of bodies *other than the Sun* at the time of birth as being based upon a fundamental misunderstanding of the sun-seasonal origin of the signs.

Constructs of Personality

Psychological definitions of 'personality' tend to differ according to the psychological perspective that's doing the defining,[458] but the 'trait' approach seems most suitable to the application of astrological sign keywords as possible descriptors of human personality. This approach essentially sees individual personality as being the distinctive pattern of a person's scores (in terms of rated strength or intensity) along measures of a number of fundamental 'traits', or characteristics of behaviour, thoughts or emotions. If such scores are relatively stable across different times and circumstances, they can be seen to combine together to describe the unique ways that individuals think, feel and behave as they do.

It's fairly easy to think of personality in terms of traits. If we're asked to describe someone's personality, we naturally tend to think of descriptive traits. We might for instance use terms such as 'outgoing', 'quiet', 'talkative', 'emotional', 'lazy', 'determined' or 'eccentric' to describe someone we know. The trait approach is, perhaps unsurprisingly, a very old way of thinking about personality. The Greek philosopher Theophrastus (371—287 BCE) wrote of various human 'characters' which can, individually, be thought of as traits.[459] Traits are however seen as distinct from the notion of people as types, as the term 'characters' might otherwise suggest. Psychologists generally conclude that the diversity of human personality cannot be characterised by a simple categorisation

---

[458] Corr & Matthews, 2009
[459] Theophrastus, 2002

202

into a fixed number of unchanging types, but that it's more accurately described as the unique way a person scores more or less along various trait dimensions.[460] A similarity at least to the astrological 'keywords' of the signs or houses here is obvious.

Psychologists have sought to determine what might be the most fundamental, separable human traits (that is, those which are not highly correlated with each other) and have devised ways of measuring them, usually by means of self-report questionnaires. The measures obtained should be 'valid' (they should measure what they set out to measure) and 'reliable' (they should be precise, reproducible, and consistent from one testing occasion to another). When one considers that such measurement of differences between people in terms of traits attempts to present 'personality' as the unique combination of such traits in an individual, it becomes notable that this is precisely what the array of keywords used in traditional astrology essentially aims to do.

People who pay scant regard to astrology may nevertheless in everyday speech refer to personality traits in terms of astrological 'keyword' terminology, even if they don't know that they're doing so. It's common practice to describe a person as 'sunny', 'jovial' or 'mercurial' in behaviour or aspect, and terms like these are derived from the astrological planets and their corresponding indicators of human temperament. Thus we see that concepts which originate from astrological symbolism are important enough to be embedded in our everyday thinking. Perhaps therefore it's sensible enough to ask: do the keyword descriptions of the signs, or of their components (polarity, quality and element) comprise potentially suitable constructs with which we might describe and measure human personality? Might they even comprise a comprehensive set of such constructs? We might also ask—sceptically but with a respectful nod to the ages-old tradition of divinatory astrology—if there is any association between the keywords of a person's 'Sun-sign' at birth and measurements of such keywords as personality indicators later on in life. To be thorough, we might ask all these questions separately for the keywords of polarity, quality, element and sign. Let's examine each of these in turn with respect to personality.

Personality & Polarity

We will firstly examine astrological sign 'polarity'. As we've seen, the twelve signs, as we enumerate them sequentially through the zodiac, alternate with regard to their polarity. Aries is a positive sign, Taurus a negative sign, and so-on. Thus there are six positive and six negative signs. We recall that signs of the positive polarity are traditionally characterised as *active, self-expressive and spontaneous*, and those of the negative polarity as *passive, self-repressive and receptive*. On a purely intuitive level it seems reasonable to suppose that some people's personalities are more 'active, self-expressive and spontaneous' than

---

[460] Asendorpf, 2003; Furnham & Crump, 2005; McCrae *et al.*, 2006; Pittenger, 2004

others, while others are more 'passive, self-repressive and receptive'—or at least that people may be seen as being inclined more or less toward one end of a bipolar dimension of such a construct, with positivity and negativity representing its extremes. Astrological polarity is reminiscent of the commonly recognised psychological construct of the 'extraversion-introversion' personality trait dimension. The notion of 'introvert' and 'extravert' *types* was first put forward by Jung in the 1920s. Jung wrote:

> In my practical medical work with nervous patients I have long been struck by the fact that besides the many individual differences in human psychology there are also typical differences. Two types especially become clear to me; I have termed them the introverted and the extraverted types. When we consider the course of human life, we see how the fate of one individual is determined more by the objects of his interest [the extravert], while in another it is determined more by his own inner self, by the subject [the introvert].[461]

Jung defined extraversion as an *"attitude-type characterised by concentration of interest on the external object"* and introversion as an *"attitude-type characterised by orientation in life through subjective psychic contents."* For Jung then, the extravert is the outgoing sort of person whose nature is determined by the 'outer objects of life' and the introvert is the more inward-looking type whose nature is determined more by their 'inner world'.[462] Jung acknowledged that the essence of the introvert-extravert dichotomy had already been grasped in varying ways by many commentators down the ages, but that, *"despite the diversity of the formulations the fundamental idea common to them all constantly shines through: in one case [of extraversion] an outward movement of interest towards the object, and in the other [of introversion] a movement of interest away from the object to the subject and his own psychological processes."*[463]

In a discussion of Jung's conception of introversion and extraversion, the psychologist William McDougall concluded that *"the introverts are those in whom reflective thought inhibits and postpones action and expression: the extroverts are those in whom the energies liberated upon the stirring of any propensity flow out freely in outward action and expression."*[464] Jung's concepts or psychological constructs of extraversion and introversion were extremely influential and have been, in various forms, incorporated into many trait-based psychological theories, models and measures of personality. These include the 'Big five' taxonomy or grouping of personality traits (also known as the 'five-factor, FFM or 'OCEAN' model),[465]

---

[461] Jung, 1923
[462] Jung, 1963
[463] Jung, 1923
[464] McDougall, 1932
[465] Digman, 1990

those of Hans Eysenck,[466] Cattell,[467] and the Minnesota Multiphasic Personality Inventory (MMPI).[468]

As we mentioned above, researchers tend now to favour the 'trait approach' to understanding personality (the unique way a person scores along trait dimensions such as that of introversion-extraversion), as opposed to viewing personalities as mutually exclusive, dichotomous types. However, in his early descriptions of introversion and extraversion, Jung at times seemed ambivalent as to whether he was presenting the introversion-extraversion construct with reference to two categorical types, or to a dimensional trait with introversion at one end and extraversion at the other. Jung wrote, *"everyone possesses both mechanisms, extraversion as well as introversion, and only the relative predominance of one or the other determines the type."*[469] Here we note that, although Jung asserts that both introversion and extraversion are seen to inhere in all people, he nevertheless also writes of a 'type' being determined from a predominance.

There doesn't seem to us however to be much conceptual difference between a degree of 'relative predominance' of one over the other, and a degree at which a person may be described along a continuous dimension between the two, and both metrics seem collapsible into one. Indeed Jung seems to equate a 'predominance' (which he seems to intend to mean as the determinant of 'type') with what might be seen as the equivalent of a persistently 'high score' in a trait-dimensional approach:

> One mechanism [i.e., introversion or extraversion] will naturally predominate, and if this condition becomes in any way chronic a type will be produced; that is, an habitual attitude in which one mechanism predominates permanently, although the other can never be completely suppressed since it is an integral part of the psychic economy. Hence there can never be a pure type in the sense that it possesses only one mechanism with the complete atrophy of the other. A typical attitude always means merely the relative predominance of one mechanism.[470]

For Jung then it seems that the introvert or extravert 'type' is the long-standing predominance in an individual of the one or the other of the construct's bipolar characterisations. More recent theorising and measurement of introversion-extraversion has tended expressly to embrace the notion of a continuum or dimension of the construct, with people scoring more to one side and thus less to the other—that is, as being more introvert or more extravert—though 'ambiverts' may be extraverted in some situations, yet introverted in others.[471]

---

[466] Eysenck, 1953

[467] Cattell & Schuerger, 2003

[468] Butcher *et al.*, 1989

[469] Jung, 1923

[470] *Ibid.*

[471] Cohen & Schmidt, 1979

In general, 'extraverts' are seen to be more outgoing and assertive, whilst 'introverts' tend to be more reserved and inward-looking. The astrological polarities appear to mirror these constructs extremely closely; thus the fitness of polarity as a personality construct seems to reduce to that of introversion-extraversion. The latter construct is widely evaluated in psychometric tests, typically in the form of self-report questionnaires, wherein the score of scaled responses to certain questions is taken to indicate the degree of introversion or extraversion. Such tests generally appear to have good 'validity' and 'reliability'; that is, they measure what they set out to measure, and they accurately produce consistent results over repeated occasions.[472] We might assert therefore that, in so far as the astrological positivity-negativity polarity parallels the extraversion-introversion dimension of personality, it has as good empirical justification as a meaningful construct of personality.

We might now consider the possibility of polarity at birth as a predictor of personality. Neurobiological factors have been correlated with individual differences in extraversion and introversion scores.[473] In one sense this may be said to be an uninteresting truism: *any* behaviour or emotion must have *some* sort of correlate in the brain. However, given a potential relevance in divinatory astrology of seasonal factors, it may be of interest that some research has suggested that extraversion-introversion scores (and thus, one might presume, by conceptual extension, possible ratings of astrological polarity) are associated with sensitivity of the brain to the neurotransmitter dopamine,[474] and that dopamine levels have been found to fluctuate according to season, at least in terms of a difference between autumn/winter and spring/summer.[475]

One cannot however co-implicate natal astrological polarity with seasonal dopamine levels, since zodiacal polarity alternates from one Sun-sign (approximately a one month period) to the next, not between one major seasonal period of the year and another. It has been shown that dopamine genetic differences are linked to stressful climates,[476] but not to such abrupt and short changes of seasonality. To fully implicate astrological polarity with seasonal variations in dopamine levels, one would require evidence showing that such neurotransmitter levels fluctuate between single Sun-sign periods, which, to our knowledge, is not forthcoming. Thus although it may be that dopamine levels might influence changes in introversion-extraversion between *major* seasons of the year (such as between summer and winter), there's no evidence to suppose that they do so from one month (or sign-period) to the next. It's also worth noting that, in order for such a biological effect to underlie polarity in natal divinatory astrology, it would also be necessary to specify some mechanism whereby *being born* at a certain period could mediate the bringing about of such an effect, to endure

---

[472] Thompson, 2008
[473] Eysenck, 1967; Depue & Collins, 1999; Johnson *et al.*, 1999; Stenberg *et al.*, 1993
[474] Depue & Collins, 1999
[475] Eisenberg *et al.*, 2010
[476] Fischer & Verzijden, 2018

(presumably) through a person's lifetime, but to our knowledge, not even a hypothesis to propose any such a mechanism is forthcoming.

Some evidence has nevertheless been put forward to suppose that the extra-version-introversion dimension does indeed correlate with astrological polarity at birth, and in the expected way. Mayo *et al.* (1978) found that people born with the Sun in signs of the positive polarity scored higher than average (that is, they were more extravert), while those born with the Sun in signs of negative polarity scored lower than average (being more introverted).[477] This study however suffered from a fatal methodological flaw, in that a sizeable proportion of the participants had prior interest and knowledge in divinatory astrology; indeed some had already asked the lead author (who was himself an astrologer) for 'astrological predictions'; thus it's feasible if not probable that the results were biased by participants having completed the extraversion-introversion self-report questionnaire, consciously or unconsciously, in ways that modified their self-image according to what they believed it should be, from a pre-existing astrological perspective. It's fair to point out that the researchers were indeed aware of the possibility of this confounding effect of the subjects' prior knowledge of astrology, though they largely dismissed it, remarking:

> ...about one-third of the [participants] had some knowledge of astrological principles, two-thirds did not. An analysis of the scores obtained from these two groups did not show any significant differences, suggesting that knowledge of astrological principles was not a casual factor. We cannot in the nature of things rule this alternative hypothesis out completely, but it does not seem to us to account for the facts. It is a weakness of the study that only [subjects] are included who requested astrological predictions from the senior author-i.e. who were not a random sample of the population. It is difficult to see how any selection along these lines could have produced the results obtained however, and we do not believe that this constitutes a serious weakness of the experiment.[478]

The authors' 'difficulty' in seeing how a selection of subjects with a pre-existing interest in astrology could have influenced results seems at best short-sighted and at worst disingenuous. While other studies have also found that extraversion scores were higher for positive signs, some results were statistically significant,[479] while others were not.[480] Two studies found extraversion scores to be actually *lower* for positive signs, though in both cases the differences were not

---

[477] Mayo *et al.*, 1978
[478] *Ibid.*
[479] Smithers & Cooper, 1978; Van Rooij *et al.*, 1988
[480] Veno & Pamment, 1979; Clarke *et al.*, 1996; Fourie, 1984

statistically significant.[481] One study in particular showed that the results of Mayo *et al.* (1978) were reproducible for participants who *were* familiar with the keyword symbolism in divinatory astrology, but *not* for those who were not—apparently confirming the contamination of the study's results due to the uncontrolled selection of subjects.[482]

Hamilton (2015) found a significant effect of birth polarity of sign (termed 'brightness' of sign in the study) on the likelihood of later *celebrity* in life, with those born in positive Sun-signs being more likely to become celebrities than those born in negative Sun-signs.[483] Hamilton speculated that the observed effect of 'brightness' (polarity) may be a proxy effect for that of extraversion-introversion or sociability, though the manifest unreliability of the Mayo *et al.* (1978) study and the contrary findings of the further research may be said to bring that speculation into doubt.

In the case of astrological positive/negative polarity of sign therefore, we can see that it does seem to be an acceptable construct of personality, in so far as it is extremely similar, if not virtually identical, to the now-established psychological construct of extraversion-introversion, which has been widely used in many psychometric tests. We must also note however that in terms of its ability to predict a facet of personality, not via self-report questionnaire, but from its traditionally corresponding Sun-sign at birth (the aim of 'divinatory' astrology), alternating from positive to negative through the twelve signs, the evidence is at best equivocal, since prior knowledge of astrological symbolism has been strongly implicated as a confounding factor; in addition, some results were contrary to the hypothesis, while others were statistically non-significant. The finding by Hamilton (2015) of a significant effect of Sun-sign polarity at birth on the likelihood of later celebrity cannot be disregarded, though to our knowledge it has not been replicated and thus remains isolated and anomalous in the literature.

We are not particularly surprised by the ambivalence (at best) of the available evidence for a correspondence between polarity of Sun-sign *at birth* and later extraversion-introversion (which latter seems conceptually coextensive with polarity). On the one hand it seems beyond doubt that there are seasonal effects upon prevailing moods, as anyone experiencing the transition from a joyful summer to a melancholy or at least more grounded, 'sensible' feeling in autumn will attest. Further, if seasons affect humans in such ways, it neither seems wholly beyond the realms of possibility that they just might in some way affect the nature of a new life that erupts in them. Even a seasonal effect to cause a prevailing mood which alternates back and forth from positive to negative as the months progress through the year (i.e., that of polarity) doesn't seem absolutely impossible. For example, one often really does feel more hopeful (and thus more 'positive') generally around that time of the year in which the Sun moves from

---

[481] Saklofske *et al.*, 1982; Mohan & Gulati, 1986
[482] Pawlik & Buse, 1984
[483] Hamilton, 2015

208

the sign of Capricorn to that of Aquarius, and one may presume that it is the lengthening days and the hopeful feeling of 'spring somewhere on the horizon' that gives Aquarius the corresponding positive polarity of its theme.

Nevertheless, even if these subtle differences of feeling can in some mysterious way stamp their natures upon births, they are nevertheless too indistinct or too vaguely differentiated between strictly-defined monthly periods to be measurable by (possibly too insensitive) personality tests in later life. In short, the existing empirical evidence clearly doesn't support the notion that polarity of the Sun-sign at birth, alternating between single-month periods, has any correspondence with later personality measures. Perhaps for the moment all we can say is that the pattern of the zodiac signs has developed to include in its composition a construct of polarity (positivity and negativity) which seems to have conceptually anticipated the more recent psychological construct of extraversion-introversion. This in itself is noteworthy; however, the notion that being born in 'positive' or 'negative' times of the year might actually be associated with later correspondent measures of extraversion-introversion is not well supported by the evidence, which can only be described as equivocal.

Personality & Quality ('Quadruplicity')

We will remember that each astrological sign has an associated 'quality' (or 'quadruplicity'). We will also recall that there are three of these qualities, namely: cardinal, fixed and mutable, and that they progress in that order through the twelve signs, such that Aries is a cardinal sign, Taurus a fixed sign, Gemini a mutable sign, and so-on. Thus there are four signs of each quality (and hence the name '*quad*ruplicity'). Cardinal signs denote those that begin one quarter of the year, and generally, a new season; thus it may not be surprising that cardinal signs are seen as 'outgoing and enterprising', as reflecting the beginning of a new phase of the year. Fixed signs mark 'mid-season' periods of the year, when seasonal conditions are relatively established; this appears to be reflected in the description of the fixed quality as 'steadfast and resistant to change'. Signs of the mutable quality indicate periods that mark the ending of a season, echoed in the thematic portrayal of the mutable quality as 'variable and open to change'.

Can these three astrological 'qualities' be seen as constructs of personality? It certainly seems reasonable to suppose that some people may be more or less 'outgoing and enterprising' than others, some more or less 'steadfast and resistant to change', and some more or less 'variable and open to change'. However if these three constructs are to be seen as candidate descriptors of distinct psychological personality traits, one would not expect there to be too much overlap between them, either conceptually, or as they might be assessed in individuals who, by virtue of some suitable testing, proved to represent each particularly.

Considering initial conceptual comparisons, there is an obvious mutual exclusion between the fixed type as 'steadfast and resistant to change', and the mutable type as 'variable and open to change'. There also appears to be at least something of a contradistinction between the fixed type's 'steadfastness and resistance to change' and the cardinal type's 'outgoing and enterprising' attitude, since one might fairly suppose that it would be difficult to be both. In addition it's intuitively possible to imagine individuals who partake of both the cardinal and the mutable qualities; that is, people who are not only 'outgoing and enterprising' but also 'variable and open to change'. One might therefore feel that the mid-season quality of fixity might be said to have more of a certain distinction amongst the three constructs.

The three qualities may seem more separable conceptually however if the cardinal quality were recast in the original seasonal sense as "being mainly concerned with the commencement and successful initiation of important new conditions, phases or projects" and the mutable quality as "being mainly concerned with the ending, completion or final consolidation of existing conditions, phases or projects and the anticipation of the next". We might therefore, with the right phraseology, be more likely to accept astrological 'quality' (which we might term 'phase interest') as a candidate personality construct, with three dimensions: firstly, a predisposition to be concerned with the commencement and successful initiation of important new conditions, phases or projects (cardinal quality); secondly, a predisposition to be concerned with the ongoing establishment or continuance of existing conditions, phases or projects (fixed quality) and thirdly, a predisposition to be concerned with the ending, completion or final consolidation of near-accomplished conditions, phases or projects, and the anticipation of the next (mutable quality).

These three aspects of astrological 'quality' (or as we have termed it, 'phase interest') don't seem to restate any existing constructs of personality. However, empirical research would be needed to see if they are indeed not subsumed by other constructs, that they actually inhere in individuals in any meaningful way, to assess their validity and reliability, and to see if they predict relevant behaviour (as assessed by say, self-report questionnaires).

Qualities at Birth as Predictors of Personality

As was the case with polarity, we feel obliged to ask: is there any evidence to suppose that behavioural or other indicators are predictable from the cardinal, fixed or mutable quality of an individual's Sun-sign *at birth*? Hamilton (2015) found that there was an association between a person's natal Sun-sign 'quality' component and their likelihood of *celebrity*. In particular, significant differences were found between cardinal and fixed signs, and between mutable and fixed signs, especially in a person's maturity, apparently strengthening the notion of a greater conceptual distinction for the fixed quality, as noted above. Hamilton remarks upon this apparent greater likelihood of celebrity in later life for the more 'stubborn and persistent' fixed signs, noting that this 'depth of season' effect *"might be a proxy for a personality factor associated with a preference for the status quo such as rigidity or even one of its consequences, aggressiveness."*[484] This *post hoc* proposed explanation for aspects of the results of a single study seems to us however somewhat questionable: is celebrity fostered by an aggressive style of personality, in turn driven by a fixed attitude? Of course, we do not know, and perhaps at least we should respect an hypothesis that is prompted by empirical results, even if they are counterintuitive (or perhaps especially if they are counter-intuitive).

Hamilton's combined findings that both *positive and fixed* natal Sun-signs are more likely to result in later celebrity (see *Personality and Polarity* above) would indicate that births in the two 'positive-fixed' signs, namely Leo and Aquarius, are the most likely to result in later celebrity. But such findings clearly need replicating—and explicating: it still remains completely open as to exactly *how* being born in a Sun-sign of any given 'quality' (or 'phase interest') might bring about such personality differences in later life. We would be surprised indeed if such granular seasonal conditions at birth were responsible, and we would in any case want to know what mechanisms could possibly mediate any such effect.

Personality & Element

We have seen that, in addition to polarity and quality, each of the twelve astrological signs is also associated with one of four 'classical' elements, namely fire, earth, air or water (a sign's 'triplicity'). The first sign Aries is associated with fire, the second sign Taurus with earth, the third sign Gemini with air, and the fourth sign Cancer with water. The signs thereafter continue in this repeated sequence of four-fold element association, so that a total of three signs are associated with each of the elements (thus the name 'triplicity'). Fire signs are said to denote an attitude or mode that is *ardent, keen, energetic and assertive*; earth signs one that is *practical, cautious and restrained*; air signs one that is *intellectual, communicative and mentally active*, and water signs one that is *emotional, sensitive and intuitive*. The four elements have their root in the thought of the Greek philosopher Empedocles (c. 494—c. 434 BCE) who took them to be the four most fundamental substances in the cosmos, and which, according to their combina-tion in different things, make up everything else.

Various four-fold primary factors seem to have been posited throughout man's conceptualisation of himself and the world around him. From the works of early Greek physician-philosophers such as Hippocrates (460—370 BCE), Polybus (c. 400 BCE) and Galen (129—210 CE) there developed the idea of four basic bodily 'humours' or fluids of the body (blood, yellow bile, black bile and phlegm).[485] Each of these four humours were seen to be composed of a unique pair of the four classical 'qualities' (hot-moist, hot-dry, cold-dry and cold-moist,

---

[484] Hamilton, 2015
[485] Jouanna, 2012

respectively).[486] This physiological scheme, particularly as developed and promoted by Galen, maintained that physical health depended upon an equal proportion of these perceived humours or 'fluids' in the body, and that illness was a result of their imbalance.

These four humours, along with their associated pairs of 'qualities', began to be linked to four psychological 'temperaments', namely, *sanguine* (linked to blood), *choleric* (linked to yellow bile), *melancholic* (linked to black bile) and *phlegmatic* (linked to phlegm), each seen as being accompanied by a preponderance of its associated bodily fluid. The four humours were also linked to the four seasons, as blood to spring, yellow bile to summer, black bile to autumn and phlegm to winter, each humour supposedly being generally more predominant in its corresponding season,[487] as well as to the four developmental stages or 'seasons' of a person's life (infancy, youth, adulthood and old age respectively), with a similarly presumed preponderance of the associated humour and temperament at each stage.[488] Eventually the four-fold concepts of temperament, classical qualities, humours, seasons and age-stages became tied to Empedocles' four elements, as 'elements of man'.[489] These ideas thus cohered culturally in the western world into a scheme which comprised all of these ancient four-fold notions of primary constitution,[490] and which are summarised in Table 8.[491]

Table 8. Correspondences Between Classical 'Element', Temperament, Season, Life-Stage, Bodily 'Humour', Classical 'Quality' & Astrological Element

Element	Air	Fire	Earth	Water
Temperament	Sanguine	Choleric	Melancholic	Phlegmatic
Season	Spring	Summer	Autumn	Winter
Age-stage	Infancy	Youth	Adulthood	Old age
Humour	Blood	Yellow bile	Black bile	Phlegm
Classical qualities	Hot, moist	Hot, dry	Cold, dry	Cold, moist
Astrological key-words of element	Intellectual, communicative and mentally active	Ardent, keen, energetic and assertive	Practical, cautious and restrained	Emotional, sensitive and intuitive

---

[486] These ancient 'qualities' associated with the humours are not to be confused with the astrological 'qualities' of the zodiac signs, being cardinal, fixed and mutable.

[487] See Polybus' *The Nature of Man* and Galen, in Jouanna (2012).

[488] Galen, in Jouanna (2012).

[489] As propounded by Nemesius of Emesa (c. 390 CE) in *De Natura Hominis*; see Morani (1987).

[490] Jouanna, 2012

[491] It was some centuries after the time of Galen that the correspondences fully cohered to maintain the neat appearance that they have in Table 8; see Jouanna (2012).

In the 'Golden Age' of the theorising of the four humours and associated temperaments, in the sense of psychological as well as physiological aspects, an early anonymous Greek source, *On the Constitution of the Universe and of Man*, published in the mid-nineteenth century by J. L. Ideler,[492] described the characteristics of the four humour-temperaments, much as they appear in Table 8 above. Those whose constitution is seen to be predominantly that of 'blood' (of the 'sanguine' temperament) are described as *"always friendly, joke and laugh; regarding their bodies, they are rose-tinted, slightly red and have pretty skin."* This type corresponds to the 'sanguine' designation that has roughly the same meaning to this day, as one who is optimistic and affable in character. One sees the correspondence to a stereotyped image of the spring and infancy. Those whose constitution is seen to be predominantly that of 'yellow bile' (of the 'choleric' temperament) are described as *"quick-tempered, bitter, daring; regarding their bodies, they are greenish and have yellow skin."* This type corresponds to the 'choleric' nature that we still understand by that term today, who is deemed to be susceptible to a quick temper and a certain forward rashness. One might also see the supposed correspondence to a stereotyped image of the summer, perhaps more certainly to youth.

Those whose constitution is seen to be predominantly that of 'black bile' (of the 'melancholic' temperament) are described as *"indolent, pusillanimous and sickly; regarding their bodies, they have black eyes and black hair."* This is the 'melancholic' type—though the latter term today perhaps more often simply denotes one more than usually given to a depressive illness. There is a certain correspondence to a stereotyped image of the 'sad' autumn, as well as to the responsibilities or trials of later adulthood. Those whose constitution is seen to be predominantly that of 'phlegm' (of the 'phlegmatic' temperament) are described as *"despondent, forgetful; regarding their bodies, they have white hair."* The term 'phlegmatic' has developed from that description to one that is today more understood as 'having an unemotional, dispassionate or calm disposition, especially in the face of adversity', though a certain thematic link to the older meaning is nevertheless still apparent. There is a parallel with a stereotyped image of the bleakness of winter and the forgetfulness that can often be apparent in old age.

The notion of the four 'humours' and their supposed effect upon health persisted until as late as the 17th century, when physicians such as William Harvey (1578—1657) began to use more rational, empirical methods to understand human anatomy and physiology. Prior to that time, the belief in a surfeit or deficit of one humour over another as the principal cause of illness resulted in disastrous forms of medical intervention, such as 'bleeding', where blood was deliberately 'let' (drained) from a patient to rectify what was seen to be an imbalance. Needless to say, such medical interventions were frequently far more dangerous than the illness, and even now serve as prime examples of the perils of relying on theory alone without empirical evidence. Despite the egregious mistakes

---

[492] Jouanna, 2012

involved in blindly applying the 'humour theory' to medical practices without empirical verification, it's nevertheless intriguing to consider that the long-evolved system of the 'four factors' as summarised in Table 8 may in some way represent mankind's collective attempts to identify archetypal factors in his nature. If such is the case, then we might reasonably ask if these factors might contain useful constructs with which we might describe human personality. It would seem, after all, sensible enough on the face of things to suppose that some people are consistently more 'ardent, keen, energetic and assertive' than others, that some are more 'practical, cautious and restrained', that others are more 'intellectual, communicative and mentally active', while yet others are more 'emotional, sensitive and intuitive'.

In comparatively recent times, various philosophers and scientists have been intrigued by these ancient short-forms of describing human typology or disposition; intrigued enough to explore the possibility of systematising the four factors as potential constructs of personality. The great German philosopher Kant (1724—1804) proposed a model which aimed to elucidate the classical notion of the temperaments. Kant saw the sanguine and melancholy temperaments as bipolar aspects of 'feeling', which are strong but short-lasting in the case of the sanguine, while weak and longer-lasting in the case of the melancholic. The choleric and phlegmatic temperaments were in contrast seen by Kant as similarly bipolar aspects of 'activity', highly active though not persistent in the case of the choleric, and relatively inactive but more enduring in the case of the phlegmatic.[493] Later, the German psychologist Wilhelm Wundt (1832—1920) proposed that the four factors were measurable according to 'emotion' and 'changeability'. For Wundt, the choleric and melancholic temperaments are disposed to strong emotions, while the sanguine and the phlegmatic to weaker emotions. Wundt saw the sanguine and choleric temperaments by contrast as inclined to high levels of changeability, while the melancholic and phlegmatic to low levels of changeability.[494]

Kant's concepts of 'feeling' and 'activity' are clearly very similar to Wundt's notions of 'emotion' and 'changeability' though there is an important difference. For Kant, the choleric and phlegmatic temperaments were the sole product of the concept of 'activity', while the melancholic and the sanguine temperaments were the sole product of the notion of 'feeling'. For Wundt however, each of the four temperaments was referable to both strength of 'emotion' and to degree of 'changeability'. In Kant's scheme, a personality is (somewhat surprisingly to the modern mind) quite categorically either sanguine or melancholic or choleric or phlegmatic. In Wundt's two-dimensional model however, a personality varies along both axes simultaneously, and so may lie anywhere within one of the quadrants which might result schematically by overlapping the constructs on two orthogonal axes (Figure 36).

---

[493] Kant, 1798
[494] Wundt, 1874

It was a small step from Wundt's two-dimensional model of the four temperaments to their application to the two psychological and dimensional constructs of extraversion-introversion and neuroticism-stability as propounded by Hans Eysenck.[495] Eysenck described the theory of the four temperaments as embodying, in its great antiquity, *"a large slice of excellent clinical observation, without which it would never have been accepted or have lasted longer than any other psychological theory."*[496] We view this statement of Eysenck as decidedly disingenuous, as we would suspect that Wundt's concepts were the result of ingenious theorising, rather than 'clinical observation'. However this may be, Eysenck pointed out that the personality dimensions of extraversion-introversion and neuroticism-stability may easily be substituted for Wundt's dimensions of 'changeability' and 'emotion' respectively, thus producing a two-dimensional description very similar to that of Wundt, and moreover containing comparable quadrants that may be seen to recapitulate the four temperaments.[497] A schematic representation of the four classical temperaments or factors as envisaged by Kant, Wundt and Eysenck is shown in Figure 36.

Researchers have put forward evidence to suppose that the four classical 'temperaments' comprise real, orthogonal constructs of personality,[498] and that in procedures of measurement they show adequate validity and reliability.[499] Further, it has been shown that the 'humour quadrants' formed by the bisection of the extraversion-introversion and neuroticism-stability dimensions correlate with measures of subjects' moods (as measured by self-report mood scales) and that these associations are in agreement with the traditional descriptions of the moods linked with each humour. Thus for instance, those whose scores on the extraversion-introversion and neuroticism-non-neuroticism scales indicated a 'choleric' tendency (high neuroticism and high extraversion) also scored highly on an 'anger' dimension of the mood scale, in line with an expected traditional description of that 'humour'. Similar results found significantly higher optimism scores for those of the 'sanguine' tendency, lower state anxiety for those of the phlegmatic tendency, and higher state anxiety for those of the 'melancholic' tendency.[500] Howarth & Zumbo (1989) supported these findings with more precision, confirming that the old constructs of the 'four temperaments' are recapitulated in the quadrants that emerge from the two dimensions of extraversion-introversion and neuroticism-stability.[501]

---

[495] The 'neuroticism' dimension refers to a measurable personality trait which is purportedly characterised by high levels of negative emotionality such as depression and anxiety at one extreme, and emotional stability at the other.

[496] Eysenck *et al.*, 1981

[497] *Ibid.*

[498] 'Orthogonal', meaning independent of and not subsumable by each other, as determined by statistical procedures. Thus both conceptually and metrologically distinct from one another.

[499] Cruise *et al.*, 1980

[500] Howarth, 1988

[501] Howarth & Zumbo, 1989

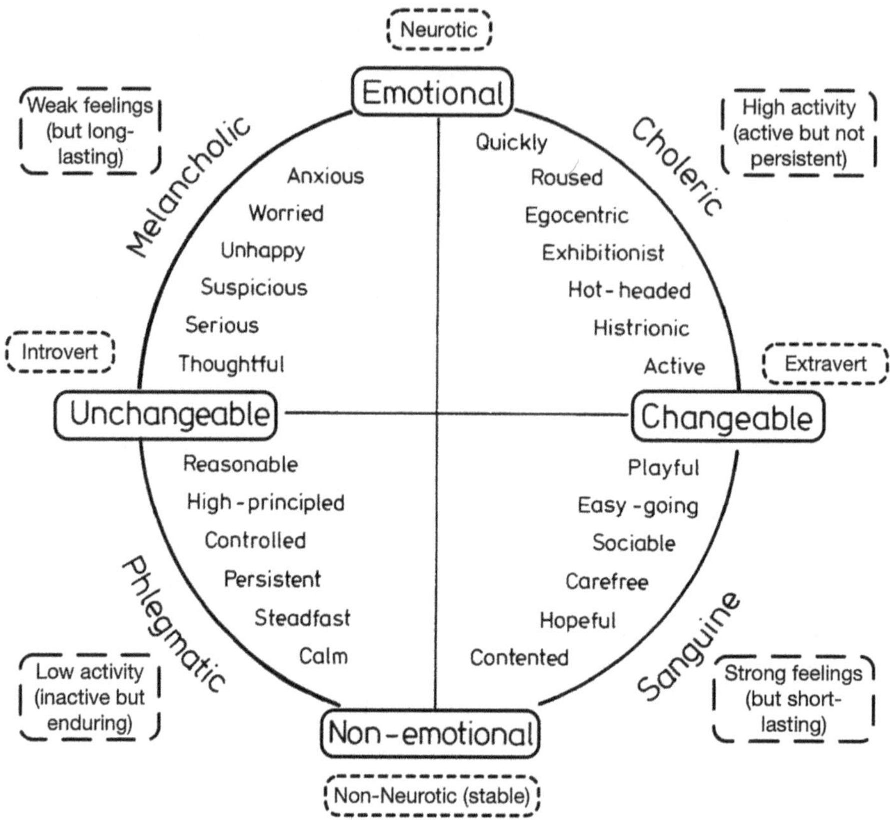

Figure 36. The Four Classical Temperaments and Other Correlating Factors as Envisaged by Kant (dashed), Wundt (solid) and Eysenck (dotted)

In Table 8 we might, therefore, should we wish to do so, add an 'introversion-extraversion/neuroticism' column, with 'extravert-stable' in the 'sanguine' row, 'extravert-neurotic' in the 'choleric' row, 'introvert-neurotic' in the 'melancholic' row, and introvert-stable' in the 'phlegmatic' row. The astrological keyword associations of the four elements seem to correspond fairly well, thematically, to the associated seasons and age-stages as set out in Table 8, thus reinforcing a view of astrological archetypes as agreeing with the year as a metaphor for human development, which we shall discuss at more length in the next section.

It is of course tempting to see if the individual signs of the zodiac in their sequence might be discernible in the circle of Figure 36, taken as a representation of the year. There does appear to be a certain correspondence between the keywords of the *temperaments* in Figure 36 (being those of Eysenck, derived from Wundt),[502] and those of the zodiacal signs, as one traces through the four quadrants of the circle as a year. The correspondence is not exact, but one can see a broad association: we recognise a general essence of the keywords of the spring signs in the 'sanguine' quadrant, of those of the summer signs in the 'choleric'

---

[502] Eysenck *et al.*, 1981; Wundt, 1874

quadrant, of those of a descent into the 'melancholic' autumn signs in the 'melancholic' quadrant, and of those of the winter signs in the 'phlegmatic' quadrant. This overall seasonal fit to the *temperament* keywords is quite compelling, and many of the signs' keywords stand out in just about the right place.

We see therefore that there seems to have developed mutually agreeing thematic and sequential correspondences between the four factors in Table 8, as exemplified by the elements, the 'humour-temperaments', the seasons and the age-stages. We note however that, although one can see a fairly convincing correspondence between the keywords of the elements and the four seasonal *quadrants* (spring-air, summer-fire, autumn-earth and winter-water), there seems to be no principled relationship between that four-season fit and the way that the elements are represented sequentially through the twelve zodiacal *signs*. That is, although the keywords of the elements seem to be meaningfully represented in the four seasonal quadrants in the sequence shown in Table 8, and also meaningfully represented separately in the individual signs in their progression through the year (not shown in Figure 36), there seems no principled relationship between these two ways in which the elements are characterised in the course of the year.

There *would* be such a patterned relationship if, say, each 'middle quadrant' sign (for instance) was represented by its 'quadrant element' (e.g., Taurus by air, Leo by fire, Scorpio by earth and Aquarius by water), but such is not the case. Thus the thematic meanings of the astrological elements stand as good metaphors for the four quadrant-seasons of the year, *and* they fit well thematically to the pattern of the keyword structure of the individual signs, but these two types of thematic relationship for the elements through the year are not connected in any principled way that we can discern. Despite this, the symbolic roles of the elements in the seasonal quadrants and those symbolic roles in the signs, separately, seem to hold sensibly for their referents.

The temperaments, taken by themselves, appear to reflect valid personality constructs, in that they can be mapped conceptually onto the modern extraversion-introversion and neurotic-stable dimensions. This conclusion is not vitiated by the fact that the 'elements as temperaments' do not agree with the 'elements as components of zodiacal signs', and is supported by research.[503] This being so, we can identify the elements as proxies for the valid extraversion-introversion and neurotic-stable dimensions, in so far as they associate with the temperaments in their seasonal quadrants. It would remain for further empirical research to determine whether or not the elements, *as described by their traditional astrological keywords alone*, would be found to be acceptable as valid psychological constructs. We could of course be content to propose an identification of the elements with their corresponding temperaments, and thus elevate them immediately to the status of valid personality constructs (air as sanguine/extravert-stable, fire as choleric/extravert-neurotic, earth as melancholic/introvert-neurotic, and water as

---

[503] Howarth, 1988; Howarth & Zumbo, 1989

phlegmatic/introvert-stable), though research based on the elements' astrological keywords alone would plainly be more revealing.

Would such proposed empirical research be likely to see the keywords of the astrological elements as separate, orthogonal constructs as we here propose them as proxies for the already-validated temperaments? It seems sensible to say that people who are primarily 'ardent, keen, energetic and assertive' (fire sign) are less likely to be 'practical, cautious and restrained' (earth sign); and equally that those who are primarily 'intellectual, communicative and mentally active' (air sign) are less likely to be 'emotional, sensitive and intuitive' (water sign). However, there are intuitive overlaps as well as differences, for it *may* seem reasonable to assert that at least some who are 'practical, cautious and restrained' (earth sign) might also be 'emotional, sensitive and intuitive' (water sign); and we might also imagine someone who is 'ardent, keen, energetic and assertive' (fire sign) and yet also 'intellectual, communicative and mentally active' (air sign). We note that a proposed instantiation of the elements as *dimensional* constructs may overcome such distinctions of conceptual independence to a degree.

In general there seems therefore to be a good deal of conceptual compatibility between fire and air, and between earth and water (being the 'kindred' pairs of elements that we mentioned in Chapter 4), but less congruence between fire and earth, or between air and water. Here we are reminded that, in apparent agreement with that intuitive observation, all fire and air signs are of the positive polarity, while all earth and water signs are of the negative polarity. Considering the conceptual associations of fire with air, and of earth with water, we might perhaps even expect to find that those two groupings—fire and air, and earth and water—are more likely to constitute separate primary personality constructs (i.e., rather than the four elements separately), though no data is at present forthcoming to support or doubt such a supposition.

We therefore note the viability of the ancient 'temperaments' as psychological constructs, and their thematic association with the four elements and the four seasons (as in Table 8). We are forced to acknowledge however that the way the elements fit the four quadrants of the seasons of the year is quite different to the way they fit the signs. We also note that straightforward psychometric research on the elements' keywords alone is necessary to see whether or not the astrological elements *per se* can be considered as viable psychological constructs of personality. Intuitive observations of overlaps between element pairs (as discussed above) would constitute interesting experimental hypotheses to test.

Elements at Birth as Predictors of Personality

We might finally ask: is there any empirical evidence which supports the notion that the four astrological elements are predictive, in terms of the applicable Sun-sign *at birth*, of later personality? Mayo *et al.* (1978) claimed to find that people born with the Sun in signs of the water element scored significantly higher along the 'neuroticism' dimension, a psychological trait characterised by high levels of negative emotionality such as depression and anxiety, which is arguably in agreement with the 'emotional' keyword description of the element.[504] However, as was discussed above in the context of this paper's purported evidence of an association between birth sign and polarity, the results were most likely contaminated by participants' prior knowledge of astrological principles. In addition, a number of other researchers have failed to replicate these results.[505] When the four elements were, as is frequently the case, recast as the four psychological functions proposed by Jung,[506] namely, fire as 'intuition', earth as 'sensation', air as 'thinking' and water as 'feeling', no correspondence was found between ratings of such functions (as measured by the Myers-Briggs Type Indicator or MBTI) and the element of the Sun-sign at birth.[507]

Hamilton (2015) found that being born whilst the Sun was in water and air signs was more likely to be associated with later *celebrity* in life, and that birth in air signs showed this tendency significantly more so than birth in water signs.[508] Combining this result with Hamilton's other finding that birth in the fixed and positive signs has a similar effect would seem to indicate plainly that it is the sign composed of positivity, fixity and air—namely, Aquarius—which is the birth sign most likely to result in later celebrity. This results in an hypothesis that seems eminently capable of empirical determination, though no support for it seems to be forthcoming.

We would conclude that if the astrological elements (as described by their keyword definitions) can be identified with the temperaments, as shown in Table 8 (sanguine-air, choleric-fire, melancholic-earth and phlegmatic-water), then by virtue of the findings of Howarth (1988) and Howarth & Zumbo (1989), which established experimentally that the temperaments were indeed "*clearly discriminable in a meaningful manner*",[509] the elements are at least reputable candidate personality traits. These studies essentially came to their conclusions by proposing that both the temperaments and the elements are identifiable conceptually with the introversion-extraversion and neuroticism-stability dimensional constructs. This identification may however be too simplistic. It may perhaps be more helpful if empirical research tested more directly whether or not the actual keywords of the traditional astrological elements represent valid personality constructs in their own right, and then separately whether these correlate significantly with the quadrants produced by the axes of extraversion-introversion and neuroticism-stability. If such a study was undertaken and correlations were indeed obtained, then identity would be implied between:

---

[504] Mayo *et al.*, 1978
[505] Saklofske *et al.*, 1982; Mohan & Gulati, 1986; Veno & Pamment, 1979; Clarke *et al.*, 1996
[506] Jung, 1923
[507] Myers & McCaulley, 1985; Van Rooij, 1993
[508] Hamilton, 2015
[509] Howarth & Zumbo, 1989

- The 'neurotic extravert' and the 'ardent, keen, energetic and assertive' keyword description of the fire element.

- The 'neurotic introvert' and the 'practical, cautious and restrained' keyword description of the earth element.

- The 'stable extravert' and the 'intellectual, communicative and mentally active' description of the air element.

- The 'stable introvert' and the 'emotional, sensitive and intuitive' keyword description of the water element.

Although it might be argued that there are 'vague shapes' of correspondence in these four associations, different identifications between quadrants and elements are clearly possible. The apparent association reported by Mayo *et al.* (1978) between the element water and neuroticism is not in agreement with the relevant 'quadrant identification' above, though we note again that this study seems doubtful due to likely flawed experimental methodology and lack of replication. Again, it would perhaps be better to disregard the identification of the elements with the quadrants seen in Figure 36 and instead simply conduct the requisite empirical research to see if the four 'element key-phrases', viewed apart from other apparently associated factors, can be seen as truly independent personality constructs, if they have sufficient validity and reliability, and moreover if they possess predictive value. The answers to these questions cannot, ultimately, be extrapolated from identifications with other constructs, though the basic research to obtain these answers has not, to our knowledge, been undertaken.

Another overall difficulty of accepting such correspondences between existing personality constructs and the astrological elements is that the latter tend to be seen in terms of typology rather than dimensional measures. The translation or identification of dimensional measures to types is fraught with difficulty and can be generally misleading. For instance, the personality descriptor 'neurotic' was not originally meant to convey a pejorative term but rather a notional extreme on the neurotic/non-neurotic personality dimension; however it's likely that many people who identified with a Sun-sign that could be said to describe a 'neurotic' typology would nevertheless take it as such and resent the nomenclature.

The Status of the Signs as Personality Constructs

At this point we might wonder if the twelve signs themselves might be seen as viable constructs of personality. They don't seem to overlap much conceptually, and thus they appear to present as semantically isolable 'thematic clusters' or specific modalities of human expression, though only statistical procedures such as factor analysis could establish this with more certainty. We can certainly imagine the construction and assessment of a self-report questionnaire which includes the keywords that are taken to be indicative of each sign.

Used on a large and varied enough sample population, one might then see if people scored significantly more highly on some signs's traits rather than on others. If individual differences seemed apparent, one could then go on to see if such results proved consistent over time, and moreover if they could predict behaviour with regard to these candidate personality traits. One could also of course attempt to see if there were any significant correlations between such keyword ratings and the 'Sun-sign' at birth—the old claim of 'divinatory' (predictive) astrology. The stubborn cultural persistence of 'Sun sign' divinatory astrology in a science-oriented age seems to warrant such study.

The suitability of the signs' keywords as fundamental terms with which to describe personality should in any case first be assessed. Do each of the signs' keyword terms constitute meaningful candidate personality traits? We might restate the question and simply ask: what terms would? From a purely intuitive point of view, anyone may ask: what traits make up someone's personality? If we were asked to jot down a list of words that we think might be used to describe people's personality generally, what might we include? Perhaps we might consider their degree of:

- Emotionality
- Nervousness
- Creativity
- Sense of responsibility
- Kindness or empathy
- Intelligence
- Need for material security
- Bravery or fearlessness
- Passion, intensity or determination
- Aesthetic sensibility or talent
- Desire or need for emotional security

From such an *ad hoc* list it seems evident that many of the keywords of the zodiac signs are already apparent. One might recognise the theme of Cancer in 'emotionality', Gemini in 'nervousness' or 'intelligence',[510] Leo in 'creativity', Aries in 'bravery or fearlessness', Capricorn in 'sense of responsibility', and so-on. But the obvious criticism to this view of our extemporised list is that it comes from authors already interested in the characteristics of the zodiac signs. Perhaps we unconsciously added terms that corresponded to them. Whether we did or not, a less potentially biased list would be better obtained from empirically derived normative data; a set of the most fundamental traits which are commonly seen as applicable to personality description, from a large population sample. If a list of 'primary' personality traits from such data was subsequently identified

---

[510] Researchers have traditionally viewed intelligence and personality as distinct and separate aspects of human psychology, though this conceptual separation has recently been called into question (see Kaufman 2014).

from statistical procedures, it could be compared to the sign keywords. If it was found to mirror the themes of the signs, then we would of course be in a position to say that the sign keywords do indeed encapsulate some of the fundamental aspects of human personality and experience. It could then be subjected to empirical testing, such as by the analysis of self-report questionnaires.

Much of the work to establish such a 'primary list' of personality keywords—the most fundamental or basic dimensions or traits of personality—has of course already been carried out, though without reference to or comparison with those of the zodiac signs. In particular the British-American psychologist Raymond Cattell (1905—1998) used a statistical technique known as 'factor analysis' to identify sixteen such basic, 'primary' or 'source' traits. Cattell's set of sixteen personality traits has been shown to be comprehensive, in so far as it appears to contain the dimensional constructs of all other major personality tests.[511] From this list Cattell went on to develop a self-report questionnaire, the *Sixteen Personality Factor Questionnaire* (or '16PF'), to measure how individuals score along these sixteen basic personality trait dimensions. Each factor can be seen as having descriptors of high or low range.

In Table 9 we have listed Cattell's sixteen factors (termed 'primary scales'),[512] alongside their high- and low-range range descriptors (the extremes of each factor). We've also noted what we think may be the likely equivalent zodiac signs that correspond with the high and low range descriptors in each case, as well as the zodiacal relationships that subsist between the signs. Our astrological assignments are of course subjective, since they're not derived from any formal normative procedure, though we feel that the correspondences seem reasonably accurate. Others may see some different correspondences of signs to descriptors, though we would suggest that many or even most of our assignments are the obvious ones to make. In any case, it can be seen that the zodiac sign-themes in general do seem to have a thematic applicability to the extremes of Cattell's primary factors.

Table 9. Cattell's 16 Personality Factors, With Suggested Corresponding Signs for Descriptors of Extreme Ranges ("Opp." = opposite signs; "Adj." = adjacent signs)

Cattell's Primary Scale	Descriptor of Low Range	Equivalent sign	Descriptor of High Range	Equivalent sign	Signs' Relationship
1. Warmth	Impersonal, distant, cool, reserved, detached, formal, aloof	♒ Aqu	Warm, outgoing, attentive to others, kindly, easygoing, participating, likes people	♌ Leo	Opp.

---

[511] Conn & Rieke, 1994
[512] *Ibid.*

Table 9. Cattell's 16 Personality Factors, With Suggested Corresponding Signs for Descriptors of Extreme Ranges ("Opp." = opposite signs; "Adj." = adjacent signs) — (Continued)

Cattell's Primary Scale	Descriptor of Low Range	Equivalent sign	Descriptor of High Range	Equivalent sign	Signs' Relationship
2. Reasoning	Concrete-thinking, less intelligent, lower general mental capacity, unable to handle abstract problems	♉ Tau	Abstract-thinking, more intelligent, bright, higher general mental capacity, fast-learner	♊ Gem	Adj.
3. Emotional Stability	Reactive emotionally, changeable, affected by feelings, emotionally less stable, easily upset	♋ Can	Emotionally stable, adaptive, mature, faces reality calmly	♑ Cap	Opp.
4. Dominance	Deferential, cooperative, avoids conflict, submissive, humble, obedient, easily led, docile, accommodating	♎ Lib	Dominant, forceful, assertive, aggressive, competitive, stubborn, bossy	♈ Ari	Opp.
5. Liveliness	Serious, restrained, prudent, taciturn, introspective, silent	♑ Cap	Lively, animated, spontaneous, enthusiastic, happy-go-lucky, cheerful, expressive, impulsive	♐ Sag	Adj.
6. Rule-Consciousness	Expedient, nonconforming, disregards rules, self-indulgent	♒ Aqu	Rule-conscious, dutiful, conscientious, conforming, moralistic, staid, rule-bound	♑ Cap	Adj.

Table 9. Cattell's 16 Personality Factors, With Suggested Corresponding Signs for Descriptors of Extreme Ranges ("Opp." = opposite signs; "Adj." = adjacent signs) — (Continued)

Cattell's Primary Scale	Descriptor of Low Range	Equivalent sign	Descriptor of High Range	Equivalent sign	Signs' Relationship
7. Social Boldness	Shy, threat-sensitive, timid, hesitant, intimidated	♋ Can	Socially bold, venturesome, thick-skinned, uninhibited	♊ Gem	Adj.
8. Sensitivity	Utilitarian, objective, unsentimental, tough-minded, self-reliant, no-nonsense, rough	♈ Ari	Sensitive, aesthetic, sentimental, tender-minded, intuitive, refined	♓ Pis	Adj.
9. Vigilance	Trusting, unsuspecting, accepting, unconditional, easy	♎ Lib	Vigilant, suspicious, skeptical, distrustful, oppositional	♏ Sco	Adj.
10. Abstractedness	Grounded, practical, prosaic, solution oriented, steady, conventional	♉ Tau	Abstract, imaginative, absent-minded, impractical, absorbed in ideas	♊ Gem	Adj.
11. Privateness	Forthright, genuine, artless, open, guileless, naive, unpretentious, involved	♐ Sag	Private, discreet, non-disclosing, shrewd, polished, worldly, astute, diplomatic	♏ Sco	Adj.
12. Apprehension	Self-assured, unworried, complacent, secure, free of guilt, confident, self-satisfied	♈ Ari	Apprehensive, self-doubting, worried, guilt-prone, insecure, worrying, self-blaming	♓ Pis	Adj.

Table 9. Cattell's 16 Personality Factors, With Suggested Corresponding Signs for Descriptors of Extreme Ranges ("Opp." = opposite signs; "Adj." = adjacent signs) — (Continued)

Cattell's Primary Scale	Descriptor of Low Range	Equivalent sign	Descriptor of High Range	Equivalent sign	Signs' Relationship
13. Openness to Change	Traditional, attached to familiar, conservative, respecting traditional ideas	♑ Cap	Open to change, experimental, liberal, analytical, critical, free-thinking, flexibility	♒ Aqu	Adj.
14. Self-Reliance	Group-oriented, affiliative, a joiner and follower dependent	♎ Lib	Self-reliant, solitary, resourceful, individualistic, self-sufficient	♈ Ari	Opp.
15. Perfectionism	Tolerates disorder, unexacting, flexible, undisciplined, lax, self-conflict, impulsive, careless of social rules, uncontrolled	♓ Pis	Perfectionistic, organised, compulsive, self-disciplined, socially precise, exacting will power, control, self-sentimental	♍ Vir	Opp.
16. Tension	Relaxed, placid, tranquil, torpid, patient, composed low drive	♉ Tau	Tense, high-energy, impatient, driven, frustrated, overwrought, time-driven	♊ Gem	Adj.

We noted above how adjacent signs in the zodiac are indeed characterised by being completely different from each other, more than by any other sign-to-sign relationship, differing in terms of all the zodiacal components of polarity, quality and element. This particular mark of mutual difference in theme or character seems congruent with their being appropriate to the opposing extremes of Cattell's primary personality factors.

We have seen how opposite signs, on the other hand, are 'different' more by virtue of subsisting as complementary 'extensions' of each other, the characteristics of the first six signs dealing with a theme applying to 'the self', and the characteristics of the last six deal with those same themes but 'extended', by being applied to 'others'. It's not entirely clear to us how the attribute of 'difference through extension' might be more related to Cattell's high and low extremes of the factors of warmth, emotional stability, dominance, self-reliance and perfectionism, though many of these do seem to be social dimensions. However, a mark of 'difference' still applies in each case for these opposing signs, and their relationship as 'polar opposites' at least seems appropriate.

Generally it seems therefore that signs of the zodiac which are the most 'different' from each other appear to be applicable in a rational way to the extremes or poles ('high' and 'low' ranges) of Cattell's most fundamental traits of personality. It thus appears that there are at least some recognisable points of contact or resemblances between the themes of the zodiac signs and the most basic personality factors empirically derived by the most carefully objective methods of psychometric research—at least in terms of those derived by Cattell.

It might of course be argued that one could pick any *ad hoc* list of personality traits and assign them with some degree of success to the high and low extremes of Cattell's primary factors. This seems certainly possible in principle, since Cattell's factors were not derived as being completely orthogonal to each other (some degree of correlation between them is possible) and thus another arbitrary list of factors may be likely to have a certain applicability to a number of them. However, the signs of the zodiac are a particular, longstanding, delimited and specific list of personality traits or themes, with a recognisable internal structure of coherence, yet all of them are assignable specifically to the high and low ranges of Cattell's factors, and moreover in ways that are in agreement with the zodiac's own internal system of 'difference'—adjacency and opposition (at least in our uncontrolled comparison in Table 9).

In answer therefore to the question, "Are the keyword associations of the twelve signs suitable trait-constructs with which we might describe fundamental aspects of personality?" we must conclude that they certainly do seem to be, from their recognisable kinship to existing personality constructs which have been derived from statistical methods. They don't completely restate Cattell's 16 primary factors, though it's certainly interesting that, at least with our *ad hoc* notation of sign-to-factor correspondence, the thematically appropriate zodiacal phenomenon of 'sign adjacency' seems to account for most (69%) of the difference between Cattell's 'high' and 'low' range, while the similarly appropriate zodiacal phenomenon of 'sign opposition' accounts for the rest (31%).

Signs at Birth as Predictors of Personality

We may now turn to the perhaps inescapable question of whether there are any associations between the keywords of the Sun-sign at the time of birth and later measurements of personality traits. It's worth mentioning that there is indeed evidence for associations between longer, more general seasonal periods of birth and later personality, in particular for behavioural-personality factors such as schizophrenia, bipolar disorder, major depression and manic-depressive psychosis (an excess for winter/spring births in all cases),[513] panic disorder (an increase for births in September to December),[514] novelty or sensation seeking (an increase for winter-born males)[515] and suicide (a peak occurring in late spring or summer).[516] Although the differences between seasons are statistically significant, the risks of developing such conditions from being born in these seasons are nevertheless low.

However our question is more specifically concerned to ask if there is any evidence for an association between the keyword-themes of the shorter, approximately one-month-long periods of *the Sun-sign* at birth and corresponding personality traits measured in later life. If there was, one would of course be able to predict developed personality simply by noting the relevant keyword characteristics of the individual's natal Sun-sign, in a similar way to how one should be able to predict aspects of personality from measured ratings on Eysenck's 'extraversion-introversion and 'neuroticism-stable' dimensions, or on those of Cattell's factors. Any reliable associations found between natal Sun-signs and later personality trait measures would result in more predictive ease and power than 'mainstream' measurements of traits in psychometric tests, since all one would have to do to assess personality would be to note the date of birth! This is of course tantamount to asking if there is any evidence to support traditional divinatory (predictive) astrology—at least that part of it that deals with the *Sun-sign* at birth.

There have in fact been empirical studies which have looked for correlations between keyword personality factors and keywords of the Sun-sign at birth. Over a number of years, Michel Gauquelin gathered keyword personality traits from the biographies of 2,000 sports champions, actors, scientists and writers, and compared these with the astrological keywords of the Sun-sign, the Moon-sign, and the sign rising on the eastern horizon (the 'ascendant' or 'rising sign' in astrological terminology) of each subject at birth, as provided by leading astrological textbooks.[517] Gauquelin found no significant degree of matching between the subjects' biographical trait keywords and the keywords of their natal Sun-signs (or those of their Moon-signs or ascendants).

The study's methodology was perhaps not ideal: the comparisons looked for were word-for-word matches, yet there seems no guarantee that biographers would have chosen to use the keywords that are given as exemplars of the signs by the astrological textbooks, or indeed that the biographers' assessments were always correct. There may be more merit in constructing a self-report questionnaire to assess ratings of the relative strength of all the signs' keywords, adminis-

---

tering this to a large and randomly-selected population of 'normal' individuals (not just to those unusual enough to be peculiarly gifted in certain areas), and looking for any correspondence of their ratings to the keywords of their natal Sun-signs. An additional comparison might be made between ratings made by the subjects' close partners or friends (instead of from the subjects' self-report) and the subjects' natal Sun-sign keywords. However, gathering such large quantities of normative data is not easy, and we would be the first to admit that Gauquelin's results, even if based on less than ideal methodology, are most unfavourable for the notion of a correspondence between natal Sun-sign and personality.

Other studies have been conducted which may be said to shed light on whether the Sun-sign at birth (amongst other factors of natal astrological horoscopes) is associated with or is able to predict or foreshadow personality. One study found no association between Sun-sign at birth and scores derived from the California Personality Inventory (CPI), except for the inventory's measurement of a 'femininity' scale, for which an association was found.[518] However, further studies failed to replicate the finding of an association between natal Sun-sign and the CPI's 'femininity' scale.[519]

Some studies, taking it as their premiss that divinatory astrology unerringly sees the natal Sun-sign as a predictive clue to a person's later life *occupation*, have sought to test such an association empirically. The assumption is however questionable, even from the astrologer's point of view: the astrological symbolism of the Sun, as we've discussed, concerns a person's *general* nature, the central yet overall creative faculty that attempts to integrate all parts of the person into wholeness of being; the core spirit which strives to reproduce the stamp of a person's spirit into an impressive and unique individual, represented by the *whole* pattern of the psyche. A person is lucky indeed if their occupation (taken as their 'officially', socially recognised and financially reimbursed career) is actually based upon this integrative and creative ability, but such of course is not always the case. Many errant chance factors no doubt actually determine people's socially recognised occupation, and people's real core interests may perforce be relegated to hobbies, or even by dint of necessity, sadly neglected. In addition, as regards one's official occupation, a great many astrologers are in actual fact more likely to lay emphasis on planets and other factors concerned with the 'tenth house' in natal birth-charts as its significators.[520]

It may be that some astrologers have asserted that natal Sun-signs are indeed associated with occupation, while others may have emphasised other astrological

---

[518] Pellegrini, 1973

[519] Illingworth & Syme, 1977; Tyson, 1977

[520] The astrological 'houses' are, like the signs, twelve anticlockwise divisions of the ecliptic, but beginning from the point on the eastern horizon at the time of birth. Interpretatively, the houses are in effect the themes of the zodiacal signs in the same order, but restated in terms of equivalent 'spheres of life'. The tenth house is said to be a sphere of life particularly characterised by matters to do with one's career, ambition and occupation (see Capricorn in Chapter 3).

228

associations in the birth-chart (such as factors to do with the 'tenth house'). However, regardless of these different and questionable assumptions in divinatory astrology of the association between various natal factors in the birth-chart and a person's later occupation, those studies which have looked for evidence of such associations between Sun-sign and later occupation in life have found none. Such researchers have thus added to the accruing scientific stockpile of evidence against the claims of divinatory astrology.[521,522]

Other studies which have claimed to show that divinatory astrology has no empirical support have been founded on more fundamentally incorrect assumptions, the worst being the assessment of any form of 'divinatory astrology' which concerns itself with anything other than Sun-signs. Now, we plainly understand that many 'serious' astrologers would vigorously disagree with a 'delimiting' of divinatory astrology to Sun-signs, and would argue that, not only the Sun in sign, but also the Moon in sign, the planets in signs, and the intricate angular interactions between all of these, and more, hold the 'real' key to astrological personality prediction. There are indeed many psychological researchers who believe they are being very *au fait* and 'up-to-date' with astrology as it is practiced, by insisting on assessing complete horoscopes, rather than 'simplistic' Sun-signs. But we vehemently disagree: from what we view as a strong theoretical basis, we assert that *only* Sun-signs may *possibly* be considered as associable with personality. We set out our reasons for this at more length in the next section, *The Status of Divinatory Natal Astrology.*

An exemplary study which tested whether the keyword traits of a person's natal Sun-sign might correspond with later personality, at least as it may be measured by a multiple choice questionnaire, was conducted in 1999 by Jan Van Rooij.[523] In this study, participants completed a questionnaire which asked them to rate how well certain keyword traits applied to them. The participants were not told that the keywords used were those understood by astrologers to be descriptive of the twelve Sun-signs. Following this, their astrological knowledge was assessed by the completion of a second questionnaire, asking them if they knew their Sun-sign, and if so, if they could name some keyword traits that were associated with it. The results of the study showed that participants described themselves in terms of their actual natal Sun-sign—*but only if they had some astrological knowledge* (as measured by the second questionnaire). Participants who had no astrological knowledge of Sun-signs did not describe their personalities in terms of their Sun-sign.

---

[521] McGervey, 1977; Tyson, 1980

[522] Rather curiously, the study by Tyson (1980) which failed to find any significant association between date of birth (which captures Sun-sign) and occupation, assumed a conceptual distinction between 'astrology' (which we take to be 'divinatory astrology') and 'season of birth'. We have here demonstrated that the Sun-signs, which are at the basis of any form of divinatory astrology, originated precisely from twelve seasonal times of the year; thus we see how far removed some studies are from understanding 'astrology' and thus in turn from being valid assessments of the subject.

[523] Van Rooij, 1999

The study thus strongly suggests that Sun-signs at birth do not predict personality (and therefore are unlikely to instil it at birth in any way), but only appear to do so in the case of those who have acquired some knowledge of astrology. It would therefore seem that knowledge of (and by implication, some acceptance of) astrological theory alters people's self-attribution or concept of themselves to be in agreement with that knowledge. As the author remarks, it would be interesting to see if the same effect extends to a person's behaviour, in addition to the way it affects their internalised view of their own personality, as measured by the self-report ratings. It would also be interesting to see if the effect extends to a person's attributions of *other people's* personalities, contingent on their knowledge of those others' Sun-signs.[524]

Indeed, Van Rooij's study seems to invite many interesting additional conditions. One may for example imagine an extension of the study where, before ratings took place, one group of astrologically naïve people were falsely led to believe that their Sun-sign indicated something completely different to the astrological textbook meaning (if indeed such a manipulation was possible). If such a group rated themselves as having the falsely primed characteristics, then the role of cognitive bias would be even more exposed and underlined. The existing results of the study on their own nevertheless persuasively suggest a strong personal cognitive bias from prior knowledge.

On the basis of our description of how the signs originated, and moreover on the basis of the empirical evidence cited above, we conclude that the Sun-sign at birth (that is, the characteristic time of year at birth) does not form nor affect personality, and therefore neither predicts it. Rather, the *belief* that it does, originating from an assimilated knowledge of divinatory astrology amongst certain people, becomes a strongly instilled self-concept, which is reflected in self-report ratings. Indeed, the outcome of any study which attempts to determine if natal Sun-sign affects personality would seem to depend upon the proportion of its participants who have a prior knowledge of astrology.

Signs as Constructs of Personality Without Regard to Birth

In considering the twelve signs themselves as potential constructs of personality, we conclude therefore that, while the Sun-signs of the zodiac appear to be an impressive descriptive repository of archetypes which encapsulate some of the most fundamental facets of human personality, there is no evidence to suppose

---

[524] Van Rooij's (1999) study thus highlights the potentially confounding factor of prior astrological knowledge for the testing of a potential association of any natal astrological factor (not just Sun-sign) with personality, as was revealed to be the case by Pawlik's (1984) clarification of the study by Mayo *et al.* (1978). Indeed it seems to us that Van Rooij's (1999) study has a bearing on the validity of self-report questionnaires as measures of personality factors generally—at least in the case of respondents who are knowledgeable about their own natal astrological configurations such as their Sun-sign—since in such cases it may be that such prior astrological knowledge could contaminate ratings of any personality factor that has a bearing on, or is conceptually related to, that prior astrological knowledge.

that one may actually predict personality simply by noting in which particular 'Sun-sign' period a person is born, as is claimed by divinatory traditions. Indeed it would appear that self-attributions of one's personality that apparently agree with the natal Sun-sign are most likely to be self-attributions or self-concepts which have been altered by an assumption of the ability of the natal Sun-sign to instil personality. Apart from such considerations of cognitive bias, it is not at all clear by what physical mechanism such a personality-forming process could exert its influence from the natal association of a seasonal period of the solar year, even if uncontaminated evidence was found. We would furthermore stress that there is certainly no basis whereby the natal zodiac sign placement of celestial bodies *other than the Sun*, such as the Moon or the (actual) planets, could *possibly* have any relevance to, let alone any association with, later personality traits, since such placements are independent of the seasons, which are the very origin of the signs. (In the case of Sun-signs, any effect would be an effect of the season—not an effect of the Sun itself. In the case of extra-solar planets, there is no seasonal effect to be considered, and none likely from the celestial body itself.)

Divinatory astrology thus stands quite apart from our thesis that the keyword themes of the zodiac signs are remarkably cogent and comprehensive constructs with which to *describe* the most basic facets of personality. This is perhaps what one might expect from pre-scientific yet millennia-old heuristics, projected from the most important human concerns of the seasons of the year onto the unstructured stimulus or 'canvas' of the random patterns of the stars. The array of keywords in the signs of the year—the zodiac—has crystallised, as it were, to become a wonderfully descriptive palette of archetypes that summarise human life, personality, behaviour and development, coming as it has from the collective unconscious over many ages. Over millennia, what humankind has fancifully imagined by looking above has been a discovery of the most fundamental aspects of its own nature below. The seasonal zodiac signs capture, thematically, the basics of human personality; they do not, however, capture or instil people's personality merely because those people are born during them, as divinatory astrology might otherwise imply.

Metaphors of Development

Just as the planets became the deified projections of humankind's most basic urges, functions or principles, so the tropical zodiac by a similar process became crystallised into a rich repository of archetypal human concerns. The zodiac's signs present as a coherently structured array of fundamental modes of human expression, while their interpretation as 'houses' recapitulate those concerns as equally fundamental spheres of human life. Given this foundational and universal nature of the signs, we have been prompted to examine them to see if they, or their constituent components of polarity, quality and element separately, can be looked upon as workable constructs of personality.

We've seen that the component of polarity (positive or negative) can indeed be seen as a viable construct of personality, in so far as it subsumes or restates the widely acknowledged extraversion-introversion dimension. It's not so clear if the component of 'quality' (cardinal, fixed or mutable, or as we have restated it as 'phase interest') can be viewed as a viable personality factor. Though one study seemed to find an association of the astrological quality of the Sun-sign *at birth* with personality,[525] it remains isolated in the literature and has not been replicated. The astrological quality (or as we term it, the 'phase interest') component does not appear to correlate with any other known and validated personality factors, and whether it can be looked upon as a viable personality construct therefore remains to be evaluated. The 'element' component of the signs can be viewed as a construct of personality, in so far as it has been shown to recapitulate the classical (and now authenticated) construct of 'temperament', as well as aspects of the more modern construct of introversion-extraversion.[526] The twelve signs themselves can be viewed as personality constructs in so far as they seem very closely related, and in principled ways, to the most fundamental or primary personality factors as carefully derived by Cattell,[527] though as we have indicated, more direct research would be more enlightening. The signs and their components therefore certainly look promising as potential constructs of personality and, despite the stigma against research into astrological symbolism, they certainly warrant further, more direct and clarifying empirical study, rather than mere indications of agreement or correlation with other known factors of personality (as intriguing as such results seem to be).

We now turn to ask: do the archetypes inherent in astrological symbolism relate meaningfully to human *development*? It is a curious fact that the symbolism of the astrological *planets*, when seen in sequence from the Moon to the more distant, seems to recapitulate a basic scheme of human development. We saw in Chapter 2 how this was referenced by William Shakespeare in Act II Scene VII of his pastoral comedy *As You Like It*:

> *"All the world's a stage,*
> *And all the men and women merely players;*
> *And all the men and women merely players;*
> *And one man in his time plays many parts,*
> *His acts being seven ages. At first the infant,*
> *Mewling and puking in the nurse's arms.*

Here the image of the infant can be seen to represent the Moon, with its accent on birth, maternity and infancy.

---

[525] Hamilton, 2015

[526] Cruise *et al.*, 1980; Howarth, 1988; Howarth & Zumbo, 1989

[527] Conn & Rieke, 1994

232

"Then, the whining school-boy with his satchel
And shining morning face, creeping like snail
Unwillingly to school.

The schoolboy represents Mercury, from its association with Gemini and early intellectual learning.

"And then the lover,
Sighing like furnace, with a woeful ballad
Made to his mistress' eyebrow.

The lover is Venus, the deity of love, redolent of romance and partnerships.

"Then, a soldier,
Full of strange oaths, and bearded like the pard,
Jealous in honour, sudden, and quick in quarrel,
Seeking the bubble reputation
Even in the cannon's mouth.

The soldier is youthful Mars, the ardent and recklessly brave warrior.

"And then, the justice,
In fair round belly, with a good capon lined,
With eyes severe, and beard of formal cut,
Full of wise saws, and modern instances,
And so he plays his part.

The justice is clearly Jupiter, from the association with Sagittarius and the affinity with the expanded physique, justice, wisdom and (here, comically) maturity.

"The sixth age shifts
Into the lean and slippered pantaloon,
With spectacles on nose and pouch on side,
His youthful hose, well saved, a world too wide
For his shrunk shank, and his big manly voice,
Turning again toward childish treble, pipes
And whistles in his sound.

The sixth stage represents Saturn, spare, old and ascetic.

The symbolism of the Sun does not seem to feature in Shakespeare's stages, perhaps because it is difficult to portray its overarching, general, perhaps even spiritual nature. Shakespeare and the authors who influenced his writing would only have known of the seven 'classical' planets; nevertheless the poet seems strangely to adumbrate Neptune and its association with the spiritual, self-dissolving and other-worldly Pisces (albeit comedically) in his seventh 'stage':

> *"Last scene of all,*
> *That ends this strange eventful history,*
> *Is second childishness and mere oblivion,*
> *Sans teeth, sans eyes, sans taste, sans everything."*

Shakespeare's conception of the 'seven ages of man' thus closely parallels the astrological symbolism of the planets in their sequence from the Sun to Saturn and beyond, and is thought to have been based upon, or at least influenced by, the *Zodiacus Vitae* ('the Zodiac of Life'), a book of twelve poems, one for each sign of the zodiac, written in the early 16th century by the Neapolitan poet Marcellus Palingenius Stellatus, otherwise known as Pier Angelo Manzolli, or more simply 'Palingenius' (c. 1500—1551).[528] The Zodiacus Vitae was a regular feature of the curriculum of grammar-school education in 16th century England, and would have been familiar to Shakespeare.[529] It's interesting to note that the passage in Shakespeare's play is spoken by Jaques, who has been described as *"the only purely contemplative character in Shakespeare"*,[530] as if he was conceptually 'above' humankind's developing nature and not a part of it, but merely describing it, philosophically and dispassionately.

Could it be said that we, as well as, perhaps, Palingenius and Shakespeare, are merely 'reading-in' an account of human development in terms of the symbolism of the planets in their sequence? In one sense of course we are, but we wonder why the metaphor of development seems so readily and obviously apparent. Could it be that the planets' symbolism, like those of the zodiac signs, have for long been not only the projected characteristics of some of the most basic archetypes of human nature (being thus in any case good material for any contemplation of human development), but have also been somehow instinctively projected in a developmental *order*, from the nearest and most obvious planets, to the more distant and obscure, as the awareness of them progressed? The symbolic characteristics of the planets in their sequence is certainly there for all to see, and they do seem to have entered folkloric wisdom as ready heuristics with which to describe the most basic aspects of human nature, and in a way that undeniably mirrors the milestones of human development.

What of the zodiac signs? Does their progression through the year relate meaningfully to human development? It's interesting to note that prenatal and postnatal infant development in terms of growth and motor control usually follows a 'cephalocaudal' pattern; that is, from head to toe. The earliest and fastest growth in size, weight, and feature differentiation starts at the head, and

---

[528] Soellner, 1972
[529] Baldwin, 1944
[530] Hazlitt, 1854

234

works its way down from top to bottom: to the neck, then the shoulders, the trunk and so-on, downwards.[531] This obviously mirrors the sequence of physiological associations of the signs as they progress from Aries to Pisces. But intriguing as this is, it is perhaps not the stuff from which humankind would develop a collectively unconscious metaphor for the significant developmental stages of his life.

We noted in Chapter 4 how life on Earth has necessarily adapted to the seasons of the year, apportioning its behaviours appropriately to the 'easier' and more 'difficult' times (spring and summer, and autumn and winter, respectively). Many creatures have for instance evolved to favour the spring and early summer as times to give birth to and rear their offspring, when the climate is more equable and food is thus more abundant. While humans do not regulate their mating to the seasons, they have had to seasonally conform much activity that is geared towards the procurement of food, both vegetable and of livestock, with important times of planting, harvesting, breeding, rearing and stockpiling. The different conditions of climate and the varying resources available throughout the year influenced not only human activity but also attendant psychological states, from the energised feeling of the glorious rebirth in spring, to the joy of summer, to the poignant and even fearful 'fall' of the year at autumn, and to the more testing and difficult time of winter which was often less appropriate for practical or strenuous endeavour but more suited to introspective, even spiritual experience.

Human life has therefore not surprisingly chosen different parts of the year cycle for appropriate activities, and in doing so has necessarily adopted concomitant attitudes which are associated with those activities. These activities and attitudes have thus long characterised a fundamental representation or myth of man's place in the 'story' of the Sun's annual journey, from stages that concern bare survival to those which relate to more spiritual awareness. This basic myth has driven the establishment of an *overall* picture or metaphor of human development as one progresses through the year, as in the general succession from birth (in the spring), to fruition (in the summer and at the harvest), to decay (in the first 'sting' of Scorpio into autumn) and to 'death' (in the winter). It does not seem surprising therefore that people have internalised this fundamental year-pattern as a representation or metaphor of their lives, since its overview is a broad narrative view of *life* generally, which ubiquitously follows the same basic common trajectory (it seems sensible for instance to talk of 'the seasons of one's life'). There is of course more detail however, both in human development and in the zodiac signs, than in the simplified, global year summary. We might therefore pose the question, does a more detailed sequential progression through the zodiac signs show a correspondence with typical human development?

If one dispenses with an attempt to tie the signs to their ruling planets (that is, an attempt to evince a 'sign version' of the 'Shakespeare-Palingenius' *planetary* scheme of development), but rather looks more plainly for a developmental

---

[531] Santrock, 2014

sequence in the regular progression of the signs from Aries to Pisces, then there does seem to be a developmental pattern. Aries may be seen to represent the essentially 'egocentric' early infant, who is overwhelmingly concerned with minute-to-minute urgent personal survival: its immediate needs are the only things that matter, and being helpless, the world revolves around it. Taurus shows us the later pre-school infant who is no longer so much concerned with immediate personal survival, but more with the security and continued posses-sion of the familiar things around them that make them feel safe. Gemini shows a still later stage, where very young children's cognitive functions develop; where experience is taken up with early learning, the relationship to the immediate environment and the development of the intellect and communication. Cancer shows the pivotal importance of the domestic sphere, especially in terms of the sign's inherent conflict in needing the safety, emotional security and sense of belonging in the home, and yet needing to make tentative excursions beyond it. Leo reflects the young adolescent, who wishes to engage in happy recreation; to play with and impress their peer group, and to develop a personal and unique creative nature. Virgo shows the young adult as novitiate, whose major and perhaps often worrisome concerns are with practical matters such as serving usefully in employment, being a skilled and serviceable part of the community, thus laying the groundwork of a promising basis for a relationship.

Libra shows the young adult in a relationship, whether of marriage or otherwise, relating to a 'significant other' and establishing harmony in a partner-ship. Scorpio shows the older adult who, having had the scales of romance lifted from the eyes, is now familiar with sex, birth (and thus, unconsciously, death) and the 'grittier' and more realistic aspects of life. Sagittarius shows the mature adult, who expands experience to deeper and wider philosophical and moral concerns, where 'the foreign' becomes explored. Capricorn shows the ageing individual who is more concerned with advancement in career, status and reputation, and, facing the inevitable limitations and afflictions of later life and reflections upon old age, is a little pessimistic and characteristically more conservative and austere. Aquarius shows the even older individual, whose long life experience has now enabled a more open outlook that can finally dispense with notions of status, and who can embrace unorthodox attitudes and the dropping of what are now seen to be outmoded prejudices in favour of more humanitarian objectives. Pisces shows the individual at the end of life, who feels a liminal need to dissolve the attachment of the self to now virtually irrelevant material concerns, and who may finally embrace a spiritual and renunciative outlook.

On the one hand, this representation of development through the regular zodiac is open to the easy criticism that we have merely 'shoe-horned in' a contrived picture of a developmental sequence into the progression of the signs. On the other hand, one simply can't help seeing it: there does indeed appear to be a tantalising outline of development, of the major stages of life, in roughly the correct sequence, which one might perhaps expect from a collectively projected

236

synthesis of the year, being one of the most basic determinators of life and its concerns. It seems to us that it would be difficult to 'read in' the same pattern from any arbitrary sequence or series.

A picture of human development thus certainly appears to be discernible in the sequence of the signs, one which seems both easily familiar and fairly comprehensive. There is also however another way in which we may view the signs in the regular sequence from Aries to Pisces, which shows how they can be relevant to 'personal human development', and that is how they relate, not to development as a fixed temporal order of maturation stages, but to 'development' as a hierarchy of human needs, and this is the subject of our next section.

The Signs as a Model of a Hierarchy of Needs

In the previous section we saw two astrological-symbolic representations or metaphors of the sequence of human maturational development, firstly in a somewhat condensed or abbreviated way in the themes of the planets (taken in their succession of apparent visual distance progressively from the Moon to the more distant planets),[532] in what we have termed the 'Palingenius-Shakespeare scheme', and separately, in a more detailed way, in the regular succession of the themes of the zodiac signs. The latter picture, of life from the earliest years, devoted to 'basic' activities, to later age-stages given to 'higher' philosophical endeavours, seems to possess a certain hierarchical nature in a valuative sense, and resembles the theoretical account of a hierarchy of human developing needs and motivations put forward by the American psychologist Abraham Maslow.

In 1943 Maslow proposed, based upon observations from his clinical experience, a theory of human motivation, which set out what he saw as the most basic or fundamental *needs* that are common to everyone.[533] Maslow thought that the 'integrated wholeness of the organism' should be a prime foundation of an account of human needs, and that no single need can be treated in isolation, but is related to the state of satisfaction of all of the others. This view is redolent of the 'integrating' principle of the Sun and of the inter-relatedness of the sign-components of the zodiac in astrological symbolism. Despite his recognition of a holistic approach, Maslow nevertheless saw the most fundamental human needs as arranged in a 'prepotent' hierarchy; that is to say, a particular need will usually only arise when earlier, more pressing ('prepotent') needs are mostly satisfied. Maslow saw the 'basic' human needs, in order of prepotency, as:

• Physiological needs. Maslow sees the basic necessities for physiological survival as the pre-eminent or most prepotent needs. These constitute the body's immediate need to maintain the homoeostasis it requires in terms of air, food, water, warmth and sleep. Maslow also included sex in the physiological needs.

• Safety needs. When the purely physiological needs have been satisfied to an acceptable degree, then there arise what Maslow termed the safety needs—the

---

[532] In astrological terminology, the Moon is referred to for convenience as a 'planet'.
[533] Maslow, 1943

requirements for a reliable, predictable and stable state; a physical 'ground' of security, free from danger or from a constant fear of threat. Factors that mitigate situations of danger or the threat of danger are things like a strong, secure and familiar personal territory, and adequate possessions and money to offset a want of resources.

• Love needs. If both the physiological and the safety needs are satisfied to a reasonable extent, then there emerge the needs for love, affection and intimate belonging. The individual then feels the need for friends, partners, lovers, family and children; for mutually regarding and rewarding intimate relationships generally. Maslow emphasises that, although often intertwined in practice, the need for love is not the same thing as the need for sex, the latter being seen as a purely physiological need.

• Esteem needs. When the physiological, safety and love needs are met to an adequate degree, then there arises the need for esteem, both in terms of self-esteem (or self-respect) and the esteem of others. Maslow emphasises that true self-esteem is 'firmly based', or the result of 'real capacity, achievement and respect from others'. According to Maslow, the need for esteem can be seen as having two aspects. Firstly there is *"the desire for strength, for achievement, for adequacy, for confidence in the face of the world, and for independence and freedom. Secondly, we have what we may call the desire for reputation or prestige (defining it as respect or esteem from other people), recognition, attention, importance or appreciation."*[534]

• The need for self-actualisation. Even when the needs of physiology, safety, love and esteem are all satisfied to acceptable degrees, there arises another need for something which Maslow termed 'self-actualisation'. Generally, the term refers to self-fulfilment in the realm of one's own unique life spirit, one's chosen vocation, or as Maslow termed it, *"to become everything that one is capable of becoming"*. Maslow acknowledged that the form of this need would vary from individual to individual, according to his or her own personal predilections. For one person, such self-fulfilment may lie in ideal parenting, for another in an athletic pursuit, for yet others in artistic or inventive endeavours. Self-actualisation certainly sounds like the fulfilment of a creative urge, and although Maslow did not think of it as a necessarily creative need, he acknowledged that *"in people who have any capacities for creation it will take this form"*.

Maslow accepted that, although most people seek to satisfy these basic needs in the 'prepotent' order that he proposes, the order is certainly not always rigidly sequential. A 'lower' need may be only partially met before a 'higher' level need strenuously emerges. For instance, there are those who value self-esteem more than love, possibly as a result of believing that self-esteem is in fact instrumental in obtaining love. Again, there are people who are so strongly creative that they engage in creativity despite a lack of earlier needs. People often have different needs that are only partially satisfied at a given time. The prepotent sequence is, in effect, in the form of an 'ideal template' that would be followed were other things

---

[534] Maslow, 1943

equal, though of course they rarely are.[535] As he developed his theory of needs, Maslow also drew attention to other important and relevant factors, in particular noting that *"there are certain conditions that are immediate prerequisites for the basic need satisfactions"*. The first of these is freedom, such as in freedom of speech, freedom to act as one pleases (as long as no harm is done to others), and freedom to enquire and seek information. Maslow doesn't quite give freedom the status of a basic need, apparently because it is not, strictly (but only 'almost') an end in itself. He nevertheless asserts that, without freedom, *"the basic satisfactions are quite impossible, or at least, severely endangered."*[536]

Maslow does however seem to consider another 'precondition' as having the status of a basic need in itself, and that is cognition (the perceptual, learning and intellectual capacities). Although, like freedom, a set of 'cognitive capacities' is initially seen only as a precondition for the basic needs, Maslow nevertheless does employ the term 'cognitive needs' and even explicitly argues for 'the reality of cognitive needs'. Maslow almost but never fully conflates the need for 'cognitive capacities' with the wider and deeper need 'to know and understand'. Concerning the latter, he states that, *"the desire to know is prepotent over the desire to understand"* and that both are *"as much personality needs as the basic needs."*[537] As his theory developed, Maslow's hierarchy also included aesthetic needs, as in the need to experience and even create beauty, harmony, balance, form and so-on. Maslow remarks:

> I have attempted to study this phenomenon on a clinical-personological basis with selected individuals, and have at least convinced myself that in some individuals there is a truly basic aesthetic need. They get sick (in special ways) from ugliness, and are cured by beautiful surroundings; they crave actively, and their cravings can be satisfied only by beauty. It is seen almost universally in healthy children. Some evidence of such an impulse is found in every culture and in every age as far back as the cavemen." Maslow asks, "What, for instance, does it mean when a man feels a strong conscious impulse to straighten the crookedly hung picture on the wall?[538]

Maslow also later identified 'transcendence' as a basic need in human motivation. This refers to the motivation a person has to transcend the personal self, in such activities as sexual union, aesthetic experiences, feelings of union with nature, in service to others, or in religious faith or mystical experience, where there is a need to be united with what is felt to be transcendent or divine.[539] It

---

[535] Maslow, 1943
[536] *Ibid.*
[537] Maslow, 1954
[538] *Ibid.*
[539] *Ibid.*

appears that Maslow developed the notion of the need for transcendence from aspects of the 'self-actualisation' need. For instance, his description of 'peak experiences', which can be attained by 'self-actualising' individuals as states of profoundly positive, whole experience, often of rapture, love and happiness, and *"complete mindfulness of the present moment without influence of past or expected future experiences"* sound decidedly spiritual or transcendent in nature. Indeed it's been argued that Maslow effectively amended his model to place self-transcendence as a motivational step beyond self-actualisation.[540]

We present an extended model of Maslow's hierarchy of needs in Figure 37 (including the 'cognitive', 'aesthetic' and 'transcendence' components, as there seems no doubt that Maslow wished to incorporate these), also showing the zodiac signs (as the 'houses'), in a way that we see as their likely identifications with Maslow's needs. It can be seen that there is undoubtedly a general resemblance between Maslow's hierarchy and the progression of the keyword themes of the signs, even in terms of sequential order. The comparison is not one of perfect identity. Maslow's 'cognitive' needs seem to encompass both Gemini and Sagittarius, which are a distance apart from each other in the zodiac sequence.[541]

Maslow's 'love' need also seems applicable to two signs; namely, to Cancer ('love' in the sense of emotional nurturance, security and belonging, as in a family) and to Libra ('love' in the sense of more romantic partnership-type relationships). The creativity inherent in Leo might seem thematically close to Maslow's 'self-actualisation', though in the scheme of 'the signs as needs' it appears as a period of joyful self-expressiveness, creativity and recreation that one is able to enter into once the more pressing needs of survival, security, learning and emotional security have been met. Engaging in recreational activity, such as sports, games and creativity generally, as represented by Leo, is surely a universal human need. We would tend not, however, to see Leo's need for creativity and recreation as necessarily the most potent and perfect goal of life, as might have been attributed to 'self-actualisation'.

Virgo and Scorpio do not seem to find a ready home in Maslow's scheme—unless in the latter case we simply identify Scorpio with the sexual urge. Indeed we would be more inclined to associate Scorpio with the sexual urge separately, and not to include it in the prior 'survival-oriented' physiological need as was the case in Maslow's scheme. Maslow's physiological needs seem to be those more immediately required for *survival*, such as air, food, water, warmth and sleep; the need to gratify the sexual urge, though extremely powerful, does not seem to us to be attributable to those 'survivalist' needs, for we can surely survive without sexual gratification (at any rate as individuals).

---

[540] Koltko-Rivera, 2006

[541] We are nevertheless reminded that Maslow seemed to distinguish between "cognitive capacities", which phrase reminds us of the keywords of Gemini, and "the desire to know and understand", which is more reminiscent of those of Sagittarius.

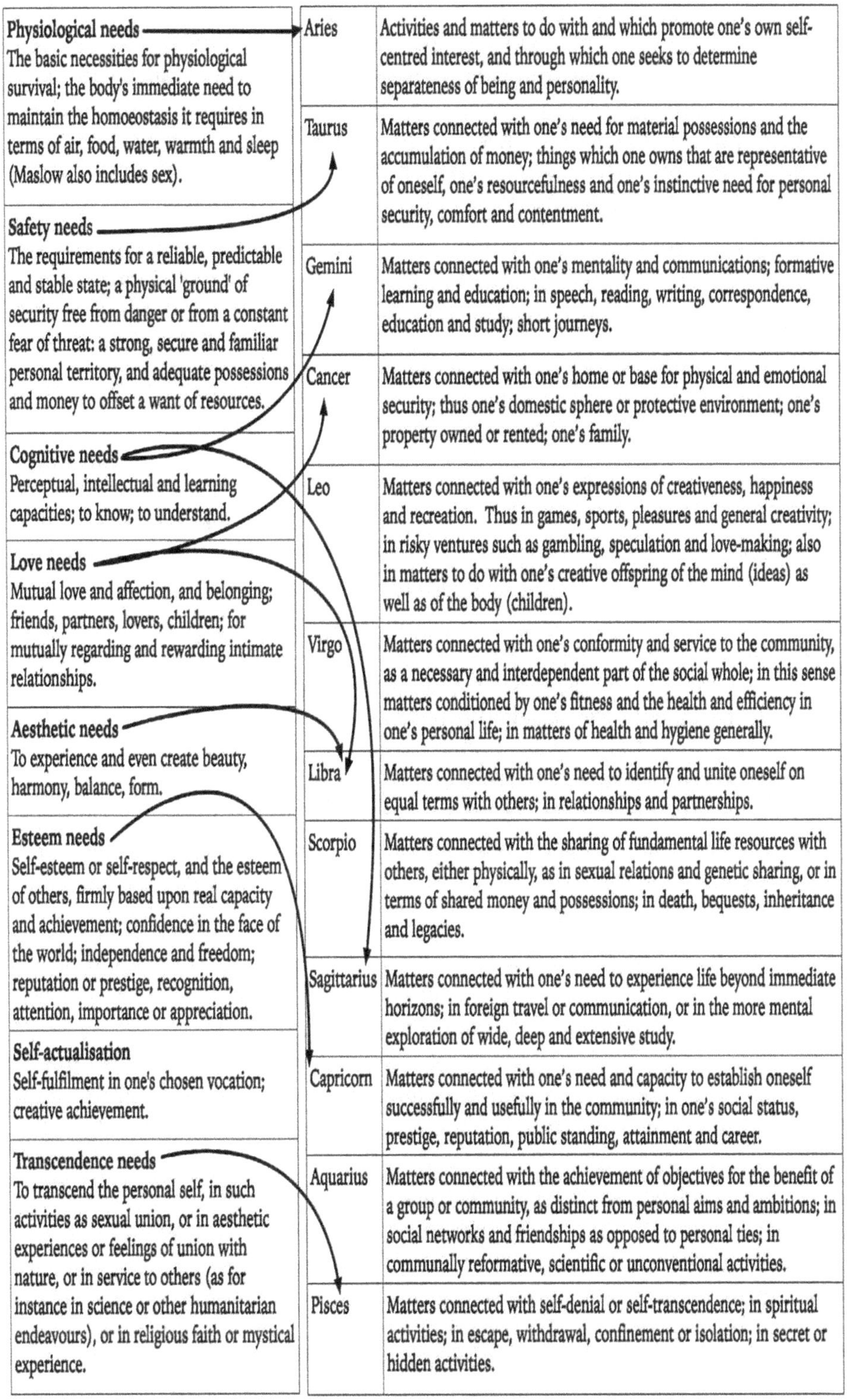

Maslow's Hierarchy of Needs	Sign	Sphere of Life
Physiological needs The basic necessities for physiological survival; the body's immediate need to maintain the homoeostasis it requires in terms of air, food, water, warmth and sleep (Maslow also includes sex).	Aries	Activities and matters to do with and which promote one's own self-centred interest, and through which one seeks to determine separateness of being and personality.
Safety needs The requirements for a reliable, predictable and stable state; a physical 'ground' of security free from danger or from a constant fear of threat: a strong, secure and familiar personal territory, and adequate possessions and money to offset a want of resources.	Taurus	Matters connected with one's need for material possessions and the accumulation of money; things which one owns that are representative of oneself, one's resourcefulness and one's instinctive need for personal security, comfort and contentment.
Cognitive needs Perceptual, intellectual and learning capacities; to know; to understand.	Gemini	Matters connected with one's mentality and communications; formative learning and education; in speech, reading, writing, correspondence, education and study; short journeys.
Love needs Mutual love and affection, and belonging; friends, partners, lovers, children; for mutually regarding and rewarding intimate relationships.	Cancer	Matters connected with one's home or base for physical and emotional security; thus one's domestic sphere or protective environment; one's property owned or rented; one's family.
Aesthetic needs To experience and even create beauty, harmony, balance, form.	Leo	Matters connected with one's expressions of creativeness, happiness and recreation. Thus in games, sports, pleasures and general creativity; in risky ventures such as gambling, speculation and love-making; also in matters to do with one's creative offspring of the mind (ideas) as well as of the body (children).
Esteem needs Self-esteem or self-respect, and the esteem of others, firmly based upon real capacity and achievement; confidence in the face of the world; independence and freedom; reputation or prestige, recognition, attention, importance or appreciation.	Virgo	Matters connected with one's conformity and service to the community, as a necessary and interdependent part of the social whole; in this sense matters conditioned by one's fitness and the health and efficiency in one's personal life; in matters of health and hygiene generally.
Self-actualisation Self-fulfilment in one's chosen vocation; creative achievement.	Libra	Matters connected with one's need to identify and unite oneself on equal terms with others; in relationships and partnerships.
	Scorpio	Matters connected with the sharing of fundamental life resources with others, either physically, as in sexual relations and genetic sharing, or in terms of shared money and possessions; in death, bequests, inheritance and legacies.
Transcendence needs To transcend the personal self, in such activities as sexual union, or in aesthetic experiences or feelings of union with nature, or in service to others (as for instance in science or other humanitarian endeavours), or in religious faith or mystical experience.	Sagittarius	Matters connected with one's need to experience life beyond immediate horizons; in foreign travel or communication, or in the more mental exploration of wide, deep and extensive study.
	Capricorn	Matters connected with one's need and capacity to establish oneself successfully and usefully in the community; in one's social status, prestige, reputation, public standing, attainment and career.
	Aquarius	Matters connected with the achievement of objectives for the benefit of a group or community, as distinct from personal aims and ambitions; in social networks and friendships as opposed to personal ties; in communally reformative, scientific or unconventional activities.
	Pisces	Matters connected with self-denial or self-transcendence; in spiritual activities; in escape, withdrawal, confinement or isolation; in secret or hidden activities.

Figure 37. Maslow's Hierarchy of Needs, Compared to the Signs of the Zodiac (As 'Houses' Or 'Spheres of Life')

We have assigned Maslow's 'esteem needs' to Capricorn, though we realise that this need does perhaps have descriptors that may be relatable to Aquarius (e.g., 'independence' and 'freedom'). Maslow's important 'precondition' of freedom, which didn't quite meet his criteria for inclusion as a 'basic need', also seems to emerge in the freedom-loving Aquarius.

Despite the imperfect correspondence between the two schemes, a similarity is clearly discernible. With respect to Maslow's need for 'self-actualisation', we feel that we cannot assign this to any particular sign; rather, we seem to see that it's possible to assign it to any of them—in fact, to any sphere of life at all; for it is surely the case that a person may find 'self-actualisation' in almost any life endeavour. We feel that this is a point which Maslow himself did not adequately address in his system of the needs hierarchy. Therefore, for the most part we leave 'self-actualisation' alone in the comparison, as we see it as applicable to virtually any life-sphere domain, according to personal predilection.

When we consider the signs that do not seem to fit neatly into Maslow's basic needs—Leo, Virgo, Scorpio and Aquarius—we might speculate that these nevertheless do represent basic human needs, but ones which Maslow either omitted or specified tangentially. Leo seems to embody Maslow's notion of the 'creative achievement' component of 'self-actualisation'. One might realistically argue that the sign Virgo represents a fundamental human need: there is of course, as in many animals, a basic human necessity for personal attendance to grooming, washing, health and hygiene; furthermore, humans are social animals and there is arguably a case to be made for a need to cultivate and maintain a 'fitness' that enables one to be of service to one's community. In the case of Scorpio, we undoubtedly see a most basic human need in the sexual urge, but also in its more subtle, less overtly conscious yet more profound aspect of the universal need for a deep communion or acknowledgement of the sharing of common life-resources with others—material as well as genetic—reflected in the ceremonies and rites that surround birth and death. Finally in the case of Aquarius, though its 'science and humanitarian endeavours' elements may seem to intrude into the 'transcendence' need, it would appear to us to have a greater affinity with Maslow's 'precondition' of freedom, and we would be inclined to assert that we can better see it as a separate basic need to engage in like-minded social networks and to identify with new, progressive and free-thinking group objectives.

We therefore see that the keyword descriptions of all of the zodiac signs can be seen as fundamental motivational needs (perhaps most accurately when taken in their descriptive forms as the 'houses' or 'spheres of life'); that they are very closely allied to the hierarchy proposed by Maslow and, like the components of Maslow's scheme, they emerge in a roughly prepotent sequence. They appear applicable, at one time or another in life, to all humans universally, and none in particular should be seen as the especial province of particular individuals, as might be implied in divinatory astrology (excepting of course for the usual variations in individuals from a normal distribution). We would assert that each are fundamental, and independent of one another in their essential natures.

The essence of Maslow's theory of prepotent needs seems to have a perennial appeal, despite the fact that its constituent components were specified in a somewhat loose manner as the theory developed. But we might not wonder at this. Anyone may take the time to jot down what they think are the 'most important things' or 'the most important needs' in life. In doing so, many people might evince similar, basic things, such as health, money, love, creativity, spirituality. That limited list may of course not be complete for everyone. Most probably it would also be rare to find someone who would firmly and finally settle on a strict order of importance of such factors. But we are attracted to the idea that the twelve signs of the zodiac, taken as a whole or interconnected 'set', look very much like mankind's collectively unconscious and historical approximation of all the 'departments' of life (like the imaginary ones 'jotted down' in the list above), which all need to be satisfied, and probably equally, because of their inter-dependent nature. They may not all be satisfied at the same time—that may be practically impossible—though it seems correct to say that some needs (such as transcendence) are very often explored when other more pressing and mundane factors have been settled (e.g., material stability), but are nevertheless ideally equal in a whole life. This is very like Maslow's idea.

Maslow's theory was not based on what we think of as strictly controlled empirical evidence—yet it continues to resonate with people intuitively, in the realms of personal development, education and business.[542] Thus it has persistent popularity despite the want of a strict empirical basis—much like astrological symbolism. We might go so far as to say that the zodiac signs, particularly as they are interpreted as spheres of life, constitute a more complete and integrated account of basic human needs than that of Maslow's familiar hierarchy. In addition we are reminded that, unlike Maslow's hierarchy, they don't reflect the theory of any one individual, but are the refined product of millennia of collective human myth and archetypal symbolism. Perhaps the pattern of the signs—stages of life through the year, projected by a globally collective unconscious—is a more profound and more comprehensive picture of humankind's needs than one thrashed-out consciously by one individual, however insightful that individual was.

The Status of Divinatory Natal Astrology: Sun-Signs & Planet-Signs: Theory & Evidence

As we mentioned at the outset, astrology continues to find a popular presence even in a modern age supposedly dominated—at least in mainstream academia—by science. Very few people are interested purely in the symbolism of astrology; that is to say, without also subscribing to the belief that one can describe and

---

[542] Wahba & Bridwell, 1976

predict an individual's personality from the position of the Sun, the Moon and the planets in the signs of the zodiac at the time of that person's birth. (We refer to this practice as 'divinatory astrology', for want of a better term.) The present authors however do belong to that select few who are fascinated by astrological symbolism, but who reject the practice of divinatory astrology as wholly misleading. We might hope that we have made reasonably clear why we take divinatory astrology to be false; it has no empirical support, but more importantly, for anything other than natal Sun-signs (the zodiacal sign that the Sun was in when a person was born), it is based on a traceable misunderstanding of the origin of the zodiac signs. We hope we will not try the reader's patience if we once more attempt to make crystal clear how this is the case.

The significance of the Sun being 'in' a sign is, as we have seen, nothing more than a characterisation of a particular time of the year (specifically, a roughly thirty-day section or 'time-slice' of year, approximately corresponding to a month period—see Chapter 1). This form of characterisation has been employed because long ago, the current time of the year was marked by observing (or inferring) the star-pattern which lay behind the Sun and projecting a salient or meaningful picture or 'sign' onto it—salient in that it was emblematic of the mundane characteristics of that time of year. This process of marking year-periods by projecting appropriate celestial pictures was put into practice by ancient peoples who did not on the whole apprehend such psychological processes of cognition. This being so, it is understandable that, after some time, the projected picture was treated as if it were a naturally occurring concomitant of the time of year—as if the picture wasn't a man-made, projected image of that time of year in the first place, but a co-occurring 'sign' of the season, being somehow part of the natural order of things.

These 'pictures of the times of year' therefore became long-established in the popular understanding of the changing nature of the annual cycle and of the environment or cosmos generally. When they began somewhat problematically to shift away from their old seasonally-referenced times in the year, due to precession, a change was eventually made to restore them once again, by adopting the 'tropical' zodiac (at least in Western astrology), where twelve equal signs always started at the spring equinox; thus the thematic agreement between 'sign' and the corresponding conditions of the time of year was reinstated and made invariable. But the ideas that these signs were still connected with the star-constellations and that they were somehow natural concomitants of the time of year still remained. Thus for instance when the Sun was in the sign of Virgo, people considered that the 'picture of stars' roughly in the region of the Sun's path in the zodiac, long understood as 'the virgin holding the ear of grain', was a heavenly token of that time of year, when the virgin earth was indeed ripe to give up its fecundity as a precious harvest.

It was a short step from there to conflating the meaning of a sign as 'the time of year in which certain things happened' with 'the time of year in which certain people were born', and further, to 'what those born at that time must be like'. A person born 'in the sign of' Virgo, for instance, was seen as somehow necessarily *personally* possessing the characteristics which were associated with and necessary for the mundane activities of that harvest time of year; thus, such individuals were taken to be practical, diligent, discriminating, etc; in short, like the actions and attitudes that were seen and required at harvest-time, and like the fecund, receptive earth itself which will produce the fruit of that harvest. Although strictly we have to view such a proposition about birth and personality as an hypothesis, capable of being subject to empirical testing, it is obvious how the erroneous idea of natal correspondences grew out of this misconstruing or inappropriate extension of the concept of 'Sun in a sign' as meaning 'the conditions of the time of year', into a meaning of 'the character of people being *born* at that time'. One is free indeed to test such a poor hypothesis, but as the misconstrual of the concept itself would predict, one finds no support for it. Such a misconceived hypothesis is, in addition, devoid of any accompanying account of the physical mechanism that might be supposed to mediate such an effect—though speculation about this hardly seems necessary given the likely way the belief came about.

Once the unfounded assumption that the 'sign that the Sun is in at birth' (being in origin a short-form for 'the time of year of birth') entailed the notion of 'seasonally fixed personality', such extended usage of the concept of 'the Sun in a sign' was compounded further into truly inadmissible dimensions by also considering *planets other than the Sun* as relevant to the fixing of personality at the time of birth. If 'the sign that the Sun was in' at birth (that is, 'the time of year at birth') cannot in fact predict personality (by way of seasonal effects), the sign that these other bodies were in at birth certainly can not (there are no seasonal factors involved). It is worthwhile expanding even further on these points.

At certain times of the year it is possible for an observer to point to the position of the Sun against its backdrop of stars and declare, *"When the Sun has those stars behind it, then people generally are happier,"* (for instance, when people are, by and large, happier in the more agreeable conditions of summer, rather than in the conditions of winter). This is just another way of saying that meteorological or climatic conditions characteristic of one part of the year (e.g., summer) *tend* to have an effect upon people *generally* (e.g., make them happier than in winter). It is a reflection of the changing relationship of the Sun and the Earth's climate—in other words, it is a *seasonal* effect. At other times of the year—for instance the beginning of spring—it is similarly possible for an observer to point to the position of the Sun against its different backdrop of stars and say, *"When the Sun has those stars behind it, then new life returns to the earth and people generally feel better and more confident,"* (being the time of spring when life is reborn). These examples, and others like it, are *seasonal* effects; the seasons are merely marked, for convenience, by the Sun being observed to be 'in' different star-patterns (which patterns may be stylised as 'signs' with thematic pictorial representations that are appropriate to the 'feel' of the time of year).

There is no reason however to suppose that *being born* in such different seasons is associated with or causes an indelible stamp of a thematically similar personality. This idea is a fanciful and unwarranted extension of the concept of 'the Sun in the sign'—as a reference merely to the characteristic seasonal conditions of the time of year—into 'the person of the sign' as a reference to a supposedly inevitable corresponding personality of those born at that time. It is the assumption that people born, for instance, in the summer are forever going to be 'summery' people, or that people born in the autumn are forever going to be 'autumn-like' people.

This idea that there is some 'instilling' of personality from the characteristics of the season of birth (the time of year which is marked by a 'Sun-sign') may or may not be true (though it appears that it is not: there is no empirical support, nor is there any physical mechanism to account for it; indeed it looks very much as if the whole notion indeed arose confusedly from the concept of 'Sun in sign' as 'time of year' being spuriously extended to 'person of sign'). But when the *Moon* or any of the distant *planets* appear in one of those stellar backdrops (are 'in' signs), no season with attendant characteristics is even being indicated by that celestial configuration, and thus no similar effect, associable to the 'Sun's time of year', is possible even *theoretically*, since those bodies, whatever their geocentrically apparent location in the ecliptic, have no relation to the seasons of the year whatsoever. In such a case involving the planets, we are seeing the usage of the term 'the Sun being in a sign' (as a short-form for the time of the year, with its known seasonal characteristics) being extended even more illogically, with no seasonal characteristics involved (and thus no possibility of 'this-season-like people').

The idea of 'planet in sign' 'piggybacks' conceptually on the idea of 'Sun in sign', but without the reasons that might have given the latter a seasonal effect to people generally. The phrase 'the Sun in Aries at birth' means *a time of year of birth* (which time or season might have been held to affect personality); the phrase 'Uranus in Aries at birth' means nothing more than a fortuitous geocentric measurement; no time of year or season is being referenced at all (and the signs *are* times of the year). One might as well talk of 'the sign that the International Space Station was in' at the time of birth (if its trajectory was always geocentrically inside the ecliptic); it would be as meaningless in terms of the signs, or times of the year, as the planets are meaningless in terms of the signs or times of the year; neither the space station nor the planets have any relevance to the seasonal times of the year, *which are the origin of the signs themselves.*

It may be one thing to conjecture that people born in the Sun-sign of (say) Aries at spring will receive such a strong impression of that wonderfully resurgent time of year at their life's beginning, that they will, by some unknown means, personally harbour those seasonal characteristics all their life long (though even this is fanciful). It is quite another however to conjecture similar things of *planets* which happen to be in a zodiacal sign at birth: the position in the zodiac of a planet, unlike that of the Sun, has no relationship with a season. It is clear, from the thematic correspondences here reviewed between the signs and the twelve 'time-slices' of the year which they represent, that the signs had their origin in the seasons. Thus, given the seasonal origin of the signs, it is only the Sun-sign (that is, the time of year) that could *possibly* be considered to be associable to a seasonal effect, whether transient or lifelong.

If the conjecture of the lasting effect of a natal 'Sun-sign' (a way of saying 'the effect of a seasonal time of year') is fanciful, the proposal of a lasting effect of a natal 'planet-sign' is plainly reasoning gone astray: it is applying the original speculation of potentially lasting effects of a natal 'Sun-sign'—a seasonal time of the year—incorrectly to a celestial body which has no relationship whatsoever to the seasonal time of year. The planets' locations in the zodiac signs simply do not betoken the seasons, as the Sun's location in the zodiac signs does. Thus we see that the signs owe their very existence and meaning solely to the Sun, not to the Moon or planets. Nevertheless the planets, those heavenly projections of archetypal human functions, became the objects of an unreasoning perseveration of that 'lifelong stamping of the season' conjecture, even though 'the sign a planet is in' does not indicate a season at all. The Sun 'being in a sign' is an indication of a seasonal characteristic, and is therefore subject to that (admittedly doubtful) conjecture that such a characteristic may be 'stamped onto' the newborn and last the whole life long. A *planet* 'being in a sign' has no relevance at all to the seasonal time of year, so the conjecture does not apply, though it began erroneously to include any celestial body according to 'what sign it was in'.

This then is our summary of the misguided basis by which divinatory astrology came into being—misguided at least in so far as it proposes more than the possibility that natal Sun-signs might somehow reflect an 'impression' of their associated seasonal conditions indelibly at birth into personality, though even for this possibility we have seen no empirical evidence, nor is there any known physical mechanism whereby such a process might be mediated. In the case of the zodiacal position of any celestial body *other than the Sun* at birth, for the reasons just stated, and especially regarding the very origin of the zodiac signs, we reject any notion of a divinatory effect *a priori*; thus it does not surprise us that the empirical evidence we have reviewed to test the possibility that the position of extra-solar bodies at birth might predict personality have neither shown any support.

Belief in Sun-Sign Divinatory Astrology

There is, therefore, no empirical support for the notion that the geocentric locations of the Sun, the Moon or the planets at birth are in any way associated with, or can predict, human personality. Indeed we have traced the unwarranted assumptions which have lead traditions to infer that they might be (fallacious views of the signs as causative entities as opposed to purely seasonal markers, and the absurder extension of this error to extra-solar planets 'in signs' when these bodies are not even connected with the seasons). The question thus presents itself: why do very many people nevertheless subscribe to divinatory astrology, or at the very least grant it ready acceptance, even if only in the most basic way of natal Sun-signs, in the complete absence of positive evidence and in the presence of reasons not to?

In our experience those who do so are not unintelligent or more than usually credulous. They are normal, everyday people, like ourselves. To put it simply, one's own and other people's natal Sun-signs very often really *do* seem to be indicative of their personalities. The present authors have not been immune to this belief. The first author has found that, when studying the birth-charts (horoscopes) of people he personally knows, he often seems to see correspondences of the keyword symbolism of their Sun-signs in their personalities and in their behaviours. We might illustrate this with some anecdotal examples. The horoscope or birth-chart of one friend showed that the Sun was in the sign Cancer at the time of birth. We will remember that Cancer and its ruling 'planet' the Moon is associated with sensitivity and the imagination; the friend in question is a highly sensitive type of person who writes poetry. Cancer is also associated with maternal lactation, and is physiologically associated with the chest area; as an infant the poetic friend was accidentally scarred on his chest by scalding-hot milk. The friend eventually became a dairy farmer. Another friend's birth horoscope also showed the Sun in the sign Cancer. Cancer is associated strongly with emotional sensitivity, the domestic sphere and the collecting of perceived resources, while its ruling 'planet' is the Moon. The second 'Sun-in-Cancer' friend was well-known for his dislike of venturing outside his home, suffered from a 'hoarding' obsession and spent much of his time manufacturing calendars which showed the phases of the Moon.

Another friend's birth horoscope was shown to have the Sun in Aries. We will remember that the Aries 'personality' is characterised as self-oriented, often of a quick-tempered disposition, and physiologically associated with the head. This friend was characteristically self-centred in outlook and experienced the complete loss of all the hair on his head at an unusually young age, causing him to expose a completely bald pate throughout adult life. Another person, a family relation, also born with the Sun in Aries (which we recall is also characterised by impulsivity) once as a child tumbled downstairs, cutting her head, only to confess later that she had in fact impulsively and deliberately launched herself from the stairs in an unthinking moment of recklessness. Another friend, born with the Sun in Leo, whose sign's 'personality' is seen to be proud and needing to impress, but nevertheless generous and gregarious, was exactly that in character, as though in caricature. A relative whose Sun-sign was in the sign Virgo, which is associated with an especial regard to hygiene and modesty, was obsessed with cleaning and was prudish in the extreme. The horoscope of another friend showed the natal

Sun to be in Libra, a sign described as charming and disliking discord. This friend was indeed enchanting and agreeable, in appearance as well as character, and possessed a notable aversion to disharmony and conflict to the point of squeamishness. Another friend was born whilst the Sun was in Sagittarius, which sign is associated with extensive travel, and physiologically with the hips. This friend was a global traveller who required surgery for a hip replacement.

These examples are open to the obvious objection of the charge of confirmation bias: not all bald people are born with the Sun in Aries, nor are all people who require hip replacements born with the Sun in Sagittarius! It nevertheless *seemed* to the author that the number of confirming examples appeared to occur at a level greater than would be expected by chance. The examples above do not constitute an exhaustive list of apparently confirming examples where the author has been able to see an association between the keywords of their Sun-signs and their personalities. Indeed, for the great majority of the author's friends whose Sun-sign he has ascertained, he can see an association between the keywords of their Sun-signs and their personalities. We are of course aware that these observations present here as purely anecdotal; for all the reader knows, they might have been fabricated. The reader is thus invited to try the same experiment with personal friends or relatives whose Sun-signs are known, consulting the keywords of the appropriate signs from those listed in Chapter 3, and comparing these with the personality characteristics of the known persons. If the reader finds similar correspondences, then he or she is discovering the same apparent associations that many others have also perceived.

The curious situation thus presents itself where, even when we limit our discussion to natal Sun-signs, on the one hand we are aware of the fact that empirical studies overwhelmingly do *not* support an association between these and personality; yet on the other, we nevertheless often seem personally to be surrounded by apparent examples of just such an association. What might account for this? Some might feel inclined to suggest that there really is a correlation between natal Sun-sign and personality, and that the empirical research has just not been conducted in a manner suitable enough to expose it sufficiently. But as we have seen, a number of careful studies have examined the possibility and found no supporting evidence. One might otherwise suggest that there is an association, but only for some people; that is, a delimited number of people (but a number higher than would be expected by chance alone) have personalities that do indeed correspond to the keyword characteristics of their Sun-signs, and that among these are the people who become impressed by Sun-sign astrology and who may go on to develop an interest in it. But such a possibility would of course add the further question of what differentiates this particular class of people from everyone else. For both these possibilities—'an effect not properly explained' and 'an effect only for a few people'—it remains the case that the conceptual jump from 'Sun in sign as disposition of the time of year' to 'Sun in sign as the lifelong disposition of a person *born* at that time of year' still seems an unwarranted leap.

Both possibilities also still leave open the curiously unanswered question of what physical mechanism mediates the instilling of personality from the characteristics of a seasonal period of the year.

One commentator has suggested that belief in divinatory astrology happens through people simply paying undue attention to a keyword that is understood to be a descriptor of their Sun-sign. In other words, people learn what the Sun-sign 'means' from a single adjectival description (for instance, going through the signs in succession from Aries to Pisces: *"assertive, possessive, changeable, sensitive, creative, critical, harmonious, secretive, adventurous, cautious, detached, intuitive"*). From thereon, because we are *"interested only in our own sign"*, we 'home-in' on the adjective that supposedly describes our Sun-sign, see that it does indeed tally with a trait which we sometimes have and, forgetting that all the other single traits may equally apply to us at times, we believe that the astrological Sun-sign trait in particular does indeed describe us well. As the author puts it, *"...we fail to notice what astrologers aren't telling us, namely, that these traits are universal. Everybody behaves in each of these ways at various times; so, no matter what your sign is, it will agree with a trait you already possess. Lo! Astrology works—and you have started on the road to belief."*[543]

It could be argued that, if people did learn the basics of the Sun-signs from single keywords, it would in reality be hard for them to accept that their overarching natures conform exclusively to that single descriptor and never to others. The personality traits associated with the signs, as presented in newspapers, books, magazines and the internet, are in fact commonly presented as prose descriptions of the multiple keyword 'clusters' of which they are composed, with their interconnected thematic associations, rather than single terms. Furthermore people no doubt *do* learn what other signs 'mean', when they initially learn something of astrology, if only out of interest for their friends or family; in such a way they're able to compare and contrast their own Sun-sign keywords with those of others.

If the Sun-sign 'keyword-clusters' appeared applicable to everyone, the average person would not be so stupid as to not notice this. It seems more probable that people very often notice that certain other 'sign keyword clusters' do *not* apply to them. It's possible for instance to imagine someone assessing that their overall personality characteristics belong *either* to (for instance) the Gemini 'keyword cluster' (mainly intellectual, logical, communicative, etc), *or* to, say, the Cancer keyword cluster (mainly emotional, instinctive, introspective, etc). True, everyone may exhibit either keyword-cluster at some points in their life, but if someone is asked whether the one or the other thematic cluster characterises their *general* personality, it's doubtful that either would suit; since they are so different, it could only be the one or the other (or neither). The objecting author quoted above apparently fails to see the notion that, while all the sign-traits might indeed surface at one time or another in the same person, some will apply *more than*

---

[543] Dean, 1987

others (indeed, it would deny the very concept of human personality to suppose otherwise).

If the keyword descriptions of the signs were indeed all quite homogeneous, then a confirmation bias known as a 'Barnum effect' could be said to come into play to affect people's attributions and beliefs about Sun-signs. The 'Barnum effect' is a psychological phenomenon where people believe that given personality descriptions apply specifically to them, when they are in fact vague enough to apply to most people, or even everyone.[544] This might be more likely to become the case with a presentation of the signs as single keywords, since these would indeed more readily appear to apply to most people at least some of the time; but as we have pointed out, this is not how the signs are in fact typically portrayed or explained; they are rather presented in thematically-related 'clusters' of traits. It seems less likely that these more specific and descriptive 'domains' of keyword-clusters would appear to apply to everyone, or even to most people, especially when taken in the Sun-sign sense as 'traits which *generally* apply significantly more than others'.

Readers are invited to examine the clusters of keyword descriptions for each of the signs as described in Chapter 3 and decide for themselves whether they appear conceptually distinct from one another (for instance, the example we cited of the difference between the keyword-clusters of the sign Gemini and those of the sign Cancer). For our part we feel that the average reader would be easily able to discern the themes of each and to distinguish between them, and that such themes are sufficiently mutually exclusive for the broad accusation of an inevitable 'Barnum effect' to be misplaced.

But the question remains: *"Why do people subscribe to divinatory (natal) astrology, even taken just as the idea that the theme of the Sun-sign at birth reflects an 'instilled' general personality, when empirical evidence shows no support for this?"* A clue to the answer comes from the study we touched upon earlier, conducted by Van Rooij (1999), which found that those who have prior knowledge of the descriptions of their astrological Sun-sign tended to rate their own personalities in agreement with those Sun-sign's keywords (via a self-report questionnaire), while those with no such prior knowledge did not.[545] These findings suggest that exposure to astrological knowledge of the keyword interpretations of our own Sun-sign brings about a powerful cognitive bias, an altered self-concept, which persuades us that our natal Sun-sign does indeed describe our personality.

The study has some interesting implications for tests of personality traits *per se*, given its implication that the measurement of personality seems able to be influenced by, or, as one might say, 'indoctrinated' by, pre-existing ideas and beliefs. We might even say that the study has implications for what we refer to as 'personality' itself, since it might be assumed that personality, as revealed (or even designated) by such tests, very commonly itself has components that could be said to be made up of prior belief systems or indoctrination.

---

[544] Brittanica, 2024
[545] Van Rooij, 1999

The telling difference in self-ratings between Van Rooij's knowledgeable and non-knowledgeable groups certainly seems to show that prior knowledge indeed had some differentiating, indoctrinating influence upon self-attribution. The difference leads us fairly reasonably to assume that the knowledgeable group's different responses were conforming to that prior knowledge; that their responses were not in a sense 'real', but that they rather represented ways in which they were 'talking about' or in some way affirming the self-concept bias arising *from* their prior astrological knowledge. If we assume this to be correct, then we feel we should also say that we don't know what the knowledgable group's personality-rating responses would 'really' have been like without the prior knowledge, because such information was masked by the 'indoctrinating' cognitive bias. We similarly tend to assume that the 'non-knowledgeable' group's responses were the true, 'real' reflections of *their* personality, since they were *not* biased by prior knowledge.

These assumptions would therefore imply that a trait-rating test is only reliably able to assess personality in the absence of prior biasing knowledge—unless, that is, we would be happy to say that such a test 'just does' measure self concept—or even 'personality'—correctly, as it is at the point of testing, whether it is altered by some biasing prior knowledge or not. It might be said that such an approach is more acceptable than one which takes an overweening regard to biases from prior information or belief—to 'indoctrination' which has altered self-concept, since arguably there will always be such biases and one can never control for all of them (or even know them). How much personality is *not* shaped by biased indoctrination of prior belief systems? That said, we cannot help noting the stark difference in Van Rooij's study between the group who had prior *astrological* knowledge and the group who did not. That prior knowledge clearly seems to have been a variable of interest to us in its power to alter self-concept, and may go some way to explaining why people persist in accepting Sun-sign astrology despite a complete lack of evidence.

Van Rooij noted that it would be interesting to investigate whether the prior knowledge affects a person's *behaviour* as well as their measured self-concept. If the knowledgeable group in addition went on to 'act out' the personalities prompted by the prior knowledge, we might be even more tempted to say that such attitudes and behaviours *really are* their personalities; that the cognitive biases, brought about by astrological knowledge, had actually determined at least part of their personality. However, even if we accept this, *it would not be the season, reflected as the Sun-sign, that would have been the cause of such a 'change' in personality;* it would only have been the originating indoctrination—a self-fulfilling prophecy which might in principle have arisen through any similarly convincing 'doctrines' (an 'indoctrination' of self-confidence, for instance, instilled by parenting, may in the same way cause actually 'confident personalities'). The important thing for us to consider here is that the doctrine, the prior information, could have been any one of a number of things of a greater or lesser power to instil belief; it did not have to be anything particularly to do with the seasons or their thematic markers, the signs.

The results of the study seem quite conclusive, though it may be interesting if the experiment could be repeated with an additional condition where close friends or partners ('close informants') also rated participants' traits. The ratings of close informants are generally reliable.[546] If such close informants consistently rated differently to the way the knowledgeable group of participants rated, then we would perhaps be able to say with even more confidence that it was indeed the 'indoctrination' and the subsequent formation of an alternative self-concept on the part of the knowledgeable participants that was being 'acted out' in the test. It might just be possible that close informants themselves might draw on *their* knowledge of the participants' Sun-signs, and that such knowledge might be reflected in *their* ratings. If there were sufficient numbers of close informants to constitute groups who were and who were not knowledgeable of the participants' Sun-signs, further comparisons might be made between the ratings of these additional groups (it may be, for instance, that knowledge of *someone else's* Sun-sign may not act so strongly as a bias). Participants or close informants who were misinformed as to Sun-sign might also constitute additional revealing conditions. Of course 'indoctrinated' participants might 'act' their internalised personalities to the point where their close friends would assume such reified traits to be the real thing.

To speak to the author's perception of his friends that we mentioned above, the trait-rating study would indeed need to be extended in a way that could establish the existence or otherwise of a similar bias of personality-attribution of other familiar people's personalities, where their Sun-signs are known and not known to the raters. Given the strength of the bias which knowledge of one's own Sun-sign has been demonstrated to have to alter one's own self-attribution or self-concept, it certainly seems a reasonable hypothesis to suppose that, for those with some prior astrological knowledge, awareness of *others'* Sun-signs may equally bias one's judgement of others' personalities. If that extended hypothesis were tested, it would not surprise us if the results would lead us to conclude that when people become aware not only of their own but also of other people's Sun-signs (together with something of a resumé of the signs' characteristics), they may often modify, to a greater or lesser degree, their appraisal or belief of their own *and* other people's personality traits to suit the characteristics of these known Sun-signs. There may be more nuanced differences, of course: it may be more difficult to appraise (rightly or wrongly) one's own personality, rather than others'. Indeed, a general difficulty of appraising one's own personality may explain the ease with which one adopts a self-concept or self-attribution that is prompted by an apparently structured, knowledgeable source—that is, divinatory astrology.

At this point our question, *"Why do people subscribe to divinatory astrology, even if just to the idea that the Sun-sign at birth is associated with personality, when the*

---

[546] Kim *et al.*, 2019

evidence shows no support for this?" appears to be at least partly answered with regard to beliefs about our own Sun-signs: a strong cognitive bias, being a change of self-concept or self-attribution, comes into play when we are conversant with our own Sun-sign and the rudiments at least of its keywords. But our question then seems to be immediately replaced by another: why is the cognitive bias so powerful? Why does such prior knowledge so readily alter our self-attribution or self-concept, to the point where we believe that our natal Sun-sign keywords really do summarise our personality? We might suggest that we are so vulnerable to a cognitive bias of attribution in the case of divinatory astrology because of at least two reasons.

Firstly, although we have a natural desire to understand and evaluate ourselves in relation to other people and the world around us, we nevertheless find it generally difficult to appraise our own personalities. Even when we attempt to do so, we can't be sure that our opinion is verified by others. Thus an easily calculated system with widespread usage and which appears to have an ancient authority may be tempting to adopt as a guide, its *modus operandi* often seeming immune from absolute doubt precisely because it is unspecified, tacit, mysterious, opaque, not critically explained, and its origins not understood (people are generally unaware of the original seasonal denotation of the signs, or of the fallacious use of 'planets in signs', as discussed above).

Secondly, as our review here has shown, the system of the astrological zodiac signs seems to comprise descriptions of the most basic aspects of human nature— the most fundamental or archetypal 'semantic clusters' or images of the human psyche. This makes it an attractive framework which speaks very readily to an appraisal of personality. It is also *comprehensive* with regard to these archetypes. The zodiac, which characterises the signs as a whole system, is probably the most comprehensive set of such factors ever used to provide an image of the human psyche, incorporating virtually all of the most basic facets of human activity and experience. The things it deals with make sense to us, and even includes aspects of life that are not matters for everyday discussion but which no doubt feature in our own introspections. Whatever characteristic of human nature you seek to understand, it is projected, somewhere, in the planets and signs; thus the all-inclusive nature of this array of astrological symbols lends the divinatory practice even more credence.

It is just because because divinatory astrology deals with this 'complete array' of the most archetypal human functions, the most basic aspects of development and life needs, that a sort of effortless resonance or a ready willingness to identify with its forms is easily forthcoming, as is the similarly easy inclination to engage with an apparent personal summary of these matters and to ignore contrary evidence by way of biased self-concept or self-attribution. The fully comprehensive scope of this 'round table' of archetypes makes cognitively biased discrimination more likely and more potent, since the symbols represent the foundational things that we are primed to identify with; in a sense, they are very often precisely the things that constitute the default matters which confirmation bias is inevitably prejudiced to look for.

After all, what may be said to influence confirmation bias, other than the factors which are the most basic, most fundamental and most important to our nature? These are the primal factors everyone is biased to see. In this sense, the confirmation bias of identifying with the symbolic function of a particular sign or planet can be seen as another form of psychological projection—as usual, of the most salient or fundamental issues that concern the human psyche. We therefore naturally tend to project without much effort into the symbolism which divinatory astrology incorporates, employing cognitive bias more readily.

In a way this is a secondary projection: humankind's basic functions were first projected onto the planets and into the random patterns of the stars, which latter coalesced into a kaleidoscopic image of the important and even crucial matters reflected in life's journey through the year. Once codified in an almost crystalline fashion into the schematic of the zodiac, another form of projection was brought about—the divinatory aspect, looking inwards into the interconnected network or array of those symbols.

We have to remember, however, that divinatory Sun-sign astrology—the assumption of seasonally specific symbolism inhering as lifelong characteristics of those born at the relevant times of the year (e.g., 'spring babies always retain something of the spring')—though perhaps understandable, given the impact of the seasons and the primary symbolism that grew out of them—is nevertheless based on unwarranted and fanciful reasoning. A mistaken, accretive belief took hold that *anything* taking place at the 'time of the sign' (the births of people occurring at such times, and even the completely unrelated positions of the *planets* in the signs) would be somehow bound up with, or take on the nature of, those essentially seasonal characteristics. Unsurprisingly, empirical evidence does not support such hypotheses.

As we hope we have shown, there is good reason to believe that one's Sun-sign at birth (that is, the characteristic time of year at birth) is not associated with, and does not predict, personality. The evidence, particularly that of Van Rooij (1999), suggests that the curiously stubborn persistence of belief in Sun-sign divinatory astrology (that the natal Sun-sign reflects lifelong personality) despite the absence of evidence, reflects a strongly internalised self-concept in those who once begin to be aware of the keywords involved and the divinatory assumption. When based on the signs—a powerfully descriptive and comprehensive array of the most basic human traits—the allure of an association of Sun-sign with personality is thus extremely tenacious. In the absence of better or readier methods, but left with a strong desire to understand ourselves and our place in the world, we therefore still tend to give it credence. The easy propensity of the zodiac signs in particular to make real descriptions of personality (even if unsystematically assigned to individuals) and so to foster cognitive bias is commented upon by Van Rooij:

> ...astrology is one of the few, if not the only, widely used systems for describing personality at a layman's level. It is a personality system with which many lay people are familiar, at least as far as the sun-sign is concerned. Generally, people who have an interest in personality find in astrology a simple but elaborate flexible description which makes use of the same language (traits) that people use in their daily life.[547]

When someone identifies with the description of a Sun-sign it is never a wholly negative attribution (except perhaps for those unfortunate persons whose self-image is so poor that *any* proffered description is disliked). Whatever sign is indicated is a universally recognised aspect of life, with primordial and archetypal features and characteristics. It may seem engaging and thought-provoking that this one sign with its interesting facets apparently applies to you. It appears to offer a glimpse into identity, and cognitive biases will seem to verify this. The identification can obviously be profound—strong enough to 'punch through' the results of experiments such as those conducted by Mayo *et al.* (1978) and Van Rooij (1999) as a readily mediating variable.

A fully drawn up birth chart is even more gripping: it has the appearance of detailed yet highly personal, even unique information, which claims to provide the ownership of a whole picture of the self—an almost miraculous thing. The archetypes are all there, and furthermore they are arranged as if personally for you and you alone. What else can offer such an apparently exclusive and comprehensive picture of your life and inner being? One encounters something replete with information concerning fundamental human functions, and as these pertain apparently uniquely to oneself. It is more powerful than a Rorschach inkblot, as it comes with structured archetypal components, which can become convincing prompts. It is, once again, projection: one naturally wants to make sense of one's life, and one is apparently able to do so with recognisably fundamental human attributes. Nothing peculiar is being said; on the contrary, one recognises these functions in one's own being, and one may easily accept the relative importance of an emphasised or weighted subset of them, since they appear as one's very own. This is powerful enough to override notoriously unreliable knowledge of the self: if someone has, perhaps with some sense of bewilderment, sought knowledge of their inner being, and they are subsequently told by way of an ancient authority that they are in essence highly emotionally sensitive, might they not very often go along with such an idea?

Despite the substantial evidence against divinatory astrology, we nevertheless feel that we must guard against a certain fashionable yet unpleasant vilification of anything that is even related to the subject, and we do so for good reasons. At the outset we drew attention to the danger of disregarding astrology to the point that we avoid anything even remotely concerned with such a 'pseudoscience', tainted

---

[547] Van Rooij, 1999

as it appears by notions of divination. We would rather advocate an outlook whereby, while we can rationally acknowledge the evidence against the claims of *divinatory* (natal) astrology, we can nevertheless appreciate that the symbolism which 'astrology' has systematised is anterior to divinatory practice, being a fundamental expression of the nature of human needs and cognition, and is of profound importance in gaining a holistic view of the most basic structure of human life, and of the human psyche.

One gets the impression from many researchers that they suppose astrological symbolism must have sprung somehow quite fortuitously out of a vacuum; that it should be treated as nothing more than the random noise that must be controlled in scientific experiments; not that it represents the primal attempts of humans to understand and conceptually organise facets of the cosmos which surrounded them and which moved around them. One might even think that some commentators assume that the Babylonians, the Greeks and others just 'made up' their celestially-painted myths almost at random, or because they were ignorant, dull, frightened, wild or irrational. It might seem absurd to such researchers for us to propose that these symbols were the first renderings, the first pattern-seeking cognitive footholds with which humans sought to construct a meaningful perception of the cosmos, to make sense of the world around them and as it related to them.

Researchers may be loath to appear involved even by association with such 'superstition' and so to become mistrusted by their peers. Even in a condescendingly quasi-sympathetic appraisal of astrology as a form of 'entertainment', one commentator who still crudely limits judgement of the subject in terms of 'influences from the stars' writes, "[It would not matter] *if astrology is used like Rorschach inkblots to provide insight: Just as there is nothing really there in inkblots, so we need have no concern if there is nothing really there in celestial inkblots"*,[548] thus unfortunately missing the central role of projection in pareidolia—the cognitive process which has been the greatest clue to ancient human psychology, the fount of astrological symbolism and the very origin of the signs.

---

[548] Dean, 1987

6

The Way of the Zodiac

In our present review we have seen how the signs of the zodiac have evolved from pareidolia-based cognitive projections of important seasonal conditions into a coherently structured symbolic repository or distillation of humankind's most basic or archetypal life concerns.[549] The pattern of the signs and their components contains fundamentals of what we now understand as dimensional constructs of human personality, such as introversion-extraversion, neuroticism-stability, and the major factors of personality as determined by Cattell.[550] We can also discern an overall symbolic reflection of human maturational life-development, in the projected themes of the planets as they're enumerated successively in terms of their distance from the Sun (the 'Shakespeare-Palingenius' scheme), in the overall seasonal progression of the year, and in a more detailed way through the complete sequence of the signs of the zodiac. We also see a strikingly close correspondence between the general sequence of the zodiac signs and the prepotent hierarchy of human motivational needs as proposed by the psychologist Abraham Maslow.[551] Furthermore, we suggest that the symbolic representations of needs in the complete sequence of the zodiac signs can be looked upon as an improvement on Maslow's original conception.

The widespread conception of divinatory astrology—the notion that the zodiac sign which the Sun is 'in' *at birth* can actually predict aspects of later personality, according to the thematic characteristics of the sign (presumably by some effect of the environmental conditions of the sign-season on the newborn) seems at the very best highly doubtful: not only is there no empirical support for the hypothesis, but moreover no plausible candidate theory of physical mechanism to explain such a phenomenon is forthcoming. The notion that the geocentric placement of a planet *other than the Sun* in a zodiac sign at birth can predict aspects of later personality, according to the principles of that planet and of the sign, we dismiss as reflecting an egregious misconception of the origin of the signs: it was solely the apparent position of *the Sun* against the stellar backdrop through the year that gave rise to the signs as markers and characterisations of

---

[549] To clarify, we consider that the planets became deified projections of humankind's most fundamental *urges, functions or principles*, while the signs became projections of *modes of expression of archetypal life concerns*.

[550] We would be interested to learn of further empirical work to determine the possible status, as constructs of personality, of the astrological sign-component of 'quality', or as we have reformulated it as 'phase interest', of three types: the predisposition for interest in currently new, fresh conditions; the predisposition for fixity of interest in existing conditions; and the predisposition for interest in the ending of current conditions and the anticipation of new ones; which three correspond to the 'cardinal', 'fixed' and 'mutable' 'quadruplicities' or 'qualities' of the signs, respectively, in astrological symbolism.

[551] Maslow, 1943; Maslow, 1954; Maslow, 1970

the seasons, and no other astronomical body. The Moon and the other planets play no role in the origin of the seasons, or thus, the zodiac signs, which are in essence markers for seasonal periods or divisions of the *solar* year. In addition to the conceptual error, there is, unsurprisingly, no empirical support for such an idea.

At the risk of prolixity but in the interests of emphasis, we might clarify this further. As we have seen, the signs of the zodiac (whether in their original form as constellations, or as post-Hellenic, tropical, equal 'segments of the year') have their origin in the changing *seasons*, which are caused by the obliquity of the ecliptic (the roughly 23.4° angular tilt between the Earth's own rotational axis and the axis of its plane of orbit around the Sun—see Figure 1). These various seasonal periods of the year gave rise to the signs as 'heavenly signatures' of these periods—fancied pictures projected onto the random star-patterns behind the Sun at these successive stages of the year, being unconsciously imagined markers for, or symbols of, the conditions of those seasonal periods.[552]

Any causal effect of the sign-time of year on individuals (if any association were found and thought to be causal in nature) could only come from the terrestrial condition of the season (e.g., the prevailing climate, or necessary activities of that season), not from the stars behind the Sun which served simply as canvases or backdrops for those imagined seasonal pictorial markers in the heavens. The idea of the Sun as having some terrestrial effect 'through the sign' is based upon a fundamental misunderstanding of the cause of the seasons and thus the signs. To extend and compound that misunderstanding by thinking that planets *other than the Sun* could have such a significance is to protract the error even further into an extreme and absurd sense. While these conclusions will no doubt seem a disappointment to adherents of divinatory astrology, we would rather draw attention to the intrinsic value of the prototypical symbols of human life which have been projected onto the planets and the zodiacal signs, in their own right.

In the symbolism of the deified planets, and in the array of seasonal characteristics of the zodiac signs through the year, we see age-old heuristics or metaphors for the most fundamental human urges or functions, for archetypal modes of expression, for the typical stages of individual development, and for universal human needs. Since these symbols stand for such basic characteristics of human nature, they will of course be recognisable in aspects of personality, but we conclude that it is an egregious mistake to think there is a particular connection between the configuration of the planets and the signs *at the time of birth* and how their symbolic associations are represented in an individual. We feel there may be more to be learned from this wealth of symbolism from a personal growth perspective, rather than from a misleading assumption of some divinatory or predictive correspondence.

---

[552] 'Sun in Scorpio' (for instance) simply refers to that part of the year when, behind the Sun, there is a star-pattern that was, long ago, pictured as a scorpion and given the name 'Scorpio' to characterise and signify that time of year.

We should not disregard important symbolism when we rightfully reject predictive, 'horoscopic' assumptions. We may be able to learn to assess our lives with reference to astrological symbolism, regardless of when we were born. Indeed it is the universality of the symbolism of the zodiac that we find compelling.

The reader may have noted that we have discussed how each zodiac sign can be seen as having a 'good' and a 'bad' expression. The signs can thus be seen in an instructive or therapeutic sense, in so far as one may try to tend towards the 'better' expression of each one, and towards a more balanced or 'democratic' functioning of each in relation to all the others as a whole. In view of the apparently comprehensive nature of its human symbolism, it is therefore conceivable that the zodiac may be viewed as a framework or basis to assess one's way of living. We therefore now finally propose that the progression of the year through the zodiac signs, and the way it relates so closely to universal human personality, development and needs, can be characterised as a 'path' of human experience, which we might term the 'way' of the zodiac. Let's now examine that path.

The Way of the Zodiac — Aries

Aries, like the beginning of spring which it marks,[553] embodies the fundamental, primary need for self-projection and for personal survival. The accent is on the promotion of the self—the most basic requirement simply to live, before other activities can even be attempted. Before we can begin to think about comfort, abstract ideas, emotional affiliations or recreation, and long before we might consider the 'higher' luxuries of aesthetics, philosophy, social issues or spirituality, we must perforce simply *survive*, as individuals.

In order to survive personally, especially in situations of extreme urgency, it's very often necessary to be quick, decisive, bold, brave and courageous. The qualities that we need to find within ourselves in order to set about the primary business of surviving are often necessarily urgent, impulsive, forceful—even savage in nature. They are the characteristics which Aries teaches us to have when circumstances are critical for our continued existence. The Aries attitude is one of initiative, courage and enterprise. Without that foremost, self-assertive, often adrenalin-fuelled impulse to fight, flee, or to just keep blindly going on in the face of danger, we are lost, and all of the more developed and nuanced aspects of life that we might look forward to in later experience are forever denied to us.

In a situation where we are confronted with imminent danger or the need to take action, the primary Aries compulsion for fight, flight or for some other immediate action, without regard to subtleties, is the one that will save us. If we found ourselves alone in a burning building, the Aries drive for decisive, instant and assertive action in order to save ourselves, even under the extreme stress,

---

[553] That is, and as we have noted, in the northern hemisphere.

would be essential. It's not just in circumstances of personal survival however that the characteristic Aries expression may be valuable. In many important social situations the sign's self-asserting attitude may prove necessary. One might imagine a medical team working together to diagnose and treat a patient with a complex condition. In such a situation, if a healthcare professional possesses important expertise, critical information or a potential solution that could save the patient's life, then a self-assertive and forthright attitude which has the resolve to speak out and not be cowed by self-doubt or peer pressure becomes crucial and may save the patient's life.

If someone appears to possess the quality of bravery under most circumstances, then we think of such a person as being an indisputably 'brave type'. It should be remembered however that the courage that is embodied in Aries might be hidden from view: while we can admire overt bravery, there may be many others who are quietly but bravely battling punishing circumstances or burdensome health conditions, their struggle lying largely beneath the surface, but nonetheless heroic for that. Bravery may also emerge unexpectedly in a person who finds themselves suddenly thrust into a critical situation which abruptly warrants decisive assertion. One may be surprised to find that a person whom one has hitherto seen as unassuming finds a courage that the outside world (and indeed perhaps the person themselves) did not know they had. It is not always obvious who will be the courageous actor, or who will fulfil the role of the decisive leader or the pioneer when, in unexpectedly desperate or life-threatening circumstances, Aries-type qualities such as bravery and self-assertion become essential.

We may sometimes be puzzled as to whether to look upon some actions as brave or foolish. Often indeed, they may appear somehow to be both. The Aries qualities might thus sometimes be judged negatively, perhaps appearing as merely selfish, reckless or frankly idiotic to an observer who may not perceive or appreciate the pressing need for self-preservation which makes them necessary. The less dire we judge the needs surrounding the circumstances (perhaps having no knowledge of their urgency), the more we will tend to view the action as being merely self-seeking, egotistical or foolhardy. A tendency to underestimate the necessity for the impulsive 'Aries need' may be especially apparent in those who are caught up in later needs, and who have perhaps forgotten (or who have fortunately not had to confront) the experience of the need simply to survive.

There are of course many instances where the self-seeking Aries principle would not commonly be seen as justifiable; when the impulse for self-projection is merely gratuitously applied, or overused without due necessity. In such cases we encounter crude selfishness, over-optimism and recklessness. This is the Aries need being applied without reference to other contrasting and modifying needs; it is the sign's operation without integrity; that is, without contextual integration within the whole psyche as exemplified by the zodiac. Considering a sign-need's integral place within the whole of the psyche, it's insightful to compare its attitude with those of other signs—especially its adjacent and opposite signs—to examine more closely its characteristic mode of action and its interacting role. The principles of these other signs can act as contrasting perspectives, tests or checks on the appropriateness of a sign's attitude in given situations.

Aries contrasts notably with its adjacent and preceding sign, Pisces. While the essence of Aries is the projection and promotion of the self and of self-interest, that of Pisces seems quite the opposite, being one of self-abnegation and self-sacrifice—the *dissolution* of the self. We might contrast the two by revisiting our imaginary example of a medical team working together to treat a patient. If the self-abnegating attitude of Pisces dominated in such a way as to deny our own personal initiative, to downplay the importance of our actions and the potential utility of our own skills—meekly waiting for others to act, or assuming that others will act—then harm may come out of our reluctance to take the initiative. This is more likely to be the case in larger groups of people: since the 1960s social psychologists have been aware of the phenomenon of the 'bystander effect', where the greater the number of people there are present, the less likely people are to help a person in distress.[554] In many scenarios one might hesitate to act if one tries to envisage the likely outcome for all involved, yet an urgent situation may preclude the opportunity for such ethical reflection. If alternatively the Pisces need provokes us to act, but blindly and from a naïve and artless sense of moralistic self-sacrifice, without regard to practicality or competence, then lives may actually be put in danger. The self-promoting Aries need can at times therefore act as a modifying check on the self-denying Pisces need, when the latter might be gratuitously overemphasised or sought inappropriately.

It can be argued that, in order to be able to help others, one has to be capable of doing so, and this will obvious necessitate caring for—and thus promoting—oneself, at least to some degree. Moral choices between self assertion and self denial will inevitably have to be made throughout the course of a person's life, and sometimes the more vital Aries need may have to come first. The Aries need is at basis a primal need for personal survival, and in that sense it shows its prepotency over that of Pisces. There is a time to promote oneself as well as a time rather to favour a regard to one's fellow man; indeed there are times when one must promote oneself *in order to be able* to help others. Thus although a balance of mutually modifying attitudes may frequently be required, the preferment of oneself may sometimes be the right choice.

Aries also contrasts significantly with its other adjacent and following sign, Taurus, but in a different way, Where Aries is direct, adventurous and even reckless in asserting itself, Taurus is cautious and restrained, and values security. In our earlier imagined scenario of finding ourselves alone in a burning building, a plodding over-reliance on caution and security procedures may well be less important than the initial impetus to escape.

---

[554] Darley & Latané, 1968

We can see the prepotent nature of the two needs in a more general sense: the main concern of Aries is the most primary concern of basic animal survival, which may at times need to take precedence over caution; once survival is more likely, attendance to matters concerning material security can be thought of, but not until the compulsion for survival and a readiness to take risks is at least animated.

Another sign that contrasts notably with Aries is its opposite sign, Libra. Where Aries pertains to one's own sense of *self* and singularity as a separate, individual person, Libra is specifically concerned with one's sense of relatedness to, and unity with, *others*, as in partnerships. Although the Aries need is primarily concerned with matters to do with personal survival, its importance in social situations may become apparent.

In some critical group situations, an individual's self-assertive and self-promoting attitude can be preferable when it comes to decision-making, taking charge and effectively leading the group, especially if that individual alone possesses relevant special skills or knowledge. An attitude uncompromisingly concerned with relatedness and unity could lead to delays in decision-making if the group feels obliged to reach a consensus on every action, especially where time is of the essence and action becomes crucial. As in our comparison with Aries and Taurus, the prepotent nature of the Aries need nevertheless in a general sense remains: the need for social relatedness embodied by Libra comes long after the primal necessity of personal survival.

We can therefore see that perspectives which clarify the place of the 'Aries need' and which help us to view its function as a part of the whole are particularly highlighted by a consideration of the contrasting characteristics of its adjacent signs Pisces and Taurus, and of its opposite sign Libra. Each of us needs, first and foremost, to ensure our own survival, for without that nothing else will follow (unless we consider it necessary to sacrifice our very existence). But once the combative struggle for basic survival is tackled, we need to consider how to equip ourselves for the path ahead, the path which we struggled so hard to begin. That provision will include, amongst other things, a consideration of caution and security, an ability to relate to others instead of solely to ourselves, and ultimately a spiritual denial or letting-go of that self for which we once strove so hard to keep alive.

The Way of the Zodiac — Taurus

Taurus embodies the basic human need for the practical, material values of security, sustenance and comfort. Once we have done whatever it takes to survive, whether that was to fight in anger or flee in fear, then the next thing we naturally have to do is to find a place that is secure and which looks likely to be stable enough for our continued support, our sensory well-being and comfort; where one can feel *grounded* both physically and psychologically and 'take stock'. If you have managed to save your skin, then the next thing you have to do is to get yourself to some vicinity where you feel *safe*. No matter how high-minded or philosophical our lives may later become, we first need to be sure of a place, a region, which promises to help us establish the productive means of obtaining and protecting the basic material resources of physical security and safety, such as food, property, possessions—the valuable commodities that more often than not are purchased with money. This stage in the evolution of our needs thus puts the accent on being practical and down-to-earth; on material safety and sustenance, and the production or acquisition of the possessions that enable these, as a stable basis for growth.

The sensuality in the Taurus stage of needs includes the notion of beauty. We may perhaps wonder what practical purpose aesthetic considerations have for our material security, or whence they arise, from a constructive standpoint. The pleasant sensuous gratification derived from food is of course naturally evolved as a positive reinforcer for the continued acquisition of nourishment. But in the realm of aesthetics too, evolution has so strongly represented favourable physical conditions that they often serve as the basis for what we find as beautiful. In an experiment where naïve children were shown photographs of various landscapes, an aesthetic preference was observed for what were essentially savannahs with trees—exactly the East African landscape where much early human evolution was most fruitfully able to take place. The experimenters found:

> ... a general preference for landscapes with water; a variety of open and wooded space (indicating places to hide and places for game to hide); trees that fork near the ground (provide escape possibilities) with fruiting potential a metre or two from the ground; vistas that recede in the distance, including a path or river that bends out of view but invites exploration; the direct presence or implication of game animals; and variegated cloud patterns ... these are the very elements we see repeated endlessly in both calendar art and in the design of public parks worldwide.[555]

In another cross-cultural survey of art preferences, favourite features were found to be water, trees and other plants, human beings (with a preference for women and children, as well as great historical figures) and animals, especially large mammals, both wild and domestic. Following these surveys, composite paintings were constructed which embodied such favoured representations, and all showed a strong similarity to culturally universal forms of landscape calendar art. It has been argued that these developed aesthetic preferences underscore the evolutionary appropriateness of the scenes involved.[556] We have thus evolved a significant part of our aesthetic preferences as reflections of the practical suitability of our material world. From the viewpoint of the general Taurus theme, we can also understand how small a conceptual step it is from the sensual gratification of something that tastes good to something that is aesthetically

---

[555] Dutton, 2003
[556] *Ibid*; Balling & Falk, 1982

pleasing (that is 'tasteful') and which promises or betokens further sensual satisfaction and thus nourishment. Such material things as food and the land that provides it are naturally enjoyable—and often beautiful—in their own right, but they also serve as the basis for our strength, security and stability for further growth. If this stage in our needs is neglected, we will not establish the stability, steadfastness and support of our material environs nor the consequent physical well-being that we will need to advance further. Environmental poverty, material destitution and physical weakness do not constitute a favourable platform for moving our lives forward.

As with the other sign-needs, the appropriateness of the Taurus need will vary according to circumstances. It's possible that a genuinely pressing need for material security and sustenance might be misinterpreted as no more than avarice if an observer doesn't fully appreciate the existence of a real necessity. It may be viewed as mere greed or indulgence by someone who has never had to attend to basic necessities with much urgency, or who has forgotten what it is like to lack them. There may also be times when a need for material security unexpectedly re-emerges and demands attention, due to unforeseen but genuine insufficiency. Obviously there may also be circumstances when a desire for material advantage cannot be justified, when it is indeed gratuitously sought, being mere acquisitiveness without a genuine requirement. In such cases Taurus's principle turns into unreasoning over-possessiveness, sensualism, self-indulgence and dull, unthinking materialism. It's possible that this reflects the Taurus need caricatured, as it were, by unintegrated isolation from the other needs of the psyche as represented by the whole zodiac.

We can gain some perspective of the integrity of the Taurus need by comparing it with those of other signs—especially those signs adjacent and opposite to it. Aries precedes Taurus and contrasts with it distinctly, as adjacent signs always do. While the Aries need is to be forward, impulsive and even reckless in its quest for self-promotion, Taurus needs to be cautious, practical, patient and steadfast in order to achieve the down-to-earth security that it seeks. If a valuable commodity is sought, or if a speculation is to be entered into, then clearly Aries and Taurus would have different characteristic ways of approaching such circumstances. Aries would not hesitate, but would drive forward immediately to the goal; Taurus would rather first take time to weigh the value of the objective against possible dangers or losses before deciding whether to proceed.

Both approaches have potential advantages and disadvantages. Aries may rush headlong and succeed by dint of the sheer boldness to take action, or it may founder in the enterprise by failing to foresee pitfalls or by finding that the hastily-achieved goal was not worth the effort. Taurus may escape such dangers or losses through its characteristic caution in taking time to evaluate the worth of the enterprise; on the other hand Taurus may miss a fleeting opportunity altogether by spending too much time deliberating and failing to act immediately.

Generally however we can see that, other circumstances being equal, the emergence of the Taurus need for caution can act as a check on the most impulsive excesses of the preceding Aries need, when the latter proves unwise. Nevertheless, the Taurus need for the cautious conservation of personal material security can only be undertaken as long as the basic survivalist call of Aries has been answered.

Taurus also contrasts sharply with its other adjacent and succeeding sign, Gemini. Where Taurus is naturally slow, deliberate, practical and sensuously material in its outlook, with an emphasis upon feelings and values, Gemini's need on the other hand is naturally restless, inquisitive, communicative and concerned with intellectual, abstract and logical relationships which hold without reference to subjective feelings of worth. When we think of the zodiac as a sequence or succession of prepotent needs, we can see that the Geminian need to communicate abstract ideas requires the prior attainment of the more pressing Taurean need for a secure, concrete, material foundation (and in turn, upon the primal survivalist need of Aries).

As with the other signs, the Taurus need contrasts strongly with that of its opposite sign, in this case, Scorpio. Whereas Taurus concerns the need for one's *own* material feelings and possessions, for the peaceable and enduring comforts and pleasures these confer in the indulgence, sustenance and regeneration of the life-force (e.g., food) in one's *own* physical body, Scorpio pertains to the need to experience the feelings and possessions of *others*, and the more intense though shorter-lived feelings involved in the sharing of the common regenerative life-force with and of *others*, genetically or physically, as in sex, birth and death, as well as in other *commonly* shared physical resources, such as in jointly held money, property and inheritances. The sequential and prepotent nature of the 'signs as needs' is reflected in the Taurus-Scorpio opposition, in that the need for *personal* sustenance and material assets must be met before it can become extended in *socially* shared material resources. Some useful checks on the overuse or inappropriate use of the Taurus need can thus come from reflecting on the contrasting aspects of its adjacent signs Aries and Gemini, and of its opposite sign Scorpio. By doing so, one can gain some perspective and clarity of the place of the Taurus need within the whole psyche, as represented by the whole zodiac.

The Way of the Zodiac — Gemini

Gemini represents the strongly evolved human need for abstract thought, intellect and communication. It is the need to seek out, identify, select and gather salient information; to interpret and process that information by way of its logical manipulation as abstract symbolic representations, and to communicate clearly its meaning. This enables us to orientate and adapt to the world around us in an intelligent and versatile manner, and moreover to *communicate* interpreted aspects of such acquired knowledge to others. It is thus the fundamental need for adaptation to the environment through cognition and communication. The communication of what is learned or mentally processed happens chiefly by way of speech, reading and writing—the principal skills which enable us to express or give clear form to our conceptualisations of the outer world of appearance and of our inner world of thought. These cognitive abilities have so far conferred a tremendous evolutionary advantage to the continuance of our species, and so constitute a profoundly important human need. Psychologists have indeed identified a need for cognition, as *"the individual's need to organize his experience meaningfully," to "structure relevant situations in meaningful, integrated ways" and "to understand and make reasonable the experiential world,"*[557] even if this entails avoiding ambiguity and achieving an integrated and meaningful world *"by using heuristics and by relying on the advice of experts rather than by carefully scrutinizing incoming information."*[558]

When our needs for basic survival and security (as represented by the preceding signs of Aries and Taurus respectively) are for the most part assured, we may then turn our attention to more intellectual concerns: to perceptive examination; to learning about and adjusting to our environment; to curiosity and structured thought, and to the communication of those thoughts with others. Clearly, the lack of an ability to satisfy the need to develop and employ these intellectual faculties would severely limit our lives. Without them we are barely human, unable to derive, process or share knowledge and ideas. Some of these cognitive needs, such as speech, are so strong that they will almost always force themselves into some sort of manifestation, despite the severest circumstances. Other aspects however require schooling to raise their acquisition and competency to a satisfactory level. Just as the human neonate requires immediate nurturing and cannot survive without it, the child requires at least an elementary schooling for cognitive proficiency, certainly in reading and writing.

Despite the requirement of tuition for a proper development of some of its aspects, cognition generally can nevertheless be considered a real human need. Curiosity about the world around, the ability to mentally organise and logically manipulate that information, and the ability to communicate it in some form, are certainly innate and necessary requirements for fulfilled lives. An individual without elementary education, or one who has some drastic psychological or physiological limitation to the ability to learn, think, adapt and communicate, can be a severely frustrated individual at a distinct disadvantage, both personally and socially. For many people, the need to communicate, by any means possible, can be overwhelming.

It is of course possible for the natural Geminian need for cogitation and communication to be overdone. Perhaps more especially in the current age of the internet with its vast proliferation of data, there can too easily be lapses into superficiality and diffuseness of information and thought. Establishing the truth amidst a plethora of conflicting and often partisan information can also be bewildering and frustrating. It can also become easy to identify too much with

---

[557] Cohen *et al.*, 1955
[558] Cacioppo *et al.*, 1996

symbols, concepts and their relationships, rather than with concrete things 'in the real world' (the entry of a task in a 'to do' list does not constitute the accomplishment of that task). People may also tire of an apparently incessant need to ratiocinate, to talk, write or even read interminably (though often not very deeply) about every conceivable subject, and few would deny the value of mental quietude—a state which can seem more and more elusive to us. Nevertheless, it would be equally hard to deny the importance of the cognitive ability, even if it is at times employed uncertainly, trivially or merely too much. As with all the sign-needs, the Geminian need is real but must be tempered according to circumstances and moreover to other needs, in an integrative fashion.

We can compare the Gemini need to those of other signs, again most usefully by noting the contrast with the signs which are adjacent and opposite. We've already touched on the comparison between the Gemini and Taurus needs in our discussion of the latter. We noted that the practical, material needs of Taurus seem prepotent to those of Gemini. Normally it's only when the pressing concrete and value-laden demands of Taurus are satisfied that we can we begin to entertain Gemini's more abstract needs, which by contrast are more concerned with intellection and logical relations rather than with feelings. Security comes before curiosity, land and construction before libraries, ink and paper before books, and physical communication devices are needed to disseminate abstract ideas. Once these material considerations are met, the need for the development of the intellect and of its communicative ability can then begin to be fulfilled.

Gemini contrasts markedly with its other adjacent and succeeding sign, Cancer. Where Gemini's needs are concerned with logical cognition, abstract concepts in the intellect and their communication, those of Cancer are quite different, characteristically involving one's emotional life, intuition, imagination, and the domestic sphere rather than with a school or academic setting. When early learning and cognitive skills have achieved a certain basic competency, the instinctive need for emotional security, typically in the domestic sphere, begins to be more apparent. One might think that the need for emotional security, nurturance and the stability of the domestic setting would occur in the very earliest infancy, *before* the time when the need for language and communication skills emerges. Though we have proposed that the prepotency of the needs in the zodiacal scheme are, as in Maslow's, not rigidly sequential, the zodiac's pattern nevertheless appears to suggest that Cancer's need for emotional security in the participation in the home and family life develops a greater presence or becomes more pressing *after* the need for the acquisition of basic cognitive skills is met to foundational levels.

As with all other signs of the zodiac, Gemini contrasts markedly with its opposite sign—in this case Sagittarius. Where Gemini is concerned with the need for *personal* mental development, exploration and communication, Sagittarius pertains to the need for more *social* mental pursuits, such as law, morality and philosophy, and for deeper, wider or more extensive exploration and communication, such as in foreign language and travel.

Once again, the notion of the 'signs as prepotent needs' is reflected in the fact that the personal cognitive need must be met before it can be 'extended' into the wider, more extensive and more socially-based need for understanding that is inherent in Sagittarius. When the Geminian need for nervous information-processing and communication is overdone, or engaged in gratuitously or inappropriately, some reflections on the contrasting but equally important needs of its adjacent signs Taurus and Cancer, and of its opposite sign Sagittarius, can act as perspectives on its proper application and moreover of its place in the whole.

The Way of the Zodiac — Cancer

Cancer represents the very deep and fundamental human need for emotional security. It is thus closely related to the need for the comfort and protection of a sheltering home or base amidst the world, a familiar domestic sphere to where one may periodically resort in order to relax one's outward concerns and feel comfortable enough to engage in sentiment and the imagination, secure in a reassuring sense of belonging that's provided by family, loved ones, and even one's home neighbourhood, country or land. In the scheme of the sign-needs, when we have ensured our basic survival, secured our most demanding physical needs and possessions, and learned to interpret and communicate our immediate experience of the world, then the need for emotional security, and a safe refuge or familial home wherein such security can be nurtured, becomes important. It's also important to remember that the human emotional need characterised by Cancer is not only a need to obtain emotional security, but also to give it, in the instinctive act of parenting, or simply by way of fostering a nurturing and sympathetic attitude for others.

It seems almost unnecessary to state that emotional security is beneficial and that a lack of it is harmful to a person's life. Disruptions to the family home, particularly in the young, who are naturally the prime objects of the nurturing function of that sphere, if severe enough, can bring about lifelong psychological problems. Domestic violence frequently results in depression, anxiety and aggression,[559] and maltreatment generally has similar outcomes.[560] The emotionally negative domestic climate brought about by marital conflict typically creates unusual, trying and difficult emotional compensatory strategies.[561] These can extend beyond the home to manifest in antagonistic peer interactions.[562] Children of parents with affective disorders like depression are also at heightened risk of emotional problems, in and outside the home.[563] Even merely harsh parenting

---

[559] Rossman *et al.*, 1997; Rossman *et al.*, 2000
[560] Cicchetti & Toth, 2000; Macfie *et al.*, 2001
[561] Cummings & Davies, 1994; Davies & Forman, 2002
[562] Reid *et al.*, 2002
[563] Goodman & Gotlib, 1999; Dawson *et al.*, 2003

predicts later behavioural problems.[564] An appraisal of empirical studies of the varying state of the emotional quality of the family home has commented that:

> ... the sensitivity of young children to the family emotional climate is a double-edged sword. In well-functioning families it enhances the development of skills in emotion understanding and self-regulation, but in families torn by parental psychopathology, domestic violence, or other significant disorders, it can contribute to enduring emotional vulnerability.[565]

Even a general insufficiency or poverty of early and adolescent bonding with caregivers seems to result in a number of societal ills and maladaptive behaviours such as illnesses, addictions, violence and suicide.[566] There must be hundreds of ways in which insufficient emotional security manifests itself negatively throughout a person's life, and as many ensuing pathological behaviours and illnesses which may never be understood as originating from emotional cruelty, or even just from a neglect or absence of basic emotional sympathy. Despite this, people may all too often be derided, overtly or covertly, for emotional insecurities—or even for showing emotion generally. Perhaps they may be told to 'pull themselves together', when the togetherness or emotional integration that they need is not forthcoming. A person who rightly values the importance of the emotional life may be disparaged or even despised as having a tendency to weakness or mawkishness. Such attitudes, whether above or below the level of articulation, merely make matters worse, and moreover stifle the realm of the sympathetic imagination which is also part of the Cancer sign need.

This is not to say that it is impossible for 'emotional neediness' to be overdone in some sense or other. However, where it is, it will most likely again point to some dysfunction in the early emotional life, and even if the excessive emotional need is extremely difficult to cope with, it's hard to see how anything but a sympathetic attitude towards such originating causes (whether these are known or unknown) could be a better response. Generally there can be no doubt that the basic human need characterised by Cancer—namely, that for emotional security and belonging, often pivotal upon a stable familial home or base—is of fundamental human importance.

Once more we can compare this sign with its adjacent and opposite signs, to give some perspective on its nature and the way it integrates with the whole psyche. We have already touched on how Cancer contrasts distinctly with its preceding sign: where Gemini encapsulates the need for the intellect and overt, logical communication, Cancer's need is for emotion, imagination and covert intuition. It might be said that the two types of need could hardly be more different, though both are inherent in everyone to greater or lesser degrees.

---

[564] Rubin *et al.*, 2003; Owens & Shaw, 2003; Shaw *et al.*, 2003
[565] Thompson & Lagattuta, 2006
[566] Maté & Neufeld, 2019

As we have already mentioned, one might wonder at the prepotency of the Gemini over the Cancer need in the zodiac scheme; nevertheless, in the system of the signs, the need for a basic competency in cognitive ability is seen to precede the need for emotional bonding and domestic security.

Cancer's need also differs markedly from that of its other adjacent sign, Leo. Cancer's need for emotional security typically manifests itself in ways that are reserved, introspective, shy, moody, partisan and protective. Leo's need for creativity and self-expression is by contrast confidently outward-looking, cheerfully self-assured, outspoken and inclusive to all. In the progression of the sign-needs, Leo's need for creativity and self-expression follows and is dependent upon the resolution of Cancer's prepotent need for emotional security.

As with all signs, Cancer contrasts in a principled way with its opposite sign, in this case Capricorn. Cancer's emphasis on *personal* security in the domestic role of the familial sphere is 'extended' in Capricorn such that the latter's emphasis is rather on the security of a *social* role, and on status and standing in the outer world of society, career and ambition. One can see how the personal need for the more emotionally bound domestic status can be seen as a prerequisite for—and possibly as a determinant of—the nature of the development of the later more socially based need for success, status and reputation.

The sober formality of Capricorn's need for a 'place in the world' acts as a complementary and necessary counterpoint to the more emotional and looser familiarity of Cancer's more homespun need for a familial role—a 'place in the home'. Thus once again, a reflection on adjacent and opposite signs throws the particular sign's need into a perspective of its place within the whole.

The Way of the Zodiac — Leo

Leo represents the natural human need to express one's self joyfully through creativity; to re-create or reproduce an image of one's unique spirit; to project or impress dramatically upon the world a distilled exposition or essence of one's whole, integrated self, one's power and prowess, organised into an act of original and innovative creation. It can thus be seen as the need for 'recreation', in terms of the offspring of one's mental or artistic talents, as manifest in art, invention, sports, games, risks, speculation, drama and entertainment, as well as in terms of the physical offspring of one's body. In the system of human needs represented by the signs, when one has ensured one's basic survival, secured one's primary physical needs, learned to mentally interpret the world and gained the emotional stability that usually comes with a home and family, then the possibility arises for one to be creative and to engage in joyful recreation. In a sense, one can play.

We think that few would disagree with the assertion that both creativity and recreation are fundamental human needs. It's worth noting that Leo's theme seems to encapsulate 'creativity' and 'recreation' as being highly related if not coextensive activities. 'Creativity' has been defined by the psychologist Robert

Sternberg as *"the process of producing something that is both original and worthwhile."*[567] We would say that creativity is the act of 're-creating' one's unique spirit, the image of one's idiosyncratic self, in some outward form or activity. Since every individual spirit is unique, it would follow that every truly creative act is thus indeed original. Furthermore, the act of creativity is often considered as more than merely 'worthwhile', but rather as the singular 'target need' of a human life, given the opportunity. 'Recreation' has a dictionary definition of an *"activity done for enjoyment when one is not working,"* as well as *"the action or process of creating something again."*[568] Clearly the Leo sign-theme ties together these senses of 'creativity' and 'recreation', and the two notions do seem, at least intuitively, to be highly inter-related or thematically linked. But how, and to what extent?

Is 'producing something that is both original and worthwhile' always done for enjoyment when one is 'not working'? Some artists might point to painful struggles with the fulfilment of their original creations and may positively bridle at the suggestion that what they do is 'mere' recreation—and their activity and its fruits are commonly referred to as 'work'. Yet the creative work of the artist certainly seems closer to recreation than the work that someone is frequently obliged to do for a living. Furthermore, there is reason to believe that, very often, the more tortuous efforts of the creative artist shouldn't be seen so much as incidentally painful methods of creativity, but more as intense concentrations of the disturbing antecedents that creativity itself seeks to heal. In this sense, the healing that is sought through creativity is a 'making whole'. It's notable that the words 'heal' and 'whole' have a common root, and that the concept of 'wholeness' is central to the sense of the Leo sign-theme. The English writer Virginia Woolf, who suffered from severely debilitating episodes of bipolar disorder, commented on the healing or 'whole-making' property of creativity in her diary:

> Odd how the creative power at once brings the whole universe to order. I can see the day whole, proportioned—even after a long flutter of the brain such as I've had this morning it must be a physical, moral, mental necessity, like setting the engine off.[569]

Indeed there is evidence that expressive writing can promote healing in a diverse number of psychological and physical realms, including depression, memory, blood pressure regulation and recovery from medical procedures.[570] Research has also shown that creativity in the form of art therapy has helpful healing effects, for childhood trauma,[571] depression and anxiety,[572] and improved

---

[567] Sternberg & Sternberg, 2017
[568] Oxford English Dictionary
[569] Woolf, 1954
[570] Sexton & Pennebaker, 2009
[571] Eaton *et al.*, 2007; Ottarsdottir, 2010
[572] Thyme *et al.*, 2007; Geue *et al.*, 2010

clinical outcomes in hospitalisation.[573] Both creative writing and art therapy have self-expression in common, and it would seem that it is *self-expression*, the articulation of the whole self in essence, to 'make one's unique mark', which promotes healing and enables one to be 'made whole'.

Conversely, does a recreational activity commonly undertaken in leisure time typically bring about the making of something that is both original and worth-while? Superficially it might seem that an activity undertaken purely for enjoy-ment doesn't necessarily produce anything that's both innovative and valuable. However, although we might be tempted to think of the recreational games that we 'play' as being merely frivolous, it has been shown that play *fosters* creativity.[574] In free play one is not inhibited by the fear of making mistakes. In play, one is open to experiment; it doesn't matter what will happen, because it is 'only play'. One can ask, *"What if?"* One may happily experiment with one's own idiosyncratic—and potentially innovative—ideas without worrying whether or not they are 'right' or 'wrong'. Risk and play are both central Leo keywords, and significantly in play one can risk giving expression to ways of thinking and acting that otherwise might be thought of as silly, since silliness is acceptable in play; and those unconstrained ways of thinking and acting might be the seeds of truly creative innovation.

Recreation or play is therefore typically joyful in itself, but importantly it also helps bring about creativity and creative thinking. Furthermore, play is typically a *"behaviour* [which] *occurs in a protected context when the player is neither ill nor stressed,"*[575] reinforcing the idea that the recreational and creative need of Leo is probably best met once one is able to benefit from the stability of having already satisfied, to a good extent, the earlier, more practical prepotent sign-needs.

The need exemplified by Leo therefore seems to be one for self-expression through creativity and recreation, which can often have positive and 'wholesome' effects. As usual, the sign's need differs markedly from those of its adjacent and opposite signs, and a comparison with these can illuminate its nature by way of an integrative perspective. The adjacent and previous sign Cancer, as we have seen, exemplifies a need for emotional security which is typically evidenced in withdrawn, introspective, moody, protective and partisan ways; Leo's need for joyful self-expression is by contrast confident, outward-looking, cheerful, often risky, self-assured, open and inclusive.

In the ideal pattern of needs inherent in the sequence of the sign-themes therefore, it is only when Cancer's need for emotional security has been met to a satisfactory degree that Leo's need for joyful self-expression can be indulged in or fulfilled. Leo's need for recreation and creativity also differs markedly from the need embodied by its other adjacent but succeeding sign, Virgo.

---

[573] Stuckey & Nobel, 2010
[574] Bateson & Martin, 2013; Garaigordobil, 2006
[575] Bateson & Martin, 2013

Where Leo's need is for a proud and authoritative expression of the whole, overall, or general self, that of Virgo, as we shall see, is by contrast a need for attending critically to detail, to parts, and is shown in characteristically self-effacing and modest ways, often to do with unostentatious service. Leo's creative recreation typically takes place in times where there are no duties to perform, whereas Virgo closely concerns duty and service. In the system of the sign-themes as needs, it seems that Virgo's need for critical attention to detail is best taken in hand when some degree of the Leo need for an expression of the whole self has been achieved.

As with all the signs, the need embodied by Leo contrasts in the principled, 'socially extended' way with that of its opposite sign, Aquarius. Leo's need to outwardly express an organisation or integration of the whole *personal* self in a act of creativity or recreation is extended in Aquarius, where there is a need for organisation and integration in and of *society*, as in community groups and affiliations, and in socially progressive, creative or inventive scientific or techno-logical concerns. If Leo's need for impressive creativity and recreation is over-emphasised or dwelt upon too much, a consideration of the very different but equally important needs of its adjacent and opposite signs can provide a perspective of its place in the overall scheme of the needs of the whole psyche.

The Way of the Zodiac — Virgo

Virgo represents the human need to attend conscientiously to detailed, discriminating, practical matters to do with work, service, health and hygiene. It is the need to attend critically, meticulously and responsibly to mundane but necessary duties which ensure the efficiency of the functioning of the whole; to conform modestly and to be of useful service, to ourselves and as a part of our community. In the system of needs presented by the signs, when our needs for survival, security, cognition, emotional stability and creativity are met, we're able to turn our attention to the pragmatic need for personal fitness and service. As the last of the six 'personal' sign-needs, Virgo seeks to ensure that the individual is fit for inclusion in socially shared experience. This need represented by Virgo doesn't feature in Maslow's hierarchy of needs,[576] but the system of the zodiac signs nevertheless includes it as an integral archetype, and we find its status as a basic human need compelling. While we are aware of the danger of merely looking at the signs and seeing each and every one as a fundamental human need simply by way of some sort of confirming bias, we would nevertheless assert that Virgo's sign-theme can be plausibly seen as a real human need, and that our inclusion of it as such is not vitiated merely by its omission in Maslow's scheme.

For each of us there is the need to attend to small, practical matters that, while modest and undramatic in outward appearance, fulfil an important role in promoting our health and efficiency. We need to maintain the purity, cleanliness and hygiene of our persons and of our environment—to some degree of mainte-

---

[576] Maslow, 1943

nance at least. Washing and grooming are behaviours that have evolved from the earliest times in humans and many other animals.[577] These practices guard against infection—historically the most significant threat to human health. In a more general sense there is a need to attend to the humdrum yet important chores of everyday life, to achieve a state of cleanliness, orderliness and moreover of *efficiency*, without which our practices would become unhealthy, imprecise, chaotic, inept and unsustainable. This methodical and pragmatic attention to detail and fitness has a wider manifestation in the necessity to be of modest but helpful and conformant *service*; to be dutiful, useful and fit to serve the community as an effective constituent part, often in relatively unassuming positions of diligent care and probity.

It would be hard to overstate the importance of a need for a close and thorough attention to the personal service of health and hygiene. A need to be of some useful service to the wider community is also certainly laudable and even necessary. It is possible, of course, for attention to cleanliness to become overdone, notably in cases of pathologically compulsive washing or obsessive orderliness, which can be seriously debilitating. As with most psychopathologies, such disorders are not 'the norm' in that they seem to be exaggerations of common behaviour; indeed, the mere fact that such abnormal exaggerations exist suggests the fundamental and inherently necessary nature of the originating (normal) behaviour.

As with all the signs, one can gain some insight into the role of the Virgo need within the whole scheme of the zodiac by comparing and contrasting it with its adjacent and opposite signs. We have seen how Virgo's adjacent and preceding sign Leo needs to generalise and see the 'overall picture'; how it is outspoken, self-expressive, proud and dignified. This is in sharp contrast to Virgo, which rather needs to attend critically to detail, and is self-effacing, serving and modest. Leo's playful recreation typically takes place in times where there are no duties to perform, whereas Virgo is very much concerned with the orderly carrying out of duty and service. The pattern of the signs as human needs seems to suggest that when the self has been given the opportunity to express (or 'recreate') itself in playful creativity, then one can turn one's attention to the more modest but equally important aim of fulfilling practical duties which enable one to be a fit, usefully serving and efficiently functioning part of the community. The Virgo need also differs markedly from that of its other adjacent and succeeding sign, Libra. Where the Virgo need involves close discrimination and the seeking of differences between things, that of Libra, as we shall see, involves a strong need to evaluate relatedness, agreement, harmony and similarities. Like all the sign-needs, Virgo contrasts in the characteristically 'extended' manner with its opposite sign, in this case Pisces. Virgo is the need for self-effacing practical service, often in terms of the protection of physical health, or the guarding against the 'evil' of illness that might threaten the *material* person serving in the community.

---

[577] Curtis, 2007

Pisces, as we shall see, embodies the need for self-effacing *spiritual* service, to an absolute sense of 'the other', to the 'absolute spirit', or God; for the protection of 'spiritual health', or the guarding against the evil that might threaten the *spiritual* realm. Thus we see that, as with all the sign-needs, a consideration of the adjacent and opposite signs can be helpful in considering whether or not the need is being over-emphasised or sought inappropriately, and helps to give some perspective of its place within the whole psyche, as represented by the whole zodiac.

The Way of the Zodiac — Libra

The sign Libra—the first sign of the 'extended' second half of the zodiac—represents the fundamental human need for relatedness, balance and harmony, which manifests itself in the urge to attract, identify and unite oneself with significant others in partnerships on equal terms, as well as in that impulse to admire the attractive relatedness that is inherent in evaluations of aesthetic harmony. This need to value attractive relatedness, whether personal or aesthetic, is ancient and universal. In the system of needs exemplified by the signs, when we have to a satisfactory degree managed to meet our needs for basic survival, material security, mental cognition, emotional stability, joyful creativity and fit service, we can then seek to satisfy the need for relatedness and relations with others, and particularly in close, affectionate and harmonious relationships, in order that we may unite ourselves with 'significant others' whom we attract and who attract us; with whom in some sense there is mutual agreement, or agree-ableness. This urge has obviously evolved in order for us to bond peaceably enough with what we take to be a suitable 'other', in preparation for our repro-duction into offspring, but also for immediate social and environmental amica-bility generally.

The urge for relatedness has been identified as the basic psychological need for a *"connecting to and feeling significant to others"*, and *"the desire to feel connected to others—to love and care, and to be loved and cared for"*, relevant and important across developmental periods, cultures, and personality differences. Its satisfac-tion is seen as *"essential for wellness, both developmentally ... and situationally ... across ages, contexts, and cultures,"* and its absence as resulting in *"a sense of social alien-ation, exclusion, and loneliness"*.[578] In *"perhaps the largest study conducted on needs and well-being"*,[579] sampling 123 countries, researchers reported that relatedness featured as a highly important factor in affecting well-being. This held true even when the researchers controlled for the satisfaction of other needs such as sufficient safety, food, shelter and respect,[580] showing the integral role and immutability of Libra's need for relatedness amongst the other sign-needs.

---

[578] Vansteenkiste *et al.*, 2020; Deci & Ryan, 2000
[579] Vansteenkiste *et al.*, 2020
[580] Tay & Diener, 2011

Libra's need is for harmony and attractiveness in aesthetics as well as in social relationships. In a general sense we tend to be attracted to, and judge as aesthetically positive, those forms and arrangements whose elements harmonise, not necessarily by virtue of possessing simplistic symmetry, but by displaying proportionate *balance*, and thus an agreement, or absence of discord between two or more entities. Compositions which 'agree' in this way we find aesthetically 'agreeable'. Even the 'agreement' of mathematical equations has been seen to reflect a positive aesthetic quality, even from a neuroanatomical perspective.[581] These key conceptions of balance, agreement and harmonious relatedness in positive aesthetics are clearly restatements, in the sensory realm, of 'relatedness' in the sphere of close interpersonal relationships.

As was discussed above, Maslow asserted that *"there is a truly basic aesthetic need"*, with some individuals becoming *"sick ... from ugliness, and ... cured by beautiful surroundings"* with certain cravings being *"satisfied only by beauty"*.[582] We are probably safe in asserting that Maslow therefore implicitly included Libra's need for harmony (both as in affectionate relationships and as in aesthetics) in his 'love' and 'aesthetic' needs (see Figure 37). It's interesting how the cluster of keyword definitions for the Libra sign-need seems to specify and tie together these two related needs of Maslow's, we might say perhaps more meaningfully.

As with all the signs, the characteristics of the Libra sign-need are thrown into sharp relief when compared to the adjacent and opposite signs. Libra's adjacent and preceding sign Virgo represents a need to attend closely to particular detail, to discriminate and to look critically for *differences* between things; by contrast Libra's need is to seek relatedness, agreement and the points of *similarity*.

The system of needs in the signs seems to imply that, once the foundations of Virgo's need for practical diligence, service to detail and duty have been laid, then Libra's need to seek agreement and similarities in relationships can be undertaken. The novice adult has to find their useful place in the community before they can be in a position to seek relationships. The Libra need also differs sharply from its adjacent and succeeding sign, Scorpio. Where Libra is attuned to relatedness, being pre-eminently oriented to 'the other' and desirous of the smoothing over of differences, Scorpio's need, as we shall see, is one-pointed, single-minded, and wishes to uncover and expose a commonly-shared *singleness* of experience.

The Libra sign-need contrasts in the characteristic 'extended' way with that of its opposite sign, Aries. We have seen that Aries represents one's need to be concerned primarily with the assertion of one's *self* or one's singularity, whereas Libra's is the need for relatedness to *others*. The need for relatedness, love, affection, balance, harmony and aesthetic enjoyment may well be seen as superfluous or over-rated by those in whom other, prepotent needs are holding sway—particularly that of the opposite sign Aries, whose need is necessarily bound up with the self.

---

[581] Zeki *et al.*, 2014
[582] Maslow, 1954

In this point in the succession of the signs as needs however, we have come a long way from Aries's need for self-assertion, and at Libra we can see how human need has become fully 'extended' from 'self' to 'other'. The consideration of the Libra sign-need to its adjacent and opposite signs thus gives us some perspective of its role within the whole psyche, as that is represented by the whole zodiac.

The Way of the Zodiac — Scorpio

The expression of the sign Scorpio closely resembles the principle of the planet Pluto. Both astrological symbolic archetypes represent the intensely powerful human need, at critical times, for renewal or regeneration, by urgently disclosing, unearthing, bringing to light, facing and participating in, hitherto hidden, deep-seated matters or urges, which have grown to such extremes that they have become burdensome and which can no longer be ignored, contained or allowed to remain as they are, and which must be expelled, eliminated or transformed.

The Scorpio need is for an identification with, and a participation in, acts of mutual communion with the commonly shared generative and regenerative life-force, manifest as the feelings, possessions and resources which are shared with, held in common with, or gained through, *others* in some way, such as in birth, sex, death, genetics and inheritance, as well as in other types of shared resources or legacies held in common, such as jointly managed, appropriated or inherited money or other wealth (including property, taxes or 'shares'). Such acts and matters are frequently hidden or censored, but the Scorpio urge is the pressing necessity at exigent times to disregard and violate such taboos and to uncover, reveal and participate in these things. The need is typically manifest in forms of passionate, critical, determined action; in urgent expulsion, single-minded probing, investigation, or mystical endeavour.

When we have, to an appropriate degree, satisfied our needs for survival, material security, mental cognition, emotional stability, joyful creativity, fit service and harmony in relationships—then the veils of innocence are, so to speak, lifted from our eyes, and the urge arises to participate in the deeper, more profound, intense and perhaps darker aspects of the shared commonality of the life-force. The most obvious or typical manifestation of the Scorpio need is in the formidable sexual urge. It is of course a commonplace truth that the need for sex is a deep and powerful impulse in humans—perhaps *the* most deep and powerful. Its power and intensity is the guarantor of the continuance of the species, for without the desire for procreative sex there would be no next generation. Millions of years of evolution have selected a fierce compulsion for sexual procreation, more strongly than any other trait, since only those who possess the genes that carry that passionate impulse will survive by creating a new generation. Without sexual reproduction, the human species would face extinction.

In terms of the individual's need for sex, a wide-ranging meta-analysis of studies has found that increased frequency of penetrative sexual intercourse is associated with greater satisfaction with one's mental health, better quality of intimate relationships, better ability to perceive, identify and express emotions, reduced frequency of maladaptive immature defence mechanisms, lower incidence of depression, lower incidence of prostate cancer and better sperm health in men, positive analgesic effects, better vaginal and pelvic function in women, better musculoskeletal health, a slimmer physique, better cardiovascular health, decreased risk of breast cancer and even improved life expectancy.[583] It is perhaps a truism to say that humans have evolved a need for positive sexual behaviour and its concomitant gratification (indeed it is the *sine qua non* of human evolution) and that sexual activity is thus a fundamental human need.

Since it is such a powerful urge, its repression can cause violent and negative psychological consequences in the individual. As was mentioned in the section on the planet Pluto (which recapitulates much of the symbolism of the sign Scorpio), the nature of the Scorpio need is strikingly recapitulated in Sigmund Freud's psychoanalytic theory, which proposed that the repression of the powerful sexual urge can bring about psychological neuroses and obsessions, which, Freud proposed, can only be eliminated or transformed through the uncovering, revealing or expulsion of the urge into consciousness (the parallel with the astrological symbolism of Pluto-Scorpio here being virtually identical).

The notion of sexual repression was new as a subject for public discussion in Freud's day. In modern times, now that sexual matters are so much less repressed from public consciousness, we are inclined to think that Freud over-emphasised sexual repression as the exclusive cause of neurosis, but in Freud's time such repression may well have been more of a factor in causing psychological illness, and the potential of such repression of course always remains. The great power of the sexual need nevertheless also means that humans in social groups naturally also have to ensure that its satisfaction only occurs in mutually consensual acts, and that any damaging dysfunctions, such as pathological and physiologically inappropriate desires for pre-pubescent or intra-familial sexual encounters, are strictly curtailed.

As with all the sign-needs, insight into the place of the Scorpio need within the whole psyche (as represented by the whole zodiac) can be gained by comparing it with its adjacent and opposite signs. Scorpio's adjacent and preceding sign Libra represents a need that is oriented to 'the other', attuned to relatedness, and which wishes to smooth over singular differences; Scorpio's need by contrast is one-pointed, uncompromising, and wishes to uncover and expose a single, commonly shared substratum of experience and a singleness of purpose. Scorpio's need also differs markedly from that of its adjacent and succeeding sign, Sagittarius.

---

[583] Brody, 2010

Where Scorpio's need entails a one-pointed, single-minded attitude, which seeks to penetrate intensely into a commonly shared, single, inner focus, and is typically serious or even suspicious, Sagittarius's need by contrast is for a wide, extensive and open attitude which seeks broad, expansive space in which to range freely, and is characteristically forthright, candid, frank and jovial.

When we compare Scorpio with its opposite sign, Taurus, we once again see the characteristic difference of 'extension'. Taurus concerns the need for *personal* feelings, as in the comfort of possessions and other pleasant material things, where Scorpio's need is towards the feelings and possessions of *others*, and those commonly shared with others, as in transformable or convertible currency or money, and the 'possession of others' as in sex. The Taurus need seeks to engage in the *personal* sensual indulgence of food and of similar enduring pleasurable physical sensations; Scorpio extends this into the 'pleasant sensual indulging' in the tastes and sensations of and with *others*, as in sex, which is intense but short-lived. The Taurus need is the need to experience the life-force that regenerates through the sustenance of the personal body, as in food; Scorpio's need extends this by needing to experience and confront the life-force that is regenerated through and commonly shared with others, through birth, sex and death. These comparisons of Scorpio with its adjacent and opposing signs give us some idea of how this powerful need operates within the totality of the psyche, as represented by the whole zodiac.

The Way of the Zodiac — Sagittarius

The sign Sagittarius represents the human need for exploration, adventure and discovery. It is that optimistic and opportunistic urge to expand the horizons of one's experience to wider and more extensive realms; for deeper meaning and understanding, both physically through travel and mentally through study. When we've met our requirements for basic survival, material security, mental cognition, emotional stability, creativity, fit service, harmonious relationships and the communion of shared resources, then we're able to address our need to explore far beyond our immediate experience and to gain a broader and more profound understanding of the world and of ideas. The need to venture beyond the commonplace certainly seems to have been a basic human need for millennia. No doubt early humans gradually migrated from their places of origin in eastern Africa as factors such as better food supply and changes in climate dictated, though this didn't exactly reflect a need for exploration for its own sake. There must however have been individuals amongst them whose natures, being more than usually far-sighted, optimistic and explorative, made them eminently suitable as members of small, mobile parties who were ready to be 'advance scouts'—those who sought further than their peers for new lands which might afford improved environments for living, as circumstances varied.

This type of activity is indeed *exploration*—travel for the sake of discovering new places and new knowledge. Interestingly, the word 'explore' itself derives from the Latin *explorare* and is likely to have originated from a hunter's term meaning to 'give out a loud cry' (from the Latin *ex* meaning 'out' and *plorare* meaning 'to cry') or *"to scout a hunting area for game by means of shouting"*.[584] Since the trait for such explorative behaviour often had survival value, evolution by natural selection would have favoured its continued existence in each generation, producing individuals who would readily venture forth to bring news of promising and improved environments beyond the horizons of their fellows. In time the necessity of this activity would be commonly and communally internalised as a recognised need, open to anyone who was willing to try their luck in adventure.

Exploration in new geographical and physical environments of course brings about cultural discovery in addition to the physical resources of those environments themselves, which widens one's philosophical framework or mental outlook with new practices, new ways of thinking and novel insights. The long era of the hunter-gatherer had involved physical exploration for good and better hunting grounds, but the transition to settled agriculture during the Neolithic revolution some 12,000 years ago brought about not only an appreciation of the benefits of fertile land but also the beginnings of food surpluses, enabling the existence of a priestly caste in newly established urban and city areas which could devote much of its time to new mental horizons of a philosophical nature. When such settled cultures encountered one another through exploration, either peacefully or otherwise, there was also the opportunity for the cross-fertilisation of ideas between developed cultures.

Philosophical needs seem quite 'rarified' after the earlier life-or-death needs like bare survival and material security, but it is precisely because those more urgent (and thus earlier or prepotent) needs have been met that exploration (both physically in terms of travel and mentally in terms of wider or philosophical thought) can emerge as a true need. It's notable that historically, explorations in philosophy have often become developed when basic needs have been relatively assured, as when they were fulfilled by slaves for the comparatively leisured and more philosophically-inclined classes in ancient Greece. The world is of course an infinitely better place without slavery, and more organised and integrated solutions to meeting those earlier needs can be better employed to enable the subsequent fulfilment of the more 'exalted' needs of physical and mental exploration.

The Sagittarian need for exploration in its mental aspect seems to be subsumed by Maslow's finer description of the cognitive need's facet as the *"desire to know and understand"*.[585] The need described by the theme of the sign Sagittarius seems more appropriate to the notion of 'understanding' (as opposed to Geminian pure abstraction or 'cognition'), in the way it envelops both physical and mental exploration, as these latter so often advance and indeed bring about the other. Generally we feel that the Sagittarius sign-need distinguishes 'understanding' from 'cognition' more plainly and thoroughly than does Maslow's account.

---

[584] de Vaan, 2008
[585] Maslow, 1943

As we have seen, the need that is embodied by each sign can be viewed in a more holistic or 'whole-zodiac' perspective by comparing and contrasting it with other signs—especially those adjacent and opposite to it. Sagittarius's adjacent and *preceding* sign Scorpio is characteristically a one-pointed, single-minded need, seeking to penetrate intensely upon a commonly-shared, single, inner focus, and is grim, grave, secretive and suspicious. Sagittarius by contrast is a need for a wide, extensive and open attitude, seeking broad, expansive spaces in which to range freely, and is open, cheerful, optimistic, candid and frank. The difference between Sagittarius's need and that of its adjacent but *succeeding* sign, Capricorn (which we discuss below) is also marked: the Sagittarius need is jovial, adventurous, explorative and broad-minded, whereas that represented by Capricorn is serious, cautious, prudent and more narrowly conforming.

The characteristic 'difference through extension' is once again apparent between Sagittarius and its opposite sign, Gemini. Where Gemini's need is concerned with logical, abstract and above all *personal* mental activities, and short, orienting communications or interactions with the *immediate* environment, Sagittarius is rather a need for wider and more *socially* oriented mental pursuits (such as in philosophy), and involves more *extensive* communications and journeys (such as travel to distant lands). A comparison of the sign's need with the adjacent and opposite sign-needs once more therefore affords some perspective of its place in the whole psyche, as represented by the whole zodiac.

The Way of the Zodiac — Capricorn

Capricorn represents the human need to establish oneself securely in the wider community beyond the protective domestic environment, in terms of public role, attainment, career, the achievement of social status, reputation and prestige. It is typically therefore a need to conform to obligations and responsibilities, to work, and to maintain sustained efforts which take a long time and which require patience, self-restraint and forbearance. The sign thus symbolises the need for the sort of sober conduct, persevering self-discipline and respect for authority which promotes reputable social standing, and which collectively enables a socially structured, civilised life. When the more prepotent needs of survival, material security, cognitive competence, emotional security, creativity, fit service, harmonious relationships, the sharing of common resources, and physical and mental exploration have been met, there then emerges the need for long-term achievement and the promise of positive recognition and repute in the social sphere.

Ever since humans have cohered together in extra-familial social groups there have been forms of public roles to which they have conformed, with which they have identified and in which they have strived to excel in the eyes of 'society at large'. The need to achieve in terms of public career and social standing is understandable, in so far as it confers the confidence, independence and security that comes with a social 'place in the world' as well as the attendant material stability. The need however goes beyond purely material matters and involves a desire for positive social acknowledgement or approbation for its own sake. The sense of prestige which comes with public achievement is not necessarily that of great fame or celebrity, but is nevertheless a gratifying perception of increased status that comes with social approval, acclaim and the public recognition of accomplishment through having adhered to some convention of structure and probity. In this sense it is the need for a respected public image or identity—a respectable answer to the question, *"What do you do?"*

We saw how Maslow identified the existence of an 'esteem need' and how he viewed it as involving two aspects; firstly, *"the desire for strength, for achievement, for adequacy, for confidence in the face of the world, and for independence and freedom,'* and secondly, *"the desire for reputation or prestige (defining it as respect or esteem from other people), recognition, attention, importance or appreciation."*[586] Maslow's two aspects of the 'esteem' need restate our above description of the Capricorn need as being composed of both the necessity for material and psychological strength and confidence, and for positive social recognition.

The concept of *status* seems central to the nub of the Capricorn sign-need. A review of a wide range of studies across social scientific disciplines, including psychology, sociology, anthropology, economics, public health, and organisational behaviour concluded that, *"The importance of status was observed across individuals who differed in culture, gender, age, and personality, supporting the universality of the status motive ... taken as a whole, the relevant evidence suggests that the desire for status is indeed fundamental."*[587]. Status may be seen as the perceived possession of a level of merit or competency in comparison to others in a social group; of some commonly recognised form of rank.

Achievement is of course something to be desired personally for its own sake. But like many other social animals, humans have also naturally evolved a general need for the achievement of high status because it has afforded them survival and reproductive advantages.[588] In seeking mates, although human *males* generally prioritise physical appearance,[589] females tend to look for male partners who have high status, since it indicates an enhanced ability to control resources across many situations. Thus, natural selection has favoured *"evaluative mechanisms in women designed to detect and prefer high-status men,"* since choosing such men enhances a woman's survival and reproductive potential.[590] No doubt natural selection has also in turn favoured the reciprocal tendency in men to strive for elevation in status for similar reasons of reproductive success.

---

[586] Maslow, 1943

[587] Anderson *et al.*, 2015

[588] *Ibid.*

[589] Gregersen, 1982

[590] Ellis, 1995

A high level of competency or merit is also desirable because of the material and psychological security that derives from the authority, power, respect, influence, enhanced rights and access to resources that the accruing high status (or at any rate its perception) confers within the context of the social group.[591] It is notable that status is highly context-dependent: a person might have high status in one social situation (such as the workplace, or in a sports arena) but low status in another (such as in the home);[592] thus there are different situations in which the seeking of high status can manifest. Status is therefore a need that is sought on the species-level to maximise reproductive success, and on a more individual level to gain the tangible benefits of security that come with a common recognition (or perception) of greater competency. The price of the attainment of such status and prestige, of a positive public image, attendant on merited social standing, is however by necessity often that of patient, long-suffering, sustained and even painful toil; of restraint, conformity, obedience and self-discipline.

How does the rather severe but nevertheless strong Capricorn need relate to the other needs inherent in other signs? As before, we can reveal useful contrasts by making comparisons to adjacent and opposing signs. Capricorn's adjacent and *preceding* sign Sagittarius embodies a need for jovial, adventurous, extensive and broad-minded attitudes and behaviours—a need to expand, explore and to be free; Capricorn's need, by contrast, is a need for a serious, sober, prudent, conventional, even narrow conformity and a 'knuckling down' to the disciplines and restrictions necessary for long-term achievement. A similarly contrasting but different relationship is seen between Capricorn and the need inherent in its adjacent and *succeeding* sign, Aquarius. Where Capricorn's need requires conventional, conservative and necessarily biddable attitudes and practices, Aquarius (as we shall see) represents a strong need for perspectives and pursuits that are essentially unconventional, progressive, original and freedom-loving.

The characteristic 'difference through extension' is once again observable between opposite signs in the case of Capricorn and its opposing sign Cancer. The opposing sign Cancer embodies a need to establish one's standing and role in the somewhat closed-off arena of *personal*, domestic affairs. Capricorn's need is rather to strive for and construct one's role, place and reputation in the outer, *social* and public world. In the case of Capricorn, as with all the signs, we see once more therefore that a consideration of adjacent and opposite signs gives some perspective of the sign's place in the whole zodiac.

The Way of the Zodiac — Aquarius

Aquarius represents the need for freedom to view matters dispassionately, objectively and scientifically, and thus, where necessary, to think, and to be, different; to be able to deviate drastically from the conventional; to be free to question potentially outmoded ways of thinking or doing in order to gain wholly

---

[591] Anderson *et al.*, 2015
[592] *Ibid.*

new insights; to identify with and put into practice independent, original, innovative, progressive, unconventional and radically new ideas, new technologies and new modes of behaviour—often especially as these pertain to groups or the community as a whole. Frequently it manifests as a need to identify and associate with like-minded people who are fellow-members of wider social groups, movements or causes which have common humanitarian horizons or objectives, often of an unorthodox or 'alternative' nature, and typically with a view to social or technological innovation or reform. The Aquarius need may be said to be the need for the freedom to think without bias and if necessary to be different from the crowd—a need for an openness in social creativity. The Aquarius need did not exactly feature as one of Maslow's basic human needs, though he did strongly assert 'freedom' to be the very first of the *"conditions that are immediate prerequisites for the basic need satisfactions"*,[593] and as this 'prerequisite', freedom seems to be the one concept emphasised by Maslow which is closest to the Aquarian theme's need.

The Aquarius need might be regarded as something of a 'luxury', in so far as a person usually only seeks to entertain it when the more pressing or prepotent needs of the earlier signs have to some degree been satisfied. It seems far removed from many of the basic needs of life, and in the progression of the sign-needs, it certainly is. If a person's immediate survival is at stake, they're unlikely to take the time to consider the advancement of progressive modes of thought, technology or social reform. True, a person may be in the position of needing to ensure immediate survival *and* to be said to be of this unconventional Aquarian type; conceivably such a person might therefore endeavour to employ relatively unconventional means with which to survive. But, such things being equal, in the ideal progression of human needs as they appear to be represented in the zodiac signs, the Aquarius need in its own right is nevertheless seen to emerge when the more pressing or prepotent needs of survival, material security, cognitive competence, emotional security, personal creativity, fit service, harmonious relationships, the sharing of common resources, physical and mental exploration, and the pursuit of social position and status, have all been to some satisfactory degree accounted for.

Though perhaps rarely essential for immediate survival, the need for a readiness to question 'received wisdom' is nevertheless important to us, both on individual and societal levels, because our understanding of the nature of the world typically proceeds by the successive establishment and breaking-down of paradigms of knowledge. We perceive the world around us by making hypotheses based on the assumption that what is happening is more or less likely to resemble what has happened before. Even when we do something as simple as walking we unconsciously predict the presence of the ground at each step; but if new experience suggests that the road is unexpectedly uneven, we begin to question the presence of a firm surface. Therefore at times we need to change our

---

[593] Maslow, 1943

assumptions when enough evidence occurs which is contrary to what we normally expect. Thus our beliefs become questioned and they change, based on what sort of 'fit' observed events have with our preconceptions. But it often takes a careful and dispassionate assessment of the current state of things, together with a definite readiness to jettison old modes of thinking, to put into practice these 'checks' on our existing assumptions.

Humans seem more to be able to develop free, questioning attitudes at certain stages in life. The psychologist Jean Piaget noticed that children typically persist in apparently fixed ways of thinking, even when presented with evidence that is plainly to the contrary, until they reach a certain stage of cognitive maturity, when they are then able to accommodate the new evidence.[594] At other times, we tend to see what we expect to see. The psychologist Ulrich Neisser emphasised the contribution of the perceiver to perception, writing, *"there must be definite kinds of structure in every perceiving organism to enable it to notice certain aspects of the environment rather than others."*[595] Neisser saw perception as a *process* whereby a 'schema' (a form of pre-existing set expectation in perception, based on earlier experience) directs exploration of the available information. That available information is subsequently often interpreted *in terms of* the schema (that is, in terms of existing experience and therefore of existing assumptions). But sometimes the match between the existing schema and the available information becomes too discrepant: in such a case, the schema or expectation itself must be modified to accommodate the new information. Thus, according to Neisser, this 'perceptual cycle' carries on, by turns expecting to see—and thus seeing—the world in terms of known patterns, but eventually changing those expectations themselves when new information stubbornly will not fit old models, and thereby seeing the world differently.

The basic process of cognition in humans might therefore be characterised by a general tendency to expect to perceive as one has experienced before, but also by a need to modify such expectations (and thus the perception of the world) when new information is plainly too discrepant with past experience. This evolving process of perception occurs every day at an individual level, but is formalised socially as 'science'. Science makes hypotheses and predictions based on what has gone before, as best guesses, but then crucially *tests* them, by controlled, dispassionate experiment. Even in the formal societal cognition that is science, habitual assumptions prevail for long periods, but eventually become overturned by the intransigent persistence of new and contradictory observations which result in the coherence of completely new paradigms—until these in turn are tested by further contradictory observations.[596] The Aquarius need especially emphasises the dispassionate 'testing' or 'questioning' part of this cyclical process of social cognition—the need or readiness to entertain or accommodate wholly new observations and ideas which cast doubt upon or plainly contradict old

---

[594] Ormrod, 2014
[595] Neisser, 1976
[596] Kuhn, 1970

assumptions; in this way drastically new and unorthodox paradigms of knowledge and practice have a chance to be tested, and if found valid, to be integrated.

The need embodied by the sign Aquarius is the need to partake of this general process, often in association with like-minded peers, in order to question and even reform old ways of perceiving, thinking, doing and being, in an impartial manner and in a dispassionately friendly integration with all others without distinction—others who are also willing to question and reformulate matters despite the weight of old standards and orthodoxy. The Aquarius need may thus be said to be the need for social and technological creativity.

Clearly there can be instances when a strong need to break with established modes of thought and behaviour can be misguided or simply overdone, either individually or socially. Like any need, the need to think and 'be different' can be merely exaggerated, when it is thus not *wholesome*; that is to say, when it takes its own way without relating to the balancing principles of the other sign-needs in the psyche (as represented by the whole zodiac). There is often an unclear boundary between innovative genius and mere eccentricity, and yet another between eccentricity and frank madness. The points along that spectrum all share the same Aquarian characteristic but the polar extremities reflect successful and unsuccessful expression. As with the other sign-needs, we can get more of a feel for the place of the Aquarius need within the whole zodiac (i.e., within the whole psyche) by comparing it with other signs—most usefully with those that are adjacent and opposite to it.

Aquarius's adjacent and *preceding* sign Capricorn embodies a need to be conventional, conforming, conservative, traditional and authority-respecting. Aquarius's need, by stark contrast, is the need to be unconventional, original, progressive and questioning of authority. As usual with adjacent signs, the characteristics couldn't seem to be more different, yet *for each to function well*, both need to take into consideration the other's place in the whole. A similar contrast is seen between the Aquarius need and that of its adjacent and *succeeding* sign Pisces: where Aquarius's need is necessarily detached, impartial, clinical and scientifically-inclined, that of Pisces (as we shall see) is emotional, impressionable, compassionate, intuitive and even spiritually inclined. A sharply-defined difference once more emerges here between adjacent signs, though again, both need to operate in some sort of mutually tolerant and balanced coexistence in order to be able to function at their best within the entire psyche as represented by the zodiac as a whole. The characteristic 'difference by personal-to-social extension' is again apparent when we compare opposing signs, here in the case of Aquarius and Leo. Where Leo represents the need for the organisation, integration and innovative creative exposition of *personal* matters (e.g., in personal creativity and recreation) in the whole *self* without distinction of its constituent parts, Aquarius embodies the need for the organisation, integration and innovative creative exposition of *impersonal* matters with *others* (e.g., in community groups, scientific associations, etc) and the whole of *society* without distinction of *its* constituent parts.

As with all the sign-needs, to describe the role of Aquarius's need within the whole psyche as represented by the whole zodiac would ultimately necessitate innumerable and lengthy comparisons between it and every other sign-need, but in the absence of such complex and perhaps over-involved expositions, the comparison of the Aquarius need with its adjacent and opposing signs provides some of the most important aspects of such a perspective.

The Way of the Zodiac — Pisces

Pisces, the last sign of the zodiac, represents the need for selflessness, self-denial or self-abnegation; for the transcendence of the everyday material existence of the self; the need for the disassociation or dissolution of one's self or personality into a greater, subtler, other-worldly realm, often in situations of withdrawal, retreat, isolation, surrender or seclusion. Self-denial is widely seen to be a hallmark of what people commonly take to be 'spirituality'. As a token of spirituality, it can manifest as the self-denial inherent in the doing of charitable acts for others (rather than for oneself), or as the 'forgetting of the self' (or, some might say, of the surrendering of the illusion of the self) that is inherent in meditation. Pisces is therefore that need for a self-negating or surrendering dimension to one's life which is variously termed 'spiritual', 'religious' or 'mystical'. Very often we may view the notion of 'surrender' adversely, or even with contempt. As competitive animals, forced to survive against the odds, we wish to win through. Yet there is a spiritual side to Pisces's notion of 'surrender'. It is in fact the beginning of spirituality when, in the words of the Jesus figure, we *"resist not evil"*;[597] that is, when we don't react or retaliate to it, and thereby escape our involvement in it; when we surrender our ego-involvement, our immersion in and identification with the world of phenomena, by way of spiritual meditation.

It may seem strange to see an urge towards self-transcendence as a human need, especially when it is contrasted with the markedly practical needs represented by the earlier signs, such as those involving survival, security, protection and ambition, yet there can be no doubt that, all other things (or needs) being equal, there is undoubtedly a perennial *need* in humans to transcend the self. Of course the spiritual, self-abnegating Pisces need could, theoretically, be felt or encountered at any point in the sequence of the signs (and this same applies to any other need),[598] but in the somewhat idealised scheme of the zodiac, it is nevertheless generally the case that only when the various other prepotent facets or needs of life have been, to a greater or lesser degree, met or passed over, that humans will ultimately gravitate to a need for a spiritual transcendence of the self, for a dissolution of the self into a greater realm of being, an ineffable state or

---

[597] Matthew 5:39

[598] Maslow remarked, *"I find not only self-actualizing persons who transcend, but also non-healthy people, non-self-actualizers who have important transcendent experiences."* (Maslow, 1971)

domain of something we might term the divine. As we have noted, Maslow in his later work did identify 'transcendence' as a basic need in human motivation,[599] though he was not particularly specific about it and tended to conflate it with other needs, such as sexual or aesthetic urges, service to others, progressive social aims, etc. We feel that Maslow was in the process of moving towards a conceptualisation of a human need or urge for the numinous which the Pisces emphasis upon self-transcendence embodies more emphatically.

As with any other need, the need for self-transcendence may be practiced in 'good' or 'bad' ways. One may transcend the self in a good way by doing unselfish works for others, or in spiritual meditation; but one may also transcend the self in a bad way by merely obliterating the self through suicide, or through drugs or alcohol, and it is no coincidence that intoxication is frequently referred to in common parlance as 'getting out of it'—that is, getting 'out of oneself'. It can be appreciated that at least some fulfilment of the earlier prepotent sign-needs of the zodiac (e.g., supportive social needs) may serve to improve the way in which the need for self-transcendence may be met.

In Chapter 3, in our discussion of the developed characterisation of the sign Pisces, we saw how the psychologist Carl Jung looked upon alcoholism as a very crude and harmful form of the fundamental desire for self-transcendence. We might repeat and enlarge upon this here, in order to explicate further this point about the different ways (harmful or uplifting) that the urge for self-transcendence can be put into practice. In 1961 Bill Wilson, a co-founder of the organisation Alcoholics Anonymous, wrote to Jung, revealing that the latter had unknowingly played a 'critical role' in the founding of the organisation, through a consultation the psychologist had once had with an apparently hopeless alcoholic, one Rowland Hazard. In the consultation, Jung had advised Hazard that nothing could help his alcoholism—except for an immersion in spiritual experience. This immersion Hazard proceeded to accomplish, within the Christian organisation known as the Oxford Group, whose principles emphasised surrender of the self to God, service to others, meditation and prayer (all of which practices may be subsumed under the term 'self-abnegation'). Hazard subsequently found that these practices took the place of his alcoholism and largely freed him from the illness.

As we touched on in Chapter 3, in reply to Wilson's letter, Jung wrote that he thought Hazard's *"craving for alcohol was the equivalent on a low level of the spiritual thirst of our being for wholeness, expressed in mediaeval language: the union with God."* Jung went on, *"You see, Alcohol in Latin is 'spiritus' and you use the same word for the highest religious experience as well as for the most depraving poison. The helpful formula therefore is: spiritus contra spiritum."* The Latin phrase at the end of Jung's reply translates loosely as 'spirit against spirits' and points out, not only the curious coincidence of the word 'spirit' being applied both to alcoholic spirits as a poor way to self-abnegation and to 'spiritual' practice as a good way, but also to the

---

[599] Maslow, 1970

fact that actions deriving from 'spirit as alcohol' and those from 'spirit as spiritual practice', though both originating from the same urge for self-transcendence, were competing 'against' each other in his patient as modes of expression *of* that urge, the message being that the patient needed to substitute the latter 'higher' expression for the former 'lower' form. Hazard can be seen to have thus successfully gone on to replace a bad mode of gratifying the need for self-transcendence (alcoholic stupor) with a good one (spiritual practice).

It is a commonplace observation that both drug or alcohol use, and spiritual or religious practices, are pretty much universal in human societies.[600] We can see therefore that, like any other fundamental human need, the need for self-transcendence is universal, but it can be expressed in harmful or wholesome ways. It is more likely to be practiced in a wholesome way when it is supported by a good degree of integration with the fulfilment of the other prepotent needs, which give it a better foundation of expression *within the whole*. When these other needs are lacking or frustrated, it is more likely to be practiced poorly. The need is there, but the relative merit of the *way* it is fulfilled, as with any other need, is dependent on how well it is integrated as a part of the psyche as a whole, as represented by the other needs in the zodiac. With this in mind we can only reflect that modern society does not foster such integration very well, and we might repeat our quote from Chapter 3 of Aldous Huxley's comment that *"Most lead lives at worst so painful, at best so monotonous, poor and limited that the urge to escape, the longing to transcend themselves if only for a few moments, is and has always been one of the principle appetites of the soul."*[601]

The manifestation of the Pisces need for self-denial or self-transcendence can therefore range from despairing suicide, or crude attempts at 'getting out of oneself' by way of intoxication with drugs or alcohol,[602] to profound contemplations of the natural world, to intense physical activities, and—perhaps most ideally—to the 'higher', 'spiritual' practices of self-abnegation that are to be found in kindly and charitable altruism and service to others, and in the self-transcendent practices of meditation.

That the sign-needs, although quite distinct in themselves, are nevertheless mutually dependent upon one another may be illustrated by reflecting on certain characteristics of the 'higher', spiritual aspects of the Piscean need for self-abnegation or self-transcendence. The self-denial of altruism is not only difficult to practice but also difficult to conceptualise when taken on its own and without

---

[600] It should go without saying that none of the foregoing is intended to exonerate all practices that might be subsumed under the term 'religion'. Indeed, organised religion has time and again brought about inequality and untold suffering to humanity. It is only when a 'religious' person is truly and disinterestedly involved in self-abnegation or self-transcendence that the term 'religion' applies to the sense in which it is intended here.

[601] Huxley, 1954

[602] We may concede that, for the right individuals, under proper guidance and expert medical supervision, there may be medicinal or even 'spiritual' utility in the use of hallucinogenic drugs such as psilocybin or LSD, though we would also draw attention to the fact that there are also potential risks and real dangers involved.

reference to other needs and urges, whose natures, being quite different or even positively contrary to self-abnegation, necessarily clash with it. There has of course been the puzzlement of why altruistic behaviours exist at all in organisms which are constrained by the apparently selfish course of evolution by natural selection, though such conundrums are largely only apparent: more nuanced consideration and research often shows that many altruistic behaviours do indeed have survival value, if not to the individual, then to some important hereditable factor.[603] It may be a moot point whether altruism could be seen as the 'selfishness' of the gene in a self-abnegating disguise, but there are other problems and paradoxes of altruism that arise when considering the subject from purely logical, moral philosophical, religious or theological viewpoints.

There is a joke that says religious people only do good in order to get to heaven, so really, they're very selfish. Perhaps a true saint, hearing this jest and seeing a potential grain of truth in it, might defiantly and self-righteously reject heaven (taken either as a place in the 'afterlife', or as a state of beatitude in this life). Being so scrupulously self-abnegating, the saint may choose the ultimate self-denial: the rejection of the personal salvation of heaven or Nirvana and instead wish to go on suffering—even by deliberately committing bad actions. In doing so he would therefore suffer the same fate as the worst sinner. So in this deliberately simplistic example where sainthood is taken to be equivalent to absolute self-denial, the fate of the perfectly unselfish saint and the most selfish sinner are apparently one and the same.

One can of course fall into other paradoxes and conundrums about self-abnegation and altruism. One might imagine a society which is populated exclusively by perfectly altruistic saints (not a distasteful fancy, one would have thought, from a religious point of view). But what would such a society be like? Life for its perfectly altruistic members would be impossible, since each would be trying to out-do the other in terms of self-denial. *"Let me do this for you,"* one saint would say to another. *"Oh no,"* the other would reply. *"I don't want anyone to do anything for me! I don't want anything good for myself! I only want to do good for others!"* To which the other might reply, *"No, no! I must do something for you!"* So the upshot of this incessant altruistic bowing and scraping would be a multitude of saints who are desperately wishing to abnegate their own interests by doing things for others, but who are unable to do so, because those others, even if suffering terribly, are also saints and won't hear of it. So the 'ideal' of an Earth populated by saints without sinners is in fact a recipe for the impossibility of *any* self-denial. Such an 'ideal' state of universal self-denial could therefore serve no purpose whatsoever: no-one could employ altruism, and no-one could be its recipient.

This deliberately oversimplified example may seem remote and fanciful, though certain schools of Buddhism seriously entertain the notion of a *Bodhisattva*, a saint who is certain to achieve Nirvana but who abruptly rejects it

---

[603] Okasha, 2020

in favour of compassionately helping his fellow humans. But the function of a *Bodhisattva* is similarly dependent upon the existence of sinners (those who are not wholly self-denying), or at any rate upon suffering people. Does all this mean that in order for there to be real, practicing saints, there is also a need for sinners (that is to say, people who are not willing to be totally self-abnegating) and for suffering? It would seem so.

One might consider another moral paradox or dilemma of altruism. One can imagine two people who love each other very dearly, and who both cherish the knowledge that their love is equally reciprocated. Each also knows that one of them will die before the other, leaving the survivor with the agonising grief of bereavement. Either of them might think, *"If I died first, it will be a terrible thing that such grief would be visited upon my beloved partner. So perhaps I should kill my partner painlessly, so that I shall be the one to suffer bereavement instead?"* But the idea of killing the beloved partner doesn't sit at all well with their love for them, so it's unclear what they should do or think. Like the paradoxes of the saints on earth and in heaven, it may seem, from such scenarios, that true, self-denying love may depend on some non-loving act or imperfect state in order for it to exist.

It seems reasonable to assert that human lives generally involve less suffering than they did a few hundred years ago. Perhaps we might wonder how self-abnegation as 'the alleviation of the suffering of others' might further evolve if that alleviation became ever more successfully employed. Ultimately a time might come when the only suffering in the world that is left may be at the level of someone experiencing what we now consider as the discomfort of a mild stomach ache. In this imagined future, before long, the notion of someone suffering the 'stomach ache level of suffering' would be seen as the most dire, awful and emotively horrific thing imaginable. Tear-evoking symphonies may be seriously composed and solemnly played to evoke the essence of such 'suffering', all worse suffering being long forgotten. But what if even the 'mild stomach ache' level of suffering is done away with? What if society became mechanised and automated to a point where people are permanently numb to any sensation and thus permanently pain-free? Is that the intended consequence of the alleviation of others' suffering? For some reason it doesn't sound like a natural or even a good existence. If it isn't the intended consequence of 'the alleviation of suffering', then does that mean that some suffering is necessary or desirable in the world? If so, how much, of what nature, how often and for how long?

What of the spirituality of self-abnegation that is inherent, not in the 'forgetting of the self' involved in doing charitable acts for others, but in the 'self-forgetting' that's intrinsic to meditation? One might learn to meditate and rest in a blissful state of pure consciousness, uncontaminated by content. Wouldn't it be incumbent upon a person to deny themselves that state or interrupt it, at least from time to time, either for ethical or for practical purposes? In our example above of the 'loving couple' it's reasonable to suppose that both might wish for the other to be able to meditate and to rest in a serene state of peace and joy. But, being self-abnegating, either of the two may hesitate to reside in such a blissful meditative state if the other is unlikely to do so as well (that is, if the other is still in a state that, by contrast, seems to be a state of suffering). So each might avoid any practice that leads to meditative bliss, for fear of being in such a state of joy whilst the other is, even if only by contrast, still suffering. Each, therefore, through altruism for the other, would avoid a self-denying, spiritual, meditative state. But that would paradoxically lead them both away from the meditative form of self-denial—and ostensibly for the sake of self-denial itself. And this argument is extensible from the example of the couple to human society generally, such that everyone wishing to be self-denying should be a *Bodhisattva*—though we remember that the function of the *Bodhisattva* is dependent upon the existence of sinners.

What is the alternative to being a *Bodhisattva*? If we choose to pursue a path of meditative bliss and ignore the suffering of others, will we then be furthering an ugly and unfair world, where only those who are (we might say) 'selfish' enough to meditate are those who achieve that bliss, while the rest do not and continue to suffer? An ugly world where apparently 'spiritual' people actually only look to themselves and not to the welfare of others? The injunction to reject or at least postpone a state of spiritual bliss, if one sees others suffering and one is in a position to help, was commended by the German mystic Meister Eckhart (c. 1260—c. 1328) when he taught that one should forego a personal 'rapturous state' if one sees a necessity to attend to one's sick brother if the latter needs a cup of soup.[604] Should we follow Eckhart's advice? If we choose to concentrate on the alleviation of suffering, then perhaps we will never get the chance to rest in meditative bliss, as the world is full of suffering; our lives would be wholly and forever taken up with the welfare of our fellows.

Eckhart also enjoined us to surrender all personal will and extolled the virtue of obedience.[605] Whilst one can see this aspect of self-abnegation as a characteristic perhaps likely to promote a selfless, 'spiritual' state, one may nevertheless have qualms about following its advice without reservation. If one perceives or strongly suspects that the authority that one is surrendering to is actually setting out to do evil (as for instance in following the cruel and inhuman demands of a totalitarian state) then one might well think to suspend one's 'self-abnegation of obedience' for the sake of those who may suffer as a result.

Both the 'self-forgetting' involved in charitable actions done in favour of another's well-being and the 'self-forgetting' involved in the attainment of a meditative state evidently recapitulate the central Piscean ethos of self-abnegation, but in the scenarios and examples given above, they often appear opposed to each other. It seems therefore that some forms of self-abnegation are contrary to others. How can we settle this paradox? One suspects that the avuncular response of an orthodox religious priest to these musings would be merely to assure us that there will always be sinners, and always opportunities

---

[604] Blakney, 1941
[605] *Ibid.*

for self-denial. It's notable however that this would be an implicit admission on the part of the priest that his saintly ideals for his fellow man will never be achieved—as well as a tacit concession that sinners are required for pious self-denial.

Perhaps the most practical answer to these conundrums of self-abnegation is that one should try, as far as possible, to be self-denying both in terms of outward charitable acts *and* in terms of contemplative meditation, where these seem possible without too much detriment to each other. Perhaps there is a state of meditation that can be employed at the same time that one is striving practically to help others. Furthermore, perhaps it is sometimes necessary *not* to be wholly self-denying, as when we need to ensure our personal survival, basic sustenance or security, for if we do not, we are hardly likely to be able to employ the self-abnegation either of altruism or of meditative contemplation at some point in the future. Perhaps one needs to be 'selfish' sometimes (that is, concerned with one's own welfare), even if only to be able to begin to be helpful to others.

This approach seems in accordance with the general notion of balancing one sign-theme with all the others, even when they seem to be in mutual contradiction (for instance, in this example, contrasting the Pisces and Aries needs). Of course, we could say that, in the natural order of things, some people (or some people at some times) just *are* self-abnegating, and others just *are* self-preserving, and that's the way things are. But the scheme of the sign-needs of the zodiac seems to suggest that these apparently opposing needs inhere in a single individual. We might propose that, how a person fulfils their need for self-transcendence will depend on how well they have integrated the other needs in their psyche, as represented by the whole zodiac. Indeed, the 'morality' of life might ideally be composed of *all* the 'modes' of all the signs, working in concert, albeit often according to a rough hierarchy of sequence as reflected in the zodiac.

The answer may therefore be in commending the Piscean ethos of self-abnegation *as it relates to the whole psyche* (as represented by the whole zodiac). With such a holistic view in mind, and as we've noted with every sign, we hope to obtain a clearer picture of the way the sign relates to the whole by comparing it to the other sign-needs, particularly to those that are adjacent and opposite to it. We have seen how the sign adjacent to and immediately preceding Pisces—Aquarius—is characteristically one of a need for a detached, objective, dogmatic, clinical or scientifically-inclined attitude. Pisces by contrast is a need for an emotional, subjective, impressionable, compassionate, spiritually-inclined outlook. The difference is stark and even seems mutually exclusive. But, and as we have argued, for each sign-need to be satisfied appropriately, it cannot be truly *exclusively* sought, but must accept, balance and relate to the characteristics of all the other signs, in a consideration of the psyche as a whole.

The other sign adjacent to Pisces is Aries, at the beginning of the zodiac, and once more we see the characteristically marked difference that always applies to adjacent signs. Aries is essentially a need to be *self-assertive,* survivalist, concrete, direct and straightforward, whereas Pisces by contrast is a need to be *self-sacrificing,* surrendering, intangible and other-worldly. Again however, despite the seemingly irreconcilable difference between the highly contrasting attitudes involved, both need to find some form of *rapprochement* or balance of relation with each other, in order for each to be able to function at their best within the whole psyche, as represented by the whole zodiac.

The characteristic 'difference by extension' between opposite signs is again apparent in the case of Pisces and its opposing sign, Virgo: where Virgo emphasises a need for *personal* practical service of the self to the community, Pisces involves a need for absolute self-effacement, self-abnegation or self-transcendence; for the total denial of the (perhaps merely apparent) self and its dissolution into 'the all', the boundless divine, or God. In the case of the Pisces sign-need, its comparison with the others, once more represented most fruitfully by the adjacent and opposing signs, provides us with some important perspectives of its place within the whole psyche.

The Way of the Zodiac — the End of the Rainbow

We have explored the signs of the Western tropical zodiac in some detail. They have been developed and refined over millennia to become a coherently inter-connected framework or pattern of twelve important seasonal themes, collectively projected as fancied pictures onto the random patterns of stars that lie behind the Sun at each corresponding time of year. Taken together as the progression of life through the year, these archetypal images of major life concerns appear to have embodied the most basic facets of human life and experience. It would not be too much to say that they have encapsulated or summarised the most fundamental aspects of the historic human psyche. It may not be surprising therefore when we find that they reflect meaningful constructs of human personality, often anticipating those of modern psychological theory. Their progression though the solar year—the 'stations' of the annual cycle of life in the natural world—appears to be a convincing metaphor of the developmental stages of human life. In that progression they may also be aptly seen as a hierarchy of basic human needs, similar to that put forward by the psychologist Abraham Maslow,[606] though indeed we see them as a more comprehensive and coherent series than those which made up Maslow's account. As in Maslow's hierarchy, we see a general prepotency in the sequence of the signs as needs, where one need is ideally attained (and in practice most probably *usually* attained) before succeeding needs emerge and are satisfied in turn. Also like Maslow's scheme, we do

---

[606] Maslow, 1970

not however see this prepotent sequence as necessarily fixed or rigid, but as an overall approximation, or, one might say, as an ideal.

We might ask, however: what does one do when all these needs have been fulfilled (if such a thing is possible)? What is that state? Is there some sort of teleological 'end-point' to the system of needs inherent in the signs, and thus to humankind's collective psyche? One seems to 'finish' at Pisces, but thereafter there seems nowhere to go, other than to start the cycle over again. If the signs could be said to comprise the various 'colours' of the psyche, then is Pisces the end of the rainbow? In one sense, Pisces, with its other-worldly, spiritual, self-dissolving aspect, does seem as if it might be the 'highest' state, perhaps an end or aim of the human condition. But we cannot ignore a strong intuition that the human psyche might rather be better represented as a *whole*, served by each and every one of its parts, and that to detract from the significance of the unity of all its components in favour of just one—even if that one is the transcendent Piscean ethos—may be seen in a sense to deny that whole. We might say that, at the appropriate times, we need the self-oriented Aries, just as much as at other times we need the selfless Pisces. In this view, Pisces isn't 'the' way to be, but just one of the ways needed for us to function as whole individuals.

The nature of wholes or holistic systems may be said to be an emergent property of coherently inter-dependent parts, working in concert. How does this apply to the human psyche in the context of interconnected needs? If one asks people informally what they consider to be the most fundamentally 'important' factors in life, in our experience they invariably enumerate factors such as health, money, love and creative work. (We note that money is not always the same as creative work. It might perhaps be seen as ideal if the need for money is satisfied *by* creative work, but we understand that, generally, such is rarely the case.) The order of priority ascribed to these re-occurring 'important' factors tends to vary, though some are almost always placed before others; for instance, health is almost always given priority over money. (We also note that 'health' might often in fact be used, consciously or unconsciously, as a convenient 'catch-all' term adduced to cover the most important facets of life generally, as if, arguably, 'health' might conceptually subsume any other important factor, as in 'the health of the body', 'the health of one's finances', 'the health of one's love life', and so-on.)

Such a list of factors also seems to have some inter-relatedness of its components. One's health for instance may realistically depend upon one's disposable income. One's ability to satisfy love needs may also depend on one's money—or on one's health, or one's money *and* health, and so-on. In the case of such an informal survey of life's 'important factors' we feel we'd like to have some sort of 'whole', overall or holistic understanding which takes into account the inter-dependence or inter-connectedness of all the constituent needs or functions *as well as* whatever their prepotent succession may be, and the same seems true of the zodiac signs as needs. Indeed we have here repeatedly put forward the notion that, over and above their prepotent sequential nature, the signs seem only fully comprehensible as a *whole*; that is, as a coherent and inter-dependent system. A strictly sequential attainment of all the sign-needs up to and including Pisces thus may not necessarily be a view which fully explicates the zodiac, or the 'ideal state' of the *whole* human psyche, since the sign-needs are then seen as being constantly superseded or relegated in importance or significance.

Often added to such *ad hoc* lists of 'important factors in life' is another component, which we might generally refer to as 'spirituality'. This seems to be a restatement of the need that Maslow recognised as that for 'transcendence'. By 'spirituality' people generally seem to mean the embracing or inclusion of a non-material aspect to life (viewing 'spirit' as a non-material thing), and this seems coextensive with 'transcendence', in so far as, when we talk of 'transcendence', it is the material that is seen to be transcended. It is important to note that we are here *not* referring to 'religion', but particularly the need for transcendence, whether that is sought in a 'base' way through drugs or in a 'higher' way through practices such as meditation. In Chapter 5 we identified the need for 'spirituality' or 'transcendence' with the need that is inherent in Pisces, and this certainly seems to be the case, in so far as the Pisces need does indeed emphasise the urge for self-transcendence. But we might see a 'spiritual', 'transcendent' or 'highest' aspect of the zodiac (and thus of the human psyche) in more nuanced ways; indeed in three ways.

Firstly, we may see it in the culmination of the sequential progress of the zodiac in the final self-sacrificing theme of the final sign Pisces, as described above. Secondly, we might alternatively see it in an ideal conception of the zodiac *functioning as a whole* (as the state of 'all signs functioning well and equally well', and thus 'as one'). Thirdly, we may also see the 'highest', spiritual or transcendent aspect in a surrender of attachment from *all* of the component parts of the zodiac or psyche, in an escape or retreat from *any* particular part or distinction, to an empty and unmoving centre. Each of these seems to point to a 'spirituality' or 'transcendence' that can be seen of as a sort of stillness or nothingness. It is in the 'nothingness' of the zodiac's end in the final self-dissolving theme of Pisces; it is in the 'nothingness' of the whole, when all particularity of forms 'disappear' in that sole (and therefore 'non-particular') totality; and it is in the absolutely undifferentiated 'nothingness' of the retreat from *all* themes to the still mystical centre. But let us take a closer look at these three ways of characterising 'spirituality' in the zodiac.

The Goal

It seems clear that there is some sort of sequential 'progression' in the zodiac signs, from the needs of the survivalist, self-seeking Aries to the more transcendent needs of the surrendering, self-denying Pisces. This reflects the developmental metaphor of the progression of life through the seasons of the year, from the vigorous birth (or rebirth) in the spring through to the spare and other-worldly time of late winter. So does this mean that, when there are no more needs to fulfil, the 'spiritual' Pisces emerges as 'the goal'? Many may indeed be inclined to agree that Pisces, if seen as the sign which pre-eminently signifies self-denial, is perhaps the highest, most 'spiritual' need or state of affairs that one can aspire to. It is true that the essence of the Pisces sign-theme seems to recapitulate that 'spiritual' process whereby one lets go of sensations, impressions and thoughts which are held in mystic traditions to merely masquerade as the 'self', and perhaps one can view the preceding signs as 'life preliminaries' to that end, whereby more 'basic' needs are first taken care of.

Is one therefore left with the Piscean self-abnegation or self-transcendence as the 'point' of the zodiac—and thus the 'point' of the human psyche? If so, then one might perhaps think that, having satisfied the Pisces need—the ultimate need of the zodiac—that one has somehow therefore 'automatically' attained the whole in some sense, since most if not all precedent needs have probably been accomplished. It is, after all, the end of the zodiac, and seems to denote a 'spiritual' sense in its emphasis on self-abnegation or self-dissolution (and of course preferably not in its 'poorer version' of self-dissolution as mere oblivion through intoxication). After Pisces, in a motivational sense, there is nothing left to which one might aspire. When all the sign-needs are accomplished, even theoretically, then there does seem to be a sort of nothingness in this final Piscean realm of self-transcendence.

But can one attend to this apparently spiritual need of Pisces, exclusively? The inmates of spiritual retreats, such as monks or nuns, may *attenuate* other needs (such as those for food, communication, recreation, fastidiousness of health, sexual desire, travel—all the preceding needs of the zodiac), to an extreme extent. But circumstances nevertheless must surely still arise when some of those preceding sign-needs again require attention, at least to some degree, even when one has finally embarked upon the rarified life of spiritual self-sacrifice. Can those other prepotent needs ever really be completely extinguished? Perhaps some of them—for instance, sexual desire—can be 'sublimated' or transformed, though how this is to be done is difficult to specify; but perhaps others, such as the need for physical sustenance and security, surely cannot, while life is to be maintained. Even the anchorite needs to eat. It would seem that even the most spiritual person still needs to turn their attention on occasion to mundane exigencies such as material subsistence, health and a modicum of relationship with the material world.

Even if we accept that the last sign Pisces partakes of a paragon of sublimity that seems inherent in the theme of self-sacrifice, one might nevertheless feel uneasy or sceptical in viewing it as the ultimate mode of human existence. One might feel that there is some truth in the notion that, taken alone, the Pisces theme may not be the 'whole point' of human nature as portrayed by the zodiac signs. Attending exclusively to the Pisces need would be, after all, by definition, not attending to any of the others. Perhaps none of the signs on its own can be thought of as *the* answer to all our questions, yearnings, or indeed, needs. It could be said that, no matter how attractive a sign's essential theme is on its own, it will always be a 'particular thing' and thus forever wanting. Even the numinous sign Pisces is a 'particularity', even if we can't help but feel that there is that about it which does directly beckon us in the direction of spirituality, in the form of surrender as the final precursor to transcendence.

The Whole

Against the view that the Pisces sign-theme, being the endpoint or final goal of the zodiac sequence, is the 'highest' aspect of the human psyche, it could rather be asserted that Pisces is in truth no more important than any other sign. Instead, perhaps the value of *wholeness*—the complete integration or the inter-connected functioning of the entire array of sign-themes in the zodiac *taken together*—might alternatively be emphasised as the true 'spiritual' endeavour. In any individual, some sign-functions will no doubt be in want of development (or will be be over-developed), while others will be better expressed.[607] The zodiac as the total picture of needs and accomplishments is likely therefore to be more or less balanced in the individual—largely attained in some areas but not in others. Wholeness or integration may thus perhaps be sought by identifying the poorly-developed (or over-developed) sign-needs and improving these to their correct proportions in relation to the whole, as necessary. Since the sign-themes of the zodiac seem to comprise such a comprehensive picture of the most fundamental functions of the human condition, their states in an individual, taken together, might therefore be seen as an index of a person's tendency towards wholeness. Wholeness would presumably be achieved when the best form of expression for each and every sign is attained, in a good and equal relationship with all the others.

In Carl Jung's view, wholeness consists of *"the union of the conscious and the unconscious personality"*.[608] In an analogy to a mandala-like symbolic wheel of the zodiacal year, Jung's interpretation might correspond to a union of the 'lighter' signs (between the winter and summer solstices) and the 'darker' signs (in the other 'darker' part of the year). Indeed, we have seen how such a duality is echoed in much myth, wherein the protagonist needs to descend into the 'under-world' of the death-like winter and become reborn in the spring. It's not clear whether such mythical journeys can be seen as quests for wholeness in terms of the reconciliation of the dichotomous parts, or whether they are no more than unquiet portrayals of the necessary passage through darkness and danger, serving as psychological palliatives or abreactions by way of a collective acknowl-edgement. The attainment of *épopteia* in the Greek Eleusinian Mysteries seems to come close to being an appreciation of a holistic view, via the contemplation of

---

[607] This is no doubt how the practitioner of divinatory astrology sees the individual's horoscope.

[608] Jung, 1969b

the naturally antagonistic (or complementary) halves of the year.[609] But in this our present discussion of 'wholeness', we are considering the ultimate value of a more all-inclusive sense—an integrated synthesis of *all* the twelve zodiac signs in a synchronously or simultaneously functioning equality.

Without equal development, things can go horribly wrong. Think, for instance, of possessing a great amount of material resources in your life, but a complete absence of love, or a serious cognitive impairment, or poor health of a serious nature: suddenly those material resources may lose a lot of their value. If you had love but very few material resources, things may soon become sour. If you had remarkable intellect but few material resources, life wouldn't be as good or stable. If you had love but poor health *and* very few material resources, things generally would be very bad. So the greater the number of depleted 'departments' of life, the greater the impact upon what we think of as life itself (as the whole of life).

Earlier we noted that, of our 'rough list' of the 'important things in life' (namely, health, money, creative work and love), it is possible that the term 'health' may be used to encapsulate all the others as a 'catch-all' term (the 'health of one's finances', the 'health of one's love-life', etc). One might similarly view 'spirituality' as encapsulating all the 'factors' (of health, money, creative work and love), and obviously more easily so if we identify wholeness as spirituality. Wholeness as a criterion of spirituality would rule that the principle of any one sign should not be under- or over-developed out of proportion, at the expense of any other, at least not in a way that could be said to delimit or caricature the person. A person's wholeness would depend on how far they satisfy or achieve each sign-theme 'well and equally with every other'. If one particular life-function predominates, then the whole person could be seen as unnaturally influenced or distorted by it, and the person's wholeness of being might thus be viewable as compromised by that function. A criterion of wholeness would dictate that, as long as we are uneven in this way, we are imperfect, in that we are dominated and misrepresented by such inequalities in our lives.

Thus the sign-themes of the zodiac, which *taken together* seem to be a comprehensive picture of the composition of our nature, may be a guide to wholeness, which itself may be thought of as a 'spiritual' aspect of life. If the individual self is anything, it is the totality of all the elements that make up one's body, one's psyche and one's life. The desirable wholeness of the self could be said to subsist when all those parts are functioning 'well and equally well together', in mutual equipoise. When all the sign themes function in such a way, then one could say that there is no particularity, and the separateness of the signs in the zodiac may be said effectively to 'disappear' as obstacles to the oneness of a spirituality that is seen as wholeness.

---

[609] See Chapter 4.

This is reminiscent of the way the various organs or parts of the body, when 'whole' or operating in good health[610] and thus in harmony with one another, result in no painful experience of 'particularity' or 'dis-order' of illness. We are typically only aware of any particular part of our body when we are unwell, when something is wrong with that part; that is, when our physical state of wholeness is compromised. When the body is healthy or whole, one is not aware of any particular part. It may possibly be argued that, equally, one is psychologically or spiritually healthy or whole when no particular aspect of our psyche dominates, intrudes, holds sway, or causes undue self-consciousness. We talk of a healthy personality as one that is 'balanced' or 'well-adjusted', again seemingly indicative of wholeness. Etymology and common usage encourages an identification of what may be said to be spirituality with wholeness: to be 'holy' is to be 'holistic'—indeed, to be whole, just as to be 'healthy' is to be 'whole'. Organic life is a self-integrating whole or system. It is of course also self-reproducing, but it is the pattern of the whole that must be reproduced. Each system—every one of us—is a reproduction or impression of an idea, of a pattern, of a whole.

One can see an example or analogy of this commendable idea of wholeness or the integration of the signs, in the action of practicing physical exercises, such as in Yoga postures. When striving to adopt and maintain a Yoga posture, one often learns that one firstly has to overcome one or more 'lop-sided weaknesses' that one has been born with, or which one has acquired through habit or injury. A beginner may find that they are weaker on one side, or that they tend to be less effective when needing to employ certain limbs, muscles or positions. Thus they have to pay especial attention to making extra effort or care to those areas. Having worked to overcome these imbalances, they then strive to maintain that wholeness in the pose, such that each muscle and limb is working well *and equally well*, to hold the pose correctly.[611] Similarly, in striving to achieve the wholeness of the zodiac signs in one's life, one would firstly have to overcome one's natural weaknesses in (or 'poor expressions' of) certain sign-themes, for example, in being over-nervous or mentally diffuse as a poor expression of the Gemini theme. Thus one would try, to the best of one's ability, to correct such 'lop-sided' expressions, and thereafter one would strive to maintain that integrated state of the signs being expressed 'well and in harmony with each other'. In our personal actions and habits generally, such an integrative view of life may enable us to be free of the various imbalances that can cause much pain. It would not be controversial to suggest that many people go through life for years weighed down by the suffering that is caused by unwholesomeness—by a disproportionate preoccupation with certain behaviours or aspects of life. When we say something is an 'unholy mess' we're tacitly acknowledging the meaning of 'holy' as organised, integrated, holistic or whole.

---

[610] One might coin an etymologically cognate neologism 'wholth'.

[611] The same principle may of course be applicable in various other forms of sports, athletics, callisthenics or other aptitudes.

The practice of striving to achieve such wholeness for the fundamental parts of life that are embodied in the zodiac sign-themes would in addition bring home to us the fact that every sign has a 'good' and 'bad' expression, and may conceivably help us to be more tolerant and understanding, both of ourselves and of others. In the normal way of things, we might see in other people an aspect of a sign-theme being expressed which seems quite different to our own nature; we may look upon that form of expression unfavourably, as a 'pet hate'. We may, for example, see an expression of the Taurus sign-theme which, if quite different to ourselves, we might characterise purely negatively. But if we develop a conception of the zodiac as a whole, emphasising the equality and necessity of *all* the signs, we may come to understand that such an expression is part of, and required by, that whole; that individuals who emphasise the Taurus sign-theme are needed as well as any other. Thus there is wholeness in groups as well as in individuals. The prejudices we might have against certain personality types would recede in the appreciation of tolerance that comes from living in an awareness of the need for wholeness. This is not to say of course that we shouldn't recognise a 'bad' or exaggerated expression of a sign-theme or understand that it could be better expressed. But a conception of the whole system of signs may enable us at least to appreciate the integral nature of personality expressions, when we might otherwise have taken their imbalances to be somehow 'bad' in themselves.

The notion of a 'balancing towards wholeness' would also serve to remind us of the utility of pre-potency in the sign-needs, for instance in that we are probably not fit to go about self-sacrificing works if our very survival, health or competence is at risk. Perhaps a certain equality of functioning of all the signs is required for any proposed end-point to be realised. One loses the value of the holistic aspect of the zodiac if the characteristics of one sign are grossly over- or under-developed to the expense of the others; thus, the attainment of a 'goal' of spirituality would depend upon the maintenance of a certain wholeness. Regarding wholeness for its own sake, the 'ideal' is for 'all sign-needs to be working well, and equally well in relation to each other'—the constantly sought-for homoeostasis, upon the attainment of which the whole emerges, alone. Perhaps the whole psyche, seen as in that single, holistic, integrated or systemic state, may be that which might best approximate to our idea of 'the best expression of the zodiac', and to Maslow's 'self-actualisation'. It is true that Maslow seemed to view self-actualisation as a discrete, separate need, though he nevertheless somewhat gnomically appeared to tie the sequence (the 'goal') and the whole together in his writings on the place of transcendence in his hierarchy of needs, when he remarked that *"Holism in the sense of hierarchical integration is assumed."*[612]

If spirituality is seen in this way as wholeness, it might perhaps be most aptly represented in astrological symbolism by the Sun, since the Sun's associa-

---

[612] Maslow, 1971

tions, as we have seen, are with wholeness and integration, and of course the Sun, as the central hero of the year-journey, has represented divinity in most myth. In the ancient Indian scriptural text the *Isa Upanishad, Brahman* (the personification of ultimate spiritual transcendence) is symbolised by the Sun, as if it were Brahman's proxy or example in the material realm, and thus at the same time our own core spiritual nature:

> O life-giving sun, off-spring of the Lord of creation, solitary seer of heaven! Spread thy light and withdraw thy blinding splendour that I may behold thy radiant form: that spirit far away within thee is my own inmost spirit.[613]

Of the organising principle of wholeness, which we might here identify with the integrating principle of the Sun, the Neoplatonist philosopher Plotinus wrote:

> We are like a choir of singers who stand round the conductor, but do not always sing in time because their attention is diverted to some external object; when they look at the conductor they sing well and are really with him. So we always move round the One; if we did not, we should be dissolved and no longer exist; but we do not always look towards the One. When we do, we attain the end of our existence, and our repose, and we no longer sing out of tune, but form in very truth a divine chorus round the One.[614]

The 'whole' which may be said to emerge with a comprehensive parity of all the signs 'working well and equally well together' is a unity: the spirit of the Sun and its attendant planet-functions operating in homoeostasis; the single wholeness of *all of the parts functioning in concert*. Such a state of wholeness might be said to be one where 'particularity' (other than the whole itself) is obliterated. This seems possible if one can accept that such an ideal state of wholeness somehow causes an indistinguishability or a disappearance of any separate component part, and that only the 'one oneness' then emerges as apparent. It is a state akin to all the colours of the rainbow being blended together to produce a single, undifferentiated white light. This state might be said to be spiritual in itself, for it is a non-componential whole, which characteristic is certainly allied to the notion of 'spirit'. In traditions of spirituality there is said to be no differentiation or 'particularity' in the spirit. In a sense, therefore, this state of spiritual wholeness is also a form of nothingness, in that it has no identifiable 'particularity'.

But having here gone to some length to illustrate the idea of spirituality as 'wholeness in life' (and thus in the zodiac signs, since we take these to be a comprehensive set of the exemplars of life's particular 'parts'), we can nevertheless see problems with the notion. On the one hand it seems conceivable that

---

[613] Mascaró, 1973
[614] Inge, 1918

304

wholeness might be considered a transcendental spirituality, if one could accept that, when it is achieved, all particular forms 'disappear' in the one singularity that remains, and if we can view that oneness as equivalent to the transcendent state of 'union' in the mystic. But does anyone actually achieve a spiritual state by these means? Does anyone indeed actually attain wholeness? Of course it can be argued that a widespread failure to achieve wholeness is not evidence against it as being the essence of spirituality in life. But realistically one may nevertheless also argue that, even if such a state of perfect wholeness or homoeostasis can be viewed as transcendent spirituality, the struggle to achieve it—and moreover to *maintain* it—is likely to be eternal. How and when is the whole grasped and retained?

We all feel the need at certain times to escape or step away from the dreary and frequently conflicting doings of 'this and that'—the wretched round of *particular things* that seem never to end; the 'slings and arrows' which harry, fret and threaten to consume our lives. In such a case we might take a 'holiday', which word derives from the Old English *hāligdæg*, meaning 'holy day'—cognate with 'whole'; a time when we forget particulars and take a more leisured and overall view of the wholeness of things. In some relevant sense, we take a *holiday* for the good of our *health* as a *whole*. But despite the value of the health-giving unity of a holiday, we nevertheless note that it is only a transient state. Symbolically the zodiac, as a wheel, always turns, and there seems to be an eternal repetition of the cycle of birth, death and rebirth. Perhaps the 'whole' may be imagined, but never actually realised.

Wholeness of the zodiac implies a democratic equality between the signs—that no one sign is intrinsically better than any other. This may be difficult to interpret spiritually. For instance, one must say that, in justifying Aries's expression (which must be justified as much as any other sign), one must sometimes be a little bit selfish or self-oriented; yet in doing the same for Pisces, the particularly spiritual call of self-abnegation in Pisces seems to say, *"No; one must indeed be dead to the self."* So, how can we attain a true and simultaneous wholeness of all the signs, if some are frank contradictions of others? Furthermore it could be argued that it is natural and desirable that some individuals may excel remarkably in one or more specific 'sign areas', even at the significant expense of others. Perhaps psychic imbalances—even if they are frequently painful—can be unique founts of exceptional creativity, as long as they are not merely pointless obsessions or other 'unwholesome' exaggerations which cannot be characterised as anything but plain illnesses (and even if that latter type may be the more common). How might we choose between a 'safe' but potentially vapid homogeneity of wholeness and the possibility of an infrequent but spectacular product of creativity resulting from the domination of one particular sphere?

Against this criticism it has been suggested that the highpoint of creativity, at least, is essentially a function of the whole individual, all separable parts working in concert. Maslow felt that *"creating tends to be the act of a whole man ... he is then most integrated, unified, all of a piece, one-pointed, totally organized in the service of the fascinating matter-in-hand. Creativeness is therefore systemic; i.e., a whole—or Gestalt—quality of the whole person."*[615] Although this agrees with our analysis of the place of creativity and wholeness in the context of the sign Leo earlier in this chapter, it is nevertheless a moot point whether exceptional artists such as Michelangelo would have been seen as well-balanced, 'whole' individuals when they produced their extraordinary creative works. Furthermore we acknowledge that wholeness as *creativity* and wholeness as spiritual transcendence of particularity might not be seen as the same thing.

The Hole

From a different perspective it may be said that, although 'wholeness' is what we might strive for, dynamically, in everyday life, and that from an overall perspective it is necessary to do so for harmonious living (and perhaps for creative endeavour); and that, although if successfully accomplished it might, as an undifferentiated entity, in one sense transcend particularity, it is nevertheless not the spirituality of the mystic state which truly transcends the multifaceted characteristics of the sign-themes. Perhaps we might look upon wholeness only as a prelude, facilitator or secular proxy to the truly transcendental spirituality of mysticism. In 'spirituality as wholeness', we wish for the whole array of signs to operate in an equal fashion, until a state of oneness is realised; but perhaps such a transcendence, supposedly inherent in the 'disappearance' of particularity when we achieve that singular wholeness, is in fact chimerical and never to be achieved, or at any rate never maintained, or simply not suitable to be identified as true transcendent spirituality. Perhaps there is another way of seeing 'spirituality' as it pertains to the zodiac as the structure of the components of the human psyche, which relates more closely to the ancient mystical tradition of 'the void' of pure consciousness (that is, consciousness without any 'particularity' of content).

This 'mystic way' is without doubt strongly hinted at in the sign Pisces. The mystical-spiritual 'emptying', 'dissolving' or 'disregarding' of the mind (and perhaps one might say, of the life) of all thoughts, impressions, volitions or emotions—the deliquescence of all forms of multiplicity or distinction which disturb or 'contaminate' the absolute freedom of pure consciousness, as reflections 'disturb' or 'contaminate' the purity of the mirror—this appears to epitomise quite remarkably the tendency that is inherent in the theme Pisces, with its emphasis on self-dissolution, self-abnegation or the surrender of the notion of 'self'. Indeed, a résumé of the characteristics of the Pisces sign-theme recapitulates the essence of the means whereby the mystic state is traditionally obtained or rather disclosed by the surrender of any and every particular thing. We have seen that Pisces seeks seclusion, escape, and the transcendence of the self and the

---

[615] Maslow, 1971

material, even if this is sometimes only crudely expressed by means of mere intoxication. At basis, the Pisces urge, in whatever form it takes, is to completely forget the self. Libra was the first to turn attention to 'the other,' but in the final outcome of the zodiac at Pisces, in one way or another, the many is dissolved in the oneness of the spiritual void. In other words (and in this view), Pisces is the epitome of the evolution of man from basic success in life to spiritual transcendence, and recapitulates the renunciation which discloses the mystic state. The linear sequence of the zodiac sign-themes therefore 'tends towards' spirituality.

But are we not here backtracking our argument and once more making the case for spirituality as inhering *in* the 'goal' of the attainment of the 'higher' aspect of Pisces exclusively? We are, almost, but not quite. If the Piscean ethos is not absolutely developed in its 'higher' spiritual aspect, the step beyond it can be characterised as leading back to 'rebirth' in Aries, to start the cycle of life again. But if the Piscean transcendence of the apparent self *is* realised, then perhaps the invisible path beyond it can be characterised symbolically as leading to the *centre* of the zodiac, as in the inward path of a concentric labyrinth. The caesura between Pisces and Aries may represent the choice between the ultimate mystic escape or a rebirth into the selfish, survival-oriented world. If the path of surrender is maintained, *even for itself*, then that path leads beyond Pisces, but inwards, to the disclosure of that mystical state where the self with all its outward attendant expressions is realised as illusory—to the still centre of the zodiac. If it is not taken, then rebirth into Aries takes place.

The crucial point is that, for the attainment of the true spiritual void at the still centre, Pisces must give itself up as well. The spiritual goal ultimately leads to the empty centre; that still centre around which the phenomenal world of the various signs revolves; the still centre that the poet T. S. Eliot referred to as being:

> At the still point of the turning world ... neither movement from
> nor towards, neither ascent nor decline ... except for the point, the
> still point, there would be no dance, and there is only the dance ...
> the inner freedom from the practical desire, the release from action
> and suffering.[616]

The notion of a transcendent spirituality or perfection as residing in a still centre is not a new representation. As we saw in Chapter 1, in the period between 4,400-2,200 BCE the figures of the bull, the lion, the eagle and the angelic man were projected onto the four stars which most nearly marked the important cardinal points of the year (the two solstices and the two equinoxes), before these principal four eventually came to 'anchor' the full circle of the twelve projected signs of the zodiac. These four significant pictorial representations gained more developed cultural and symbolic significance in Christian iconography as 'tetramorphs', where they were commonly depicted as four corner-pieces

---

[616] Eliot, 1943

representing the similarly 'important' followers of Christ, the four evangelists Matthew, Mark, Luke and John, with Christ as the image of the spiritual centre-piece which they surround (see Chapter 1). The four figures of the tetramorphs can and have been seen as representing the four 'pillars' of the entire phenomenal world (the latter symbolised by the complete array of the various forms and 'ways' of the signs), surrounding the still centre of that swirling profusion of multiplicity, which focal point is a central image of the godhead, the absolute, the void, a personification of perfection, which, unmoving and unmoved, is thus holy and wholly transcends that changing world.

The 'tetramorph', the image of the four 'representatives' of the phenomenal world surrounding the unmoving spiritual centre, has been represented, either consciously or unconsciously, in various examples of secular and religious iconography, where the secular blurs with the religious and the mystical in representational art. A subtle example of such a representation is in Hieronymus Bosch's painting *Christ Crowned with Thorns*, wherein four tormentors, one at each corner of the painting, surround the contrastingly serene figure of Christ in the centre. The corner figures have been identified as portrayals of the four humours (and thus, the various 'four factors' which we discussed in Chapter 5), and although different commentators have assigned different positional orders of these factors for the four figures, they are almost certainly representations of them.

It has been remarked of Christ as the spiritual centre in Bosch's painted representation, *"Here is the stillness that we find in the heart of Bosch's painting: the face of Christ, unmoved and unmarked by his assailants."*[617] In this mediaeval Christian example of the timeless image of the central transcendent godhead, we see the four cardinal points as prime exemplars of the signs; as would-be but ultimately ineffectual 'assailants', in the phenomenal world, of the stillness of the soul, the inviolable mystic void. The same authors remark, *"This is the stuff of meditation, and the real function of devotional image."* They also cite the Dutch Christian humanist Erasmus (1466—1536) as restating the same essential message of the spiritual centre (here as Christ) as the antidote to entrapment in the phenomenal world, as *"indeed a very centre or middle point unmoved."* This sort of mystical, contemplative iconography seems to us to be the ultimate human impulse and need, and thus in spirit anterior to partisan religious doctrine.

The third way of the zodiac is therefore a path beyond Pisces, but not to a rebirth in Aries, and neither in an endless struggle to maintain an integration or homoeostasis of all the parts as a singular whole, but a path to emptiness which we can only call the 'hole'. This can be seen as the transcendent aspect of spirituality that we see in the roots of Hinduism and Buddhism, which don't just describe the best way to be whole in one's life, amongst one's fellow men, but also a way to disclose the true transcendence of the spiritual void. The ancient Indian *Prasna Upanishad* describes Brahman (the embodiment of the mystic state)

---

[617] Foster & Tudor-Craig, 1986

in a way that is reminiscent of the still centre of the zodiac, when it says that the manifold aspects of the world of phenomena are but *"spokes projecting from the Self, who is the hub of the wheel. The Self is the goal of knowledge. Know him and go beyond death."*[618] That most central hub of the wheel is empty and unmoving. As the wheel of the zodiac can be characterised as the array of archetypes that constitute the various 'particular' or prejudiced states of attachment of the phenomenal world, so the one true self can be seen as the still, empty and motionless centre of that wheel. That still centre is pure consciousness, the 'blank sheet of paper' upon which the manifold ideations of the signs are, so to speak, potentially written or impressed.

After Pisces there can therefore be, symbolically, a rebirth into Aries and therefore yet another return to the potentially endless wheel or progression of the various activities of life as represented by the component signs of the zodiac, with a poor hope, realistically, of ever attaining—let alone maintaining—the non-particularity of its whole expression. Alternatively however, there can be a denial of this rebirth, and instead a retreat from every one of the various phenomena associated with the signs (the 'ten thousand things' of Taoist and Buddhist philosophy), to the uncontaminated, still centre, symbolised as the centre of the zodiac wheel: the void of the mystical experience, being pure consciousness without content. It may be said that the only way out of a circle is through the centre. To cease to revolve on the wheel of the zodiac, one has to avoid being 'reborn' eternally from Pisces to Aries, and instead turn inwards—perhaps indeed at any point along the sequence—to the centre, to that which is nothingness.[619]

If the self-abnegation of Pisces was the 'goal', and the maintenance of a simultaneity of the 'good and equally well functioning' of the signs in their totality was the 'whole', then this surrender to the still centre is the 'hole'. This is the centre of the zodiac, as pure consciousness without content or object; an indisputable oneness by virtue of its absolute emptiness, untainted by any modification from any impression (as represented by the signs). It is the original 'mystical' state; the disclosing of the 'blank sheet of paper' upon which all the various impressions which emanate from the various signs (and which together give the illusion of selfhood) might otherwise be 'written'. Perhaps that mystical retreat can be sought at any point along the progression of pre-potency, at whatever 'goal-seeking' state we happen to find ourselves; after all, it is always there.

We find this notion compelling symbolically. However, we noted above that the maintenance of spirituality or transcendence, either as the 'final' self-abne-gating theme of Pisces, or as the state of wholeness or homoeostasis of the totality of the zodiac, may be difficult or impossible to *maintain*, and perhaps a similar difficulty applies to the practical attainment of spirituality or transcendence as

---

[618] Prabhavananda & Manchester, 1947

[619] We say *"perhaps at any point"*, though mystical endeavour is perhaps typically under-taken by older people towards the later part of the 'need sequence'. But this is not to deny the possibility of the spiritual 'disclosure' of the mystic state or void at any stage of life.

'the hole', the surrender of all needs, of everything, for instance in meditation. Perhaps this 'escape to the centre' can also be nothing more than an intermittent practice—*unless* it inheres in a form of 'meditation in action' which can be employed no matter what is happening 'out there' in the phenomenal world.

Completion, Wholeness and Renunciation

We find difficulty in stating a precise description of what we mean by 'the end of the rainbow' with reference to a 'spirituality' in the sign-themes of the zodiac. Because we see in the signs a credible pattern of personality characteristics, because we see something that looks very much like a developmental sequence, because we see a realistic prepotent succession of needs; because, in other words, we seem to see a comprehensive account of the most fundamental components of the human psyche, we are naturally led to wonder: does this repository of archetypes tell us something of the 'point' of human life, or less teleologically, of its best, 'highest' or most spiritual expression? Thus we are here guilty, like so many others, of seeking a meaning to life, and we wonder if the zodiac, since it appears to be such an all-inclusive representation of the human psyche, can give us clues. What is that point, that highest or most spiritual expression? What is that meaning?

We might see it as simply the 'end' or 'goal' of the sequence. There does indeed seem to be a very appropriate metaphor of the human condition in the sequence of the zodiac signs, from Aries to Pisces, as of a 'journey through life', with obviously earlier concerns and obviously later or more mature concerns. However, although that teleological notion might in some sense sound suitable, it may nevertheless not be appropriate, since we then ultimately find ourselves 'stuck' at Pisces to the exclusion of all other signs; denying any holistic viewpoint. As sublime as the self-transcending Pisces is, we recall that the zodiac of the year is a wheel, and like all wheels it moves on, from beginning to end, and from end to beginning again, without ever truly finishing. We might alternatively see it in the complete integration of all the sign-needs, where 'all are expressed well and equally well', characterisable as the 'whole'—the whole of the human psyche, the unity of the One Spirit, where the biased particularity of any separate component 'disappears' in such united integration, though if such a state is ever achievable or permanently maintainable in any real sense—and whether it truly represents spirituality—is open to question. We might thus be more inclined to think of it as the 'hole'—the mystical and still centre of the zodiac wheel; for here we quite certainly detach from each and every separate sign, and find ourselves liberated in the unmoved and unmoving centre, while the component parts move as they will, with a repeating sequence that is irrelevant. Indeed then, the parts of the whole operate, and the whole itself moves as it will, around us, without affecting or afflicting us.

We also reflect however that such a form of meditative 'escape' from, or transcendence of, the manifold aspects of the phenomenal world (as they are

310

represented by the zodiac signs) may seem likely to be only intermittent, considering the exigencies of life that the sign-needs meet—*unless* there can be a meditative practice of such a nature that can be continually maintained regardless of the influence of the signs, taken singly or together. In one sense of course that empty and still centre is there all the time. One only needs a meditative way of fully becoming it or disclosing it which is forever immune to any and all of the worldly phenomena of the signs.

Epilogue

We have examined variously interpreted forms of a basic myth which re-enacts the solar year in the northern hemisphere: a journey from growth in the spring, to fruition in the summer, to a 'falling' decay in the autumn, to a death-like state of suspended animation in the winter, back to a rebirth of growth once more in the spring. Customs, myths and legends have accreted around this central story of the cyclical progression of Earthly life, which recapitulates many aspects of human development, needs and the psyche generally. The myth-story is that of the Sun, journeying through the signs—the stations of the year, each with its characteristic theme. The solar personification in myth is typically a heroic figure who in one form or another re-tells or represents the evolution of that journey, adventuring through the significant aspects of its overall cycle.

The story often appears quite dramatic and elaborate in its various mythical forms, but in essence it tells the basic tale of life on Earth, which is able to overcome entropy by means of sexual reproduction and death, thus enabling the survival, not of the individual, but of the repeating pattern, the 'spirit' of the Sun. This miracle of continuing life however necessarily entails the personal death of the individual, which humans, having consciousness and logical intelligence, do not particularly like the thought of. Thus the creation of a myth in the context of 'life through the year' to acknowledge that story, and to emphasise rebirth, as a form of collective therapy. The repeated narrative pattern in the myths of Inana (Ištar) and Dumuzid (Tammuz), Osiris, Adonis and Aphrodite, Attis, Demeter, Persephone-Proserpina, Jesus and various other tales bears witness to this process.

The parts of the year that comprise the progressive stages of this ever-recurring cycle have been projected and refined as the zodiacal signs. The zodiac as a whole constitutes a remarkably coherent pattern which deserves our admiration, despite unfounded but understandable wanderings into notions of natal divination. The language of divinatory practices has nevertheless made a great deal of human sense to people who have sought to understand their physical and psychic nature with reference to time and space within a perspective view of the cosmos, and has clearly still not lost that appeal. When we speak with those who practice 'serious' divinatory astrology, we're struck by the fact that the concepts and methods they use, though, as we have seen, unable to predict personality, nevertheless comprise an orderly, sensible and insightful language of the human archetypes.

An astrologer who, for instance, appraises a person who has Mars in the sign Aquarius in their birth-chart, might describe this configuration of symbols as signifying that *'their urge and ability for activity, to work and to be enterprising'* (i.e., the Mars function), is for them characteristically *'unconventional, forward-looking and questioning of authority'* (i.e., expressed in the Aquarius mode). If nothing else, this is a wonderfully concise familiarity with some of the most basic human functions and modes of expression. Knowing the symbolism, we understand the way the prose description has been constructed from the 'planet in sign' short-form. Indeed the language used would often allow us extrapolate the 'planet-in-sign' form from the prose description. It is therefore a meaningful shorthand way of summarising a mode of expression (the sign) of a basic function (the planet). However, because empirical research tells us that there is no evidence for the association of someone's personality with their Sun-in-sign *at birth* (let alone planet-in-sign at birth), we cannot and should not use such short-forms to describe individuals' personality on the basis of their birth-charts (horoscopes).

We realise that 'absence of evidence does not mean evidence of absence', but we have to acknowledge that the existing studies do not give support for natal divinatory astrology; quite the contrary. Perhaps we could wait for even more sophisticated research, though even if such were funded and carried out, it seems unlikely to us that it would be any more supportive of divinatory astrology, even in terms of seasonal (Sun-in-sign) effects. It seems likely that the idea of a possible 'Sun-in-sign-theme at birth' effect upon a person's lifelong personality came about by way of an over-zealous abstraction of the nature of the zodiac signs. The signs represent many fundamentally important human factors, but there is no evidence to support the notion that merely being born in them in any way fixes for life their associated factors in terms of personality. The language of the universal symbolism used in the divinatory endeavour nevertheless remains eminently comprehensible, which is perhaps one reason why that endeavour is so susceptible to cognitive bias and why it persists.

We note that we couldn't help suggesting, above, the need for more and better empirical evaluation. We wonder if we do so from a rational motivation of completeness, acknowledging the fact that there still may be an effect of the natal Sun-sign which is strangely elusive but which may nevertheless be ultimately determined through proper empirical research, or whether we are showing ourselves to be still in the grip of a strangely powerful cognitive bias. If it is, as is likely, the latter, then perhaps the bias is so easily evoked—especially amongst those conversant with astrological symbolism—because the fundamental functions and ways of expression described by astrological symbolism are precisely those factors that tend to influence cognitive bias itself.

In a similar way sometimes indeed we feel the need to pinch ourselves and ask: has humankind really been *that* affected by the seasons, those climatic effects of the fortuitous obliquity of the Earth's plane of ecliptic, that their effects have spoken to its most fundamental myth-making? Despite the seemingly absurd simplicity of the cause, we believe that this is indeed the case. Life on Earth has been vastly affected by this factor and forced to adapt to it, so perhaps it doesn't seem quite so strange that humankind has been no exception to its influence. The

314

major features of the year—the seasons—reflect major requirements for the adaptive behaviour of life on our planet generally, so it should be no surprise that they are used as metaphors to express the way individuals develop through their lives. The year-journey meaningfully reflects needs and practices that organisms require and what they can glean from season to season in their cycle of life.

One wonders how things might be for exoplanets (planets of other solar systems) with different orbital characteristics; where, for instance, the celestial equator is *not* tilted from the plane of the ecliptic and where there are therefore no seasons, as on Earth; or on planets with markedly different equatorial obliquities; or planets with no axial spin, so that one side permanently faces the parent star and the other lies permanently in darkness. What activities, customs and ways of thinking would evolve, dictated by the available means of procuring energy for life and reproduction, and thus what societies, what myths and internalised representations of them in the psyche might there be? Would the inhabitants of such worlds, like us, be concerned deeply with 'completion, wholeness and renunciation', or would *completely alien* forms of internalised symbolical importance predominate?

We admit that, when we find ourselves entertaining such speculations, however rational and meaningful they may be, we are nevertheless somewhat brought up sharply, as if we had caught ourselves in some florid fantasy. We ask ourselves, is it all nonsense? Do our surveys and cogitations contain a tendency to perceive meaningful connections between actually unrelated things (a cognitive phenomenon known as 'apophenia')—a 'reading-in' or selectively narrow and prejudiced perception of human nature, so that we over-emphasise the significance of these symbols of the year-story that we have investigated? But having pinched ourselves to make sure we are not dreaming, and having reassessed the long history of custom and myth, we are inclined to conclude that these concepts and interpretations are indeed valid, and represented in many cultures which have left a record of myth.

We have seen in our review how the 'myth-story' of humankind has indeed been one which internalises symbolically the major factors which affect Earthly life, of which humans have been an integral part, the most salient and powerful of which is the Sun's journey through the year. The type of things that we *would* naturally 'read in' to our view of the cosmos around us are precisely those things that have been symbolised as the 'functions of the planets' and the 'ways of the signs', the very things that have formed our lives and thus our myths. We have projected our fundamental functions and expressions into the planets and signs, cast these universal facets of our natures into myths, and attributed the greatest importance to them, because they are ways in which we integrate our innermost natures into wholeness of spirit in Earthly life. Thus even as myths they are primary sources of human spirituality.

Our final thought is that, although we are all different, indeed unique individuals, in terms of the human needs we have studied, whether of Maslow's scheme or of that of the zodiac signs, it is nonetheless the case that, whatever the names or labels that we give to the pieces of land that we inhabit, whatever the colour of our skin, the sound of our speech, or the cultural milieux in which we find ourselves, we nevertheless all have the same *needs*, as we tread the same path from the cradle to the grave. We all—each of us, and all of us together—need to survive; we all need to be secure in our little places; we all need to be able to perceive and communicate; we all need the comfort and love of a home and family; we all need recreation and creativity; we all need to be able to ensure our health and fitness; we all need to love and be loved; we all need at critical times to confront and commune with the depths of the life-force of our common nature; we all need to explore, either physically or mentally or both; we all need to endure hardship and knuckle down for ambition, status and a place in society; we all need to recognise and embrace the radically new; we all ultimately need to dissolve our individual spirits in the One. The basic functions and ways of being that we have projectively distilled into the heavenly planets and signs have helped us and continue to help us to articulate these needs.

Appendix 1: Mithraism

Mithraism was a Roman religious cult which began a little before the rise of Christianity, some time around the first century BCE, thereafter spreading throughout the Roman empire (especially among the military) during the 1st century CE. The Greek philosopher Plutarch (c. 46—119 CE) recorded in his biography *Parallel Lives* that in 67 BCE the Roman general Pompey encountered pirates from Cilicia in south east Asia Minor and discovered that they were practising 'secret rites' of *Mithras*; that is, a religion of a deity Mithras in which one was initiated and subsequently sworn to secrecy.[620] Such a secret and initiatory cult is known as a 'mystery religion', the term deriving via the Latin *mysterium* from the Greek *mystêria* and in turn from that term's root *myo*, meaning 'to close or shut'—in this sense, to shut one's mouth and keep the rites secret.

The devotees of Mithras met secretively in temples now known as *Mithraea* (singular: *Mithraeum*) which were fashioned from, or in the appearance of, underground caves. Such Mithraea have been discovered all over Roman Europe. The signature iconographic characteristic of the Roman cult of Mithras is the unique array of features that are always present in the Mithraea. Apart from always being contrived to be, or to appear to be, situated inside a cave-like space, the Mithraeum features at one end a carved and often painted stone scene known as the 'tauroctony'—a scene depicting the god Mithras slaying a bull (often a white-coloured bull), accompanied by other figures in set choreographed positions which appear symbolic. These other figures always include a dog, a snake, a scorpion (which is biting the bull's testicles) and a raven. Mithras himself is always depicted wearing a Phrygian cap, and is shown turning his head to his right, away from the bull, as he kills it. On either side of the bull there are almost always found two human figures carrying torches; on one side the figure is depicted with his torch pointing upwards, while that on the other side has his torch pointing downwards; both of these figures, known as *Cautes* and *Cautopates* respectively, are usually depicted with their legs crossed.

Busts of the Sun and the Moon, the Sun with the rays of its corona emanating from the head or crown, and both Sun and Moon frequently depicted driving chariots, are almost always found in the upper corners of the tauroctony scene. The figures of a lion and a cup were also sometimes added to the sculpted scene, and the bull's tail often had an ear or ears of wheat emanating from it.[621] Sometimes the twelve signs of the zodiac are portrayed above the figures at the top of the Mithraeum, and in other instances they are displayed around the figure of Mithras and the bull in a circle (with Scorpio's scorpion, in the correct zodiacal

---

[620] Plutarch, 2012
[621] Beck, 2006

sequence, biting the bull's testicles). Busts showing the seven classical planets were also often incorporated, either above the head of Mithras, or on his cloak, or somewhere in the space surrounding him, or on the benches provided for the select congregation.[622] On occasion seven asterisk shapes are depicted above the head of Mithras, which may be stellar placeholders for the classical planets. Sometimes the roof of the Mithraic temple is decorated with stars. A figure of a lion-headed god is also found in many Mithraic temples. He has a human-like (though winged) body, yet a lion's head. In his right hand he holds a key, whilst in the other he holds a long rod at an oblique angle. He stands upon a globe which has a skewed cross overlaid upon it diagonally (similar to that seen on armillary spheres), while a serpent entwines his whole figure. His body is also marked by the signs of the zodiac.

Understanding the symbolic meaning of the Mithraic tauroctony has taken a very long time indeed. One factor seems evident: that its iconography points to a fundamentally celestial or 'heavenly' symbolism. The features have many correlates in astronomical bodies, constellations and the zodiac. We certainly see the Sun, the Moon, the seven classical planets and two recognisable zodiacal constellations, namely, Taurus the bull and Scorpio the scorpion. The Neoplatonic philosopher Porphyry (c. 234—c. 305 CE) recorded that the Mithraic temples were made to be cave-like in order for them to represent 'an image of the cosmos.' Porphyry further mentions that the figure of Mithras is placed symbolically in the vault of the cave 'along the celestial equator with the North on his right and the South on his left.'[623]

The early Christian scholar Origen (c. 185—c. 253) quotes the 2nd-century Greek philosopher Celsus as describing celestial symbolism in 'the mystery of Mithras' wherein there is represented 'two orbits in heaven, the one being that of the fixed stars and the other that assigned to the planets.' The former appears to be another allusion to the celestial equator whilst the latter seems to point to the ecliptic. Origen also cites Census as describing another Mithraic symbol, 'a ladder with seven gates and at its top an eighth gate', which in the celestial context obviously suggests the seven classical planets.[624]

In 1869 the German scholar K. B. Stark was the first to be bold enough to propose that the tauroctony scene does indeed depict heavenly bodies and constellations. Stark pointed out that every single element in the scene can be seen to represent a constellation or body in the night sky. As noted above, the Sun and the Moon are represented, and the bull can be seen to represent the zodiacal constellation Taurus (the bull), and the scorpion that of Scorpio (the scorpion). In addition, the dog has a parallel in the constellation Canis Minor (the dog), the snake in the constellation Hydra (the snake), the raven in the constellation Corvus (the raven), the lion in the constellation Leo (the lion), the cup in the constellation

---

[622] Beck, 2006
[623] Porphyry, 1983
[624] Origen, 1980

Crater (the cup) and the ear of wheat erupting from the bull's tail parallels the star Spica (the 'ear of wheat') in the constellation Virgo.[625]

A celestial theme therefore appears central to the symbolism in the Mithraic temple and the tauroctony, and we may be surprised to think that Stark's claim was ever seen as being radical. However, between the end of the 19th century and the 1970s it had been assumed by most scholars that the Roman mysteries of Mithras simply had their origin in a much earlier cult of a Persian god named *Mithra*, an Indo-European deity worshipped at least as early as 2,000 BCE. This assumption was largely due to the perceived authority of the scholarship of Franz Cumont in the 1890s, who had assumed that the later Roman Mithras had merely developed from the Persian Mithra, based on the similarity of the names.[626] Cumont's view however ignored frank differences between the two traditions: firstly, there is no element in the Persian religion of any element of initiation or secrecy, as in the Roman Mithraic 'mysteries'; secondly, the signature iconographic characteristic of the Roman Mithras—the unique array of celestially-themed features that are always depicted in the 'Mithraeum' temple—are completely unassociated with the Persian deity of the similar name.

Cumont nevertheless saw no differences between the Persian Mithra and the Roman Mithras, despite the celestial iconographic characteristic being unique to the latter. Cumont did try to assemble various unrelated Persian myths that referenced bull-slaying, dogs, snakes and so-forth, but none of these scattered Persian mythological elements cohered together as in the hallmark Roman Mithraeum depiction. Indeed, there is no known Persian myth wherein Mithra kills a bull. There is a Persian myth where *Ahriman*, a force of cosmic evil, kills a bull, and Cumont somewhat lamely attempted to argue that the Ahriman myth must have been somehow transformed into a myth in which Mithra replaced Ahriman.

Such was Cumont's apparently unassailable scholarly repute, however, that the stark difference between the two religious traditions remained ignored until 1971, when scholars attending an international congress on Mithraic studies in Manchester, UK, pointed out that the only resemblance between the two was in the name of the central deity figure—Mithra in Persian and Mithras in the Roman mystery religion. These scholars agreed that the Roman cult of Mithras was a new religion created in the Greco-Roman world, which had merely adopted the name of the ancient Persian god, perhaps to bestow upon it a certain exotic flavour. Thus it began to be seen that Roman Mithraism was indeed a wholly new religion, with its own unique and apparently puzzling celestial iconography which was absent from ancient Persian mythology. The iconography of the Mithraeum was found in very many places throughout the Roman empire, and became a cult, which at its height challenged the rise of Christianity.

Scholars continued to debate the actual meaning of the Roman Mithraic bull-slaying iconography, but it wasn't until 1991, when David Ulansey analysed its

---

[625] Stark, 1869
[626] Cumont, 1903

characteristics in a new light, that the secret of the 'mystery cult' began to be unravelled.[627] Like Stark before him, Ulansey noted that every figure in the bull-slaying scene had a parallel in celestial factors, which pointed to its having a particularly astronomical or astrological significance. In trying to establish what that significance was, Ulansey asked why a certain delimited number of constellations were represented in the main bull-slaying scene. What was so special about that particular section of constellations? Ulansey then realised that all the depicted constellations in the main Mithraic tauroctony scene lay along the celestial equator. The celestial equator is the circle that would be described against the background of stars by an imaginary projection of the plane of the Earth's equator, from the point of view of an Earth-bound observer. The celestial equator intersects with the ecliptic at the two equinoctial points, the important spring and autumn equinoxes; a diagram of this intersection would take the form of the two planes—the celestial equator and the ecliptic—forming a skewed cross.

Now we also remember that, due to the phenomenon known as the 'precession of the equinoxes' (or simply 'precession'), the constellations in the backdrop of stars which appear to lie along the celestial equator at any given time of year do not remain fixed, but, like those which lie along the ecliptic, though appearing more or less fixed for most observers within their lifetimes, will nevertheless appear to be slightly different for observers of successive generations. Since the spring and autumn equinoxes are those points at which the celestial equator and the ecliptic intersect, the apparent constellation or star-picture in the stellar backdrop which 'mark' those points also slowly changes, moving in a circle, roughly once every 25,000 years. Thus, the constellations 'along the celestial equator' slowly change over time.

This being so, one can calculate, as did Ulansey, that, although it is true to say that the constellations depicted in the tauroctony are those that appear to lie along the celestial equator, they are indeed so, but not as the celestial equator is now, nor as it was 2,000 years ago in Greco-Roman times when the secretive cult of Mithras actually existed, but as it was in the time of ancient Mesopotamia, when the (Sun at the) spring equinox was 'in' (appeared against or in front of) the constellation that we know as Taurus the bull, and the autumn equinox lay in the constellation that we know as Scorpio. In addition, at that ancient time, all the constellations portrayed in the tauroctony scene lay between these points along the celestial equator. Thus Ulansey saw that that the tauroctony portrayed the constellations along the celestial equator as it appeared in ancient Mesopotamia.

This interpretation may also explain the presence of a lion and a cup in certain examples of the Mithraic tauroctony: when the constellations of Taurus the bull and Scorpio the scorpion were positioned at the spring and autumn equinoxes respectively in the time of ancient Mesopotamia, the summer and winter solstices would have been marked by the constellations Leo and Aquarius respectively; the lion would have represented Leo's marking of the summer

---

[627] Ulansey, 1991

solstice, while the cup (as the 'water-bearer') would have represented Aquarius's marking of the winter solstice.

It is tempting to see the two torch-bearers Cautes and Cautopates as representations of Castor and Pollux of Gemini. However Ulansey considered that these two figures more likely symbolised the equinoxes; Cautes holding the torch up, indicating the birth of life or the Sun rising above the equator at the spring equinox, and Cautopates holding the torch down, indicating the 'dying' time of the light at the Autumn equinox. But what is the reason for the depiction of Cautes and Cautopates as having their legs crossed? Ulansey guessed that this is a repeated depiction of the great skewed cross described by the intersection of the ecliptic and the celestial equator. This supposition is supported by the discovery of Mithraic reliefs which also show what the torch-bearers are carrying: the one on one side is carrying the head of a bull; the torch-bearer on the right is carrying a scorpion - these are the constellation markers of the equinoxes at the time indicated by the astronomical symbolism of the bull-slaying theme. Furthermore, in another Mithraic relief we see the torch on one side pointing down, next to a tree with fruit on it, representing the Autumn harvest equinox; on the same relief we see the torch on the other side pointing up with a bull and a tree in leaf, representing the spring equinox.

Ulansey at first thought that the knowledge of the 1st century BCE configuration of the celestial equator which the tauroctony's representation contains must have been preserved from ancient Mesopotamian times as a secret, mysterious and ancient body of knowledge, but he soon rejected this hypothesis, since the ancient Mesopotamians did not have a concept of the celestial equator and thus they would not have known what constellations lay along it. Indeed, it was not until around 128 BCE that the Greek astronomer, geographer and mathematician Hipparchus discovered precession. This suggested that the originators of the tauroctony iconography and the mysteries of Mithras were amongst the few who, shortly after the time of Hipparchus, understood precession, along with how the phenomenon had caused the shifting of the spring equinox out of the constellation of Taurus the bull in about 2,000 BCE. Indeed, it seems that the tauroctony scene depicts this very shift—the 'demotion' of the constellation Taurus as the marker of the spring equinox, represented by the slaying of the bull.

The knowledge of precession, even after Hipparchus, would only have been known to a select few scholarly or priestly individuals. Furthermore, it would have been seen as an important event astrologically, since, as we have seen, although all the symbolism of the signs were originally fixed when a picture was psychologically projected onto a constellation when the Sun was 'behind' that sign at the appropriate time of the year, the seasonal origin of the zodiac sign-naming had been forgotten and obfuscated by a tradition of 'marking by the stars'; thus the named constellations that had once happened to mark these times of year had been given precedence.

Today we know that the phenomenon of precession is caused by various gravitational forces upon the irregular shape of the Earth,[628] but in the time of Hipparchus this was not understood. At that time, when the geocentric view of the cosmos prevailed (the belief that the Earth was the immovable centre of the cosmos), the phenomenon must have appeared to show that the entire system of heavenly spheres had been shifted or turned by some tremendous, supra-cosmic force—perhaps somehow from outside it.

Around the time of Hipparchus it was also believed that, after death, the soul attempted to rise up through the ascending planetary spheres, to the heavenly realm of the fixed stars, in an important and potentially perilous journey, sometimes even requiring knowledge or passwords to unlock subsequent stages upwards. Here we may recall the lion-headed god that appears in the Mithraic temples, who stands on the globe of the cosmos (which shows the intersecting lines or skewed 'cross' of the celestial equator and the ecliptic), holding a key, represented that being who holds the keys to unlock the heavenly gates through which the soul must ascend after death. The serpent, which symbolised wisdom in many ancient contexts, wreaths his body, and the key that this god held may well have symbolised the 'key' of the secret knowledge required to make a successful ascension after death.

It may be that the lion-headed god was the deity that was seen as so powerful that he could 'shift' the entire cosmos, which resulted in the concomitant shifting of the equinoxes in precession, such that the spring equinox left the constellation of Taurus the bull. Indeed, in one Mithraic relief, Mithras is depicted holding the cosmic sphere in one hand, while in the other he is rotating the zodiac. He would have also perhaps been capable of granting salvation to those who worshipped him—perhaps by helping them ascend through the seven planetary spheres after death. The iconography of the Mithraic tauroctony scene symbolically depicts the constellation-shift of the (Sun at the) spring equinox from that of Taurus to Aries which occurred in much older Mesopotamian times (c. 2,000 BCE), since, at the time of the cult's beginning, this was the most recent shift to have happened. As Ulansey explained:

> Hipparchus's discovery of the precession made it clear that before the Greco-Roman period, in which the spring equinox was in the constellation of Aries the Ram, the spring equinox had last been in Taurus the Bull. Thus, an obvious symbol for the phenomenon of the precession would have been the death of a bull, symbolizing the end of the 'Age of Taurus' brought about by the precession. And if the precession was believed to be caused by a new god, then that god would naturally become the agent of the death of the bull: hence, the 'bull-slayer.[629]

---

[628] The Earth is not quite a sphere but rather an oblate spheroid, bulging in the equatorial region.

[629] Ulansey, 1994

In addition Ulansey proposed that, even though the cult grew up and continued to flourish during and after the time that the equinox moved from Aries to Pisces (when the iconography of the tauroctony would not have 'fitted' that spring equinox precessional shift), its proponents might in any case have believed that the precessional transition to Pisces would occur later, at a traditional 8° into a constellation, following an ancient Babylonian rule; thus they would have thought that they were still well within the 'Age of Aries', and that therefore the last pertinent 'slaying' would have been that of Taurus the bull.[630] Had the cult arisen later, after the spring equinox had moved out of the constellation Aries and into that of Pisces (which occurred around the 1st century CE), then the symbolic depiction of precession in the tauroctony might possibly have shown the slaying of a lamb (Aries), as if to say pictorially, 'the spring equinox has moved out of the constellation of the ram (Aries) to that the fish (Pisces)'. But it's likely that the cult arose when the spring equinox was still in the constellation Aries; thus its earliest adherents and iconographers merely portrayed the last known equinox sign-shift, which was from Taurus to Aries.

What of the figure of Mithras himself? Who or what is he? In the representations, he appears just above the bull; so what constellation is just above Taurus? The answer is the constellation *Perseus*, who in ancient mythology is a young Greek hero typically depicted wearing a Phrygian cap, and wielding a dagger. Perseus was, in antiquity (as far back as the 5th and 6th centuries BCE), believed to be the founder of Persia.[631] This is where the Persian link, in the form of the choice of the Persian 'Mithra' as the name of the bull-slaying god, could have occurred. Notably, in Cilicia, from where the earliest known practitioners of the Mithraic mysteries came, but before the origins of those mysteries, there was practiced an ancient cult which worshipped Perseus.[632]

Interestingly, the bull depicted in constellations is always shown facing to the left, whereas the bull depicted in the Mithraic bull-slaying scenes is always shown facing to the right. Ulansey proposes an insightful explanation for this seemingly trivial but actually important difference, which is as follows. If Mithras is a god capable of shifting the entire cosmic sphere, then he must have been imagined as residing, in some sense, *outside* the cosmos. This explains the traditional 'rock birth' of Mithras: the cave was meant to be an image of the cosmos, as seen from the inside; this means that the 'rock' from which Mithras is frequently depicted as being born represents the cosmos as seen from the *outside*; Mithras born breaking out of it represents his power to transcend the cosmos, and move it, from outside it. Very often, the rock is shown being entwined by a snake; this recalls the 'great cosmic egg' which was also entwined by a serpent, representing time, which, according to ancient Orphic mythology, was the egg out of which the

---

[630] Ulansey, 2022
[631] Herodotus, 2023
[632] Ulansey, 1991

cosmos was born. Some reliefs clearly show Mithras breaking out of the cosmic egg as he emerges from the 'rock' and surrounded by the zodiac.[633]

The ancients conceived of the cosmos of the heavens as a series of concentric spheres, surrounding the fixed Earth. If Mithras is *outside* the cosmos, on looking back into it, he would therefore (to the ancient view) see a sphere; he would see the constellations from the *outside*; he would see a reversed, mirror-image of the heavens that we see; this explains the horizontal reversal of the bull in the Mithraic scene to the one seen geocentrically as we see it. Some Mithraic monuments portray an Atlas-like Mithras holding the sphere of the cosmos on his shoulders; on it we can see the figures of the zodiac, with the constellation-figure of Taurus the bull facing to the right, as in the usual Mithraic bull-slaying scene. Thus Mithras is portrayed outside the cosmos.[634]

Other more prosaic interpretations for the Mithraic tauroctony scene have been adduced. Bruno Jacobs saw the scene as portraying the heliacal setting (i.e., the last evening visibility) of the constellation Taurus (as the bull setting or 'being killed') at the time of the spring equinox, and thus the overcoming of winter and the time of seasonal renewal.[635] However, Jacobs's theory leaves a great deal of other extraneous symbolism in the tauroctony, which is repeated in very many of its instances, unexplained. Alessandro Bausani suggested that the scene was in essence a repetition of the ancient Near Eastern 'bull-killing lion' motif of Mesopotamia, which in turn may be interpreted in terms of the seasonal cycle where the summer (as the lion in the constellation of Leo) overcomes the spring (as the bull in the constellation of Taurus).[636] But this neither explains the other multifarious symbolism in the iconography.

Roger Beck viewed the figure of Mithras in the tauroctony simply as 'the Sun in Leo', since the constellation Leo *"lies in the middle of the band of constellations intimated by most of the other elements in the tauroctony."*[637] As with Bausani's proposition, however, such a simpler interpretation, though having the apparent benefit of parsimony, does not explain the richness and variation of the symbols repeatedly seen in the tauroctony. In our view the interpretation of David Ulansey is the most cogent and insightful, being a thesis that explains just about all of the Mithraic iconography and one which is supported by otherwise seemingly unrelated elements of mythology.

One more thing concerning the secret cult of Mithras that interests us is that there were apparently seven hierarchical grades of initiation into its mysteries. These were mentioned by St Jerome (c. 342 CE—c. 420 CE) in his *Letters* and have been seen through corresponding archaeological remnants to correlate to the

---

[633] Notably, the Orphic god *Phanes* (the 'shining one') was born out the cosmic egg and is also represented as entwined by a serpent.

[634] Ulansey, 1991

[635] Jacobs, 1999

[636] Bausani, 1979

[637] Beck, 2006

seven classical planets.[638] It's possible that these ascending levels of induction to secret knowledge were intended to correspond to the 'steps' of knowledge that were intended to help the initiate in his ascension through the seven 'planetary spheres' after death. In this sense they are at least reminiscent, if not restatements, of the Palingenius-Shakespeare planetary scheme of human development that we have discussed earlier.

---

[638] Clauss, 2001

Appendix 2: The Judaeo-Christian Passover

In our section on the characterisation of the sign Aries in Chapter 3, we briefly touched upon the Judaeo-Christian spring equinox Passover festival, which is annually held for seven or eight days, starting on the 15th day of the Hebrew month of *Nisan*, which corresponds to the night of the first full moon following the spring equinox[639]—the beginning of the sign Aries and the start of the entire zodiacal year. In biblical times the religious celebration featured the sacrifice—appropriately for the sign Aries—of a ram. The festival is commonly interpreted in the Judaeo-Christian tradition as a yearly commemoration of God's sparing of the lives of the Israelites in his otherwise wholesale destruction of all the first-born in Egypt.[640] The origins of such a festival are however much older than the setting-down of these purported events, being developed from ancient spring seasonal feasts, and only later subsumed into the biblical story.[641]

The English scholar William Tyndale (c. 1494—1536), in his translation of the Hebrew Bible, coined the English word 'Passover' as a translation of the Hebrew *pesah* (פֶּסַח),[642,643] which derives from a verb root *pāsah* meaning 'to pass over', 'to skip over' or 'to hover over',[644,645] taken as meaning a reference to God's 'passing over' or sparing the houses of the enslaved Israelites when he killed the first-born of all the other people in Egypt,[646] as well as denoting the yearly festival in commemoration of that purported event around the spring equinox.[647] Tyndale forbore to translate the word as 'Easter', even though the events that were referred to corresponded to that time of year, because in Tyndale's day the term 'Easter' had a popular connotation as the season of Jesus's death and resurrection; 'Easter' therefore would have seemed anachronistic in translation, as Jesus did not exist in the times of the Old Testament. Tyndale's translation of 'pesah' as 'Passover' therefore seemed apt.

Tyndale also noticed that this word for the event in the Bible story and its yearly remembrance was *also* used to refer to the actual lamb that is slaughtered in the commemorative celebration.[648] This at first seems an odd thing: why should the name used for the *lamb* have been derived from a sense of 'passing over'?

---

[639] Due to calendrical variations the date is sometimes the second full moon after the spring equinox.

[640] Exodus 12:29

[641] Tigay, 2004

[642] Exodus 12:11

[643] Strong's Concordance: H6453

[644] Seely, 2011

[645] Strong's concordance: H6452

[646] Exodus 12:29

[647] Exodus 12:14-27

[648] Exodus 12:11, 12:21

Tyndale offered his opinion as to why two different referents were given the selfsame word in a marginal note: *'The lamb was called Passover that the very name itself should put them in remembrance what it signified.'* [649]

We do not know the basis upon which Tyndale came to this conclusion; we may only assume that it was rather neat philological guesswork. Nevertheless it is no doubt possible to imagine that the equinox festival was indeed named 'Pesaḫ' after the 'passing over' of the Israelites from God's destruction, and that later, the actual sacrificial lamb also came to be called 'Pesaḫ', idiomatically in commemoration of the event. In such a case, the word for the sacrificed animal would obviously not have actually derived from a meaning of 'pass over', as did the name of the festival; rather, it would have simply become, as time went on, colloquially known by the same name as the festival.

There is a problem with this possibility, however, as the Bible states that God himself, *before the event of the sparing of the Israelites, and thus before common usage might have caused the lamb to be known commemoratively by the same name as the event,* instructed the Israelites to *"Kill the Pesaḫ",* [650] clearly as a reference to the lamb, since the meaning was obviously not to 'kill the event'. Tyndale's marginal note therefore seems to lose its plausibility of explanation.

A solution to this difficulty would be to propose that God's words were indeed originally to the effect of, *"Kill the lamb"* (the animal), but that, *by the time the words of the scriptural text were written down,* and a colloquial correspondence between the name of the commemorative festival and the name of the sacrificial animal having become habitually established, the scribe wrote that God had said, *"Kill the pesaḫ",* using the word 'pesaḫ' to mean 'lamb', by virtue of this now customary interchangeability of the two meanings. In this case, God's original instruction could indeed have been to 'kill the lamb', but written long after as 'kill the pesaḫ'. We note that this was not the only place in the Bible that such a scriptural rendering of the phrase 'kill the pesaḫ' was used to mean 'kill the lamb' in this 'special' spring festival commemorative sense; indeed the phrase is found in no less than seven other places. [651] Tyndale would no doubt have considered that the habit of naming the lamb after the event had become widespread.

While there are, on the one hand, instances of the word 'pesaḫ' which are clearly a reference to the sacrificial animal, such as, 'kill the pesaḫ,' [652] 'sacrifice the pesaḫ,' [653] and even 'roasted the pesaḫ,' [654] there are, on the other hand, instances which certainly do *not* refer to an animal, such as 'In the fourteenth day of the first month at even is the Lord's pesaḫ.' [655] So some instances of the word 'pesaḫ' mean the actual animal to be sacrificed, and some mean the event of the commemorative festival. Tyndale would have presumably reiterated that the term

---

[649] Daniell, 1992

[650] Exodus 12:21

[651] Mark 14:12; 2Ch 30:15, 35:1, 35:6, 35:11; Ezra 6:20; Luke 22:7

[652] Exodus 12:21

[653] Deuteronomy 16:5, 16:6

[654] 2Ch 35:13

[655] Leviticus 23:5

'pesaḫ' originally referred solely to the event, but that it was also sometimes used colloquially and *commemoratively* to refer to the animal that was sacrificed. Tyndale would also have most likely endorsed our speculation that God's apparently pre-event utterance of *"Kill the pesaḫ"* probably reflected a scribe's post-event habit of using the colloquial correspondence when recording the (by then) past events.

However, in the book of Exodus we find the word for the sacrificial object being used in *two different forms in the same verse*. We read that *"Moses called for all the elders of Israel, and said unto them, Draw out and take you a **lamb** according to your families, and kill the **passover**"* (our emphasis).[656] The first instance is the word for the animal to be selected for the sacrifice ('ṣō'n', Hebrew צֹאן, Strong's concordance H6629), while the second (translated as 'Passover') is the 'special' derivative that has the (we are told commemorative) name of the object of sacrifice at the event ('pesaḫ', Hebrew פֶּסַח, Strong's concordance H6453, from H6452). The former name derives merely from a root name for a small animal (usually a sheep) as one of a flock, whilst the latter derives, as we have seen, from a root meaning 'to skip or pass over'. We may presume that the same scribe had written these words, yet he has deliberately made a distinction between two different forms with two different significations, in the same verse—one for the selected animal victim, and another for the object of sacrifice at the great event (the spring equinox 'Passover'). It seems interesting that the same scribe had been at pains to make this distinction between the animal as it was chosen and as it was specifically at the time of sacrifice, since the two referents are, we are led to believe, one and the same thing. The scribe certainly did not seem to be influenced by what Tyndale referred to as the 'commemorative significance' for the first form when he wrote the verse. This suggests that there was a distinction to be made between the common name of the selected sacrificial animal victim and the object of the sacrifice itself at the spring equinox (the 'Passover').

It may thus be equally possible and indeed perhaps more plausible to assume that the word 'pesaḫ', used for the spring event and for the 'object of the sacrifice' had always in fact been one and the same, with the same derivational root; that this Hebrew word 'pesaḫ' had an older, original meaning from which both the name of the equinox festival event (purportedly the 'passing over' of the Israelites) *and* the name of the sacrificed animal both derived. We say 'purportedly' since firstly, it is of course not easy to accept the wholesale slaughter of all first-born Egyptians as historical fact, and secondly—and more importantly—it is worth noting that scholars have attested that the Pesaḫ spring equinox festival, involving the killing of a lamb, long predated the supposed escape from massacre written in Exodus, and was originally observed by earlier nomadic Israelites on the night of the full moon nearest the spring equinox.[657] One scholar concluded

---

[656] Exodus 12:21
[657] Prosic, 2004

that, originally, the sacrificed lamb represented some form of deity which was expected to resurrect.[658]

If the name of the actual animal sacrificed at the equinox did indeed come from a root form which *was* etymologically related to the sense of 'passing over', without reference to, and before any of the 'skipping over' or 'passing over' events described in Exodus could have occurred (thus without any possibility of the name for the animal being taken as a commemorative short-form for the festival, as would have had to be the case to explain God's injunction to 'kill the pesaḫ' *before such an event would have occurred*),[659] then one might wonder if Tyndale had unwittingly stumbled upon the core meaning of a single and more ancient linguistic word root, anterior to that currently received of 'pesaḫ', which originally alluded to the *passing over* of the Sun into the lamb or ram (Aries) at the spring equinox, to begin a new zodiacal year cycle, and which later became attached to many names associated with the variously related rituals of rebirth, sacrifice and even myths of select survival of death of this time of the year.

The role of the ram certainly seems to take a central role in the 'Passover' spring equinox rite alluded to in the Christian Bible, and there seems to be a lexical distinction there between 'lamb' as 'selected sacrificial victim' and 'lamb' as 'the object of sacrifice'. With this in mind, the possibility that an ancient spring equinox festival (which was marked by the sacrifice of an unblemished or spotless ram), marking the passing over of the Sun into Aries—possibly woven into positive myths concerning the Israelites—was the prime mover of the biblical story seems too compelling to disregard. Indeed, on reflection, the 'Passover' story from the Bible is replete with the themes of Aries: the equinox, a ram, killing, red blood. The more dramatic account of God's 'passing over' (as 'sparing') the Israelites, as a mythical adjunct to the 'passing over' of the Sun into a new zodiacal year, resembles an ancient Israelite astrologer's immodest dream of the celebration of Aries the ram, prime signifier of the spring equinox, in the context of a seething resentment of Egyptian domination.

---

[658] Mowinckel, 1922
[659] Exodus 12:21

Appendix 3: Saturnalia and Kronia

To the ancient Romans, Saturn was the god of time, agriculture, wealth and social order. Time and agriculture were of course inextricably linked together in the year-cycle; upon these depended the civilising influence of sustenance throughout the year, and more especially through the otherwise precarious winter, thus enabling and maintaining wealth and social stability. The ancient Romans believed that in ages past there had once been a golden age of abundance, peace, social order and the absence of any need for toil, ruled over by Saturn. Perhaps this golden age was seen as a time when the abundant wealth and social order conveyed by the benefits of Saturn had been perfected. When the Romans conquered Greece, they identified their god Saturn with the ancient Greek deity Cronus, who in folklore was also seen as having once ruled over a golden age of social order and plenty. The Greek Cronus was also frequently identified with the Greek *Chronos*, god of time. The psychological motivation of these syncretisms may have been an acknowledgement of the importance of cycles of time in the year, in relation to agriculture, particularly as they related to the importance of adequate food provisions.

The Roman Saturn was the honoured deity of the *Saturnalia*, a celebration which took place in the days just preceding the winter solstice. During this festival, the fruits of the year's harvest were celebrated, but unusually, the normal themes of social order and responsibility, associated with Saturn, were temporarily reversed: during the festival period, general licence and merrymaking were the norm, slaves were waited upon by their masters, justice was not administered, and a 'King of Saturnalia' was elected by lot, whose arbitrary commands were to be obeyed by everyone. A figure of Saturn, having been kept all through the year with its legs bound with wool, was unbound for the duration of the festivities. Deliberately inexpensive gifts of small wax or pottery figurines called *sigillaria* were traditionally exchanged. During the Saturnalia, the enjoyment of plenteous provisions (despite the season), the general carousal, and the temporary pretence of an absence of social rank was a celebratory recalling or re-enactment of the conditions of the mythical golden age.

The ancient Greeks observed an equivalent festival known as the Kronia, which was rather celebrated in the time of the first harvest of summer. A general revelry and a temporary reversal of social rank, similar to that which took place during the Roman Saturnalia, was observed. The Kronia also traditionally recalled a golden age, when Cronus ruled a world where there was no need for labour or slaves. These festivals, with their inversion of social rank, closely resemble and are possibly the precursors of the 'Lord of Misrule' festival, celebrated in later mediaeval pagan traditions.

Despite a definite association with Saturn (or with the Greeks, the equivalent Cronus), the festivals of Saturnalia and Kronia are the most difficult festivals to place, conceptually, within the zodiacal year, especially since, despite their near identity, the Roman Saturnalia took place just before the winter solstice, while the Greek Kronia was placed at time of the first summer harvest (though we note that the importance of agriculture and its food provision was central to both). Aspects of these celebrations, such as the general revelry and the giving of gifts, are clearly reminiscent of the modern Christmas, which we have nevertheless here associated with the expansive characteristics of Jupiter in the time of Sagittarius.

The themes of the celebrations of Saturnalia are indeed those associated with the god Saturn, namely, the motifs of stern social order and necessary toil, but as we have seen, for the duration of the festival, not conventionally celebrated but instead reversed, inverted, or turned on their heads. It may be that, in harking back to an era of perfection in the realm of social order to a time when the enforcement of a harsh Saturnian ethic was unnecessary, a temporary feigning of its absence served to highlight its importance. A winter solstice festival which involved some licence and disorder may have forced the Romans, normally so cognisant of the straightforwardly stern nature of the deity Saturn, to 'unbind' him temporarily, and thus become more aware of the seriousness or importance of his nature as the fount of social cohesion—normally evidenced in the *observance* of social order, rank and labour, necessary to gain the fruits of the agricultural year-cycle. Such an interpretation appears tenuous however and seems an odd way to underline the necessity of the Saturn principle.

The emphasis on the importance of agricultural produce certainly seems to be mirrored in the near-identical Greek Kronia, held at the time of the first summer harvest, though in the case of the Greek festival, even if it had similarly functioned to underscore the importance of the human need for 'necessary toil at the appropriate times of the year' (as we identify the human 'Saturn urge'), then we nevertheless have to note the different placement of that celebration in the year-cycle. It might even be conjectured that the recalling of a supposed 'golden age' in the festivals of Saturnalia and Kronia may be a brief collective remembrance or 'retrospective celebration' of the hunter-gatherer lifestyle that preceded the rise of settled agriculture in the Neolithic era, which ushered in a need for fixed social hierarchies, harsh toil in the fields, and a system of slavery to implement a division of labour. This however remains highly speculative.

Bibliography

Ames, D. L., & Viau, J. (1965). *Egyptian Mythology*. Paul Hamlyn.

Anderson, C., Hildreth, J. A. D., & Howland, L. (2015). Is the Desire for Status a Fundamental Human Motive? a Review of the Empirical Literature. *Psychological Bulletin, 141*(3), 574-601.

Asendorpf, J. B. (2003). Head-to-Head Comparison of the Predictive Validity of Personality Types and Dimensions. *European Journal of Personality, 17*, 327-346.

Ashe, G. (1985). *The Discovery of King Arthur*. Doubleday Books.

Assmann, J. (2001). *The Search for God in Ancient Egypt* (D. Lorton, Trans.). Cornell University Press.

Athanassakis, A. N. (2004). *Hesiod: Theogony, Works and Days, Shield*. JHU Press.

Bagdasarov, R. (2001). Symbolics of the Constellations of Sagittarius and Centaurus in Russian Traditional Culture. *Astronomical and Astrophysical Transactions, 20*(6), 975-996.

Baldwin, T. W. (1944). *William Shakspere's Small Latine & Lesse Greeke*. University of Illinois Press.

Balling, J. D., & Falk, J. H. (1982). Development of Visual Preference for Natural Environments. *Environment and Behavior, 14*(1), 5-28.

Barker, G. (2009). *The Agricultural Revolution in Prehistory: Why Did Foragers Become Farmers*. Oxford University Press, USA.

Bateson, P., & Martin, P. (2013). *Play, Playfulness, Creativity and Innovation*. Cambridge University Press.

Bausani, A. (1979). Note Sulla Preistoria Astronomica Del Mito Di Mithra. In *Mysteria Mithrae* (pp. 503-513). Brill.

Baynes, T. S. (1878). Annunciation. In *Encyclopaedia Britannica, Vol. 2* (9 ed., p. 90). New York: Charles Scribner's Sons.

Beck, R. (2006). *The Religion of the Mithras Cult in the Roman Empire*. Oxford University Press.

Becker, E. (1973). *The Denial of Death*. New York: Free Press.

Bede. (1999). *Bede, the Reckoning of Time* (F. Wallis, Trans.). Liverpool University Press.

Beekes, R. (2016). *Etymological Dictionary of Greek*. Brill.

Benko, S. (2004). *The Virgin Goddess: Studies in the Pagan and Christian Roots of Mariology* (LIX). Leiden, Boston: Brill.

Bergstralh, J. T., Miner, E. D., & Matthews, M. S. (1991). *Uranus*. University of Arizona Press.

Bhutta, M. F. (2007). Sex and the Nose: Human Pheromonal Responses. *Journal of the royal society of medicine, 100*(6), 268-274.

Bhutta, M. F., & Maxwell, H. (2008). Sneezing Induced by Sexual Ideation or Orgasm: An Under-Reported Phenomenon. *Journal of the Royal Society of Medicine, 101*(12), 587-591.

Billson, C. J. (1892). The Easter Hare. *Folk-Lore, 3*(4).

Bingham, A. (2004). *South and Meso-American Mythology A to Z*. Facts on File.

Black, J., & Green, A. (1992). *Gods, Demons and Symbols of Ancient Mesopotamia: An Illustrated Dictionary*. University of Texas Press.

Blakney, R. B. (1941). *Meister Eckhart - A Modern Translation* (1st Edition thus ed.). Harper Torchbooks.

Böhme, J. (1650). *Threefold Life of Man* (J. Sparrow, Trans.).

Book, H. E. (1971). Sexual Implications of the Nose. *Comprehensive psychiatry, 12*(5), 450-455.

Bosworth, J., & Toller, T. N. (1954). *An Anglo-Saxon Dictionary*. Oxford University Press.

Breitenberger, B. (2007). *Aphrodite and Eros*. Routledge.

Briggs, K. M. (1967). *The Fairies in English Tradition and Literature*. University of Chicago Press.

Britannica, Encyclopaedia. (1911). *Bun*. https://en.wikisource.org/wiki/1911_Encyclopaedia_Britannica/Bun.

Britannica, Encyclopaedia. (2017a). *Sun Worship*. Retrieved January 02, 2019, from https://www.britannica.com/topic/sun-worship.

Britannica, Encyclopaedia. (2017b). *Moon Worship*. Retrieved March 14, 2019, from https://www.britannica.com/topic/moon-worship.

Britannica, Encyclopaedia. (2023). *Dioscuri*. Retrieved 24 August, 2023, from https://www.britannica.com/topic/Dioscuri.

Brittanica, Encyclopaedia. (2024). *Barnum Effect*. 2024, from https://www.britannica.com/science/Barnum-Effect.

Brody, S. (2010). The Relative Health Benefits of Different Sexual Activities. *Journal of Sexual Medicine, 7*, 1336-1361.

Brunhübner, F. (1934). *Pluto* (J. Baum, Trans.; Revised Edition). American Federation of Astrologers Inc.

Burkert, W. (1985). *Greek Religion*. Harvard University Press.

Burkett, D. (2002). *An Introduction to the New Testament and the Origins of Christianity*. Cambridge University Press.

Butcher, J. N., Dahlstrom, W. G., Graham, J. R., Tellegen, A., & Kaemmer, B. (1989). *The Minnesota Multiphasic Personality Inventory-2 (MMPI-2): Manual for Administration and Scoring*. University of Minnesota Press.

Byers, Michael. (2009). *Constance Lowell, in Her Prime*. Retrieved 11 September, 2019, from https://plutovian.wordpress.com/2009/12/15/constance-lowell-in-her-prime/.

Byers, Michael. (2010). *On the bogosity of Venetia Burney - or how Pluto REALLY got its name*. Retrieved 11 September, 2019, from https://plutovian.wordpress.com/2010/07/20/the-undoubted-bogosity-of-venetia-burney-or-how-pluto-got-its-name/.

Byers, Michael. (2011). *Wrexie and Percy*. Retrieved 11 September, 2019, from https://plutovian.wordpress.com/2011/01/31/wrexie-and-percy/.

Byers, Michael. (2015). *Naming Pluto*. Retrieved 11 September, 2019, from https://plutovian.wordpress.com/2015/07/10/no-venetia-burney-did-not-name-pluto/.

Cacioppo, J. T., Petty, R. E., Feinstein, J. A., & Jarvis, W. B. G. (1996). Dispositional Differences in Cognitive Motivation: The Life and Times of Individuals Varying in Need for Cognition. *Psychological Bulletin, 119*(2).

Cajochen, C., Altanay-Ekici, S., Munch, M., Frey, S., Knoblauch, V., & Wirz-Justice, A. (2013). Evidence That the Lunar Cycle Influences Human Sleep. *Current biology, 23*(15), 1485-1488.

Caramazza, A., & Shelton, J. R. (1998). Domain-Specific Knowledge Systems in the Brain: The Animate-Inanimate Distinction. *Journal of Cognitive Neuroscience, 10*(1), 1-34.

Carrier, R. (2014). *On the Historicity of Jesus: Why We Might Have Reason for Doubt*. Sheffield Phoenix Press Ltd.

Carruthers, L. M. (1994). *Kingship and Heroism in Beowulf*. Cambridge: D. S. Brewer.

Castrogiovanni, P., Iapichino, S., Pacchierotti, C., & Pieraccini, F. (1999). Season of Birth in Panic Disorder. *Neuropsychobiology, 40*(4), 177-182.

Cattell, H. E., & Schuerger, J. M. (2003). *Essentials of 16PF Assessment*. Wiley.

Cicchetti, D., & Toth, S. L. (2000). Developmental Processes in Maltreated Children. *Nebraska Symposium on Motivation, 46*, 85-160.

Cicero, M. T. (1933). *De Natura Deorum*. Cambridge, Massachusetts; London: Harvard University Press; Heinemann.

Clarke, D., Gabriels, T., & Barnes, J. (1996). Astrological Signs as Determinants of Extroversion and Emotionality: An Empirical Study. *The Journal of Psychology, 130*(2), 131-140.

Clauss, M. (2001). *The Roman Cult of Mithras: The God and His Mysteries* (R. Gordon, Trans.). Routledge.

Cochrane, E. (1997). *Martian Metamorphoses*. Aeon Press.

Cohen, A. R., Stotland, E., & Wolfe, D. M. (1955). An Experimental Investigation of Need for Cognition. *Journal of Abnormal and Social Psychology, 51*(2).

Cohen, D., & Schmidt, J. P. (1979). Ambiversion: Characteristics of Midrange Responders on the Introversion-Extraversion Continuum. *Journal of Personality Assessment, 43*(5), 514-516.

Comfort, W. W. (2000). *The Quest of the Holy Grail*. Cambridge, Ontario: In parentheses Publications.

Conn, S. R., & Rieke, M. L. (1994). *The 16PF Fifth Edition Technical Manual*. Institute for Personality and Ability Testing.

Conrad, G. W., & Demarest, A. A. (1984). *Religion and Empire: The Dynamics of Aztec and Inca Expansionism* (1 ed.). Cambridge University Press.

Corr, P. J., & Matthews, G. (2009). *The Cambridge Handbook of Personality Psychology*. Cambridge: Cambridge University Press.

Cruise, R. I., Blitchington, W. P., & Futcher, W. G. A. (1980). Temperament Inventory: An Instrument to Empirically Verify the Four-Factor Hypothesis. *Educational and Psychological Measurement, 40*, 943-954.

Cummings, E. M., & Davies, P. T. (1994). *Children and Marital Conflict: The Impact of Family Dispute And Resolution*. New York: Guilford.

Cumont, F. (1903). *The Mysteries of Mithras* (J. McCormack, Trans.). Chicago: Open Court Publishing Company.

Curtis, V. A. (2007). Dirt, Disgust and Disease: A Natural History of Hygiene. *Journal of Epidemiology and Community Health, 61*(8), 660-664.

Cutler, W. B. (1980). Lunar and Menstrual Phase Locking. *American Journal of Obstetrics and Gynecology, 137*(7), 834-839.

Cyrino, M. S. (2010). *Aphrodite*. New York City, New York and London, England: Routledge.

Dalal, R. (2014). *Hinduism: An Alphabetical Guide*. Penguin Books India.

Dalley, S. (1989). *Myths from Mesopotamia: Creation, the Flood, Gilgamesh, and Others*. Oxford University Press.

Daniell, D. (1992). *Tyndale's Old Testament*. Yale University Press.

Darley, J. M., & Latané, B. (1968). Bystander Intervention in Emergencies: Diffusion of Responsibility. *Journal of Personality and Social Psychology, 8*(4, Pt.1), 377-383.

David, A. R. (1998). *Handbook to Life in Ancient Egypt*. Oxford University Press, USA.

Davidson, B. S., Madigan, M. L., & Nussbaum, M. A. (2004). Effects of Lumbar Extensor Fatigue and Fatigue Rate on Postural Sway. *European journal of applied physiology, 93*(1-2), 183-189.

Davies, G., Welham, J., Chant, D., Torrey, E. F., & McGrath, J. (2003). A Systematic Review and Meta-Analysis of Northern Hemisphere Season of Birth Studies in Schizophrenia. *Schizophrenia bulletin, 29*(3), 587-593.

Davies, P. T., & Forman, E. M. (2002). Children's Patterns of Preserving Emotional Security in The Interparental Subsystem. *Child Development, 73*, 1880-1903.

Dawson, G., Ashman, S. B., Panagiotides, H., Hessl, D., Self, J., Yamada, E., & Embry, L. (2003). Preschool Outcomes of Children of Depressed Mothers: Role of Maternal Behavior, Contextual Risk, and Children's Brain Activity. *Child Development, 74*, 1158-1175.

de Vaan, M. (2008). *Etymological Dictionary of Latin and the other Italic Languages* (7). Leiden; Boston: Brill.

Dean, G. (1987). Does astrology need to be true? Part 2: The Answer Is No. *Skeptical Inquirer, 11*(3), 257-273.

Deci, E. L., & Ryan, R. M. (2000). The "What" and "Why" of Goal Pursuits: Human Needs and the Self-Determination of Behavior. *Psychological Inquiry, 11*(4), 227-268.

Deley, D. (2019). *Solar Mythology and the Jesus Story*. Retrieved 5 January, 2019, from https://solarmythology.com.

Delorme, A., Richard, G., & Fabre-Thorpe, M. (2010). Key Visual Features for Rapid Categorization of Animals in Natural Scenes. *Frontiers in Psychology, 1*(21)

Depue, R. A., & Collins, P. F. (1999). Neurobiology of the Structure of Personality: Dopamine, Facilitation of Incentive Motivation, and Extraversion. *Behavioral and Brain Sciences, 22*(3), 491-517.

Digman, J. M. (1990). Personality Structure: Emergence of the Five-Factor Model. *Annual Review of Psychology, 41*, 417-440.

Dionysius the Areopagite (1920). *On the Divine Names and the Mystical Theology.* (C. E. Rolt, Trans.). SPCK.

Dixon-Kennedy, M. (1998a). *Encyclopedia of Russian and Slavic Myth and Legend.* ABC-CLIO, Inc.

Dixon-Kennedy, M. (1998b). *Encyclopedia of Greco-Roman Mythology.* ABC-CLIO.

Doherty, E. (2012). *The End of an Illusion: How Bart Ehrman's "Did Jesus Exist?" Has Laid the Case for an Historical Jesus to Rest.* Ottawa: Age of Reason Publications.

Dumbrell, W. J. (2001). *The Search for Order: Biblical Eschatology in Focus.* Wipf and Stock.

Dunn, Jimmy. (2019). *The Moon in Ancient Egypt.* Retrieved March 14, 2019, from https://www.touregypt.net/featurestories/moon.htm.

Dupuis, C. F. (2001). *The Origin of All Religious Worship.* University of Michigan Library.

Dutton, D. (2003). *Aesthetics and Evolutionary Psychology* (The Oxford Handbook for Aesthetics). Oxford University Press.

Eaton, L. G., Doherty, K. L., & Widrick, R. M. (2007). A Review of Research and Methods Used to Establish Art Therapy as an Effective Treatment Method for Traumatized Children. *The Arts in Psychotherapy, 34*, 256-262.

Ehrman, B. D. (2000). *The New Testament: A Historical Introduction to The Early Christian Writings* (2nd edition ed.). Oxford University Press.

Ehrman, B. D. (2012). *Did Jesus Exist? The Historical Argument for Jesus of Nazareth.* HarperCollins.

Eisenberg, D. P., Kohn, P. D., Baller, E. B., Bronstein, J. A., Masdeu, J. C., & Berman, K. F. (2010). Seasonal Effects on Human Striatal Presynaptic Dopamine Synthesis. *Journal of Neuroscience, 30*(44), 14691-14694.

Eisenberg, D. T., Campbell, B., Mackillop, J., Lum, J. K., & Wilson, D. S. (2007). Season of Birth and Dopamine Receptor Gene Associations With Impulsivity, Sensation Seeking and Reproductive Behaviors. *PloS one, 2*(11).

Eliot, T. S. (1943). *Four Quartets.* Houghton Mifflin Harcourt P.

Ellis, B. J. (1995). The Evolution of Sexual Attraction: Evaluative Mechanisms in Women. In J. H. Barkow, Cosmides, L & Tooby, J. (Ed.), *The adapted mind: Evolutionary psychology and the generation of culture* (pp. 267-288). New York, NY: Oxford University Press.

Eusebius, & Williamson, G. A. (1989). *The History of the Church* (Rev. ed.). Penguin Classics.

Evans, J. (1998). *The History and Practice of Ancient Astronomy*. Oxford University Press.

Evelyn-White, H. G. (1914). *Hesiod: the Homeric Hymns and Homerica*. Heinemann.

Eysenck, H. J. (1953). *The Structure of Human Personality*. Methuen.

Eysenck, H. J., Eysenck, M. W., Fulker, D. W., Gray, J., Levey, A. B., Martin, I., Powell, G. E., Stelmack, R. M., & Wilson, G. (1981). *A Model for Personality*. Berlin: Springer-Verlag.

Eysenck, H. (1967). *The Biological Basis of Personality*. Transaction Publishers.

Farnell, Kim. (2005). *When and Why Did Uranus Become Associated with Aquarius?* Retrieved 23 September, 2019, from https://skyscript.co.uk/ur_aq.html.

Fenster, J. M. (2001). *Ether Day: The Strange Tale of America's Greatest Medical Discovery and the Haunted Men Who Made It*. New York, NY: HarperCollins.

Ferguson, G. (1977). *Signs and Symbols in Christian Art*. Oxford University Press.

Filaretova, L., & Bagaeva, T. (2016). The Realization of the Brain-Gut Interactions With Corticotropin-Releasing Factor and Glucocorticoids. *Current neuropharmacology, 14*(8), 876-881.

Fischer, R., Lee, A., & Verzijden, M. N. (2018). Dopamine Genes Are Linked to Extraversion and Neuroticism Personality Traits, but Only in Demanding Climates. *Scientific Reports, 8*(1).

Foster, R., & Tudor-Craig, P. (1986). *The Secret Life of Paintings*. The Boydell Press.

Fourie, D. P. (1984). Self-Attribution Theory and the Sun-Sign. *Journal of Social Psychology, 122*, 121-126.

Frazer, J. G. (1894). *The Golden Bough*. Macmillan and Co.

Furnham, A., & Crump, J. (2005). Personality Traits, Types, and Disorders: An Examination of the Relationship Between Three Self-Report Measures. *European Journal of Personality, 19*, 167-184.

Garaigordobil, M. (2006). Intervention in Creativity With Children Aged 10 and 11 Years: Impact of a Play Program on Verbal and Graphic Figural Creativity. *Creativity Research Journal, 18*, 329-3345.

Gardiner, A. H. (1927). *Egyptian Grammar : Being an Introduction to the Study of Heiroglyphs*. Oxford University Press.

Gauquelin, M. (1982). Zodiac and Personality: An Empirical Study. *Skeptical Inquirer, 6*(3), 57-65.

Geddes, G., & Griffiths, J. (2002). *Christian Belief and Practice: The Roman Catholic Tradition*. Heinemann.

George, A. R. (2003). *The Babylonian Gilgamesh Epic*. Oxford University Press.

Geue, K., Goetze, H., Buttstaedt, M., Kleinert, E., Richter, D., & Singer, S. (2010). An Overview of Art Therapy Interventions for Cancer Patients and the Results of Research. *Complementary Therapies in Medicine, 18*, 160-170.

Glass, Laurens. (2014). *The Importance of the Egg: Children and Easter*. Retrieved 11 October, 2019, from https://www.umc.org/who-we-are/the-importance-of-the-egg-children-and-easter.

Goldenberg, J. L., Pyszczynski, T., McCoy, S. K., Greenberg, J., & Solomon, S. (1999). Death, Sex, Love, and Neuroticism: Why Is Sex Such a Problem? *Journal of Personality and Social Psychology, 77*(6), 1173-1187.

Goodman, F. (1990). *Zodiac Signs* (First Edition ed.). Troddy Books.

Goodman, S. H., & Gotlib, I. H. (1999). Risk for Psychopathology in the Children of Depressed Mothers: A Developmental Model for Understanding Mechanisms of Transmission. *Psychological Review, 106*, 458-490.

Grant, M., & Hazel, J. (2001). *Who's Who in Classical Mythology* (3 ed.). Routledge.

Graves, R. (2017). *The Greek Myths: The Complete and Definitive Edition*. Penguin UK.

Green, N. (2006). Ostrich Eggs and Peacock Feathers: Sacred Objects as Cultural Exchange Between Christianity and Islam. *Al-Masaq: Journal of the Medieval Mediterranean, 18*(1).

Gregersen, E. (1982). *Sexual Practices: The Story of Human Sexuality*. London: Mitchell Beazley.

Grobman, N. R. (1981). Wycinanki and Pysanky: *Forms of Religious and Ethnic Folk Art From the Delaware Valley*. Pennsylvania Ethnic Heritage Studies Center, University of Pittsburgh.

Guardian. (2011). *Consider the Hot Cross Bun*. Retrieved 14 July, 2024, from https://www.theguardian.com/lifeandstyle/wordofmouth/2011/apr/19/consider-the-hot-cross-bun.

Guardian. (2019). *How to Eat: Hot Cross Buns*. Retrieved 14 July, 2024, from https://www.theguardian.com/food/2019/apr/12/how-to-eat-hot-cross-buns.

Guirands, F. (1967). *Greek Mythology* (D. Ames, Trans.). Hamlyn.

Hadjikhani, N., Kveraga, K., Naik, P., & Ahlfors, S. P. (2009). Early (N170) Activation of Face-Specific Cortex by Face-Like Objects. *Neuroreport, 20*(4), 403.

Hamilton, M. A. (2015). Astrology as a Culturally Transmitted Heuristic Scheme for Understanding Seasonality Effects: A Response to Genovese (2014). *Comprehensive Psychology, 4*(7).

Hansen, W., & Hansen, W. F. (2005). *Classical Mythology: A Guide to the Mythical World of the Greeks and Romans*. Oxford University Press, USA.

Harbison, P. (1995). *Pilgrimage in Ireland*. Syracuse University Press.

Harmatz, M. G., Well, A. D., Overtree, C. E., Kawamura, K. Y., Rosal, M., & Ockene, I. S. (2000). Seasonal Variation of Depression and Other Moods: A Longitudinal Approach. *Journal of Biological Rhythms, 15*(4).

Harris, J. R. (1913). *Boanerges*. University Press.

Hartner, W. (1965). The Earliest History of the Constellations in the near East and the Motif of the Lion-Bull Combat. *Journal of Near Eastern Studies, 24*(1/2), 1-16.

Hastings, J. (2004). *A Dictionary of Christ and the Gospels: Volume II (Part Two -- Profit - Zion)*. The Minerva Group, Inc.

Hazlitt, W. (1854). *Characters of Shakespeare's Plays*. London: C. Templeman.

Hesiod, & Evelyn-White, H. G. (2006). *Works and Days, Theogony and the Shield of Heracles*. Courier Corporation.

Herodotus. (2023). *The Histories*. Creative Media Partners, LLC.

Herschel, Francisca. (1917). The Meaning of the Symbol ♅ For the Planet Uranus. *The Observatory, 40*, 306-307.

Heyob, S. K. (1975). *The Cult of Isis Among Women in the Graeco-Roman World*. Brill Archive.

Higginbottom, G., & Clay, R. (2016). Origins of Standing Stone Astronomy in Britain: New Quantitative Techniques for the Study of Archaeoastronomy. *Journal of Archaeological Science: Reports, 9*, 249-258.

Hippolytus. (204). *Commentary on Daniel* (4.23.3).

Hislop, A. (1862). *The Two Babylons*. Edinburgh: James Wood.

Hodum, R. (2012). *Pilgrims' Steps: A Search for Spain's Santiago and an Examination of his Way*. iUniverse.com.

Holley, J. (2006). *George Wetherill*. Retrieved 27 July, 2023, from https://www.washingtonpost.com/archive/local/2006/07/22/george-wetherill/e47f2f52-fd34-4da2-bdee-d92612b7a081/.

Holtzmann, A. (1874). *Deutsche Mythologie*. Leipzig: Teubner.

Howarth, E. (1988). Mood Differences Between the Four Galen Personality Types. *Personality and Individual Differences, 9*(1), 173-175.

Howarth, E., & Zumbo, B. D. (1989). An Empirical Investigation of Eysenck's Typology. *Journal of Research in Personality, 23*(3), 343-353.

Hutton, R. (1996). *The Stations of the Sun*. Oxford University Press.

Huxley, A. (1954). *The Doors of Perception*. Chatto & Windus.

Illingworth, D., & Syme, G. (1977). Birthday and Femininity. *Journal of Social Psychology, 103*, 153-154.

Inge, W. R. (1918). *The Philosophy of Plotinus : The Gifford lectures at St. Andrews 1917-1918* (II). Longmans, Green and Co.

International Astronomical Union. (2006). *Definition of a Planet in the Solar System: Resolutions 5 and 6*. Retrieved 24 August, 2006, from https://www.iau.org/static/resolutions/Resolution_GA26-5-6.pdf.

Irenaeus. (1885). *Against Heresies* (A. Roberts & W. Rambaut, Trans. 1). Buffalo, NY: Christian Literature Co.

Jacobs, B. (1999). Der Herkunft und Entstehung der römischen Mithrasmysterien: Überlegungen zur Rolle des Stifters und zu den astronomischen Hintergründen der Kultlegende. *Xenia: Konstanzer Althistorische Vorträge und Forschungen, 43*.

Jansen, E. R. (2001). *The Book of Hindu Imagery: Gods, Manifestations and Their Meaning*. New Age Books.

Johnson, D. L., Wiebe, J. S., Gold, S. M., Andreasen, N. C., Hichwa, R. D., Watkins, G. L., & Boles Ponto, L. L. (1999). Cerebral Blood Flow and Personality: A Positron Emission Tomography Study. *American Journal of Psychiatry, 156*(2), 252-257.

Johnson, Heather. (2015). *Madame Guérin*. Retrieved 12 June, 2020, from https://poppyladymadameguerin.wordpress.com/.

Johnson, R. F. (2005). *Saint Michael the Archangel in Medieval English Legend*. Boydell Press.

Jordan, A. (2000). *Christianity*. Nelson Thornes.

Jouanna, J. (2012). *Greek Medicine from Hippocrates to Galen* (N. Allies, Trans. 40). BRILL.

Jung, C. G. (1923). *Psychological Types* (R. F. C. Hull, Trans.). Routledge

Jung, C. G. (1930). *Richard Wilhelm: In Memoriam* (G. H. Adler, R. F. C., Trans. 15). Princeton University Press.

Jung, C. G. (1963). *Memories, Dreams, Reflections*. Random House.

Jung, C. G. (1969a). *Collected Works of C. G. Jung, Vol. 8* (R. F. C. Hull, Trans. 2nd Ed., Bollingen Series XX ed. Vol. 8). Princeton University Press.

Jung, C. G. (1969b). *Collected Works of C. G. Jung, Vol. 9* (R. F. C. Hull, Trans. 9). Princeton University Press.

Jung, C. G. (1973). *C. G. Jung Letters, Vol. 1: 1906-1950* (R. F. C. Hull, Trans. 1). Routledge & Kegan Paul Ltd.

Jung, C. G. (2015). *Synchronicity: An Acausal Connecting Principle* (1 ed.). Routledge.

Kant, I. (1798). *Anthropology From a Pragmatic Point of View* (R. B. Louden, Trans.). Cambridge University Press.

Katičić, R. (2010). *Zeleni Lug: Tragovima Svetih Pjesama Naše Pretkršćanske Starine.* Zagreb: IBIS GRAFIKA / Matica Hrvatska.

Katz, D. (2015). *Myth and Ritual through Tradition and Innovation: Tradition and Innovation in the Ancient Near East.* Eisenbrauns Inc.

Kaufman, B. S. (2014). *How Does IQ Relate to Personality?* Retrieved 12 July, 2024, from https://blogs.scientificamerican.com/beautiful-minds/how-does-iq-relate-to-personality/.

Keeler, B. C. (1888). *A Short History of the Bible.* New York: Farrell.

Kerényi, K. (1951). *The Gods of the Greeks.* London, England: Thames and Hudson.

Kim, H., Di Domenico, S. I., & Connelly, B. S. (2019). Self-Other Agreement in Personality Reports: A Meta-Analytic Comparison of Self- and Informant-Report Means. *Psychological Science, 30*(1), 129-138.

Kloft, H. (2010). *Mysterienkulte der Antike: Götter, Menschen, Rituale.* C. H. Beck.

Koch, J. T. (2006). *Celtic Culture: A Historical Encyclopedia.* ABC-CLIO.

Koltko-Rivera, M. E. (2006). Rediscovering the Later Version of Maslow's Hierarchy of Needs: Self-Transcendence and Opportunities for Theory, Research, and Unification. *Review of General Psychology, 10,* 302-317.

Krupp, E. C. (1980). *In Search of Ancient Astronomies* (First Edition ed.). Chatto & Windus.

Kuhn, T. S. (1970). *The Structure of Scientific Revolutions.* University of Chicago Press.

Lambert, G. W., Reid, C., Kaye, D. M., Jennings, G. L., & Esler, M. D. (2002). Effect of Sunlight and Season on Serotonin Turnover in the Brain. *The Lancet, 360*(9348), 1840-1842.

Law, S. P. (1986). The Regulation of Menstrual Cycle and Its Relationship to the Moon. *Acta Obstet Gynecol Scand, 65*(1), 45-48.

Lawrence, E. A. (1994). The Centaur: Its History and Meaning in Human Culture. *Journal of Popular Culture, 27.*

Levin, J. D. (1995). *Introduction To Alcoholism Counseling: A Bio-Psycho-Social Approach* (2 ed.). Taylor & Francis.

Lin, M. C., Kripke, D. F., Parry, B. L., & Berga, S. L. (1990). Night Light Alters Menstrual Cycles. *Psychiatry Res, 33*(2), 135-138.

Littmann, M. (2004). *Planets Beyond*. Courier Corporation.

Liu, L., Li, Q., Sapolsky, R., Liao, M., Mehta, K., Bhargava, A., & Pasricha, P. J. (2011). Transient Gastric Irritation in the Neonatal Rats Leads to Changes in Hypothalamic CRF Expression, Depression- and Anxiety-Like Behavior as Adults. *PloS one, 6*(5).

Long, C. W. (1849). An Account of the First Use of Sulphuric Ether by Inhalation as an Anesthetic in Surgical Operations. *Southern Medical and Surgical Journal, 5*, 705-713.

MacEvilly, J. (2017). *An Exposition of the Gospels*. Hansebooks GmbH.

Macfie, J., Cicchetti, D., & Toth, S. L. (2001). The Development of Dissociation in Maltreated Preschool-Aged Children. *Development and Psychopathology, 13*, 233-254.

Mackenzie, D. A. (1917). *Wonder Tales from Scottish Myth and Legend*. Blackie and Son.

MacKie, E. W. (1997). Maeshowe and the Winter Solstice: Ceremonial Aspects of the Orkney Grooved Ware Culture. *Antiquity, 71*(272), 338-359.

MacNeill, M. (1962). *The Festival of Lughnasa: A Study of the Survival of the Celtic Festival of the Beginning of Harvest*. Oxford University Press.

Mascaró, J. (1973). *The Upanishads*. Penguin.

Maslow, A. H. (1943). A Theory of Human Motivation. *Psychological Review, 50*(4), 370-396.

Maslow, A. H. (1954). *Motivation and Personality*. Harper & Row.

Maslow, A. H. (1970). *Religions, Values, and Peak Experiences*. New York: Penguin.

Maslow, A. H. (1971). *The Farther Reaches of Human Nature*. Penguin.

Maté, G., & Neufeld, G. (2019). *Hold on to Your Kids*. Random House.

Mattison, H. (1872). *A High-School Astronomy*. New York: Sheldon & Co.

Maunder, A. S. D. (1934). The Origin of the Symbols of the Planets. *The Observatory, 57*, 238-247.

Mayo, J. (1964). *Astrology*. Hodder & Stoughton Ltd.

Mayo, J. (1972). *The Planets and Human Behaviour* (First Edition ed.). L. N. Fowler & Co.

Mayo, J. (1995). *Astrology: A Key to Personality*. Penguin.

Mayo, J., White, O., & Eysenck, H. (1978). An Empirical Study of the Relation Between Astrological Factors and Personality. *Journal of Social Psychology, 105*, 229-236.

Mazzatenta, A., De Luca, C., Di Tano, A., Cacchio, M., Di Giulio, C., & Pokorski, M. (2015). Swelling of Erectile Nasal Tissue Induced by Human Sexual Pheromone. *Respirology*, 25-30.

McCann, D. (2000). The Birth of the Outer Planets. *Traditional Astrologer Magazine, 19*.

McCrae, R. R., Terracciano, A., Costa, P. T., & Ozer, D. J. (2006). Person-Factors in the California Adult Q-set: Closing the Door on Personality Types? *European Journal of Personality, 20*, 29-44.

McDougall, W. (1932). *The Energies of Men*. Methuen.

McGervey, J. D. (1977). A Statistical Test of Sun-Sign Astrology. *The Zetetic, 1*(2), 49-54.

McNeill, F. M. (2013). *The Silver Bough, Vol.2: A Calendar of Scottish National Festivals, Candlemas to Harvest Home* (2). Stuart Titles Limited.

Michael, M. B. (1941). *The Miracle Flower*. Dorrance.

Mohan, J., & Gulati, A. (1986). Zodiac Signs and Personality: A Pilot Study. *Correlation, 6*(1), 11-14.

Monaghan, P. (2009). *The Encyclopedia of Celtic Mythology and Folklore*. Infobase Publishing.

Morani, M. (1987). *Nemesii Emeseni De Natura Hominis*. Teubner.

Mowinckel, S. (1922). *Psalmenstudien* (II). Oslo: Kristiania.

Murdock, D. M. (2011). *Jesus as the Sun Throughout History*. Stellar House Publishing.

Murdock, D. M. (2011a). *The Origins of Christianity and the Quest for the Historical Jesus Christ*. Stellar House Publishing.

Myers, B., & Greenwood-Van Meerveld, B. (2009). Role of Anxiety in the Pathophysiology of Irritable Bowel Syndrome: Importance of the Amygdala. *Frontiers in neuroscience, 3*(47).

Myers, I. B., & McCaulley, M. H. (1985). *Manual: A Guide to the development and use of the Myers-Briggs Type Indicator*. Palo Alto: Consulting Psychologists Press.

mythicalireland.com. (2019). *The Hill of Tara - Teamhair*. 2023, from https://mythicalireland.com/blogs/ancient-sites/the-hill-of-tara-teamhair.

Nagel, A., & Wood, C. S. (2010). *Anachronic Renaissance*. New York: Zone Books.

NASA. (2005). *Exploring the Sun Through Ancient Civilizations*. https://www.-nasa.gov/vision/universe/solarsystem/sun_earthday.html.

NASA. (2006). *The Girl Who Named Pluto*. Retrieved 3 August, 2023, from https://science.nasa.gov/people/venetia-burney-phair/.

NASA. (2018). *Solar System Symbols*. Retrieved 21 August, 2019, from https://solarsystem.nasa.gov/resources/680/solar-system-symbols/.

Neisser, U. (1976). *Cognition and Reality*. W.H.Freeman & Co Ltd.

Nelson, C. A. (2001). The Development and Neural Bases of Face Recognition. *Infant and Child Development, 10*(1-2), 3-18.

New, J., Cosmides, L., & Tooby, J. (2007). Category-Specific Attention for Animals Reflects Ancestral Priorities, Not Expertise. *Proceedings of the National Academy of Sciences, 104*(42), 16598.

Newall, V. (1971). *An Egg at Easter*. London: Routledge & Kegan Paul.

newgrange.com. (2020). *Imbolc (Imbolg) - Cross Quarter Day*. Retrieved 14 July, 2020, from https://www.newgrange.com/imbolc.htm.

Nilsson, M. P. (1940). *Greek Popular Religion*. Columbia University Press.

O'Kelly, M. J. (1982). *New Grange: Archaeology, Art and Legend* (1st ed.). Thames & Hudson Ltd.

O'Neil, W. M. (1976). *Time and the Calendars*. Manchester University Press.

O'Rahilly, Cecile. (2019). *Táin Bó Cúalnge Recension 1. Corpus of Electronic Texts* Retrieved 9 March, 2020, from https://celt.ucc.ie//published/T301012/index.html.

Okasha, Samir. (2020). *Biological Altruism. Stanford Encyclopedia of Philosophy (Summer 2020 Edition)* Retrieved 2022, 2020, from https://plato.stanford.edu/archives/sum2020/entries/altruism-biological/.

Olcott, W. T. (1911). *Star Lore of All Ages*. New York and London: G. P. Putnam's Sons, The Knickerbocker Press.

oldeuropeanculture. (2014). *Old European Culture - Henges - Rondel Enclosures*. Retrieved 29 April, 2024, from https://oldeuropeanculture.blogspot.com/2014/03/henges-rondel-enclosures.html.

Online Etymology Dictionary. (2024). *Mercantile*. Retrieved 21 July, 2024, from https://www.etymonline.com/word/mercantile#etymonline_v_14654.

Online Etymology Dictionary. (2019a). *Jove*. Retrieved 7 August, 2019, from https://www.etymonline.com/search?q=jove.

Online Etymology Dictionary. (2019b). *Neptune*. Retrieved 1 September, 2019, from https://www.etymonline.com/search?q=Neptune.

Origen. (1980). *Contra Celsum* (H. Chadwick, Trans.). Cambridge University Press.

Ormrod, J. E. (2014). *Essentials of Educational Psychology: Big Ideas to Guide Effective Teaching* (3rd edition ed.). Harlow, Essex, UK: Pearson Education Limited.

Ottarsdottir, U. (2010). *Art Therapy in Education for Children With Specific Learning Difficulties Who Have Experienced Stress And/Or Trauma*. Philadelphia, PA: Jessica Kingsley.

Ovid. (8). *Metamorphoses.*

Owens, E. B., & Shaw, D. S. (2003). Predicting Growth Curves of Externalizing Behavior Across the Preschool Years. *Journal of Abnormal Child Psychology, 31,* 575-590.

Pasachoff, J. M. (1992). *A Field Guide to the Stars and Planets*. Boston, Massachusetts.

Pauphilet, A. (1923). *La Queste Del Saint Graal*. Honoré Champion. Paris.

Pawlik, K., & Buse, L. (1984). Self-Attribution as a Moderator Variable in Differential Psychology: Replication and Interpretation of Eyesenck's Astrology/ Personality Correlations. *Correlation, 4*(2), 14.

Pellegrini, R. J. (1973). The Astrological "Theory" Of Personality: An Unbiased Test by a Biased Observer. *Journal of Psychology, 85,* 21-28.

Penglase, C. (1994). *Greek Myths and Mesopotamia: Parallels and Influence in the Homeric Hymns and Hesiod*. Routledge.

Peters, M. Danielle. (2020). *All About Mary - Wheat Ears Dress*. Retrieved 7 May, 2020, from https://udayton.edu/imri/mary/w/wheat-ears-dress.php.

Pittenger, D. J. (2004). The Limitations of Extracting Typologies From Trait Measures of Personality. *Personality and Individual Differences, 37,* 779-787.

Plutarch. (2011). *Of Isis and Osiris*. CreateSpace.

Plutarch. (2012). *Parallel Lives*. 2022, from https://penelope.uchicago.edu/ Thayer/E/Roman/Texts/Plutarch/Lives/home.html.

plutovian. (2015). *Naming Pluto*. Retrieved 3 August, 2023, from https://plutovian.wordpress.com/category/naming-pluto/.

Porphyry. (1983). *On the Cave of the Nymphs* (R. Lamberton, Trans.). Station Hill Press.

Powell, B. B. (2013). *The Iliad*. Oxford University Press.

Prabhavananda, S., & Manchester, F. (1947). *Upanishads: Breath of the Eternal*. Vedanta Press,U.S.

Prosic, T. (2004). *The Development and Symbolism of Passover until 70 CE*. T&T Clark International.

Pryke, L. M. (2017). *Ishtar*. Routledge.

Rasch, B., & Born, J. (2013). About Sleep's Role in Memory. *Physiological reviews, 93*(2), 681-766.

Raudive, K. (1971). *Breakthrough: An Amazing Experiment in Electronic Communication with the Dead*. Colin Smythe Ltd.

Reade, J. (1997). *Sumerian Origins*. in Finkel, I. L. & Geller, M. J. (Eds.) *Sumerian Gods and Their Representations*. Groningen: Styx.

Reid, J. B., Patterson, G. R., & Snyder, J. (2002). *Antisocial Behavior in Children and Adolescents: A Developmental Analysis and Model for Intervention*. Washington, DC: American Psychological Association.

Riekki, T., Lindeman, M., Aleneff, M., Halme, A., & Nuortimo, A. (2013). Paranormal and Religious Believers Are More Prone to Illusory Face Perception than Skeptics and Non-believers. *Applied Cognitive Psychology, 27*, 150-155.

Rigoglioso, M. (2009). *The Cult of Divine Birth in Ancient Greece*. Palgrave Macmillan.

Roberts, H. E. (2013). *Encyclopedia of Comparative Iconography*. Routledge.

Robinson, C. H. (1920). *The Life of Otto, Apostle of Pomerania, 1060-1139 by Ebo and Herbordus*. New York: Macmillan.

Rogers, J. H. (1998). Origins of the Ancient Constellations: I. the Mesopotamian Traditions. *Journal of the British Astronomical Association, 108*, 9-28.

Rogers, N. (2003). *Halloween: From Pagan Ritual to Party Night*. Oxford University Press.

Rossi, S., & Le Grice, K. (2018). *Jung on Astrology*. Routledge.

Rossman, B. B. R., Bingham, R. D., & Emde, R. N. (1997). Symptomatology and Adaptive Functioning for Children Exposed to Normative Stressors, Dog Attack, and Parental Violence. *Journal of the American Academy of Child & Adolescent Psychiatry, 36*, 1089-1097.

Rossman, B. B. R., Hughes, H. M., & Rosenberg, M. S. (2000). *Children and Interparental Violence: Impact of Exposure*. Philadelphia: Taylor & Francis.

Rubin, K. H., Burgess, K. B., Dwyer, K. M., & Hastings, P. D. (2003). Predicting Preschoolers' Externalizing Behaviors From Toddler Temperament, Conflict, and Maternal Negativity. *Developmental Psychology, 39*, 164-176.

Ruggles, C., & Cotte, M. (2010). Heritage Sites of Astronomy and Archaeoastronomy in the context of the UNESCO World Heritage Convention. *Paris: ICOMOS*.

Ruysbroeck, J. O. (1916). *John of Ruysbroeck: The Adornment of the Spiritual Marriage, the Sparkling Stone, the Book of Supreme Truth.* (Trans: D. C. A. Wynschenk.) J M Dent.

Saklofske, D. H., Kelly, I. W., & McKerracher, D. W. (1982). An Empirical Study of Personality and Astrological Factors. *Journal of Psychology, 110,* 275-280.

Santrock, J. W. (2014). *A Topical Approach to Life-Span Development* (7th ed.). McGraw-Hill.

Sarkar, M., & Biswas, N. M. (2005). Influence of Moonlight on the Birth of Male and Female Babies. *Nepal Med Coll J, 7*(1), 62-64.

Schindler, K. (2022). *Riordan Lecture Series: The Discovery of Pluto.* Retrieved 13 June, 2024, from https://www.youtube.com/watch?v=r7Wp-ZouHkw.

Schopenhauer, A. (1937). *Studies in Pessimism.* George Allen & Unwin.

Schrijver, P. (1995). *Studies in British Celtic Historical Phonology.* Rodopi.

Seely, D. R. (2011). *William Tyndale and the Language of At-one-ment.* Religious Studies Center, Brigham Young University.

Sexton, J. D., & Pennebaker, J. W. (2009). *The Healing Powers of Expressive Writing.* New York: Cambridge University Press.

Shaw, D. S., Gilliom, M., Ingoldsby, E. M., & Nagin, D. S. (2003). Trajectories Leading to School-Age Conduct Problems. *Developmental Psychology, 39,* 189-200.

Sheehan, W. (1996). *The Planet Mars.* University of Arizona Press.

Shinomiya, A., Shimmura, T., Nishiwaki-Ohkawa, T., & Yoshimura, T. (2014). Regulation of Seasonal Reproduction by Hypothalamic Activation of Thyroid Hormone. *Frontiers in Endocrinology, 5*(12).

Siliotti, A. (1997). *Guide to the Pyramids of Egypt.* Barnes & Noble.

Simmonite, W. J. (1890). *Complete Arcana of Astral Philosophy.*

Slipher, V. M. (1930). The Trans-Neptunian planet. *Popular Astronomy, 38,* 415.

Smith, R. C. (1828). *A Manual of Astrology, or the Book of the Stars, by Raphael.* C. S. Arnold.

Smith, Scott. (2023). *Why Does Jesus Curse the Fig Tree?* https://www.thescott-smithblog.com/2022/05/why-does-jesus-curse-fig-tree-mark-11.html.

Smithers, A., & Cooper, H. (1978). Personality and Season of Birth. *Journal of Social Psychology, 105,* 237-241.

Smyth, C. P. (1867). *Life and Work at the Great Pyramid During the Months of January, February, March, and April, A.D. 1865 (1).* Edinburgh: Edmonston and Douglas.

Society for the Diffusion of Useful Knowledge (1839). The Penny Cyclopaedia of the Society for the Diffusion of Useful Knowledge.

Soellner, R. (1972). *Shakespeare's Patterns of Self-Knowledge*. Ohio State University Press.

Sparavigna, A. C. (2008). *The Pleiades: The Celestial Herd of Ancient Timekeepers*. Retrieved 14 July, 2024, from https://arxiv.org/ftp/arxiv/papers/0810/0810.1592.pdf.

Stark, K. B. (1869). Die Mithrassteine von Dormagen. *Jahrbücher des Vereins von Altertumsfreunden im Rheinlande, 46*, 1-25.

Stearn, W. T. (1962). The Origin of the Male and Female Symbols of Biology. *Taxon, 11*(4), 109-113.

Stenberg, G., Wendt, P. E., & Risberg, J. (1993). Regional Cerebral Blood Flow and Extraversion. *Personality and Individual Differences, 15*(5), 547-554.

Sternberg, R. J., & Sternberg, K. (2017). *Cognitive Psychology* (7th ed.). Cengage Learning.

Stowe, L. E. (2010). *Stowe's Bible Astrology: The Bible Founded on Astrology*. Kessinger Publishing.

Stubbes, P. (2010). *Phillip Stubbes's Anatomy of the Abuses in England in Shakspere's Youth*. Nabu Press.

Stuckey, H. L., & Nobel, J. (2010). The Connection Between Art, Healing, and Public Health: A Review of Current Literature. *American Journal of Public Health, 100*, 254-263.

Tay, L., & Diener, E. (2011). Needs and Subjective Well-Being Around the World. *Journal of Personality and Social Psychology, 101*(2), 354-365.

Taylor, R. (2006). *The Devil's Pulpit*. Book Tree,US.

te Velde, H. (1967). *Seth, God of Confusion* (Trans: G. E. van Baaren-Pape.). Brill.

Theophrastus. (2002). *Characters* (Rusten, J. S & I. Campbell, Trans.). Harvard University Press.

Thompson, E. R. (2008). Development and Validation of an International English Big-Five Mini-Markers. *Personality and Individual Differences, 45*(6), 542-548.

Thompson, J. E. S. (1939). *The Moon Goddess in Middle America With Notes on Related Deities*. Carnegie Institution of Washington.

Thompson, J. E. S. (1998). *Maya History and Religion* (New edition.). University of Oklahoma Press.

Thompson, R. A., & Lagattuta, K. H. (2006). *Early Emotional Vulnerability*. In McCartney, K. & Phillips, D. (Eds) *Blackwell Handbook of Early Childhood Development*. Wiley.

Thompson, S. E. (2000). *Holiday Symbols* (2nd ed.). Omnigraphics.

Thyme, K. E., Sundin, E. C., Stahlberg, G., Lindstrom, B., Eklof, H., & Wiberg, B. (2007). The Outcome of Short-Term Psychodynamic Art Therapy Compared to Short-Term Psychodynamic Verbal Therapy for Depressed Women. *Psychoanalytic Psychotherapy, 21*, 250-264.

Tigay, J. H. (2004). *Exodus*. Oxford University Press.

Tombaugh, C. W. (1946). The Search for the Ninth Planet, Pluto. *Leaflet of the Astronomical Society of the Pacific, 5*, 73.

Torrey, E. F., Miller, J., Rawlings, R., & Yolken, R. H. (1997). Seasonality of Births in Schizophrenia and Bipolar Disorder: A Review of the Literature. *Schizophrenia research, 28*(1), 1-38.

Trevelyan, M. (2014). *Folk Lore and Folk Stories of Wales*. Literary Licensing, LLC.

Tyson, G. (1977). Astrology or Season of Birth: A 'Split-Sphere' Test. *Journal of Psychology, 95*, 285-287.

Tyson, G. A. (1980). Occupation and Astrology or Season of Birth: A Myth? *Journal of Social Psychology, 110*, 73-78.

Uhl, J.-F., & Gillot, C. (2015). Anatomy of the Veno-Muscular Pumps of the Lower Limb. *Phlebology, 30*(3), 180-193.

Ulansey, D. (1991). *The Origins of the Mithraic Mysteries: Cosmology and Salvation in the Ancient World*. New York, NY: Oxford University Press.

Ulansey, D. (1994). Solving the Mithraic Mysteries. *Biblical Archaeology Review, 20*(5), 40-53.

Ulansey, David. (2022). *Why Not a Mithraic Fish?* Retrieved 6 November 2022, 2022, from http://www.mysterium.com/appendix3.html.

Underdown, D. (1985). *Revel, Riot, and Rebellion: Popular Politics and Culture in England 1603-1660*. Oxford University Press.

Ushigaki, H. (1982). The Image of 'God Cyning' in Beowulf: A Philological Study. *Studies in English Literature (Tokyo)*, 63-78.

Van Rooij, J. J. F., Brak, M. A., & Commandeur, J. J. (1988). Introversion-Extraversion and Sun-Sign. *The Journal of Psychology, 122*, 275-278.

Van Rooij, J. J. F. (1993). Jungian Typology and Astrology: An Empirical Test. *Correlation, 12*(1), 28-32.

Van Rooij, J. J. F. (1999). Self-Concept in Terms of Astrological Sun-Sign Traits. *Psychological Reports, 84*(2), 541-546.

Vansteenkiste, M., Ryan, R. M., & Soenens, B. (2020). Basic Psychological Need Theory: Advancements, Critical Themes, and Future Directions. *Motivation and Emotion, 44,* 1-31.

Varley, J. (1916). Some Astrological Predictions of the Late John Varley. *The Occult Review, 24,* 40-41.

Varro, M. T. (1938). *On the Latin Language.* Harvard University Press.

Veno, A., & Pamment, P. (1979). Astrological Factors and Personality: A Southern Hemisphere Replication. *The Journal of Psychology, 101,* 73-77.

Versnel, H. (1992). *Inconsistencies in Greek and Roman Religion, Volume 2: Transition and Reversal in Myth and Ritual - Chapter 2 - Kronos and the Kronia.* BRILL.

Wahba, M. A., & Bridwell, L. G. (1976). Maslow Reconsidered: A Review of Research on the Need Hierarchy Theory. *Organizational Behavior and Human Performance, 15*(2), 212-240.

Wallenfels, R. (1993). *Zodiacal Signs Among the Seal Impressions From Hellenistic Uruk.* Bethesda, Md.: CDL Press.

Walsh, W. S., & Walsh, H. C. (1889). The Hare and Easter. *American Notes and Queries, 3,* 64-65.

Watkins, Calvert. (1969). *Indo-European and the Indo-Europeans.* In Morris, William (Ed.) *The American Heritage Dictionary of the English Language.* Boston: Houghton Mifflin.

Watkins, C. (2000). *The American Heritage Dictionary of Indo-European Roots.* Houghton Mifflin Harcourt.

West, M. L. (1997). *The East Face of Helicon: West Asiatic Elements in Greek Poetry and Myth.* Oxford, England: Clarendon Press.

West, M. L. (2007). *Indo-European Poetry and Myth.* Oxford, England: Oxford University Press.

White, G. (2014). *Babylonian Star-Lore* (3rd ed.). Solaria Publications.

Whitehouse, David. (2000). *Ice Age Star Map Discovered.* 2023, from http://news.bbc.co.uk/1/hi/sci/tech/871930.stm.

Wiggermann, F. A. M. (1998). *Reallexikon der Assyriologie und Vorderasiatischen Archaeologie* (9). de Gruyter.

Wikipedia. (2018). *Perceptions of Religious Imagery in Natural Phenomena.* Retrieved 12 December, 2018, from https://en.wikipedia.org/wiki/Perceptions_of_religious_imagery_in_natural_phenomena.

Wikipedia. (2024). *Tetramorph*. Retrieved 18 April, 2024, from https://en.wikipedia.org/wiki/Tetramorph.

Wimmer, J. (1940). *Assessment of Confiscated Astrology Literature by Josef Wimmer for Reinhard Heydrich, October 30, 1940*. https://digitalcommons.ursinus.edu/cgi/viewcontent.cgi?article=1023&context=dowsing.

Winick, Stephen. (2016). *Ostara and the Hare: Not Ancient, but Not As Modern As Some Skeptics Think*. Retrieved 10 October, 2019, from https://blogs.loc.gov/folklife/2016/04/ostara-and-the-hare/.

Winston, J. (2002). Describing the Virgin. *Art History, 25*(3), 275-292.

Woo, J. M., Okusaga, O., & Postolache, T. T. (2012). Seasonality of Suicidal Behavior. *International journal of environmental research and public health, 9*(2), 531-547.

Woolf, V. (1954). *A Writer's Diary*. Hogarth Press.

Wundt, W. M. (1874). *Grundzüge der Physiologischen Psychologie*. Leipzig: Engelmann.

Yang, G., Lai, C. S., Cichon, J., Ma, L., Li, W., & Gan, W. B. (2014). Sleep Promotes Branch-Specific Formation of Dendritic Spines After Learning. *Science, 344*, 1173-1178.

Zeki, S., Romaya, J., Benincasa, D., & Atiyah, M. (2014). The Experience of Mathematical Beauty and Its Neural Correlates. *Frontiers in Human Neuroscience, 8*.

Zettler, R. L., Horne, L. H., Donald, P., & Pittman, H. (1998). *Treasures From Royal Tombs of Ur*. University of Pennsylvania Press, Inc.

Index

Gemini (*continued*)
  composition of, 86, 104
  mythology & folklore of, 106
  origins of, 104
  personality of, 105
  physiological associations of, 105
  season of, 106
  symbol of, 104
  'way' of, 267
Geshtinanna, 165
Gilgamesh, epic of, 135
Goat-Fish (constellation), 143
God the Father, 28
gods, 2–3, 25, 59
Golden Bough, The, 163
Goronwy, 183
grain, 123–124
Great Depression, 76
Great One (Babylonian constellation), 147
Great Twins (Babylonian constellation), 104
Great Year, 23
Gronw Pebr, 183
Groundhog Day, 150
Guinevere, 186
Gunpowder Plot, 136
Guy Fawkes Night, 136
Gwydion, 182
Gŵyl Fair y Canhwyllau, 150
Hades, 53, 104
Hallowe'en, 135
Hardy, Thomas, 136
harvest time, 121, 123–124
Harvey, William, 213
heart, 32
heaven, 2
heavenly father, 30
heliacal rising or setting, 6, 89
Helios, 28

Heracles (Hercules), 109
Hermes, 38
Hermes Psychopompus, 38, 104
Herod Antipas, 152
Herodias, 152
Herschel, Sir William, 46
Heydrich, Reinhard, 70
hierarchy of needs, 237, 241
Hilaria, 169
Hill of Tara, 150
Hipparchus, 20, 46, 321
Hippocrates, 211
Hippolytus of Rome, 146
Hired Man (constellation), 89
holy grail, 185
homoeostasis, 33, 303–304
Horus, 28, 166
hot cross buns, 98
houses, astrological, 228
humility, 160
humours (bodily fluids), 211
Huxley, Aldous, 156
Hydra, 109
Hydra (constellation), 318
hypnosis, 50, 67
Ideler, J. L., 213
Imbolc, 150
Inana, 153, 164
Inca, 29, 138
Indra, 42
Industrial Revolution, 48, 64
Inti, 29
introversion, 204
intuition, 219
Isis, 95, 166–167, 177
Ištar, 95
Ištar (Ishtar), 164
Jacobs, Bruno, 324
James and John (disciples of Jesus), 106–108

Plutarch, 166, 317

Pluto, 51

Pluto's symbol, 52

Po (Moon goddess), 34

polarity, of the zodiac signs, 83

Pollux, 107, 176

Polybus, 211

poppy, 138

Porphyry, 318

positive zodiac signs, 83

precession, 17, 90

prehistory, 1

projection, 6, 10, 12

Proserpina, 53

Pseudo-Dionysius the Areopagite, 57

psychoanalysis, 73–74

Pyramid Texts, 166

qualities (classical), 211

quality (quadruplicity) of zodiac signs, 84

quarter points, 8

quest of the holy grail, 186

Queste del Saint Graal, 186

Ra, 28

Ra-Harakhte, 28

ram, 89

random patterns, 10

Raphael (astrologer), 63

Raudive, K., 12

rebirth, 92

recreation, 272, 274

Reek Sunday, 119

regeneration, 72

Regulus, 8, 115

Remembrance Sunday, 137

resurrection, 94–95

Return of Dumuzid, The, 165

Revelation, Book of, 8, 59, 96

Rorschach inkblot test, 11

round table, 185

royalty, 32, 117

Ruysbroeck, 57

sacrifice, 94

safety needs, 237

Sagittarius, 139

    composition of, 86, 140

    mythology & folklore of, 143

    origins of, 139

    personality of, 141

    physiological associations of, 141

    season of, 142

    symbol of, 140

    'way' of, 281

Šala, 121

Šamaš, 128

Samhain, 135

sanguine (temperament), 212

Sapa Inca, 29

Saturday, 59

Saturn, 3, 43

Saturn's symbol, 44

Saturnalia, 143, 147, 331

Scorpio, 132

    composition of, 86, 132

    mythology & folklore of, 135

    origins of, 132

    personality of, 134

    physiological associations of, 133

    season of, 134

    symbol of, 132

    'way' of, 279

seasons, 3, 161

Selene, 35

self-abnegation, 50, 154

self-actualisation, 238

sensation, 219

sermon on the mount, 160

Serpent (constellation), 9, 109

Set, 166

seven ages of man, 234

9 781068 756702